KINGDOM *on* FIRE

KINGDOM _on_ FIRE

KAREEM, WOODEN, WALTON,
and the TURBULENT DAYS of the
UCLA BASKETBALL DYNASTY

SCOTT HOWARD-COOPER

ATRIA BOOKS
New York London Toronto Sydney New Delhi

ATRIA
BOOKS

An Imprint of Simon & Schuster, LLC
1230 Avenue of the Americas
New York, NY 10020

First Atria Books hardcover edition March 2024

ATRIA BOOKS and colophon are trademarks of Simon & Schuster, LLC

Simon & Schuster: Celebrating 100 Years of Publishing in 2024

For information about special discounts for bulk purchases, please contact Simon & Schuster
Special Sales at 1-866-506-1949 or business@simonandschuster.com.

The Simon & Schuster Speakers Bureau can bring authors to your live event.
For more information or to book an event, contact the Simon & Schuster Speakers Bureau at
1-866-248-3049 or visit our website at www.simonspeakers.com.

Interior design by Silverglass.

Manufactured in the United States of America

1   3   5   7   9   10   8   6   4   2

Library of Congress Cataloging-in-Publication Data

Names: Howard-Cooper, Scott, 1963- author.
Title: Kingdom on fire : Kareem, Wooden, Walton, and the turbulent days of
the UCLA basketball dynasty / Scott Howard-Cooper.
Description: First Atria Books hardcover edition. | New York, N.Y. : Atria
Books, 2024. | Includes bibliographical references and index. | Summary:
"A bold narrative history of the iconic UCLA Bruins championship teams
led by legendary coach John Wooden—an incredible true story about the
messy, never-easy pursuit of perfection set against the turmoil of
American culture in the 1960s and 70s"—Provided by publisher.
Identifiers: LCCN 2023058281 (print) | LCCN 2023058282 (ebook) | ISBN
9781668020494 (hardcover) | ISBN 9781668020517 (ebook)
Subjects: LCSH: UCLA Bruins (Basketball team)—History. | University of
California, Los Angeles—Basketball—History. | Abdul-Jabbar, Kareem,
1947- | Wooden, John, 1910-2010. | Walton, Bill, 1952-
Classification: LCC GV885.43.U423 H (print) | LCC GV885.43.U423 (ebook) |
DDC 796.323/630979494—dc23/eng/20231221
LC record available at https://lccn.loc.gov/2023058281
LC ebook record available at https://lccn.loc.gov/2023058282

ISBN 978-1-6680-2049-4
ISBN 978-1-6680-2051-7 (ebook)

TO DAD

Because I am as proud of you as you were of me

AUTHOR'S NOTE

Edgar Lacy's name was misspelled as Lacey his entire high school and college career, he said after signing with the Los Angeles Stars of the American Basketball Assn. in September 1968. He apparently never bothered to correct the mistake earlier. For purposes of consistency with coverage of UCLA during his years as a Bruin, Lacey is used in the book.

Lew Alcindor was given the name Kareem Abdul-Jabbar in 1968 as part of converting to Islam. He legally changed it in 1971, after his UCLA career. The book follows the timeline in using both.

Keith Wilkes converted to Islam and changed his name to Jamaal Abdul-Lateef in 1975, after leaving UCLA, but went by Jamaal Wilkes in NBA for familiarity. In 2023, after "I kind of circled back to the Christian faith," he said his legal name was Jamaal Keith Wilkes.

Ernest Maurice (Kiki) Vandeweghe III changed the spelling of his last name to VanDeWeghe in 2013 to honor the spelling used by his paternal grandfather and namesake.

Cities in China are identified by their name when a United States basketball team made an exhibition tour in 1973. Some were later changed.

CONTENTS

INTRODUCTION

Two of the hippies planning the October 21, 1967, protest against the Vietnam War went through proper channels and requested a permit to levitate the Pentagon three hundred feet off the ground. Much of the rest of the plan was in place. About one hundred thousand people would gather midmorning on the Mall in Washington for speeches denouncing American involvement before a portion of the crowd marched four miles through the District, over Memorial Bridge, and into Virginia to reach the country's military headquarters. Once there, it had been determined, perhaps with the same mystical calculations that settled on three hundred feet as the ideal elevation to dangle a federal building, that it would take twelve hundred demonstrators to encircle the Pentagon, chant the 3.7 million square feet into the air, turn it orange, and make the structure vibrate to cast out evil spirits. The United States would then have no choice but to retreat from Southeast Asia.

The man in charge of permits turned down the petition for paranormal life to rise the length of a football field into the sky but did approve ten feet of liftoff, either playing along or so disinterested in the discussion that he surrendered to a compromise. "We shall raise the flag of nothingness over the Pentagon and a mighty cheer of liberation will echo through the land," one plotter said of the blueprints that also included nabbing Lyndon Johnson, wrestling the president to the ground, and pulling his pants off. Another organizer flew home from a speech in Iowa, the heart of corn country, with a thirteen-pound sack of purchased cornmeal in the overhead bin, because no levitation would be complete without cornmeal spread along the same circle as the chanters.

When the day finally came and the crowd estimated anywhere from thirty thousand to fifty thousand shuffled over the bridge in the afternoon and to HQ, math and gravity intruded. Even with a much larger turnout than the twelve hundred thought to be needed, protesters could not surround the mammoth structure and, alas, could not sing it into the air. By dawn the next morning, nearly seven hundred activists had been arrested for various acts of civil disobedience and the few participants who remained mostly huddled together for heat after burning their signs overnight to stay warm.

John Wooden, a week into practice for the new season with his UCLA basketball team in Los Angeles, was not made for such times. His life had been built on structure, discipline, and humility, in an idealistic world where a person's word equaled a signed contract, where politicians were to be trusted, where money was not motivation, and where the Good Book mattered a few trillion times more than the playbook. Outlandish for Wooden was allowing players to dunk in practice years later, once. He spent decades feeling bad about a 100–78 victory against Washington State in 1966–67, which came with sophomore center Lew Alcindor on the court until the end, when the game was well in hand, and Alcindor piling on with 61 points, poor sportsmanship on Wooden's part that he never forgot. He would sell the Mercedes-Benz given as a retirement gift in 1975 in favor of a Ford Taurus.

Wooden was beginning his twentieth season in L.A. as protesters gathered on the Mall, but then and forever remained the Indiana farm boy who got an English degree from Purdue, recited poetry, and coached high school basketball in small-town Indiana and Kentucky and then at the university that would become known as Indiana State. He first shot hoops on a tomato basket with the bottom knocked out and nailed to a hayloft in the barn, near the white farmhouse with his parents in one bedroom and the four brothers in the other, two to a bed. Wooden met Nellie Riley as a high school freshman, took her to the ice-cream parlor for malteds, to the movie theater to watch Charlie Chaplin and Tom Mix, and held hands while sitting on the swing on the Rileys' porch. In his senior year, they agreed to see the preacher once John finished college, and they got married in 1932, when he was twenty-two and Nell was twenty-one.

Ever since arriving in 1948, they both found Los Angeles too fast, too filled with cement and with too many fake smiles, not like true friendships back home, so imagine John Wooden strapped in as the 1960s and '70s spun furiously out of control. Worse, some of his own players were at the forefront of this new parallel universe. That coach, that program, and those times. Wooden's Bruins won ten national championships in his final twelve seasons, but the seven in a row against the backdrop of a flammable America made it a dynasty unlike anything before or since. The Boston Celtics owned professional basketball mostly at the same time, with nine championships in the 1960s, but with largely the same core of players. UCLA conquered continuously despite three roster incarnations in their seven-year run alone, plus another group in the first two crowns and yet another in the last.

What were obviously overpowering teams in the moment, from the arrival of Lew Alcindor through the departure of Bill Walton, superstar center to superstar center, can be viewed with the perspective of time as even more impressive considering they were living inside a hurricane. The simple explanation is that the Bruins won all the time because of superior talent and coaching from Wooden and his assistants, but, really, they overcame. The disorder was not behind the scenes either. Their tension was visible: Alcindor and his stand for black pride that led to his controversial move to skip the 1968 Olympics, Walton and antiwar protests, one leading to his arrest, Wooden driven to heart problems and ultimately retirement by the pressure to keep the machine running.

Alcindor was an African American from New York who hated whites and had a disdain for plastic Los Angeles, Walton a San Diego hippie who thrilled in a good rebellion, Wooden the square from Indiana farm country. How fate did so drop them in the middle of everything. Vietnam. The Robert Kennedy assassination. The Martin Luther King murder. The Kent State killings. Death everywhere. Campus riots. Richard Nixon. The

Summer of Love. The 1968 of the bloody Democratic Convention and Black Power protests and the Mexico City Olympics. Ping-Pong Diplomacy. Governor Ronald Reagan as California's ball-busting high sheriff promising to take control of campuses in his state—"If it takes a bloodbath now, let's get it over with." The slaughter at the 1972 Munich Olympics.

In truth, the Bruins often won in spite of themselves. Players grew to bristle at the expectations, pushed back at Wooden's morality code, and in many cases were bored on the court rather than reveling in a champion's existence. Steve Patterson, Alcindor's successor, later referred to it as "a grandfatherly approach" the Bruins resented, and that Wooden either scolded or excused the Bruins of the early 1970s as "victims of a permissive society." The team and the time were linked on so many levels.

Vietnam by the 1967 Pentagon protest had resulted in nearly twenty-thousand American deaths, a number that reached fifty-eight thousand throughout Southeast Asia by the time the United States withdrew in 1975. The fact that classmates, some from high school, others from college, were being drafted and sent to fight made the war personal on every campus—statistics later compiled determined the average age of death was 23.1 years and that nearly 11,500 of the 58,000 were twenty years old or younger.

UCLA as a whole was not nearly the same danger zone as other campuses around the country and wasn't even close to the biggest in its own state. The University of California in Berkeley, near San Francisco, held that distinction. Los Angeles during the Bruin dynasty was, however, central to the description of a world turning ugly. The Watts riots were in 1965, RFK was gunned down there in 1968, and the killing spree by Charles Manson's followers came in 1969. The area would have been part of the national conversation no matter what, and then Alcindor became a face of the civil rights movement and Walton succeeded in making himself part of the Vietnam debate.

Experiencing UCLA some fifty years ago requires the reader to set aside or even completely forget the Wooden, Walton, and Alcindor, later Kareem Abdul-Jabbar, of the twenty-first century. Wooden was essentially the same person in the sixties and seventies, just in a much different role, one where he needed to be demanding. He did not have the close relationship with his two best players that would come later. The sweet country gent of the retirement years would not have lasted as the head coach of a premier program, just as his players then could not have imagined that the screamer riding them in practice would one day become known as a kindly sage admired nationally for a sweet disposition.

Walton and Abdul-Jabbar, though, changed dramatically, like so many others from college years into adulthood. Their pasts are worth remembering to illustrate a fascinating life arc for both, but spotting many similarities between the adult and the student will sometimes require squinting hard. As Walton came to say of his younger days, "I did not know how to play in the game of life. And that ultimately hurt me because I was unprepared, I was unsuspecting and I was undisturbed in my life. I've learned a lot and I've hopefully grown a lot. I've changed. I've changed."

He has spent about forty of the fifty years since apologizing, on several occasions to the UCLA chancellor at the time for a particularly ugly exchange and constantly to Bruin fans for four road losses in 1973–74. But Walton has never regretted the antiwar activism that brought so much attention, just as Abdul-Jabbar, who in his later years built on his 1960s stand on civil rights, has not shied from his past. Along with several teammates, the two biggest stars of the era, the bookends for the seven championships in a row, lived both personal conflict and extreme basketball success as the world raged around them, inside the program that became a kingdom on fire.

1

ON THE EVE OF DESTRUCTION

The center of attention in a crowded room, prodding strangers, no hope of blending among fellow students for emotional refuge—he hated these moments even while mature enough at eighteen years old to handle them. Lew Alcindor was then, as he would always be, an ideal teammate in part because he preferred to deflect the spotlight, the antithesis to his dominating presence on the court. The real joys were as in early 1963, as a high school sophomore at Power Memorial Academy in New York City when fellow Panthers staged a 7-Foot Party in the privacy of the locker room. He stood shoeless and backed against a pole, a teammate stepped on a chair and placed a ruler at the top of his head to draw a line, another unfurled a tape measure, and yes: seven feet tall. Lewie, as they called him, broke into a big smile and laughed along as the others jostled him in celebration before a player unveiled a doughnut-like pastry filled with jelly and topped by a candle to mark the occasion.

On May 4, 1965, though, senior Alcindor was alone among many. He stepped from the Power cafeteria into the gym at 12:33 p.m., wearing the school uniform of white dress shirt, dark blue slacks and jacket, and dark thin tie as several hundred sportswriters, photographers, TV crews, and radio broadcasters lined the room. Amid the snaking cables and equipment of the radio and TV men in the age of rapidly expanding electronics, appearing poised and articulate beyond his years, he confronted the microphone.

"I have an announcement to make," Alcindor said with some reporters underfoot and thrusting recording devices to catch the droplets of words. "This fall I'll be attending UCLA in Los Angeles."

Alarms sounded on wire-service teletype machines in newsrooms out to the West Coast, the *ding-ding-ding* of a bicycle bell alerted an arriving bulletin ahead of the black-and-white TV images to be beamed across the country. This was historic. Ferdinand Lewis Alcindor Jr. was seven feet, three-quarters of an inch, had scored more points and grabbed more rebounds than any high schooler in a city with a celebrated basketball tradition, and had led Power, an all-boys Catholic school on Manhattan's Upper West Side, to 71 consecutive victories. Not only that, UCLA coach John Wooden quickly noted, the recruit was "refreshingly modest and unaffected by the fame and adulation that have come his way, and he plays extremely well at both ends of the floor. His physical size is as much a part of his ability as his team play, hustle, and desire." The press conference had confirmed as much. Alcindor would rather have been anywhere else, yet handled the announcement with the ease of an experienced politician.

Speaking publicly at all was a big deal after the years Alcindor was gladly shielded by his Power coach, Jack Donohue, from the media and the sixty or so colleges that charged to recruit him. The family got an unlisted telephone number and hid behind the curtain. Even they did not want to step out of line. "Can't talk anymore, Mr. Donohue said not to say anything," Cora Alcindor said that morning, just before her son's lunch-hour announcement.

When it finally came time to break the silence, when Alcindor entered the gym in the formal Catholic school uniform to change the course of college basketball forever, he was even allowed to take questions. The decision came later in the academic year than originally anticipated, he responded to one query, because he was "very confused" about whether to stay close to home. It must have been news to Wooden, who believed Alcindor had committed to UCLA about a month before, at the end of the recruiting visit to Los Angeles. He expects to focus on liberal arts in college. He chose UCLA "because it has the atmosphere I wanted and because the people out there were very nice to me." No, he replied to another, apparently serious question, there are no liabilities to being tall in basketball.

In Los Angeles, UCLA athletic director J. D. Morgan, holding back his glee, pronounced the university "tremendously pleased" and added, "Of course, this is the boy's announcement. By the rules of our conference we are not permitted to announce such enrollments." The hype machine cranked up coast to coast, from the pulsing media market of the East to the publicity center in the West. "His high school press clippings make Wilt Chamberlain and Bill Russell look like YMCA athletes," John Hall wrote the next day in the *Los Angeles Times*. "His final decision was awaited with more mystery and fanfare than the word on the first trip to the moon. The pressure on him here will be tremendous."

Except pressure was nothing new, and a white columnist in his late thirties and twenty-five hundred miles away knew nothing about the scrutiny Alcindor had been living under. It wasn't grand UCLA, with national championships in 1964 and '65, the latter only six weeks before his announcement, but New York basketball had its own challenges. The longer the Power win streak went, the more the school and its star center became a target for opposing teams, for media, and for the public. The spotlight went from bright to searing to loathsome as sportswriters made victory a foregone conclusion and Alcindor lost the joy of playing before he left high school. He was eighteen and already burdened by success.

Plus, the racism. Alcindor entered Power the same year the Freedom Riders began in the Deep South and he followed developments as protesters, white and black, put themselves at risk to desegregate interstate buses. When his parents sent fifteen-year-old Lew to North Carolina on a Greyhound in April 1962 to attend the high school graduation of the daughter of a family friend, his body wedged into an aisle seat for the six-hundred-mile ride, Alcindor saw for himself: the WHITES ONLY signs of the Jim Crow era around restaurants, drinking fountains, and restrooms as the Greyhound reached Virginia and rolled farther south. Even the businesses he saw along the way. Johnson's White Grocery Store. Corley's White Luncheonette. Scared and conspicuous—tall, even for an adult, and black—he felt the need to ask local blacks, "Are you allowed to walk on the same side of the street as white people?"

It felt like being in a different country. Alcindor read about lynchings from his parents' subscription to *Jet* magazine. The anger from hearing about four girls, none older than fourteen, being killed in a bomb blast while attending a Bible class in a church in Birmingham, what the FBI later said was an act of the Ku Klux Klan, boiled inside him for months. His stomach clenched in fear as he waded into the dangerous world and pushed Alcindor to wonder if he would be hacked to death during the ride. He couldn't help but think of Emmett Till, murdered at fourteen while visiting Mississippi.

His own coach at Power, the same Jack Donohue who portrayed himself as Alcindor's protector, left Lew emotionally scorched as a junior in early 1964 with a halftime rant. As Power led a weak opponent by only 6 points with a 46-game winning streak on the line, a frustrated Donohue pointed at his star and shouted about not hustling, not moving, not doing any of the things Alcindor is supposed to be doing, how "You're acting just like a nigger!" Donohue initially spun the furnace blast of racism into good coaching, telling Alcindor after the victory it had been a motivational ploy, and a successful one at that, and down the line would say Lew misunderstood or deny making the comment at all.

Alcindor began to find his public voice when he joined the newspaper for the Harlem Youth Action Project in 1964. He covered a Martin Luther King Jr. press conference when the preacher came to New York, listening intently while standing in the third row of people behind King. That same year, seventeen-year-old Alcindor worked a fourth consecutive summer at Friendship Farm, a camp run by Donohue in upstate New York, teaching basketball to eleven- and twelve-year-olds out of obligation to his coach while mostly wishing he were somewhere else. In the months before his senior season of high school, Alcindor again planned to drop the job to focus on work that inspired him, as sports editor of the newspaper for a New York youth organization, only to be guilted into another trip to Friendship Farm when Donohue admitted using Lew's name to attract customers. Absentmindedly doodling in the dirt with a stick one day, his mind adrift with a world spinning wildly out of control, Alcindor looked down to see what he had scratched in the earth: DEATH TO THE WHITE MAN.

A week after returning from Friendship Farm in July 1964, a year before his UCLA decision, riots swept eight blocks of Harlem and Bedford-Stuyvesant after an off-duty police officer fatally shot fifteen-year-old James Powell. The cop claimed the shooting was a reaction to being attacked by Powell with a knife, but about a dozen witnesses countered the white lieutenant had gunned down the unarmed black ninth-grader. Back in the city from the beach on a hot, muggy Sunday, Alcindor got off the subway to browse jazz records before meeting friends, stepped from 125th Street station and face-to-face with chaos. Looting, smashing windows, cops swinging nightsticks, and flying bullets overwhelmed his senses. Unsure where the shots were coming from and with few options for taking cover, Alcindor did his best to crouch behind a lamppost as people ran past. He stood in shock, frozen except for a slight trembling, until he snapped out of the trance and took off in a dash for safety, thinking only that he wanted to stay alive. Finally finding sanctuary, "I sat there huffing and puffing, absorbing what I'd seen, and I knew it was rage, black rage. The poor people of Harlem felt that it was better to get hit with a nightstick than to keep on taking the white man's insults forever. Right then and there I knew who I was and who I had to be. I was going to be black rage personified, black power in the flesh. I was consumed and obsessed by my interest in black power, black pride, black courage."

It struck Alcindor that being so tall made him an easy target. He wanted to throw a brick, partly for the lieutenant who shot Powell, partly for the racist approach of Donohue, and partly for white teachers at Power "who didn't think it important to teach us about anyone with a black face." Alcindor decided against retaliating. Instead, he went to the office of the youth group's newspaper office and helped put out a special issue on the riot, "chronicling for history what the white media was ignoring. While they were busy tabulating the property damage and police injuries, we were tabulating the cost to the community, to individuals' spirits, to the hope of easing racial tensions." Interviewing residents who lived through the flashpoint, he felt their pain and related all too well to the suffering.

It took only until his senior year at Power for Alcindor, his insides churning, to become a "very bitter young man, and angry with racism." No longer was New York a place of youthful innocence, where he started going to Madison Square Garden regularly as a seventh-grader, learning winning basketball by watching Bill Russell when the Celtics visited, admiring the way Russell played for his teammates with rebounding and passing while being a menace defending the basket. It didn't feel insular anymore, as it had for so long in the Dyckman Street projects in Inwood, the multiethnic neighborhood at the northern peninsula of Manhattan, with the Hudson River to the west and the Harlem River to the east. Alcindor's father, Ferdinand Sr., a stern man of six foot three and two hundred pounds known as Big Al, was a police officer with the New York Transit Authority with a musicology degree from prestigious Juilliard and handed down his passion for jazz to his son. Along with his mother, Cora, a seamstress, Alcindor's parents made education and manners a priority. The home was filled with books and magazines and music and they decided their only child would always attend Catholic schools with the belief they were the best in the city.

The only child had the solitude of his own room in Dyckman from three years old through high school, a rarity among his friends. Yet he was a teenager thirsting for freedom from the mother he found overbearing and a distant father who would go days without talking to Lew, sometimes opening a book wide across his face to avoid eye contact with his son longing for a relationship. Arguably the greatest player in the history of the sport from high school through college and the pros would in retirement remember playing basketball with Big Al once. He wanted out.

Alcindor narrowed his college choice to Michigan, Columbia, St. John's, and UCLA. He liked Columbia as the chance to attend school walking distance to Harlem and a subway ride to the jazz clubs he had to leave early as a high schooler to make curfew. And making it in the Ivy League would send the message of Alcindor as more than a brainless jock. But the program consistently lost and he wanted to win, not build. St. John's had the lure of Joe Lapchick, a coach Alcindor respected professionally and liked personally—Alcindor had been friends with Lapchick's son since eighth grade and was a frequent visitor to the Lapchick home. The school was forcing Lapchick into mandatory retirement, though, removing the biggest appeal for Alcindor. When St. John's also attempted to hire Donohue as an assistant, likely in hopes of a Power package deal, the school, clearly unaware of Alcindor's bond with Lapchick and broken relationship with Donohue, had deeply wounded itself for years to come.

President Lyndon Johnson, a Texan, wrote on behalf of the University of Houston and its emerging program. Holy Cross, in some coincidence, hired Donohue as head coach in April, topping the St. John's opportunity, but Donohue's star from Power gave only a courtesy campus visit and did not seriously consider continuing the relationship. The memory of the halftime language, coaching strategy or not, stormed back into Alcindor's consciousness as he stood in the middle of the Harlem riot the following summer. While he would always praise Donohue for helping develop his game, Lew had no interest in more time together.

The decision came down to St. John's, soon to hire Lou Carnesecca as head coach, or UCLA. Alcindor felt an early connection with Wooden, albeit not to the same extent as with Lapchick, and no bullets had ever whizzed past his head in California. One was in Queens, a borough east of Manhattan, close enough to imagine Cora as a constant presence in his life at a time he wanted to escape the grip of parental oversight. The other was a continent away. So, UCLA.

Los Angeles would be different. He was sure of it. Alcindor dreamed UCLA into an Eden "where I would play basketball, study, go to an occasional beer bust, stroll arm in arm on the campus with the chicks, enjoy long bull sessions in the dorm with the cats and, in general, live the collegiate life that I'd read about and been promised by all those guys I'd talked to on my first visit the April before." Maybe it was best to get away from the prejudice of New York and what he saw as a semipermanent riot situation in Harlem, Alcindor told himself, while Southern California was a land "where people were color-blind, and a man could live his life without reference to color and race." The campus in particular was in open-minded Los Angeles, specifically in Westwood, a moneyed area neighboring the hillside homes of swanky Bel Air and a few miles from Beverly Hills.

And it felt so familiar. Jackie Robinson, who broke the baseball color barrier with his Dodgers debut in Brooklyn the day before Alcindor was born in

Harlem on April 16, 1947. Robinson played four sports at UCLA, including basketball, and became Lew's first hero, at age six. Robinson was also a favorite of Cora Alcindor's, who pointed out to her son how Robinson was so articulate, implying he was someone for Lew to pattern himself after. Don Barksdale, the first African American basketball Olympian for the United States, in 1948, was a Bruin. So was Willie Naulls, in the NBA from 1956 through 1966 and sometimes with teams that would practice at Power when in town to play the Knicks. (Naulls ended up with quite the side career as a recruiter. Knicks management once sent him to Boys High in Brooklyn to convince rising star Connie Hawkins to attend college in New York so the Knicks could later acquire him via the territorial draft. Red Auerbach, the coach and general manager of the Boston Celtics, similarly pushed to get Hawkins to a New England university. Both lost—Hawkins chose Iowa.)

UCLA graduate Ralph Bunche, the first colored man to win the Nobel Peace Prize, in 1950 for his work bargaining a cease-fire between Arabs and the new nation of Israel, wrote Alcindor on March 26, 1965, to promote the school's "exceptionally fine record with regard to thorough and relaxed integration." Robinson, Alcindor's hero, also sent a letter extolling its virtues. Even if no one realized it, though, Alcindor had been won over long before by the strangest of recruiting pitches: Rafer Johnson, the decathlon gold medalist at the 1960 Rome Olympics, on *The Ed Sullivan Show*. Johnson may have been awkwardly wedged among Imogene Coca in a comedy bit, a tap dancer, and a puppet act, plus other guests, but nothing was lost on Lew as he watched an African American talk about being student body president at UCLA. That stuck with Alcindor.

In a time of few games being televised nationally, and none during the regular season, scanning newspapers for box scores allowed him to track the basketball team from across the country, taking particular note as a Power junior when the Bruins beat bigger Kansas. UCLA relied on speed and execution not height and force, an important selling point for the emerging star as a skinny high school kid who didn't think he could survive the college muscle game despite an obvious size advantage. It was just how the Celtics played when he saw them at Madison Square Garden. A season later, with the recruiting battle peaking, Alcindor watched on TV as the No. 2–ranked Bruins beat No. 1 Michigan in Portland, Oregon, for the national title the same night twelve-year-old San Diego resident Bill Walton saw televised basketball for the first time. In Westwood, an estimated five hundred students celebrated by sitting in the middle of Wilshire Boulevard, a major thoroughfare, before returning to campus unscathed for the more traditional of victory rituals, a bonfire.

The official UCLA representatives, not the big-name alumni, first connected with Alcindor in his junior season, 1963–64. It may have been long after Alcindor rose to prominence, years since he was a headliner as a ninth-grader at the 1961 Christmas Holiday Festival upstate in Schenectady as Power lost to hometown Linton High with junior forward Pat Riley, but it was also exactly the right time. The Bruins, playing fluid and playing as a team, the approach that appealed to Alcindor, were about to win the first of their back-to-back national championships. Not only that, one of the stars was an African American from the East Coast, Philadelphia native Walt Hazzard, who wore uniform No. 42 in his own salute to Alcindor's beloved Jackie Robinson.

That Donohue wrote to say he would be attending the Valley Forge Basketball Clinic in Philly, where Wooden would be speaking, was critical as Wooden stuck to his policy of not initiating contact with prospects. Wooden would not, he made clear in advance to UCLA officials when he first arrived, chase high school students, and especially not high school students beyond the Los Angeles area. "My family comes first," he explained. "I would not go away to scout. I would not be away from home. I refused to do that, and I didn't have assistants do that." If he had to leave town often to recruit, Wooden said another time, he would quit instead. He did not break the pledge in the 1951–52 season for a senior in Oakland, Bill Russell, who chose the University of San Francisco and turned the Dons into a national power four hundred miles up the California coast from UCLA. Wooden didn't break it a few years later for Wilt Chamberlain in Philadelphia, before Chamberlain picked Kansas. So, too, it would be for a New Yorker as next in line among teen-sensation centers with immeasurable potential, a stand that became harder to challenge once Wooden had a first title as proof his unique methods worked. Donohue would have to take the initiative. Perhaps, the note to Los Angeles suggested, he and Wooden could meet at the clinic.

Wooden already knew of Alcindor, of course. Everyone did, and not just street hustlers who tried to deliver Lew to different high schools and the college recruiters who followed a few years later with similar selfish motives. Even before Alcindor played an NCAA game, the owner of the Los Angeles NBA franchise was already aiming for the prodigy's exit four years in the future: "That's the year the Lakers are going to win only three games. I don't know which three, but the Lakers are going to have the first pick in the draft. Alcindor will be the start of a new era." Jerry West met him as a ninth-grader when the Lakers, like several NBA teams, practiced at Power during New York stops to face the Knicks twelve blocks away at Madison Square Garden. Alcindor never forgot the positive emotions from a conversation with Auerbach around the same time, how the Celtic boss "took enough interest in me to talk" to a fourteen-year-old.

San Francisco Warrior Chamberlain, already a dominant center after five pro seasons, and Alcindor developed a friendship in the summer of 1964, when Chamberlain owned Harlem nightclub Big Wilt's Smalls Paradise, his Bentley parked in front to announce his presence. Seventeen-year-old Alcindor would watch Chamberlain team with Satch Sanders of the Celtics and retired guard Cal Ramsey in the prestigious Rucker Tournament, then sometimes join players back at Big Wilt's for festivities known to last until 4:00 a.m. Lew would occasionally tag along as the party continued to Chamberlain's two-bedroom apartment overlooking Central Park, where Wilt provided food, usually cold cuts, and an extensive collection of jazz records that played during card games. Chamberlain liked Alcindor and handed down custom-made clothes. Alcindor, in return, "stood in awe" of Wilt. On the night the group played hearts, the rule was simple: the loser drinks a quart of water. "Drink it or wear it." Alcindor lost three in a row and ingested the punishment. By the fourth defeat, he was done, incapable of swallowing more. The others held him down and doused away.

The rest of his world was not nearly as fun loving for Alcindor, as Donohue's wall of secrecy went up during Alcindor's junior season, even though it was a year away from the most impassioned of college pursuits. Donohue heard a man say, "Hello, Lew," one afternoon at Power and sternly responded, "You know the rule! No talking to my players. Out of the gym!" It came with complete backing from the family, with phone calls referred to Donohue, before the Alcindors switched to an unlisted number as an added precaution, and mail from colleges was forwarded unopened to Donohue. "We know what getting lots of publicity has done to other boys," Cora said. "We think Mr. Donohue is a very capable man. We are with him one hundred percent. When any of those cuckoos call, we tell them they'll have to speak with Mr. Donohue." As Lapchick, the St. John's coach and a good friend, said, "Jack Donohue has the most wanted basketball property in the nation. The boy just might win the national championship for some college. Jack could probably get a half dozen college jobs if he delivered Lew."

That wasn't going to happen, certainly not after Donohue's halftime outburst the season before Alcindor signed, and UCLA had too much of a head start anyway. Seeing Rafer Johnson on *Ed Sullivan*, watching the Bruins play with precision and camaraderie in winning the 1965 national championship in Portland, loving the image of the California vibe, and the chance to be connected to Robinson, Bunche, and the other African Americans who flourished there put the school at the top of his list before Alcindor had even been to L.A. Wooden asked one thing, that Alcindor make that the final campus visit. Lew had no problem with the minor detail.

He left New York with snow on the ground and landed to find UCLA preening, so washed by sunshine, open grounds, and a seventy-degree afternoon that he couldn't imagine living elsewhere. Two players, Edgar Lacey and Mike Warren, were dispatched to the airport to drive Alcindor to campus with specific instructions not to stare in amazement, a request that sounded reasonable enough until they saw a high school kid needing to duck to exit the plane. At that point, "It's like, 'Oh my God,'" Warren said. But also, the freshman guard said in a debriefing soon after, "One of the nicest people I've ever met." Warren kept reminding himself to not stare but couldn't help it. He even checked out Alcindor in the reflection of the glass in display frames along the wall as they strode down a corridor.

Alcindor folded himself into the front seat of Lacey's Volkswagen, knees mashed to chest, for the drive twenty miles north to Westwood.

Being shown around campus by Lacey, a starting forward, Alcindor was quickly taken by the realization that if he had a twenty-minute walk to class, the steps would be on more fresh grass than he had ever seen outside of Central Park. It felt like students strolling in shorts were a parade of fashion models. Couldn't he just stay, without going home to pack? Lacey, who had been a friend since they met as part of a group appearance of *Parade* magazine high school All-Americans on *Ed Sullivan* during Alcindor's sophomore year, laughed as Alcindor rubbernecked at the ladies. Lacey also filled him in on an important detail: black guys hung together, but the whites were okay, too.

When it was time to meet Wooden, Alcindor found the coach's small office, which was part of the temporary housing for the athletic department, Quonset huts of shiny corrugated steel with a new basketball arena under construction nearby. "We expect our boys to work hard and to do well with their schoolwork," Wooden told him, traces of a slight Indiana twang coming through. "I know that should not be a problem for you, Lewis." Hearing the formal, grown-up version of his name, not Lew or Lewie the way he was used to being addressed, felt good. Wooden in pressed white shirt and black tie, with a sport jacket on the corner coatrack, appeared to be a soft-spoken gentleman of the 1800s, with straight gray hair parted close to the middle, glasses, more quaint schoolhouse teacher than head of the best college basketball program in the country. He was every bit the grandfatherly sort that *Los Angeles Times* columnist Jim Murray would come to describe as "so square, he was divisible by four."

Wooden through the years would dislike an emphasis on weight lifting for creating "heavily muscled fellows," and Auerbach would remember Wooden's response after being congratulated on Alcindor's UCLA announcement: "Oh, you mean the chap from New York? Yes, we're quite pleased to have him." Wooden the high school coach would keep his team in the locker room after games longer than necessary in hopes girlfriends would give up and leave, saving players from the late nights out they wanted. He diagrammed his philosophies into a triangle-shaped composition of so much detail and introspection that Wooden began jotting down his Pyramid of Success in 1934 while teaching high school in South Bend, Indiana, and did not finish until 1950 at UCLA after countless revisions.

Wooden immediately struck Alcindor as an elder in the best sense of the word—respected and respectful, wise but not in a hurry to impress, attentive to the task at hand. Though ordinarily quick to find faults in others, especially strangers who needed him, and despite a hostility toward white people, Alcindor liked Wooden right away. Wooden won him over with a calm demeanor that made no attempt to hurriedly win over the best recruit in the country with a power play or attempt to look smart. The white fifty-four-year-old from Midwest farm country and the black teen from East Coast concrete shared similar personalities in a lot of ways. It probably didn't hurt that Wooden was the opposite of Donohue and his gift of gab and brash sense of humor that could go overboard and would often point at the Power students. Wooden seemed more serious and almost rustic enough for Alcindor to imagine him driving a hay wagon. "He wanted to see UCLA with his own eyes, not get a painted picture from anyone," Morgan, the athletic director, said. "If we ever used a soft sell, it was on Alcindor." At the end of the visit, in the car as Wooden drove him to the airport for the return to New York, Lew—Lewis—said he had decided to attend UCLA.

Upon returning home, though, Alcindor started to agonize over the decision. He visited, and enjoyed, Michigan. He got another guilt trip from Donohue, who had taken the Holy Cross job fifty miles west of Boston and was pressuring Alcindor to visit. "You owe it to me," the coach said. Alcindor, despite telling Wooden that UCLA would be the final visit, went to Massachusetts without any intention of choosing the school, a sentiment affirmed as he took note of the lack of colored students. And when a black student was chosen to give the campus tour, the guide barely waited for Donohue to be out of earshot before advising Alcindor, "If you come here, you're crazy. This is the worst place for you to go to school. You won't have any fun at all. You'll be isolated, like I am. *Man, pick someplace else!*" Lew was going to anyway.

Wooden, still never having seen Alcindor play, flew to New York for a 1:00 a.m. meeting with his parents, after Big Al pulled a four-to-midnight shift. Morgan not only insisted Wooden continue to pursue Alcindor, even if it meant leaving Los Angeles, he also directed Wooden to take assistant coach Jerry Norman, a Catholic, in case the Alcindors had questions about church life around campus.

Morgan thought the process through in ways Wooden never did, despite the enormous stakes and despite Wooden's being an experienced coach, leading Norman to conclude Wooden did not want the nation's best prospect in many years. Wooden, Norman said, "was afraid we wouldn't win with him and then we'd get criticized." In a time few were aware Wooden could be overly sensitive, Norman had not forgotten coming to the office the first workday after the 1964 title and hearing Wooden say, "Worst thing to happen to us." The coach did not want the expectations.

The strange New York trip, going across the country for what figured to be sixty or ninety minutes of conversation, was by Wooden's count just his fourth or fifth home visit in seventeen seasons on the job. It also made UCLA the only school to be invited to the Alcindors' apartment. But the meeting felt good, a relaxed discussion among the adults while Lew waited anxiously in another room for his parents to give their final approval. Basketball was barely mentioned before Norman and Wooden flew to Kansas City for a morning introduction to the mother of another top recruit, Lucius Allen. The whirlwind itinerary would become among the most important thirty-six hours in the history of UCLA sport, before the jet-setters returned to California late in the afternoon.

Announcing his college decision remained the last major moment in Lew's life until graduation. The press conference in the Power cafeteria came seven days after Martin Luther King arrived at UCLA, stepped on the stage erected for the speech, and said in his evangelical tone that segregation was on its deathbed and "it's only a matter of how expensive the segregationists will make the funeral." Students staffed tables during the hour-long address and collected $747.98, which King said would go toward the voter-registration drive. Alcindor had covered the King press conference in New York, and now they shared at least a distant connection of putting UCLA in the headlines within a week. Awash in black pride, Lew was getting the chance to attend the school where Jackie Robinson studied, Rafer Johnson led, and King spoke.

The summer months that followed the press conference in the Power gym, his final days as a full-time New Yorker, were surrounded by what little remained of Alcindor's youthful innocence. A prominent UCLA graduate, movie producer Mike Frankovich, arranged a job for Alcindor at Columbia Pictures in New York for $125 a week, mostly delivering interoffice memos. And rarely in recent years had he been able to be a more typical kid than when New York sportswriter Phil Pepe set up through the Mets public relations department for Alcindor to go behind the scenes and watch the Dodgers, Jackie Robinson's former team, play the Mets at Shea Stadium in Queens. The *New York World-Telegram and The Sun* staffer first heard of Alcindor when a phone call tipped him off about a six-foot-eight thirteen-year-old ransacking the youth leagues. You will be interested in the grammar school game in the upcoming triple-header at Fordham, Pepe was informed, not just the main events of the high school or college contests. Over time, Pepe would become the rarest of people in Lew's life, a reporter who could be let in, an older white man who could be a friend. Now Pepe was providing Alcindor with the rare gift of being an average teenager.

On August 26, 1965, they met for an early dinner at Pepe's home. Alcindor was respectful and a little shy but did not seem uncomfortable and referred to his host as Mr. Pepe until being told to use Phil. When they got to Shea, Lew in the visitors' clubhouse was any starry-eyed kid surrounded by heroes, awestruck while being introduced to Don Drysdale, Willie Davis, Maury Wills, and Sandy Koufax, the star pitcher who once received a basketball scholarship to the University of Cincinnati before turning his attention to baseball. Some Dodgers treated the visiting teenager as the celebrity, not the other way around. The Mets, with a dreadful roster in their fourth year of existence, en route to losing 112 games and finishing 47 games out of first place in the National League, were just happy to have Alcindor at the park, even if his boyhood allegiances were to the Dodgers. A local hero, sure, but also a welcome distraction.

Back in the real world, Alcindor's dreamy vision of Los Angeles was crashing down before he could get there. On August 11, three months after the announcement to attend UCLA and the month before Alcindor would begin campus life, fifteen days before the boyish time at Shea Stadium, black motorist Marquette Frye was stopped by the California Highway Patrol for driving a 1955 Buick erratically in the Watts section. A crowd gathered on a muggy night. Authorities said he resisted arrest, resulting in Frye being clubbed with a nightstick and knocked unconscious. He said cops roughed up his mother when she arrived and tried to stop them from impounding her car. The cops countered that she jumped on another officer. The group began to throw rocks and bottles. Soon, an estimated five thousand people convened in a swath of the city that was sealed off by an estimated one hundred policemen and three hundred deputy sheriffs, with the National Guard about to be called in as pockets of violence erupted through the night. White occupants were pulled from cars by the crowd, even a cop from a police car, and a civilian was told, "This is no place for white men," as he was being dragged out and beaten. The offensive finally halted when other police vehicles arrived.

Visiting friends in Watts with his parents and two siblings, twelve-year-old Keith Wilkes heard the loud pop of gunfire on the first day of the riots. He was close enough to the mayhem to come out of the house and see looters charging out of stores with merchandise. (The Wilkes family quickly returned to their quiet beachfront town sixty miles away.) Frye was released from police custody the next day, saw the smoke rising to the sky, heard for the first time about the death and destruction on the radio, and began to cry in horror. When TV stations sent reporters—white reporters—to cover the unrest, their cars were stoned and some attackers threatened the media against returning. Given that militants had been shooting at firefighters trying to extinguish the burning landscape, these warnings were to be believed. Somewhere in there, the police were trying to restore order, although in some cases the same police who had been known to prepare for shifts in the ghetto by shouting out, "L-S-M-F-T!"—Let's Shoot a Mother Fucker Tonight. With Governor Pat Brown vacationing around the Mediterranean, it was left to Lieutenant Governor Glenn Anderson and the cops to tragically mishandle the response. Police declared the situation "rather well in hand" on the morning of the third day, when it was so not well in hand that violence resumed within hours of daylight. Anderson was more concerned about rumors that student protesters in Berkeley were plotting a lie-in to stop marching troops that he turned his back on Watts and flew north to meet with University of California regents.

Governor Brown learned from reading a Greek newspaper that the largest city in his state was in flames and quickly started the twenty-four-hour journey home. On final approach into Los Angeles International Airport, the French pilot reported the view looked similar to war zones he flew over in World War II. As the inner-city raged twenty miles southeast of Westwood, some twelve thousand members of the National Guard were patrolling the streets in troop carriers and barricading the Harbor Freeway to ensure the crucial driving artery that cut north-south near Watts remained open. That night, when television station KTLA aired the documentary *Hell in the City of Angels,* video was shown of cops in white helmets kicking suspects in the ass and poking gun barrels into other body parts and calling out, "First one drops their hands is a dead man." By the time violence was officially extinguished on August 17, thirty-four people had died, more than one thousand were injured, and six hundred buildings were damaged amid an estimated $40 million of property destruction.

Alcindor was walking straight into another racial tinderbox, the same cauldron of fury and frustration that he'd felt, like a body blow, upon stepping out of the 125th Street subway station thirteen months and twenty-five hundred miles earlier. UCLA may have been a progressive college campus, and it may have been located in a shimmering part of town, twenty freeway miles from the despair of Watts, but nothing could mask the truth that Los Angeles would not be the escape he had imagined.

Wooden's summer, meanwhile, was marked with uncertainty surrounding Alcindor. Wooden won the national championships in 1964 and '65 with teams that were scrappy and small and utilized a speed game with a pressure defense to constrict opponents into mistakes that resulted in a sprint the other way for easy Bruins baskets. The coach subtly but clearly made sure before games that referees saw he had a stopwatch, a pointed reminder to be ready to call a violation when the other team failed to get the ball past half-court within ten seconds. Even if Wooden might not ever actually look at the timer after tip-off, he wanted refs thinking about it. The first group went 30-0 without a starter taller than six-five and was so athletic that Fred Slaughter attended school on a scholarship split between basketball and track, while Keith Erickson's scholarship was shared by basketball and baseball and he would also later make the U.S. Olympic team in volleyball. "Have you ever been locked up in a casket for six days?" USC coach Forrest Twogood asked. "That's how it feels" to face the menacing defense. The California coach Rene Herrerias labeled Erickson, the last line of protection in the 2-2-1 zone, "a six-five Bill Russell."

With Alcindor, an actual Russell on defense, there would be no more scrappy. The new roster was made to stomp, not outrun, opponents after adding Alcindor, Allen, and forward Lynn Shackelford within ten days of each other. For reasons that never became clear, Wooden questioned whether Alcindor would follow through and show up in September for the start of classes, just as Wooden never believed the Bruins had much chance to win the recruiting battle in the first place. But the desire to *not* get Alcindor had become so obvious to Norman that he noted several instances during the late-night visit to the Alcindor home of Wooden saying, "If Lewis doesn't want to come to UCLA, we will understand." It was all but inviting Alcindor to change his mind. "He practically begged him not to come," Norman said, "but the kid wanted to come so bad."

To the Bruins' top assistant coach, Wooden pursued one of the most promising prospects in basketball history only because Morgan commanded him. Wooden wouldn't cross his boss even years later, after building much more clout, so he certainly wasn't going to ignore Morgan's wishes in 1965. Little did Wooden know how enthusiastic Alcindor was to get there, or anywhere beyond "the stifling shadow of my father and the emotional grip of my mother." He was sentimental in snapping a series of pictures with a 35 mm camera on the final day around New York, wondering whether he was hedging emotional bets by keeping pieces of the hometown with him or documenting the departure to prove to himself that he'd really made it out. Beyond that, Lew was anxious enough to sprint to Los Angeles.

2

UNVEILINGS

The flight descended into midday Southern California on a Saturday in September with Alcindor so deep in contemplation staring out a window that Kenneth Kelly, a friend who made the trip with plans to attend nearby Santa Monica City College, took note of the pronounced faraway gaze. Alcindor would remember only the chill of the air-conditioning while walking through the airport corridors and stepping outside to see the L.A. skyline as "a theme-park, kiddie-size version of New York," nothing like the forest of spikes in Manhattan. Palm trees did rustle in the breeze, a cliché come to life.

The first night at school was solitary, with more stares in one trip to the Student Union than in a month of subway rides at home, a dinner alone, and returning to his dorm to fall asleep. Being assigned the upbeat and outgoing Lucius Allen as a roommate on the first floor of Dykstra Hall was the fortuitous coincidence of two targets of the whirlwind Wooden–Norman recruiting trip ending up together and hitting it off. New York and Kansas converging in Los Angeles became one of the best things that could have happened to Alcindor. Before they learned what the connection would mean on the court, Allen's skilled ball handler to Alcindor's No. 1 option on offense, Alcindor found Allen's endearing disposition one of the best parts about the move that was otherwise startling. The future basketball great Alcindor in the months ahead also shot pool in Dykstra with sophomore quarterback Gary Beban, a future Heisman Trophy winner in the innocence of friendly 1965 competition with Alcindor reaching across the table to get any shot at any angle he wanted.

A phone call woke Alcindor the next morning, Sunday. The athletic department asked the front desk in the dormitory to inform him about Catholic mass at the Newman Center and that directions could be provided. He mumbled in appreciation, hung up, went back to sleep, and for the first time in his life, eighteen years old and on his own, intentionally missed church. Liberation. When he finally got up for good, it was to stroll around campus on a bright, beautiful day, a newspaper in hand, and to breakfast while noticing people relaxing on the grass having conversations before classes started.

His was a life of privilege of being escorted through orientation week while other incoming students searched on their own and receiving a rare invitation to watch football practice in advance of the season opener. He and Allen continued to hit it off talking basketball, girls, and school. Lynn Shackelford and Kenny Heitz, both part of the heralded recruiting class, and redshirt freshman Bill Sweek also lived in Dykstra and became friends. When the first-year players, ineligible for varsity competition under NCAA rules, took the court for a pickup game, four freshmen faced four varsity players, returnees from the squad that won the national championship six months before. First to 15 baskets. The freshmen won three in a row. Allen, a quick guard with the ability to drive around opponents and the counter of a dependable jump shot, proved impossible to defend.

It took three days to be walking with Kelly on campus and hear three white cats behind them.

"Hey, is that Lew Alcindor?"

"Yeah, that's him. He's nothing but a big nigger."

Alcindor wheeled around to respond as the instigator strolled off and Lew considered grabbing him. Kelly talked his friend out of escalating the situation by reminding Alcindor they had not been on campus long, as if to suggest a fight wouldn't be a good first impression. Alcindor felt stranded on a raft in the middle of an ocean. Few around him seemed fazed by the Watts riots that charred a portion of the city two months earlier. Alcindor was indignant at how Westwood, in a bubble removed from the strife, merrily went on its way. He was outnumbered by students, some twenty or twenty-one years old, whose idea of fun was to flood a hallway about four feet wide and fifty yards long in the dorm, get naked, and slide bare ass across the tiles. Other times, they would chase each other up and down the corridors to deliver goosings. Alcindor was younger yet mature enough to care about what happened in Harlem and Bedford-Stuyvesant, in Inwood, and now he looked around for the response to Watts and was disappointed to see none. "And not only did it mean nothing to most of these kids," Alcindor concluded, "but most of them were not even aware that there were hungry people in East Los Angeles. They didn't know because they didn't care to know. They were juveniles, children, babies. I just couldn't warm to people like this, and since they weren't all that crazy about me, I stayed primarily with the black brothers."

He was already souring inside, finding problems with the new surroundings barely after moving in, becoming annoyed at the world around him with great speed. The skyline was underwhelming. The plastic people were unworthy of his time. There was no hope of finding friendship among a population tucked into cars. Even the palm trees that had struck him as a grand entrance at the airport. Alcindor decided they just stuck up like rows of parking meters. Frequenting jazz clubs helped wash away the loneliness, but he connected with little else beyond the savored nights at the Lighthouse, Shelly's Manne-Hole, Marty's on the Hill, and the It Club.

"I quickly discovered that there is no special breed of people called Californians, with their own culture and background and attitudes," he said. "I discovered that most Californians came from other places, where racial prejudice abounded, and some of these Californians had the same feelings about race as their friends back home. To these bigoted people, deep down inside, I was nothing but a jive nigger. Oh, they'd try to overcome their feelings. Once in a while one of them would get up the courage to engage us in conversation, but it was hopeless. Many of these people could not relate to a black man. I realized very quickly that my attempt to outflank the racial wall had failed. I'd first observed the wall at St. Jude's in New York, and now I knew that it extended all the way from Jones Beach to Santa Monica. There was no way to outflank it." Many members of the basketball program in turn found themselves rejected by Alcindor in many failed, frustrating attempts at conversation that mostly brought a series of one-word answers.

Progressing from pickup games to the start of practice on October 15 provided a desperately needed comfort zone for the player and, surprisingly, the coach who had little experience directing talented big men and privately doubted he could bring the best out of Alcindor. Wooden gathered players in a classroom, stood before the Bruins, and delivered instructions to keep their fingernails trimmed, their jerseys tucked in, and their hair short. Shocked newcomers looked on in disbelief, matching the Day 1 reaction of some members of past classes and many to come, unaware that every John Wooden season started with a conversation on grooming. He usually also covered the topic in a summer note with slight variations sent to players in advance of reporting for the season ahead: arrive without mustaches, beards, or goatees and sideburns no longer than the top of the earlobe, and Wooden would be the final word on what constitutes suitable hair length. "From the minute a UCLA Bruin put on a UCLA uniform—even a practice uniform—I wanted him to recognize that he was now part of something special, an organization, a team, a group that did things differently," Wooden would come to write. "And it did things the right way all the time, starting from the ground up."

Wooden saw the grooming directives as the same devotion to the minuscule, not, contrary to perception, pushing back against the times. Beards and long hair get soaked with sweat in games, a player might run his hands through the perspiration, and that could lead to problems handling the ball. Longer hair also meant more to dry after showers and, therefore, a greater chance of getting sick after stepping into cold weather. Alcindor considered pointing out colds were caused by viruses, not wet hair, then thought better of speaking up.

Wooden as a coach renowned for attention to detail oversaw menus for team meals, directed that the water served be at room temperature because drinks cooled by ice might cause stomach cramps, and in the locker room before the 1967 championship game against Dayton used the chalkboard to diagram where players should stand for the national anthem. Wooden told *Sports Illustrated* writer Joe Jares he liked balanced uniform numbers, a 32 or 11 or 55. Two fat numbers or two thin numbers, but not the devil's work of a 41 or 15, as if concerned the wrong combination could cause a player to tip over.

He changed the habit of providing chocolate to players for a halftime energy boost after determining the candy left phlegm in windpipes, and decided oranges sliced into quarters would provide the same jolt at a lower risk. "Phlegm, like shoestrings that come undone, can cause distraction, which leads to errors that can get you outplayed." Student managers through the years fell into a routine of going to Food Services in a nearby building before the game, taking the box of a couple dozen or so navels set aside, and returning to Pauley Pavilion, to the manager's room adjacent to the locker room, to cut citrus. On the road, the host team would provide oranges; managers often brought a knife from the hotel and sliced away to keep to the halftime routine. Managers also had the responsibility of collecting the game programs, setting one in the stall for every player, and delivering one to each of the three coaches with more than enough time for Wooden to roll his into a long pipe on the bench just before tip-off, to be used for smacking it into a palm or hiding his mouth for covert comments.

The attention to specks became legendary. Wooden wrote each practice plan on a three-by-five index card in cursive and kept his notes to be used as a blueprint when planning workouts at the same time, sometimes even the same dates, in later seasons. If need be, he could go back dozens of years and find what the Bruins worked on at four thirty on a given afternoon because repetition would always be a prized teaching tool to him. His personal notebooks would be updated, sometimes after a game and sometimes at the end of a season, one a compilation of stats, the other a collection of drills and practices.

The staff often spent two hours in the morning discussing practices, and then in the afternoon Wooden sometimes left the floor to watch part of the session from the concourse between the first and second levels or from the top row, within arm's reach of the ceiling. He might learn something from the different perspective. The games, in the coach's mind, had already been played in the isolation of fan-free gyms in afternoons throughout the week.

Wooden the preparation freak tracked drills timed almost to the second on the logged file cards. While the varsity worked behind a partition on one end of the gym, rarely seeing the seven-foot phenom or his team-mates, the freshmen learned the crisp routine. Two minutes of layups, two minutes of reverse layups from both sides, five minutes of ballhandling work, ballhandling on the fast break for a layup, ballhandling on the fast break for a jumper, practicing shooting, practicing shooting a bank shot. And everyone did everything, regardless of position.

"Good afternoon, gentlemen," Wooden told the freshman team on October 15, 1965.

"Good afternoon, Coach."

"Today, we are going to learn how to put on our sneakers and socks correctly."

The greatest first-year class in college basketball history looked around and waited for the punch line. Wooden, never one to joke about something as serious as footwear details, bent down and removed his shoes and socks, exposing pale pink feet to light. "We are going to talk about tug and snug," he said. "Tug. And. Snug." Wooden saw the puzzled expressions coming back in his direction and grinned. "As Benjamin Franklin said, 'For want of a nail,'" he noted, as if that explained everything. Correctly sensing more confusion than before, Wooden moved forward with the Founding Father.

"For the want of a nail the shoe was lost,

"For the want of a shoe the horse was lost,

"For the want of a horse the rider was lost,

"For the want of a rider the battle was lost,

"For the want of a battle the kingdom was lost,

"And all for the want of a horseshoe nail."

Wooden shrugged. "You want to learn about basketball, read Benjamin Franklin."

His new Bruins were somewhere between stunned and confused at the introduction to actual UCLA basketball.

If you do not pull your socks on tightly, Wooden went on, finally getting to his point, you're likely to get wrinkles. Wrinkles cause blisters. Blisters force players to the sideline. Players on the sideline result in losses. Don't just tug, he directed. Be snug.

Alcindor asserted himself on the first day under assistant coach Gary Cunningham, running the freshman squad, with a display that instantly convinced Wooden his next center would dominate varsity opponents when the time came. Not stopping at pronouncing himself "amazed" by the physical presence and "extraordinary demeanor," Wooden offered the highest praise possible, that Alcindor reminded him of his beloved father in poise and self-control. Comparing anyone in a positive way to the quiet strength and dignity of Hugh Wooden would have been compliment enough.

Alcindor, though, took the opposite tack and maintained an emotional distance that never fully disappeared in their four-year partnership. Still feeling the emotional wound of his high school coach's racist halftime rant, Alcindor maintained a defensive stance to ensure he would not get hurt the same way and "kept myself a little aloof from Coach Wooden. I had been trusting once and had my heart broken. I wouldn't let it happen again. I couldn't afford to. I would force myself to be wary, especially of older white men pretending to be my friend." Cunningham, a slightly older white man of twenty-five, still found Alcindor teachable and attentive and that he "played so effortlessly that it didn't look like he was working hard, but really he just did things efficiently."

Cunningham, a UCLA guard from 1959 to 1962 back on campus taking classes toward a doctorate with plans to become a college professor, had accidentally walked into history as the first college coach of the player on a path to change amateur sports forever. On the 1965 morning that changed everything, Cunningham was getting breakfast in the Student Union when he spotted his former coach eating alone at a table. He asked to sit with Wooden and ended up in a conversation that included the news that the Bruins had just lost the freshman coach. Wooden offered Cunningham the job before the end of the meal. A high school junior varsity coach in Ohio tried to land what had suddenly become an unusually attractive role, in the program coming off back-to-back national championships, on the team with a historically good freshman roster, but Cunningham had already been hired. The best Wooden could offer was the chance to scout UCLA opponents and help Cunningham with the newcomers, an invitation Bob Knight declined.

Needing someone to challenge Alcindor, since it wasn't going to happen in practices with six-foot-five Lynn Shackelford as the next-tallest freshman, coaches brought in six-eight Jay Carty, an Oregon State player turned UCLA grad student. Carty at twenty-four years old bullied the prized recruit in a way no one else could, certainly no first-year player and maybe no one on any varsity team, either. When Alcindor faded away on his shots instead of going straight up or to the basket, Carty stressed how the student landed out of position to rebound. When he went through full college practices, he tired easily from running. Carty made Alcindor leap to touch a chalk line on the backboard eleven and a half feet high fifteen times in a row, and then, when they played one-on-one to 20, "I jumped on him. I did everything I could to try and rattle him." To Alcindor, getting bruised by a knee shot from Carty, jolted by a hip check, or cracked by a sharp elbow were obvious tests from coaches concerned basketball was coming too easy.

Lew Alcindor took the court in a UCLA uniform for the first time on November 27, 1965, surrounded by teammates who would have been an enviable recruiting class on their own but were brought to UCLA with the center in mind: Shackelford in part because his shooting range was the ideal complement for Alcindor's inside attack and partly because Shackelford was left-handed and Wooden planned to deploy Alcindor mostly on the left side of the court; Heitz, a defensive specialist whose intelligence and quickness made him a good fit to patrol the other side of the perimeter, away from Alcindor; and Allen, with the physical gifts to become as good as any Bruin guard in the Wooden years and dominate the perimeter while his roommate anchored the inside. Kent Taylor, a walk-on from Texas, was the fifth starter. The freshmen against the varsity may have been an exhibition, an annual tune-up for the older players before the real games, a glorified scrimmage in front of a crowd after practicing in solitude, but this time was different with the three returning starters and one key reserve from the NCAA champions of 1965 against the Team With Alcindor. Not only that, it would be the first game in the new on-campus arena, Pauley Pavilion.

Wooden had been promised a new building since he took the job in 1948 after two seasons as coach at Indiana State Teachers College, sixty-five miles from where he grew up among the farmlands of Centerton and Martinsville in his late teens and early 20s during the Depression. Ending up at UCLA was a fluke more than anything. He had decided to take the job at the University of Minnesota, familiar Midwest territory, not some big city in faraway California. Wooden only needed approval from the administration in Minneapolis to bring his own assistant coach rather than keep the holdover on staff and it would be done. He planned to get final confirmation from Minnesota athletic director Frank McCormick over the phone on April 17 at 6:00 p.m., accept the job in Minneapolis, and talk to UCLA an hour later to deliver his regrets. But when a storm blew through the Twin Cities and McCormick got snowed in and, unbeknownst to Wooden, cut off from communications, the Bruins phoned at the appointed time. Wooden accepted. When McCormick finally got through an hour later and urged Wooden to inform UCLA there had been a change of heart, Wooden declined. He had made a commitment.

Wooden was appalled at the facilities when he visited Westwood during the interview process, one of the reasons he preferred Minnesota and its large field house. The Bruins played on the third floor of the Men's Gym, originally able to hold twenty-four hundred fans before being reduced to fifteen hundred by the fire marshal, cold enough in winter to be known as the Ice Box, while other days it heated up with such a stench that it changed into the B.O. Barn. Wooden considered a lot of high school arenas in Indiana better. The conditions were so bad they almost drove him to accept an offer from Purdue after his second season in Los Angeles before he decided it would not be right to leave with a year remaining on the contract he, not the UCLA administration, had pushed for.

He both came to UCLA and remained at UCLA out of moral obligation or guilt, not preference, first turning away from the Minnesota opportunity Wooden preferred and then the Purdue job because he could not break his word. The reward for loyalty and building a championship program in difficult conditions was a shanty arena and empty campaign promises from school officials about a new home while the Bruins played in nine off-campus venues through the years, including the Sports Arena practically on the grounds of rival USC. The major facility would be completed within three years, they assured him, by 1951.

Edwin W. Pauley Pavilion actually opened in June 1965. Either no one realized or spoke up to note the irony of the most visible building on a progressive campus being named after a Ronald Reagan backer and vocal critic of student protests, even in later years of demonstrations within a hundred yards of the building. Once a Democratic power broker—treasurer of the national committee, friend to President Harry Truman, director of the 1944 convention that nominated Franklin Roosevelt for a fourth term—Pauley by the mid-1960s had made such a hard conservative turn as a University of California regent that the FBI planned to leak him documents to undercut the Free Speech Movement in Berkeley. In an era of J. Edgar Hoover's bureau and the CIA conducting unlawful intelligence operations together to harass students, faculty, and liberal UC regents, as well as making up false claims to destroy the career of the UC president, the namesake of the arena known as the Memorial Activities Center during its planning participated in smear campaigns and conspiracies to ruin people on the opposite side politically.

University of California regent H. R. Haldeman meanwhile embraced the role of chief fundraiser. Haldeman was a proud alum who met his future wife at UCLA, met fellow student John Ehrlichman on campus, and cheered for the basketball team and especially for the coach he admired as a man of character. Haldeman felt additionally connected as a member of the Bruin Hoopsters, who met weekly during the season in the back room of a restaurant. Wooden would speak to the booster club several of the Mondays, even the nights with as few as ten people attending, giving Haldeman the gratification of helping Wooden. They also happened to be Beta Theta Pi fraternity brothers, though from chapters half a continent apart, and Wooden was greatly pleased his vagabond program would finally have a permanent home and appreciated Haldeman's large role in making the project a reality. It was Haldeman, after all, who heard oil magnate and Cal grad Edwin Pauley wanted to make a large donation to one of the UC campuses and then corralled the $1 million for his favorite school and favorite team, such a generous contribution that the building was named for Pauley.

Just moving in created the new perception of UCLA as an energized program of the future even after losing the core of the back-to-back title teams. The timing of Alcindor and the dreamy recruiting class arriving and the gleaming arena opening within three months would have been an exciting restart no matter what, but Wooden in his eighteenth Bruin season also mostly used the same playbook that called for a fast and fun playing style. The team traveled to the Midwest at least once a season and sometimes the East Coast as well, and players lived in limelight and sunshine at home. While it may not have been worth the wait—nothing could pay back fourteen years of patience—the finished product embodied the exciting and imposing roster in the making, feeding the belief the operation with two championships in two years was not close to peaking. Pauley, Wooden came to say, "was the greatest thing to ever happen to me at UCLA," with the disclaimer that he advised on the locker rooms and adding a second full-size court perpendicular to the main surface so both varsity and freshman teams could practice at the same time. A curtain eased down from the rafters on demand for separation, and trimmings included theater-style seats in some areas and bleachers with blue-padded seating in others.

The timing, though laughably behind schedule, turned out to be perfect, coinciding with Alcindor's arrival and making November 27, 1965, a night of dual unveilings. One building hosting basketball for the first time, one skyscraper making his debut for the freshman team, countless possibilities for the future. The varsity had lost standouts Goodrich and Erickson to graduation from the 28-2 team, but the returning roster was still held in such high regard that the Bruins were an overwhelming preseason choice by the United Press International panel of coaches to win the 1966 title as well. The freshmen had never played a game together and certainly had never stood inside the hurricane of the varsity's famed panic-inducing zone press. Plus, school officials attached "Salute to John Wooden" night with the christening, with the guest of honor being feted with gifts and speeches before the 8:30 p.m. tip-off. The crowd of 12,051, which included wife Nell Wooden, son Jim, daughter Nan, and an estimated seventy-five players from his previous seventeen UCLA teams, delivered three standing ovations.

Then the freshmen won with an ease—75–60—that surprised Alcindor on his night of 31 points and 18 rebounds. It was assistant coach Cunningham, not Wooden, going easy on the opponent by clearing the freshman bench in the final minutes. The varsity press was a nonfactor. When the freshmen took the ball out of bounds following a varsity basket, the first pass often went to Alcindor at the free-throw line and the second to Allen, who would either whip the ball ahead to a teammate or use his speed to dribble beyond midcourt and break the press on his own. On the occasions the opponent double-teamed Alcindor inside, the unselfish big man found Shackelford or Allen on the perimeter for jump shots that made the experienced group pay for the strategy. Single coverage on Alcindor went even worse. One time, after a varsity reserve yelled, "I've got Alcindor!" to teammates to call out a defensive assignment, fans laughed.

On the scene to file reports for his scouting service used by NBA teams to prepare for the draft, it was clear to Bill Bertka that "you knew you were watching some history being made, because of the reaction of the crowd." Eighteen-year-old Alcindor was already better than a lot of professional centers, Bertka concluded. "He made us all look ridiculous," Warren said. "If he didn't block you, he made you change your shot. And he ran like a gazelle. He was just so graceful."

Wooden and the varsity had been so decisively taken apart that Cunningham convinced himself on the spot he would be fired for embarrassing Wooden, the only possible outcome he could imagine as a coaching rookie who had just upstaged the master, on his tribute Saturday night and everything. Unsure how to proceed but certain anything he said would increase the damage, Cunningham refused to leave the locker room to talk to the press, chronicling with great interest the rarity of a meaningful exhibition game.

The impromptu plan to hide behind closed doors for thirty minutes to wait out the sportswriters on deadline proved successful but did not address the next dilemma of being expected to attend a postgame reception in the Student Union. Cunningham attached himself to a corner and did not mingle. The next day Cunningham predicted to his wife he would be fired upon returning to the office on Monday. To then go in and have Wooden's secretary approach to say Coach wanted to talk did not surprise Cunningham. When Wooden used the meeting to praise a job well done, though, Cunningham, sure he was a goner after one game, accepted Wooden's compliments of how easily the freshmen shredded the varsity press with appreciation and even greater relief.

If the varsity had cruised to victory, Wooden reasoned, it would have been the comedown that the newcomers weren't as good as hoped. They were, in fact, as good, and "from that point on," Shackelford said in retrospect, "I think we all knew we were going to be on a wild ride. And this was not going to be ordinary times." Those players, according to the new logic, would definitely win three consecutive national championships once they advanced to the varsity in 1966–67. Not only that, they wouldn't lose a game.

Everything was seemingly settled the night of the dual christenings. Just like the Power years, grand success was quickly treated as a foregone conclusion, leaving Alcindor no room to enjoy the moments of each step forward. Watching the newcomers play before his team faced the Bruins in the varsity main event, Washington State coach Marv Harshman saw Alcindor camp out on defense around the foul line and spring into action when an opposing player made a move to the basket, taking one step into the lane and grabbing the ball out of the hands of the overpowered offensive player. Teammates had the benefit of being able to whirl and bolt down court as soon as the opponent took a shot with the confidence Alcindor could play one-on-five and still collect the rebound.

"John," Harshman finally said, turning to Wooden sitting nearby, "we're going to forfeit the next three years."

California players entered Pauley Pavilion two weeks later, needed about a half minute of watching the Bruin freshman against Santa Barbara City College in the preliminary game to see Alcindor was as special as advertised, then walked to the locker room as the home team student section stood and pointed at the Golden Bears varsity and shouted, "Next year! Next year!" Future opponents were getting taunted ten or twelve months in advance. (The fans were not wrong. UCLA won by 18 and 37 points in the

1966–67 meetings.) Washington's Mac Duckworth suggested conference coaches take up a collection to fund a Harlem Globetrotters offer to lure Alcindor away before he could wreak varsity havoc.

Wooden and Cunningham, initially unfazed by the lack of emotional fire in the prodigy, grew worried as months piled up without an opponent being able to nudge Alcindor, let alone threaten him, until finally the staff met and told Carty to rough up Alcindor. Get especially physical in one of their individual sessions of fifteen minutes on fundamentals before each freshmen practice and fifteen minutes of one-on-one after. They wanted to know how Alcindor would respond the next season when varsity talent, bigger and better, came at him in a way freshmen and junior-college squads could not.

Midway through the next workout, Carty clubbed Alcindor on the arm going up for a shot. Fire came into Alcindor's eyes, knowing the move was deliberate, but he said nothing. Carty hit him again on the next Alcindor attempt, this time harder. Still no emotional response. Alcindor got the ball back. This time, he backed Carty down, forcing the older tutor closer to the basket, using serious muscle, making it impossible for Carty to hold his ground, until the defender could feel Alcindor building toward a final surge. Carty jumped and got a hand on the ball, but stopped challenging at the last instant to get out of the way in a moment of believing his wrist would have been broken against the iron. The coaches looked pleased.

Beyond the individual sessions, though, and as much as he enjoyed syncing with his freshman teammates, it quickly became a race whether Alcindor would make it to the end of the 1965–66 season or keel over on the court from boredom due to the lack of competition. Between the Wooden conditioning drills and Carty bashings, practices tested Alcindor more than any of the Bruins' punching-bag opponents during the season. Alcindor made it only as far as December, just weeks after the freshman varsity game, before he was done with the whole scene, from the distressing immaturity around campus to struggling to keep his eyes open on the court. "At Christmastime," Alcindor wrote a few years later, "I went home for a vacation. Never in my life was I so eager to get to

New York. We played a game on Friday night and I was to leave the next morning at 9. I went back to the dorm, got dressed, packed and sat up all night. That's how excited I was."

He returned to Los Angeles after the break refreshed and determined to give student life another chance, once again open to connecting and hoping to fit in with the other cats. When Pepe called Alcindor to arrange a visit while covering the Knicks on a West Coast swing in January for the *World-Telegram and The Sun*, with the understanding it would be friends in conversation on campus and not an interview, "He seemed to be coping. He was okay." Alcindor's public comments indicated the same grudging acceptance—"I wouldn't want to live here. It's just a nice place to visit"—but privately he and Allen were already commiserating and sharing thoughts of transferring.

What Alcindor came to dismiss as typical freshmen griping was actually the start of a crisis that could have changed college basketball history. Few in the program, maybe select teammates over time, knew of the threat that began in nighttime conversation in the Dykstra dorm or, worse, that the problem had grown beyond the eventual explanation of homesick first-year students. The Bruins without realizing it were also walking into the wall of NCAA rules prohibiting players from taking money, a problem for college athletes everywhere but especially those in one of the most expensive parts of one of the most expensive cities in the country. Transferring would likely mean the financial relief of being somewhere with a lower cost of living, unless Alcindor rethought his St. John's decision, and perhaps to an athletic department willing to misplace portions of the rulebook.

At last, the season finally droned to an end after 21 games with an average margin of victory of nearly 57 points and Wooden feeling obligated to inform opposing coaches UCLA was playing its regulars thirty or thirty-five minutes a night to develop a cohesive unit for eventual varsity action. Always concerned about the image of the program, he became particularly concerned in the 1965–66 stretch that included a 103-point win over MiraCosta College of Oceanside, California. Wooden tried hard to be a good sport as he watched the Washington State freshman against Spokane Community College in February. Alcindor, Wooden said, made the Bruins "a little better" in a comparison to WSU. The less diplomatic read was that the UCLA freshman would have been competitive, and maybe more, facing a varsity schedule, and that if Alcindor had been allowed to begin at the top level, they would have delivered a third consecutive championship, instead of missing the NCAA tournament and finishing 18-8.

Beginning a romantic relationship gave Alcindor the rare chance at a normal college experience, except that dating a white girl meant having to be discreet, all the way to making a point to not hold hands in public. Sophomore guard Mike Warren had been warned by Wooden around the same time of the risks of interracial dating, a message that included Warren's being told coaches had received calls threatening him. ("I would discourage anybody from interracial dating," Wooden would say in 1970. "I imagine whites would have trouble dating in an Oriental society, too. It's asking for trouble. But I've never told a player who he could or couldn't date.") When word of Alcindor's budding romance got around, anonymous phone calls to the girl's dorm declared her a nigger lover, and the pressure became too much. They split and the loneliness piled up with the basketball season over and no sign of a love life as Alcindor decided the racist South lived in California as much as in Alabama.

Night after night of rapping with a small circle of friends, including Allen and Lacey, got old and the isolation grew worse. Alcindor, retreating into himself, also swore off the idea of getting along with white people. "I had always been such a minority of one. Very tall. Black. Catholic. I had made an adjustment to being a minority of one, and now I said to myself that I was going back to that policy. It was not necessary for me to cross the color line; my ego didn't need it. Instead, I would draw my pride from the black people, from Islam and the race of brothers. So I pushed to the back of my mind all the normalcies of college life: dancing, mixers, chicks, parties, and I dug down deep into my black studies and my religious studies. I withdrew into myself to find myself. I made no further attempts to integrate. I was consumed and obsessed by my interest in the black man, in Black Power, black pride, black courage. That, for me, would suffice."

Then reading *The Autobiography of Malcolm X* changed his life forever. Alcindor couldn't put the book down and didn't want it to end, spending day after day one week going only to class and then back to the dorm to devour more pages. He had known of Malcolm from hearing the name called out as a rallying cry during the Harlem uprising and from Malcolm calling in to the AM radio station with black listenership, but not with this insight. The book's messages struck particularly deep with Alcindor, who only fifteen months removed from the riot back home read about Malcolm being gunned down before a speech in Manhattan on February 21, 1965. They both had ancestors from the same area of the Caribbean, Alcindor from Trinidad and Malcolm from about a hundred miles away in Grenada. When the future Nation of Islam leader recalled early in the book how blacks were not allowed to be out after dark in his hometown of Lansing, Michigan, Alcindor flashed back to what he often felt in New York and had witnessed on the 1962 bus ride to North Carolina. The result was an immediate, lasting connection.

Alcindor had been fed up with Catholicism since midway through the final year of high school, turned off by the church's involvement in the slave trade, and the world that unfolded in spring 1966 as he gorged nightly on the pages of the book became an unexpectedly powerful contribution to the search for a new spiritual base. Malcolm X's life in Islam prompted Alcindor to read the Koran. That, in turn, led to the decision to likewise devote himself to Islam. The previous ten or twelve months had been nonstop swerving emotions, from the difficult college-choice decision to the excitement of leaving home to the thrill of getting to UCLA to the dread of actually being there with the Watts riots and children for classmates. But now there would be a new foundation.

• • •

Nearly four hundred miles away, a candidate for governor trying to break into politics added to the list of hidden issues. Ronald Reagan used a May campaign stop in Daly City to whack away at the University of California system, especially the UC president whom he spun into soft on communism and the Cal branch that Reagan made into the symbol of all that was wrong in the world, "where a small minority of beatniks, radicals, and filthy-speech advocates have brought such shame to a great university." It was two months after an appearance in Berkeley itself, where an estimated forty-five hundred people stomped their feet and pounded on tables in support of a Reagan speech that referenced the disgust of nudity and suggestive poses once being shown on a screen, accompanied by rock bands and the smell of marijuana in the theater. Also, the Republican challenger preached, "There were intimations of other happenings which cannot be mentioned . . . ," and, "What in heaven's name does academic freedom have to do with rioting, with anarchy, with attempts to destroy the primary purpose of the university, which is to educate our young people?"

Two-term incumbent Pat Brown went from defeating Richard Nixon in 1962, before Nixon wielded his law-and-order message, to taking on Reagan in 1966 when the sight of campus uprisings turned common. Reagan, a novice politician but superb communicator as a former actor, especially if someone handed him a script, seized the opening to make California colleges and particularly the UC system a constant punching bag, because someone had to grab the drugged-out anarchist hippies by the scruff. Reagan didn't have actual strong feelings on the subject, one of his advisers later confessed to primary target Clark Kerr, the UC head under verbal assault, but he needed talking points to build a serious campaign and a poll determined Reagan should choose from among "welfare queens," "mental-health malingerers," or Cal. He picked Cal with the demonstrations and unmentionable happenings and advanced through the months with references to "sexual orgies so vile I cannot describe them to you" and said he would appoint a commission headed by a former CIA director to "investigate charges of communism and blatant sexual misbehavior on the Berkeley campus."

Charged words—riots, sex, commies—from a charismatic speaker and the recognizable face of a former movie actor turned the regional story of the race for California governor into a national conversation. As numerous campuses across the country faced similar issues and conservative citizens kept beating the same drum regarding the troubling direction of American youth, the size of Reagan's adopted home state moved UC schools to the center of the debate. The collateral damage that followed "made it so difficult to recruit in all sports, because the perception was that it's a drug-oriented, communist campus," Cal athletic director Pete Newell said.

The fallout from Reagan making the rant a centerpiece of the bare-knuckle campaign injured college teams in the state through several years of recruiting. "No, I'm not going to send him up there and have him lose his religion and everything else," Newell's coaches reported hearing from some homes. "Or get in with that hippie culture you got up there." Many parents of recruits in various sports wouldn't even have a conversation with Cal staffers. And in case a family may not have heard about *that place* flooded with sin, some opposing coach who just happened to be chasing the same recruit would want to be helpful in sharing the news. "You don't want to send your son there because he'll become a communist, he'll become a drug addict."

Optics mattered so much that when Newell's wife went to dinner in Berkeley with the couple's youngest son and spotted a peaceful rally heading toward them on Telegraph Avenue, she told ten-year-old Greg to duck if he saw a press photographer's camera pointed in their direction. If you see something, she said, tell me and I'll duck, too. Hard-core liberal Florence Newell prided herself on keeping up with the news and may have supported the progressive cause of the moment, whatever it was, but also realized the possible blowback of Newells on the front page of the Saturday paper among demonstrators, even by accident. They avoided bad publicity, the only kind possible in the situation, and were escorted the last four or five blocks home by three protesters, former players on teams coached by Greg's older brothers, who recognized mother and child.

UCLA getting smeared in the same way, without Westwood being as close to flammable Berkeley in atmosphere, became a sign of how much Reagan's words resonated. He successfully campaigned the UCs into being run by a weak governor of the state and a limp president of the system who were holding the door open for marauding students, immorality, and an academic agenda set in Moscow. He even, without intending to be so specific, helped turn the image of Bruin basketball in the second half of the 1960s into the comedic contradiction of pious John Wooden and revolution in the streets.

The truth was in the middle, with a roster of independent thinkers wanting dramatic change in society, especially UCLA's most visible player, but who were taking peaceful actions far from the Reagan narrative of mayhem. Bruin forward Mike Lynn being arrested in fall 1966 along with his roommate for attempting to buy records with a woman's credit card, just before the start of Lynn's senior season, was the worst of it.

What schools are you considering? a coach asked high school star John Shumate and his conservative parents during a home visit in Elizabeth, New Jersey, during the 1971–72 season.

Shumate had written Wooden as a sophomore to say he wanted to attend UCLA, but in the two seasons since had eliminated the Bruins after seeing the updated roster of big men and feeling they had lost interest in him. Senior John Shumate had Michigan, Michigan State, Marquette, Notre Dame, Hampton, and USC as finalists, a list loaded with Midwest options but with the visitor in Elizabeth needing to hear only one name to turn to Shumate's mother.

You don't want your son going to California because of all the stuff that goes on out there, the recruiter counseled.

You're right, she said.

Shumate's parents, his father the preacher and his mother the spiritual woman involved in the church, watched the news enough to know the ungodly land was no place for their son. He got down to Marquette or Michigan, before his parents overruled and insisted on Notre Dame. Quinn Buckner of Dolton, Illinois, decided to sign with UCLA the same year, but his father refused, throwing the letter of intent from Indiana on the bed and ordering Quinn to sign, though more because of the distance to Los Angeles and Dad being an Indiana grad than concerns over California. (Wooden had already, in 1968, suffered his biggest recruiting loss, except it had nothing to do with location. Paul Westphal from Redondo Beach, twenty miles from Pauley, simply felt a better connection to USC and preferred trying to build something special over continuing the work others had started, forever making Westphal the one who got away.) Given the Bruins' success that followed, Reagan's attacking the state's public universities for political gain did not inflict the same damage on

UCLA as its cousin in Berkeley, with the asterisk that almost every major recruit into the 1970s came from the state, without parents needing to be assured the city had islands of decency and American ideals.

The campus turning volatile, the culture wars growing nasty—you know, Pat Brown said in a nod to his opponent's previous career, John Wilkes Booth was an actor, too—Athletic Director J. D. Morgan after the 1965–66 season declared UCLA athletics "the last bastion of student discipline on this campus." Bruin basketball in particular for years ahead "was the regularity," said Gene Bleymaier, a football player who arrived in 1971. "You enjoyed being able to go to Pauley Pavilion. There was a consistency there. No matter what was happening in the world, you knew you could go to Pauley and see a win. It comforted people. It gave them a sense that there was still some order in the world." Wooden was the definition of grounded and consistent in approach, the first-year center guaranteed continued grand success, and the new arena meant greater stability.

His Bruins by the end of the season had, if anything, become the good in a troubled world by unintentionally becoming the contrast to the lazy perception of campuses around the country turning into anarchy. While the new star was staring into a future of difficult personal times, UCLA basketball was surrounded by the positive energy of a new arena and a new roster, under the watch of a coach who banned long hair and cussing and considered self-discipline a cornerstone of success. The program was dependable to the point that varsity's 18-8 record was a letdown, more losses than would come in the next seven seasons combined, and with the best yet to come: Lew Alcindor was about to join the varsity.

3

BOY KING

If Wooden was initially hesitant to have Alcindor at UCLA, or, in Norman's harsher assessment, flat out hoping Alcindor would not come, the head coach had accepted his fate as 1966–67 approached. It may have been that the season watching freshman Alcindor erased any doubt he would fit a team system and showed Alcindor did not have the disruptive ego Wooden feared. Or, simply, that Alcindor was there and the staff had no choice but to make it work, just as Wooden for years managed playing in the B.O. Barn. Whatever the reason, he appeared committed as Alcindor joined the varsity.

His job was further complicated when a knee injury sidelined Edgar Lacey for the season and Lynn served a school suspension after pleading guilty to unlawful use of a credit card, removing the only options to handle the high post in Wooden's choice for a new offense. The option of attacking with Alcindor low, near the basket, and Lynn or Lacey closer to the free-throw line ended before it started. Left with no other choice, the Bruins moved forward with Alcindor a solo anchor inside and four teammates either on the opposite side of the lane or fanned out on the perimeter. Choosing the alignment that became an offensive Goliath was a fluke, an accidental concoction for the coach emotionally strained by the newness of building around a center.

"There was no doubt in my mind of Lewis' potential," Wooden later wrote. "If there was a doubt of any kind, it was in my ability to live up to the forecasts that were immediately made: three straight NCAAs, no defeats—

things like that. I didn't know exactly how I could use a big man to the best advantage. I had never had the chance to experiment. All I had were ideas, but with no valid way to determine whether they were sound or not. All the concepts that I believed would work when you had a big man needed one in order for me to find out." He had a list of previous failures when the buildup of a great arriving center did not lead to a title, especially George Mikan at DePaul and Wilt Chamberlain at Kansas, ready just in case.

It didn't help that Wooden lacked confidence as a game tactician, conceding that his success was built on attention to detail and preparation, not the chess matches of in-game decisions. "I am not a strategy coach," he concluded years later. "I am a practice coach." It was top assistant Norman who urged the switch to the zone press that became the catalyst of the championships with small, quick teams in 1964 and '65, one of many reasons Pete Newell, the highly respected Cal coach turned athletic director, thought Norman had a brilliant basketball mind and the makings of a star head coach. (Norman, in turn, rated Newell the greatest coach of all time.) Norman in the same early days also handled halftime adjustments in talking to players from the chalkboard. UCLA assistants rarely scouted opponents and Wooden, preferring the entire staff spend nights at home with family, even less. His idea of scouting was to read newspaper coverage to learn the offense or defense that his next victim had been using lately. Wooden his entire career focused almost entirely on the Bruins executing their system, not how to counter the other team, and opponents were almost never mentioned in locker-room talks before tip-off. The final instructions he did give emphasized effort and focus and almost never included a mention of strategy.

To Wooden, games were won or lost in the previous days of repetitive drills and an emphasis on conditioning, until UCLA, Ben Franklin in tow, had simply outprepared the adversary before taking the court to out-talent them. Wooden, Swen Nater wrote years after playing for the Bruins in the 1970s, "trained the mind to be the boss over the body. That's mental toughness. The body wants to do this but you say, 'No. You're doing that.' All practice long, we were begging to take a break. When he saw my tongue dragging on the hardwood floor he yelled, 'Get going! What are you waiting for?'

That's when my mind told my body to move. His method for getting yourself in shape was, 'Go until you can't go anymore and then go a little more.'"

Staring into the unknown new world of game-planning for a hoops force of nature, then, Wooden estimated he spent hundreds of hours in the thirteen months between Alcindor's arrival as a freshman and the start of the varsity era diagramming plays and brainstorming with coaches he respected. This time, Wooden, after never previously having a player taller than six-nine, was forced to study strategies beyond those of his own respected staff and relied most notably on Press Maravich of North Carolina State. Loud and profane, a product of the East who built his career in the South, a coach who mostly spent two years in each job, Maravich was the antithesis of Wooden and his delicate vocabulary. But he was also a friend and a trusted basketball sounding board despite the mismatch.

Losing projected returnees Lacey and Lynn, while potentially a setback in depth at forward and experience on a young roster, at least allowed UCLA to flow through center Alcindor, guard Allen, and forwards Shackelford and Heitz from the freshman team into the varsity as a single puzzle. Wooden was at least saved from any strategy decisions with the opening lineup. And the one experienced Bruin, junior Mike Warren, was intelligent, hardworking, a trusted ball handler, and dedicated to team play. Wooden considered him such a good example of the ideal Bruin and a stabilizing factor for the sophomores that he named Warren captain for the entire season, one of only four times at UCLA that Wooden went away from his usual approach of picking different captains each game. "They don't come any smarter than Mike Warren," Wooden said.

Alcindor had spent part of the summer before his sophomore season as an apprentice in the music department at Columbia Pictures' Screen Gems in New York, a job arranged with the help of Mike Frankovich, a movie producer who the year before set up employment for Alcindor delivering inter-office memos at Columbia. This time, working while living at home allowed Alcindor to save up to buy a 1958 Mercedes for $1,100, with the awareness to save the bill of sale in advance of the inevitable claims of a payoff from a booster or the school. Returning to Los Angeles with his own wheels meant newfound freedom. Moving out of the dorm—"I couldn't stand any more of those kiddies' games they played there"—and getting an apartment in Santa Monica with Lacey were early signs that life would be different as a sophomore.

For one thing, he talked to the media, after being declared off-limits as a freshman, similar to the Donohue wall at Power. The school called it Alcindor family wishes to protect their sensitive son, and a university official the year before scolded the *Los Angeles Times* for printing a picture of Alcindor watching a football scrimmage. Lew described the blackout as UCLA's idea. The rarity of speaking publicly was a news event in itself either way, the same as the press conference to declare his college choice. When the 1966–67 Bruins were introduced October 14 in Pauley Pavilion, Alcindor, befitting the buildup, was saved for last.

He walked to the microphone, adjusted it skyward to the proper height, and, fully poised as with the previous media session, prepared for the first exchange with reporters since arriving as a freshman.

"I guess you have some questions."

How tall are you? That was the first.

"I'm seven feet, one and three-eighths inches tall, and I weigh two hundred and thirty pounds."

Are you still growing?

"I have no idea."

Do you feel pressure with the much-anticipated move to the varsity?

"Yes, we are getting a lot of pressure because of what people expect of us. I'll be glad when the season starts."

"In his street clothes," Sid Ziff concluded in the *Los Angeles Times*, "Alcindor looked as slim and tall as a vaulting pole. A human slat. One foot wide and seven feet tall." Also, "If he was nervous, there was no trace of it. He seemed relaxed and under no strain. Words came to him with no hesitation. Nothing flustered him. You wondered again why all the secrecy a year ago. What did they have to hide? Obviously nothing. The guy is perfectly normal."

Press Maravich bet his friend $5 before the season that the Bruins would go undefeated the next three seasons. Wooden took the wager. The Bruins are "potentially the most awesome [team] ever assembled at any college," Jeff Prugh, one of two UCLA beat writers for the *Los Angeles Times*, trumpeted in print, with the additional assessment that other schools are "pretenders to an NCAA crown which many analysts have conceded to Alcindor & Co. for the next three years." *For the next three years*. "Why, I'd say that if he continues to improve, he'll be the greatest basketball player who ever lived," Willie Naulls, the former NBA all-star forward, said before Alcindor had played a varsity game.

"This team," Wooden said, "no team in the history of basketball had such pressure on it from the first day of practice." He could almost immediately feel the shift to the Bruins playing not to lose, and he hated it. Alcindor walked by the Pauley box office to see fans camping out two days before season tickets went on sale and learned Wooden would be doing a weekly TV show to talk Bruin hoops, until the building wave felt "bigger—and more intimidating—than I ever could have imagined," Alcindor said.

Outwardly, at least, Wooden proceeded with his usual stone face, appearing to be unfazed as interest reached new heights. There wasn't even a public reaction noted when an opposing coach suggested a rule change to raise the height of the basket from ten to twelve feet in a desperate attempt to give the mortals a chance, a proposal scrapped once word got around that it wouldn't do any good because Alcindor could elevate thirteen feet into the basketball orbit. (Another coach facetiously advocated the opposite approach of placing the baskets in the ground, as if golf holes. "That way it should at least take him longer to reach over and stuff the ball in.") Meanwhile, the Bruins were assigned the maximum number of appearances in the Pac-8 television package, three games among the ten weeks of Saturday-afternoon conference contests beamed around the West Coast.

Finally taking the court for the first time on December 3, 1966, against USC, Alcindor made 23 of 32 attempts and faced mostly man-to-man coverage on his way to scoring 56 points against a quality opponent—more than he scored in any freshman game against much weaker competition, more than anyone scored in the inaugural season of Pauley Pavilion, more than any Bruin ever. Being removed with about 3 minutes remaining in an easy win triggered a standing ovation from the capacity crowd of 12,800. Alcindor termed his shooting "adequate" but said the experience "was like test-driving a Ferrari. It was just as good-looking and fast as I had hoped." In the more telling read, Wooden was moved to instantly dump the previous approach of tempering expectations with a swooning analysis after one game: "He even frightens me." The announcement earlier in the day that UCLA would play Houston in the futuristic Astrodome nearly fourteen months later received two paragraphs on page 8.

Back-to-back victories against Duke followed, then a fourth consecutive double-digit win, against Colorado State, that included Wooden permanently earning Alcindor's confidence with a defensive adjustment in the second half that sparked the Bruins turning a 1-point lead into a 10-point victory. Hey, Alcindor thought during a time-out in the final moments and with the outcome all but complete, I'm with the right guy, and "He had a willing student the rest of the way." It was impossible to miss the irony that in-game strategy, the area Wooden felt least comfortable, had moved Alcindor to commit.

"By last week," *Time* magazine declared in mid-December, "everybody seemed willing to pronounce Alcindor 'unstoppable' and 'the best college center in history,'" even if, actually, Wooden was not, while noting short-comings on defense in particular. "He can shoot with two hands, and I still can't," no less an informed observer than Philadelphia 76ers center Wilt Chamberlain said. "He's got a great body and is well coordinated for his age. Already he's bigger than I am by an inch or so. His legs are well developed." The season was four games old. "Can Basketball Survive Lew Alcindor?," the *Saturday Evening Post* soon wondered in a headline, not limiting the projected destruction to college hoops.

Washington State coach Marv Harshman, without the benefit of a UCLA television appearance to scare his team into comprehending the approaching storm, prepared by having six-foot-six Dick Watters stand on a stool fourteen inches tall to simulate Alcindor's defensive presence. "The idea is really not as crazy as it might appear," Harshman said with the memory of watching Alcindor in a freshman game the season before. "Many of the kids on our team haven't seen Alcindor and can't imagine how much area he covers, how agile he is, and how much damage he can do." To ensure his Cougars had as accurate a read as possible, Harshman did point out Alcindor had better mobility than the stool. Other practice moments included a player strapping a one-inch-by-four-inch slab of wood to the inside of one wrist and hand to likewise prepare teammates for the great wall about to confront them, as well as holding up a tennis racquet.

The incoming spectacle of UCLA's first road game drove Washington State fans to wait in line outside in subfreezing temperatures days in advance for any of the thirty-three hundred seats available, after seventeen hundred had been allotted as season tickets. The practical student will arrive with books to pass the time studying for finals, the campus paper, the *WSU Daily Evergreen*, advised—or to build a bonfire for warmth. The host athletic director had been sounding the siren for almost a month, eliminating game-day general-admission sales and eventually requesting, probably facetiously but maybe not, that customers cut their fingernails because "we need the room." Five thousand amped fans sounded like two or three times as many assaulting ears and nerves when the opponent had the ball. Wooden already considered Bohler Gym among the two toughest places in the conference for visiting teams, along with Stanford, thanks to the arena configuration that made it feel as though Cougar backers were on top of the action, and now it would be more intense.

"And just to make sure nobody has sneaked into the gym overnight," the besieged Washington State ticket manager said the day before, "the police will search the place at seven thirty a.m. and then chain the doors shut until it's time to open."

The wheat and barley fields of southeastern Washington on January 6, 1967, were the ideal spot in many ways for the Alcindor rollout compared to the real madness that could have ensued if the first road game had been among the larger populations and conference media markets of Stanford or Cal, near San Francisco, or the University of Washington in Seattle. Oregon and Oregon State were hardly big-city, but their proximity, about fifty miles apart, meant the two schools dominated attention in a north-south swath of the state. Pullman was remote farm country, two traffic lights and 6,000 residents in addition to the 10,500 students, bumping against the Idaho border, three hundred miles from Seattle on the Pacific Ocean. The

Cougars, without a top-20 finish in the Associated Press poll since 1950 or an appearance in the NCAA tournament since 1941, did not have a rivalry with UCLA or much basketball tradition at all.

That also made Pullman the perfect early gauge of the mania of Alcindor on varsity: the rarity of students lining up outside Bohler Gym in heavy overcoats, some with hoods pulled over heads with temperatures in the thirties, others leaning against the stone outside wall of the building, none seeming to have opted for a bonfire, risking illness and poor finals outcomes to watch their 5-5 Coogs almost certainly get caught under the wheels of the Bruins already appearing dominant. Any of the seventeen hundred season-ticket holders or thirty-three hundred others hoping to shoehorn in could have avoided the cold and the chained doors to watch on TV, but instead they crammed in with great anticipation. The Bohler environment would test the Bruins starters of junior Warren and four sophomores in varsity action outside Los Angeles for the first time.

The stability the routine-driven Wooden desired in a program disappeared for good once the doors were unchained at 10:00 a.m. for the 12:15 p.m. Washington State–Columbia Basin freshman game ahead of the 2:30 main event and the dash for the first-come, first-served seats began. The challenges of the first road game for a young team and a hostile crowd made the 76–67 victory a successful outcome for UCLA even with the strangeness of a final margin in single digits, and Washington State had reasons to be upbeat in the respectable defeat. The Cougars had survived despite 28 points and 12 rebounds from Alcindor that reduced Cougars center Jim McKean to being thrilled at the sight of reserve Jim Nielsen coming in to give Alcindor a rest. "You keep thinking he's there," McKean said. "And even when he isn't, he's in your mind. He's so big. He covers so much air that you can't help but think about it. No one else can jump that high to get near him. That's just so frustrating."

"Everyone wants to see the big guy play," Santa Clara coach Dick Garibaldi said from the fortunate vantage point of not being on the schedule. "Why, people are even calling to ask if I can get them seats to the Stanford-UCLA game in March."

"Tell them they can have my ticket," Stanford coach Howie Dallmar said.

Each road stop of the regular season would prove challenging. In Chicago later in January, Alcindor was assigned police protection after receiving two threatening letters with postmarks from the city, resulting in a plainclothes cop being assigned as a discreet shadow from the Bruins' arrival on Friday until departure on Monday. "Lew's bodyguard was a fine fellow," Morgan reported after the scare became public following the return to Los Angeles, and "Lew wasn't upset in the least by the situation," with the supporting evidence of Alcindor getting 35 points and 20 rebounds against Loyola, followed with 45 points and 12 rebounds versus Illinois. The horrible snowstorm, even by Chicago standards, had proved more difficult than opponents or letter writers.

Eighteen days later, Alcindor snapped, "What's your problem?" at a newspaper photographer taking a shot of Alcindor stepping off the team bus for a practice at the University of Oregon, the same trip two coeds went to the team hotel posing as reporters in an attempt, they claimed, to win a bet with friends that they could land an interview with the Bruin center. Wooden intercepted the girls and sent them away. Two days after that, the Oregon State equipment manager said Alcindor refused to take a picture with him, and a reporter, apparently a real one, wrote of Alcindor brushing off kids wanting autographs outside the locker room, all detailed in the *Corvallis Gazette-Times*. The article made no mention of Alcindor signing thirty or forty autographs outside in the cold before Wooden interrupted to have Alcindor join the rest of the team waiting on the bus to leave. "He can't get on a plane or walk through a hotel lobby without somebody snapping a bulb in his face," Wooden said. "You say that's the price you have to pay for fame. You have to, but you don't have to like it." At California, Alcindor heard, "Hey, nigger!" and "Where's your spear?" comments black players on other teams likely received, just not as often or as openly as Alcindor.

"This bothers me sometimes, but I understand how they feel," he said around midseason of the attention. "I guess I would do the same thing if I saw somebody who was seven feet. Many times, though, I have to say No to them. It's really not very hard for me to say No either, because I have been doing it for so long." He could be more social in private, usually with the limited number of teammates he let in or friends he made at jazz clubs and found him to be a cool guy. He brought records to hang out at the Sigma Alpha Epsilon fraternity house, eating and talking music and ball. Otherwise, he often walked quickly with his head down and the devouring strides of a seven-footer on a mission, not wanting to give anyone an opening to stop him. The extreme shyness was real, but also not the complete explanation of his first months on varsity, which showed Alcindor could easily turn rude in even the briefest interactions with fans, media, and fellow students. Just looking at him while walking past could earn a return glare, the campus version of having a shot swatted away in a game.

The public-address announcer during the snowy Chicago weekend used the pregame introduction "At center . . . one of the greatest players of all time . . . Lew Alcindor!" with Alcindor's varsity career fifteen games old, and the school newspaper, the *Daily Bruin*, suggested *UCLA* should now stand for the University of California at Lew Alcindor. Others proposed LewCLA. But the subject of the adulation was descending into unhappiness at a rapid rate, even with the move to an apartment in Santa Monica and decision to avoid most anything to do with UCLA other than academics and basketball. He still found it a campus of immature kids and fakes.

Almost as troubling, Wooden even before the end of the group's first regular season together detected jealousy from teammates at the credit and attention coming to Alcindor, as if Alcindor wanted either. The initial Wooden concern two years before during recruiting, that Alcindor would become disruptive in demanding the ball and a star's gilded treatment, had instead turned out to be others causing internal strife that strained the program. Alcindor had been exemplary in fitting in and handling the downside of fame, likely better than a college sophomore could have been expected to deal with death threats, racial taunts, and overly physical defenses. Wooden more than once encouraged other Bruins that Alcindor on the team meant more publicity for all, certainly more than most would be receiving with lesser programs that weren't flying first-class or drawing tens of thousands of people on blizzardy Chicago weekends for games against mediocre Illinois or Loyola.

Wooden wasn't just playing psychologist. Underlining the positives of having such a commanding player, minus a commanding personality, became a turning point for Wooden, but, really, for the direction of the entire program. The coach concerned in October as practice began and December when the schedule opened about whether Alcindor would fit had within months become his biggest backer. Alcindor's "mere presence created problems that shouldn't have existed, but the young man himself personified cooperation," Wooden decided, and "he should never have been held responsible for the problems that seemed to surround him. Such tremendous ability often brings out petty jealousy and envy from both teammates and opponents."

Alcindor neared a breaking point even with his coach's support. Sinking emotionally and feeling the financial squeeze of being a college student in a big city, especially when the scholarship money that would have gone toward dorm payments didn't cover the off-campus apartment, he began to seriously consider leaving in a few months, after the school year. Not only that, as he found from conversations with his friend and former roommate, Allen had the same money ache and the same solution. Alcindor would go to Michigan and Allen to Kansas, forty miles from where he grew up, in 1967–68 or both would land at Michigan State. They gave different scenarios and different answers depending on the time and the speaker.

The implosion in the making became public in the February 12 *Herald Examiner* with a headline an inch tall and in bold letters stripped across the top of the front page of Sports, "Alcindor May Leave UCLA." The story included news of the Harlem Globetrotters preparing to offer what essentially amounted to a lifetime contract of $1 million for five seasons with a player option to renew the deal every fifth year and a soft denial from Alcindor that he didn't know anything about the reports. The same paper three days later screamed, "Here's Why Lew Dislikes UCLA," with the same large type and the same prominent placement, and *Life* and *Look* magazines had stories centered on his loneliness and disgust with campus life. "There are a lot of phonies out here," he said. "They pat you on the back and forget you a minute later. Back in New York, you know where you stand. If people don't like you, they don't even look." Alcindor needed five months in Westwood to move out of Dykstra Hall and decide to avoid most anything to do with his college.

Wooden and the assistants, though, still had no indication despite the headlines that two starters were unhappy, and certainly not unhappy to the point of considering transferring. Either the star center turned out to be more private than already thought, which would be hard to believe, or the staff suffered from a lack of awareness, but the dynasty was in peril before barely getting started. The option of leaving college completely to join the Globetrotters, as onetime friend Wilt Chamberlain did when he dropped out of Kansas in 1958 after his junior season, never gained momentum with Alcindor. Ann Arbor was the preference if he left UCLA with Alcindor remembering the April 1965 visit for "how beautiful the campus was, with its many trees and stately traditional buildings. To me, it felt like the kind of university I saw in movies, a place where deep thinking went on. I was also impressed by the black-to-white ratio, which I knew would make me more comfortable." The Bruin basketball program was on the brink of disaster with barely anyone aware as he thought about how New York friend Elmo Morales, a member of the track team, and basketball star Cazzie Russell "made a pretty compelling case for me to attend Michigan, which I hadn't forgotten two years later when I was considering jumping from UCLA." Michigan also happened to be "where some other hinted benefits might come my way."

At the very least, Alcindor regretted not giving the Wolverines more of a chance during the initial recruiting period when he was already 99 percent set on UCLA during his Ann Arbor stop. Rarely carried by the tide of emotions, usually deliberating major decisions rather than reacting, Alcindor weighed his college choice for a second time with the same weeks, maybe even months, of consideration as the first. There were no additional campus visits and no set timeline to reach a conclusion, only the resolve to not continue down the same path of little money and a disgust with fellow students. It had, after all, been endless contemplation of nearly two seasons, one freshman and one varsity, by the time Alcindor and Allen confided in Willie Naulls, a Bruin great of the 1950s before becoming the Knick who helped Wooden recruit Alcindor as a Power senior. Naulls spent 1966–67 mentoring basketball players and as an African American, a UCLA product, a onetime New York City resident, and a former pro had credibility no one in the program could match.

The man Naulls suggested Alcindor and Allen speak with had attended UCLA in the 1930s but did not graduate because of economic reasons. He had no titled role with the program, the athletic department, or the university, nor did he want one. Millionaire contractor and building owner Sam Gilbert preferred to operate without answering to NCAA rules. He had been on the fringe of the program as a booster identified mostly as the five-foot-seven, balding white guy sporting a Bavarian hat with a feather sitting near the home bench at Pauley games. Within the locker room, though, he was known before the Alcindor years for occasionally buying tickets from players to get them money in violation of rules. He was prominent enough that Chancellor Franklin Murphy recalled hearing the name on campus as "a friend of the basketball program," but also being assured by Athletic Director J. D. Morgan multiple times that Gilbert had not done anything that would discredit the university.

Lesser-known Bruins had been going to Gilbert's house for dinner for years while trying to scrape by financially with scholarships that prohibited jobs during the season, but, Gilbert said, he had never met the two stars until Naulls decided late in the 1966–67 season that Gilbert could broker a solution to keep the program on a winning trajectory. Gilbert was an understandable choice as someone who had a history of helping players and the Bruins, as well as a longtime acquaintance Naulls felt he could trust with what had turned into a pressing issue. "A bundle of dynamite," Naulls would call him in later years. "Sam is a heavyweight. He can take care of himself in any situation against any opponents. Whoever attacks him better be ready. Sam doesn't fear anybody." So many friends saw a connection to fictional Don Corleone that they sent copies of the novel *The Godfather* after its 1969 release, until Gilbert had fifteen hardcovers of the book in his office at one point. "He loves that image," an associate said. "He's soft-spoken, but then, godfathers don't yell, they just point."

On one of the most important nights in program history, and perhaps school history, Naulls drove Alcindor and Allen to the Gilbert home in Pacific Palisades with Allen considering the seismic double transfer a done deal and Gilbert believing the two had given the school the bad news. The group talked anything except basketball for several hours, Gilbert reported, until, by 2:00 a.m., "they had gotten it all out of their systems . . . talking to an adult who could rap with them on their own level and who understood the black-white syndrome, which most schools want to brush under the carpet." Gilbert went with the story that he convinced the pair education was more important than basketball, and both knew they were at a quality university, while Alcindor confessed in the pros, "Once the money thing got worked out, I never gave another thought to leaving UCLA." He and Allen had let off steam in conversation with each other and Gilbert and ultimately decided "that we would pretend UCLA was a job, and stick it out on that basis, the way a bricklayer gets up and goes to work in the morning."

"If not for Sam Gilbert," Allen said, "Kareem and I were going to Michigan State as a package. It was a done deal. Michigan State at that time knew how to take care of their ballplayers and I'll just leave it at that. We didn't think there was any chance we'd be taken care of like that at UCLA because of who our coach was." Alcindor remembered it as he was headed to Michigan and Allen to Kansas, but under any scenario "Lucius and I said the hell with it, we were through with UCLA." Wooden instead chose to believe the story Alcindor told him that Gilbert had no role in the decision to stay and even that Alcindor and Allen never seriously discussed leaving.

Whether the same blind loyalty bordering on naïveté caused Wooden to miss Sam Gilbert growing into one of the most crucial members of the program or Wooden simply recognized the gathering storm but chose to turn the other way never became clear. Gilbert's profile grew the moment Naulls, Allen, and Alcindor drove away from Pacific Palisades, though, without pushback from the head coach or administrators who constantly spoke of integrity. Athletic Director J. D. Morgan refused to schedule schools he saw as beneath UCLA's claimed moral high ground, except for the mandatory conference games, yet never told a blatant rule breaker to stay away from the team or to stop spending on players, perhaps because Morgan knew that would have provoked Gilbert to spend more. Wooden then appeared to defer to Morgan and began to pay with his reputation as a righteous man who went silent when it served his career. "Sam steered clear of John Wooden and Mr. Wooden gave him the same wide berth," Kareem Abdul-Jabbar wrote in 1983. "Both helped the school greatly. Sam helped me get rid of my tickets . . ."

Without anyone realizing it, Gilbert vaulted from the edge of the program to a force in one night, a status he brazenly maintained the rest of the Wooden years. Even more concerning for the university, Gilbert, rather than follow the approach of rule-breaking boosters at other schools by operating from the shadows, flaunted his involvement and laughed off NCAA regulations. The more time that passed without Morgan taking any more serious action other than occasionally reminding him of the guidelines, the wider his berth became and the more shameless Gilbert grew.

Neither player appeared distracted on the court as UCLA closed the regular season 26-0, a significant achievement amid two sophomores weighing whether to leave the team the next year. Alcindor did have the new problem of occasional migraine headaches, bad enough the day of the Washington home game that he had to lie down in the locker room about thirty minutes before tip-off, but followed with 37 points and 18 rebounds. Nothing seemed to distract the Bruins. Even the supposed test of a young roster stepping into the tournament for the first time ended with easy wins against Wyoming and Pacific on consecutive days in the regional in Corvallis, followed by dispatching Houston in the national semifinal in Louisville as Alcindor's displeasure with UCLA grew more public. "It's true, I'm unhappy there," he said at the Final Four, "but that doesn't mean I'd be less unhappy any place else. . . . I wanted basketball and an education. I think this is the place to do it."

Wooden's premonitions of Alcindor's arrival creating problems had come true, just not the way Wooden imagined. He came to call 1966–67 "my most trying year in coaching," even without being aware of the transfer crisis, even with the personal accomplishment of successfully reconfiguring the playbook, and even with the team so properly focused on the championship that Wooden's final instructions before leaving the locker room were which way to face during the national anthem and to behave properly after the win in the fifth-most immoral city in the country. Players took the court for warm-ups trying to decide what four cities were in front of Louisville in whatever ranking Wooden had found or created. Only Las Vegas came to mind.

The title came with a 15-point win over Dayton, that close only because Wooden played his bench against Flyers starters down the stretch. Alcindor blocked his man's first shot and most every subsequent contested attempt from the Dayton center seemed to come with an awkward release to avoid Alcindor's reach. Kenny Heitz, the standout defender usually beyond the spotlight of the other four starters, shut down his matchup, and emotional leader Warren noted teammates had been unselfish all season, especially Alcindor, who could have scored at will if he wanted. His first NCAA tournament, Alcindor decided, was not much more difficult than a New York City high school postseason, underwhelming to the point that his public celebration consisted of flashing a V sign with his raised right hand while jogging to the bench upon being taken out a final time.

"Who's going to beat them?" the Associated Press wondered. "That's the question everyone in college basketball is asking."

"Although it may get stale and old hat before it's over, UCLA's dynasty looks like a shoo-in for the next couple of years," United Press International, the other major news service, claimed.

And this was the transition season, minus Lacey and Lynn, without a senior and with only a few juniors in the rotation.

. . .

Muhammad Ali replaced Jackie Robinson as Alcindor's favorite athlete once Robinson retired from the Dodgers in 1956 rather than accept a trade to the New York Giants. Though only five years older than Alcindor, Ali by 1966 had an Olympic gold medal in boxing from the same 1960 Rome Games that Rafer Johnson won the decathlon and had become the world heavyweight champion with magnetism and bravado equal parts captivating and galling. To the captivated basketball sensation in Westwood, Ali was nothing less than the athlete Alcindor hoped to be, a man of supreme talent who leveraged his pedestal to speak out on social issues, however unpopular. It made no difference to Alcindor that they had contrasting personalities, an introverted college kid who disliked physical play and a motormouth boxer swinging fists for a living. He was still the thirteen-year-old Lew who watched the Olympic results come in from Italy with delight.

If finally meeting Ali after all that time wouldn't have been jarring enough, coincidentally crossing paths on Hollywood Boulevard in the first half of Alcindor's freshman year added to the shock. His world changed forever by walking into Ali performing sleight-of-hand magic tricks for fans while also enjoying a stroll with his small entourage under the city lights of a busy street. The champ away from the ring and the media machine he fed was theater even on a casual night out. Alcindor strolling with two school friends could not help but admire Ali's instant connection with strangers, a quality Alcindor would never have, and the way people giggled with delight when they parted and continued down the boulevard with a memory they'd keep for the rest of their lives.

Alcindor pushed through his usual shyness to say hello.

"Ah, another big fan of magic," Ali responded. "And I do mean *big.*"

The two groups and anyone who happened upon history in the making laughed, including the target of the joke, who typically cringed at being mocked for his height.

Alcindor found Ali charming and polite and left more enthralled than ever, even without additional conversation or an indication Ali was aware of the teenager's identity. Alcindor and his two friends walked away giddy at their good fortune. Seeing each other again at a Los Angeles party filled with college and professional athletes a few months later, though, Ali flirted with the women and charmed the men and Alcindor retreated alone to the musical instruments abandoned by the band on a break. He settled in at the drum set and tapped away, quietly but enough to build into a good beat, when Ali approached, took a guitar, and began strumming. Ali's personal photographer snapped a shot and exited, leaving the two alone.

"You sounded pretty good," Ali said, nodding at the drumsticks. "You play?"

"Nah," Alcindor replied, "I was just fooling around. My dad's the musician in the family."

"Yeah? Professional?"

"No. He's a cop."

"My dad painted signs," the champ said. Then he looked into Alcindor's eyes. "When I was little, I asked my dad, 'Why can't I be rich?' So he points to my arm, you know, meaning my black skin, and says, 'That's why.'"

Unsure how to respond, Alcindor knowingly nodded back, before Ali strummed the guitar once and smiled. "But look at us now, brother," Ali said, and the two grinned at each other as if to acknowledge their advantages compared to other young black men in the 1960s.

Only-child Alcindor felt he had a big brother from that night on—"I had plenty of coaches teaching me how to win. Muhammad Ali was the first to teach me what to do with winning." It was instantly such a valued relationship for Alcindor that he did not care it also created a conflict with Wooden, the former navy man stateside in World War II who privately criticized Ali for refusing to be inducted in the armed forces in April 1967. Though his coach never publicly spoke out against Ali as the boxer's stance on Vietnam became a national debate, Alcindor did note several snide comments by Wooden despite a growing awareness of their friendship. "First he's Cassius Clay, then he's Muhammad Ali," Alcindor once heard in passing. "Hmph." Other times, it was a rhetorical "Can't he see he's hurting the country?" as well as "It's a privilege, not an obligation, to fight for your country."

Alcindor and Wooden were not and never would be close during their joined UCLA years, despite all they had in common. They enjoyed a shared passion for baseball and reading, agreed on the importance of education, were understated and preferred life outside the spotlight but handled attention well when it did come, just as both transplants struggled to adjust to Los Angeles. "Socially I often did not fit in, because I was a teetotaler who didn't smoke or swear and on many occasions was made to feel uncomfortable about it," Wooden recalled. "On top of everything else, the traffic scared us. One day while I was driving very cautiously on the Pasadena Freeway, I looked at Nell and said, 'What in the world are we doing out here, honey?' She was kind enough not to remind me that it was all my doing." Alcindor grew up loving western movies and Wooden devoured

Zane Grey novels of frontier life. And, of course, the Bruins. But even without the warmth that would come decades later, the mutual respect in their cordial business relationship was substantial and real.

In this case, Alcindor disagreed with the anti-Ali sentiment yet thought enough of his coach after one varsity season together that "I felt like the child of divorced parents who had to listen to one beloved parent complain about the other beloved parent." Basketball was a refuge in a challenging time of insane expectations, disliking L.A., nearly transferring, needing a bodyguard, being a target of racism, insensitive gawkers, and crazies. He could only wrap himself in the sport to deal with his life, which was unlike any other teenager's. Ali's world of federal cases and debates that stretched from the United States to Southeast Asia, meanwhile, seemed an endless series of obstacles without resolution. Alcindor was conscious of the emotional swings at play and even the potential for the Ali issue to increasingly become an irritant to the coach-player relationship, with the future of college basketball at stake. He remained unapologetically and undeniably loyal to the champ anyway, without needing so much as a conversation with Wooden to explain.

The issue of Ali as a conscientious objector that particularly gnawed at Wooden had become a national argument by the end of the 1966–67 basketball season, further stoked by the racial overtones of a black man pushing back against the system and a black man who grew up attending a Baptist church converting to Islam in 1964. The emotions of the controversial war with 490,000 American troops in South Vietnam by early 1967, clashes over civil rights, and Islam scaring millions in the United States crashed together as the perfect storm of combined conflicts in the form of a brash sports star with dark skin. It had already cost Ali his heavyweight crown—boxing officials stripped him of the title when he refused to be inducted on religious grounds, despite a secret government promise that he would never be sent to Vietnam and would instead give clinics around the United States for troop morale. What others, including Wooden, saw as being un-American was to Ali and his supporters following religious teachings.

Ali had been indicted by a federal grand jury May 8, 1967, for refusing to be drafted and by the end of the month was facing a trial in Houston, site of the induction center, when his manager, Herbert Muhammad, called Ali's friend and business partner Jim Brown with a suggestion. Maybe, Muhammad told the retired star running back, you could gather other respected black athletes and influential voices to talk with Ali and advise him on a next step rather than end up in jail. Agreeing, Brown called his former Cleveland teammate and current top aide in the Negro Industrial and Economic Union John B. Wooten with the instruction, simply, "Get the gang together," without specifically naming who would be invited.

That Wooten intuitively knew to include Alcindor on the list was a clear signal of how quickly Ali had come to consider the twenty-year-old finishing his sophomore year part of the inner circle. Ali had obviously spoken of his respect for Alcindor, as a friend and valued voice despite limited involvement in the civil rights movement, in such certain terms that Wooten saw that "Ali loved Lew Alcindor." Alcindor, naturally, accepted at his own expense, as did everyone else asked to attend at the Cleveland headquarters of Brown's business—eight current or former professional football players, one current professional basketball player, one lawyer, Ali under fire, and one shy college student. Many were military veterans.

The group that checked in at the downtown Hilton on June 3, 1967, in advance of the actual meeting the next day, was a historic convergence of athletic star power joined with influence in speaking out against racial injustice: Brown as the greatest football player ever and especially popular in his adopted hometown, Bill Russell as arguably the greatest basketball player ever, Ali on his way to becoming one of the greatest boxers, future NFL Hall of Famers Willie Davis and Bobby Mitchell, and Alcindor as the best college basketball player of the moment and arguably the top college talent of any sport. (The group also included Brown's lawyer, who would later be elected mayor of Cleveland.) With the exception of Jackie Robinson and Jesse Owens, not among the unspoken list of Ali's inner circle, most every black civil rights icon from sports was in attendance, so many lions of the cause that the gathering became known as the Cleveland Summit.

The lone amateur among proven professionals in the meeting in the offices of the Negro Industrial and Economic Union was proud and flattered to be invited, but also confident enough in daunting surroundings to see the group's role as "a jury in assessing Ali's sincerity and commitment," as if they were a screening committee who would determine the validity of Ali's religious convictions as a conscientious objector. Even better that finally having a voice in an important matter would come in support of the friend who made him proud to be an African American. Alcindor went in feeling most came to persuade Ali to accept the draft. But after two hours behind closed doors that were "pretty heated as questions and answers were fired back and forth," it became obvious Ali would not change his mind. He was prepared for jail. It was enough to convince participants to publicly back Ali as a conscientious objector and not a draft dodger.

Wooten's decision to put Alcindor at the table in the front row of the press conference that followed became the greatest statement of all in elevating Alcindor as a valued voice on civil rights, a role he had desperately wanted. As if the seating assignment wasn't enough, the journey from stepping out of the subway station and into the New York City cyclone of chaos in 1964 to sharing front-row billing with Muhammad Ali, Bill Russell, and Jim Brown just three years later came at such hyperspeed that its suddenness scared Alcindor. Cub reporter at the Martin Luther King media gathering in 1964 New York City to front and center as a participant in a highly publicized conclave on race and religion in three years, a stunning timeline to match the seating assignment of Alcindor facing the audience from the left side, Brown on his right shoulder, Ali one spot over, and Russell on the right side. The eight others stood close together in a row behind them.

"I personally, and I think a lot of us, just thought he was just one of our younger brothers," Walter Beach, a retired Boston Patriots and Cleveland Browns defensive back, said of Alcindor at the historic gathering. "Far more mature in his expressions than a lot of other young twenty-year-old guys. Lew Alcindor was just a kid and we were dealing with him like he's a little brother. But at the same time, we recognized the fact that he had a level of maturity that exceeded the [twenty] years." To Beach, one of several military veterans among the current or former professional athletes, "We were the elite of the elite, and he was the elite in college basketball. But he was also the elite with the level of maturity and insight. He was really not out of place."

Cleveland brought a legitimacy Alcindor could not have reached in one varsity season. His stature on the spot went, in his own estimation, from grumbling college sophomore to national spokesperson for social issues involving African Americans. "It was what I wanted," he later concluded, "but the pressure was even greater than it was playing basketball because the stakes were so much higher. Winning a basketball game wasn't the same as trying to secure voting rights, educational opportunities, and jobs for the disenfranchised. Failing to score on a hook shot meant missing a couple of points. Failing to articulate a position clearly and convincingly could affect people's lives." He felt ready, though.

In the bigger picture, the meeting likely made no tangible difference—Ali would almost certainly have stuck to his convictions even without the show of support, he would still have been convicted sixteen days later by an all-white jury, and there is no indication the conclave altered the final outcome of the Supreme Court ruling on behalf of Ali. It likewise was not a passing of the torch to a college superstar for the next generation, not with Ali just twenty-five years old, Brown thirty-one, and Russell thirty-three with two more seasons remaining with the NBA's marquee franchise. Brown and Russell in particular would again be important in lending star power to the civil rights movement. The Cleveland Summit did, however, force Alcindor to become publicly assertive in a way his timid personality might not otherwise have allowed.

Departing Ohio also marked the end of the most eventful eight months in UCLA basketball history: the Allen-Shackelford-Heitz-Alcindor class made an easy transition to varsity play, Warren proved every bit the steady leader Wooden anticipated and needed, stomping through 30 games started a run on championships and previewed the next two seasons as limitless, Wooden demonstrated to himself he could maximize a big man as promising San Diego ninth-grader Bill Walton took note, Sam Gilbert asserted himself, and the transfer threat and the Globetrotter option evaporated. Alcindor in particular exemplified the complicated 1966–67 that from the outside mostly appeared easy, handling unreal expectations and bully defenses, deciding whether to stay, receiving death threats, and the statement of the Cleveland invitation. When Jim Brown said to get the guys together, it was understood he meant the college kid, too, as an equal member of the club of all-time greats. Alcindor would be able to look back several decades later to see the sophomore year of college as one of the important years of his life, even if it was also just the beginning.

4

CHURCHES AND STADIUMS

The racism even Alcindor on alert missed during recruiting burst into the open early in his junior year as segregationist Alabama governor George Wallace built such a formidable California base in a bid for president that campaign staffers were reallocated to the state and hundreds of Southerners followed as volunteers. "The capital of Alabama is *not* Los Angeles," the *Wall Street Journal* reported in December 1967, "but it might as well be." One of Wallace's true believers, Eric Galt, arrived the month before from his adopted home on Mexico's Pacific Coast, moved into a hotel on Hollywood Boulevard among prostitutes and drug traffickers, cruised his Mustang with a revolver under the front seat, and volunteered at Wallace headquarters in North Hollywood, drawn by the candidate's stand on white superiority. The ooze of hate he experienced living ten miles from Pauley Pavilion culminated in the spring, when the man with an alias drove his two-door hardtop to Memphis, aimed a rifle at Martin Luther King Jr. standing on a motel balcony, and fired. Only later did Galt's true identity become known: James Earl Ray.

Alcindor at the same time, even with danger in the air, had been energized by the Cleveland Summit to seek out a larger role in the civil rights movement, not just step up if one happened to come. His basketball offseason in the wake of the title as a sophomore also included attending a Black Muslim rally in Harlem followed by dinner at Louis Farrakhan's house in Queens with Ali (although Alcindor had turned away from the religious sect as an option because of its xenophobic tendencies). Working with kids on playgrounds in another Harlem neighborhood as part of a city program offered both the opportunity to reconnect with his roots and exactly the chance he wanted to become a role model, in this case by encouraging students to stay in school and avoid drugs and crime. He delivered the message as someone who could speak with credibility on education, but also as a student who had taken LSD "a couple of times" before leaving college and snorted heroin the summer after his junior year, in a Harlem park at that.

Personal growth in his hometown also included taking up aikido, a Japanese form of self-defense that Alcindor had become interested in while watching samurai movies at a theater near campus. He was struck watching the films that martial arts might benefit him in basketball. The same graceful movements the protagonists on the screen deployed to evade attacks could be used to escape the two or three defenders at a time typically sent at him, the marked man reasoned. It took only the initial sessions in New York for Alcindor to feel his senses sharpening and his reflexes quickening, such an encouraging introduction that he decided to continue after returning to Los Angeles.

The publisher of *Black Belt* magazine, a friend, recommended working with a twenty-seven-year-old struggling actor who taught martial arts for extra money, Bruce Lee. Alcindor knew of him as Kato, the crime-fighting sidekick in the one ABC season of *The Green Hornet*, so the chance to meet Lee was intriguing, albeit with the skepticism of being mentored by a TV action hero.

Lee also had a friendly demeanor and big smile that immediately thawed the introverted new pupil, unlike previous stiff instructors often demanding regular demonstrations of obedience. Alcindor this time found someone he would respect professionally and enjoy personally and gave Lee the high praise of comparing him to Wooden as a teacher who also emphasized planning in detail, endless repetition of fundamentals, and focusing on the person as well as the participant. Lee and Alcindor also discussed books at great length, a development Wooden could surely admire. "I dedicated myself to preparation by maintaining complete focus during basketball practice and my training with Bruce," Alcindor later wrote. "As a result, I became stronger, faster, and a much more intense player."

Alcindor's important advances, especially the new ferocity as defenses grew more physical, came with perfect timing in the wake of the NCAA banning the dunk shortly after the previous season. Alcindor liked adding what he considered the ballet-like moves of the on-screen samurais under siege, but the sudden rule adjustment that emphasized finesse over power made the new level of agility even more valuable. Bruce Lee, an actor, martial-arts specialist, and teacher, unknowingly impacted college and professional basketball forever.

What would always be portrayed as a seismic rule shift was actually a tweak—players could continue to use size, strength, and agility to establish position around the basket, corral offensive rebounds or lofty passes, and elevate above the rim, but could only drop the ball through the net rather than slam it down. Just the force of the finish changed. To Alcindor, though, the timing and symbolism were a blatant personal attack, the latest flailing attempt to stop the unstoppable, the 1967–68 version of the 1966–67 suggestion to raise the basket. Not only that, he read the ban as a racial issue and responded, "If I'd been white, they never would have done it. The dunk is basketball's great crowd-pleaser, and there was no good reason to give it up except that this and other niggers were running away with the sport." He accurately predicted the decision would end up a greater loss for fans than players.

Alcindor did not know, but would learn decades later, Wooden was among those who voted to outlaw the slam, even to the detriment of his own program. "The game is about teamwork," Wooden eventually told Kareem Abdul-Jabbar. "The dunk is about embarrassing your opponent." It was an "ugly shot" and "nothing but brute force" to a coach who preferred flow over muscle. Wooden didn't even agree with the premise that the rule was aimed at his star and was more concerned the NCAA would respond to Alcindor's overwhelming debut season by raising the basket after all or, in the most drastic overreaction, ban Alcindor completely. Houston coach Guy V. Lewis always believed that his players showboating and hanging on the rim during pregame warm-ups before facing UCLA in the 1967 semifinals in Louisville, with members of the rules committee watching, caused the change, not Alcindor.

Alcindor could likewise not have been aware as his junior season dawned that eliminating the powerful finishing move would become one of the best things to ever happen to his game, and one of the best developments for his future. Combining the increased flexibility and martial-arts moves gained from work with Lee, and encouraged by Wooden to use the perceived setback to grow the rest of his game, Alcindor began to develop a shot he first tried in fourth grade but had rarely used since, the hook. Wooden called it a flat hook, practically an arm's length from the basket, albeit an Alcindor arm, and without much arc, a version that relied strictly on size advantage to flick the ball above college defenders to the rim. The collaboration of professor and enthusiastic student refined the body movements and the release to float the ball more skyward, adjustments that not only made him more indefensible to opponents of the moment but would later render the reach of NBA players of similar height useless.

"We worked on it like two mechanics perfecting an engine," Alcindor described in a memoir with a joy that still came through forty years later. "It was that hook shot that brought us together on the basketball court. Working on it gave us the opportunity to spend extended time in each other's presence. Both of us spoke fluent basketball, a language free of emotion. He loved that shot and saw in it possibilities I hadn't imagined."

Whether or not the rule had been a response to Alcindor's domination and intended to be a UCLA speed bump, the Bruins were actually strengthened by the elimination of the dunk. Their center could still live above the rim, only with a softened finishing move, and an offensive arsenal improved by the addition of the skyhook. Perhaps most important, Alcindor had gone from considering transferring, if not outright deciding to leave, and a strain with Wooden over social issues to a stronger bond than ever. The new artful shot destined to become his signature move was, in the end, a symbol to Alcindor of turning adversity into advantage as well as the perfect lasting tribute to Wooden, teacher at heart and lover of the finesse game.

Growing off the court as well before the season started, Alcindor got the opportunity he wanted for years to speak out when San José State sociology professor Harry Edwards organized black athletes to discuss boycotting the 1968 Olympics in Mexico City. The combined setting of civil rights and sports, the chance to be at the forefront of an important issue eleven months away, made it an ideal moment for Alcindor to follow through on his commitment to spend some of his fame. Even the location, Los Angeles, was a match.

Approximately two hundred athletes showed up at Second Baptist Church on Thanksgiving afternoon 1967, but none with close to Alcindor's star power or megaphone. He had his cause. Alcindor was *the* name now, in contrast to his supporting role as one of several greats backing Ali, a stand in favor of the boycott that became more complicated when hero Rafer Johnson declared athletes should participate. So did Jesse Owens, the black sprinter who won four gold medals at the 1936 Berlin Olympics to ruin host Adolf Hitler's plans to turn the Games into a statement on the superiority of the white race.

A fight outside the church between Black Power advocates and a communist group turned bloody. Inside, Edwards ended two and a half hours of discussion on the second floor at 4:37 p.m. by asking, "Well, what do you want to do?" and the hundreds erupted.

"Boycott! Boycott!" thundered through the room so overwhelmingly that the decision was reached by acclamation, without an actual ballot.

Though intrigued by the chance to measure himself against the best players from other countries, some older and more physically developed, and to meet athletes of different cultures in a foreign land, Alcindor was among the proponents of the boycott. Going to Mexico City, he ultimately reasoned, would seem like he was more interested in his career than justice and that he was dodging the chance to take a stand against racism. Thinking important decisions through as always, Alcindor could not accept how winning the gold medal would bring honor to the country denying the rights of many blacks, such a bad feeling that he equated it to continuing to play for Power after Jack Donohue had crossed the line with racist language.

When given the chance to make a public stand, though, the very role he'd been wanting since early in high school, and especially since the Cleveland Summit, Alcindor tripped over himself. "If you live in a racist society, you have to react—and this is my way of reacting," he said at a press conference the next day, indicating he supported black athletes skipping the Games, except that he had not stated whether he would skip Mexico City. "We don't catch hell because we are Christians. We catch hell because we are black." The muddled statement was bad enough when he could simply have condemned civil rights abuses in America and forcefully declined to play, yet Alcindor added to the confusion by saying he remained undecided, when a *Sports Illustrated* writer inside the church heard him vote to boycott.

He even dulled the fury that followed with a strange choice of words, that the meeting caused an "unpleasant commotion." Whether the stumble was caused by his youth while still trying to find his advocacy voice or simply not being as prepared as he thought to handle a leadership role with the country watching, Alcindor fell short in his desire for straight talk on society's problems. Still, just attending the Thanksgiving rally and privately supporting the boycott triggered horrific hate mail to UCLA of racial slurs, calls that he should be thrown out of school and be barred from the NBA, and cries he was a traitor for not wanting to represent the United States after all basketball had done for him. He was, however, pleased with the school's reaction, that no university administrator, no boss in the athletic department, no head basketball coach, so much as suggested Alcindor temper his words, let alone rethink his stance.

The coincidence of the season beginning eight days later helped turn the mood away from protests, with the added boost, emotionally and physically, of the return of Alcindor's close friend Lacey from knee problems and Lynn after being suspended for the unlawful use of a credit card. The 1967–68 Bruins would be deeper, more experienced, more mettled, after the tournament run led by sophomores, and Alcindor would be more of a flaming offensive threat than ever with his new skyhook and martial-arts training. The reserve unit is the second-best team in the country, Wichita State coach Gary Thompson said. As if that weren't enough to push UCLA in a sunny direction, the opener at Purdue doubled as a homecoming for Wooden, a three-time All-American playing for the Boilermakers and

1932 Player of the Year, and so talented that he made the Hall of Fame as a guard thirteen years before being elected as a coach.

The 8-0 start that followed, while scoring at least 104 points in 6 of the wins, served as the immediate reality check that the dunk ban would provide no hope for opponents now completely out of options to slow the Bruins. Alcindor with elevated intensity and improved maneuverability regularly flicked aside both the rule change and the increased physical play by defenses he had expected since the summer aikido training. The Bruins in peak offensive flow with ball movement and their star center uncoiling the balletic skyhook were at once graceful and overpowering, appearing unstoppable in every way at 10-0 with such control that time management became Wooden's biggest challenge. Pull Alcindor with the game in hand and rob Bruin reserves of the chance to play with Alcindor—"There isn't a kid on the squad who wouldn't cut off his right arm for an opportunity to play with Lew," Wooden said—or keep Alcindor on the court and risk cries UCLA was classless in running up the score. Wooden considered it a tremendous problem, both an indication of how much he considered the feelings of others and, laughably to other coaches, of what constituted difficulty in 1967–68 Westwood.

Gary Beban won the Heisman Trophy in November and was still the second most famous athlete on campus, and perhaps behind Allen as well, without complaint. He was a realist who understood the power of Bruin hoops as much as anyone. As the school year progressed, Beban became one of the many football players who attended as many basketball games as possible and also often stopped in Pauley Pavilion after their own workout to watch from the upper deck as Wooden exacted precision on the court below.

Most of all, Beban fortunately had no interest in the spotlight, happy to be part of a program that had built from constant losers into national caliber under the direction of X-and-O savant Tommy Prothro. The announcement from the professor in January 1966 when Beban walked into Classical Music for the first time after the Bruins knocked off No. 1 Michigan State in the Rose Bowl was enough: "Beethoven. Bach. Beban." The class stood and applauded, though thankfully not for long. He was in his apartment studying for finals eleven months later when Athletic Director J. D. Morgan called with instructions to put on a sport coat and report to the chancellor's office, where Beban got word of the Heisman win. The top college football player of 1967, ahead of O. J. Simpson of USC and Leroy Keyes from Purdue, considered the grand news "just sort of a come-along," a supplement to the real reward of being a member of a special group that built itself as a top-5 program.

Beban's pool buddy from Dykstra Hall, Alcindor, washed over everything anyway, a common occurrence in Westwood already but especially in the early days of 1967 and the buildup to the January 20 game against Houston. No. 1 versus No. 2 had been pushed to the hyperbolic extreme of being billed as "the Game of the Century," before anyone knew if it would hold up as the best of the year. The Cougars with forward Elvin Hayes and guard Don Chaney had a 5-point win over Arizona, bound for an 11-13 finish, and a 2-point escape against North Texas, en route to 8-16, since Christmastime alone while appearing to be thinking more about UCLA than the opponent of the moment. The Bruins were concern-free until the 3:00 a.m. hotel room-to-room call January 13 in Palo Alto from Alcindor to trainer Ducky Drake to report a sharp pain in his left eye after getting accidentally poked going for a rebound at Cal. At the time, the game was briefly halted for Alcindor to be treated, and he played on. Six hours later, the initial soreness had turned excruciating.

Doctors after a hospital exam diagnosed a scratched iris, applied a thick bandage over the eye, and ruled Alcindor out indefinitely. Teammates had no idea until arriving at the team breakfast to news Mike Lynn would start that night at Stanford, before Alcindor sat sadly on the bench in street clothes and watched the easy win through sunglasses. Once the Bruins returned to Los Angeles, Alcindor checked into the Jules Stein Eye Clinic on campus, hour after hour confined to a dark room for treatment and not being allowed physical activity more taxing than casually shooting, with the eye still patched, at practice January 17. He sat out January 18 against the University of Portland as well, the Bruins' 47th victory in a row, then boarded the Continental Airlines charter to Houston with the rest of the team the next day for the

12:15 p.m. departure without the bandage but still dealing with double vision and reduced stamina after six days of ordered rest.

Wooden stepped onto the same flight already convinced the game was a bad idea. The basketball purist saw it as a spectacle, a first cousin to the slam dunk and excessive celebrations, but Morgan overruled and insisted the Bruins accept the invitation and that the showdown move forward with the pedal on the publicity machine mashed to the floor. A spectacle was exactly what Morgan wanted.

His boss, Vice Chancellor Charles Young, eight months from taking over the top position on campus, considered Morgan so smart, so hardworking, and so advanced in understanding the business of college sports that Morgan saw the basketball explosion coming from a distance. It wasn't just the view from Westwood and three titles the previous four seasons. In a time of regular-season broadcasts as local or, in truly grand exposure, regional, Morgan grasped like few others what national television would come to mean for the sport. He only needed the right opportunity to test the belief.

Going from associate business manager at the university to tennis coach in 1949 to head of the athletic department in 1963, a promotion after a valuable endorsement from Wooden, Morgan steered Bruin sports from financial shambles to profitable. He either initiated or marshaled existing plans to completion for basketball, swimming and water polo, tennis, crew, and track venues, failing only to get an on-campus football stadium beyond the proposal stage. He began a policy of first-class flights for the basketball team, in deference to the size of players as well as the success, and moved himself and staffers to economy before any player in the event of a seating shortage up front. And while top assistant Bob Fischer saw football as Morgan's first love, basketball was an immediate priority as new athletic director Morgan told Wooden to focus on the team and leave the schedules, budget, travel, and other administrative layers to Morgan. Coincidence or not, UCLA and its coach with fewer responsibilities off the court took off on a championship tear.

Wooden appreciated the help, respected Morgan, and maintained a positive professional relationship, but, like many, grew tired of the domineering personality overstuffed with bluster and a need to intimidate. Morgan regularly berated referees as much as Wooden, just without the camouflage of a rolled-up program, and often sped in to give the sport's most successful coach advice on what to do in games, sometimes interrupting the staff at halftime to deliver suggested adjustments. Bruin assistants grew so used to fielding eye-rolling input to be passed on that they learned the best response was simply to patron-izingly agree to forward the wisdom and then immediately ignore it.

Morgan didn't just project an imposing figure because of his low, ponderous voice that would boom out even in general conversation and his thick arms of a decades-long tennis player. He aimed to intimidate. He weaponized volume. Employees who walked into his office were made to wait silently, sometimes standing, while seated Morgan continued to work with his head down, hoping for the dream scenario of making the visitor feel uncomfortable.

In basketball terms, Morgan went as far as sitting on the bench sev-eral times, prompting the conference to declare the area off-limits to any-one other than players, trainers, and coaches—actual coaches—much to Wooden's relief. Everyone knew the target. "Boy," one coach said to an-other in the men's room, "after that rule we passed outlawing athletic direc-tors from the bench, J. D. Morgan's going to shit when he hears about this." A familiar thunder came from behind the door of a closed stall. "That, gentlemen, is exactly what J.D. is doing."

Wooden considered him "a typical second-guesser, like most fans." Aware that Morgan vented to him about various football coaches through the years meant there was a good chance that Morgan was doing the same about him. But Wooden, able to see past the "extremely forceful," "supremely confident" personality, also rated Morgan the best athletic director in the country, no small praise for someone Wooden did not like much personally. The conflicts they did have were resolved in civil terms, unlike Morgan's showdowns with other coaches where he pounded his fist on his desk and gave them bark-ing lectures. On occasions Wooden disagreed with the schedule, Morgan responded with the logic of "Well, you're doing all right, aren't you?" and the coach had no choice but to agree. And when Morgan pushed Wooden to be more aggressive in recruiting, frustrated at Wooden's being too passive in refusing to initiate contact with prospects and rarely making home visits, Wooden borrowed the same "Well, we're doing all right with the players I'm recruiting," and Morgan had to begrudgingly accept the rationale.

Morgan's positive influence on the success had become as impossible to miss as his bullying, from insisting UCLA pursue high school senior Alcindor to correctly strong-arming Wooden into the Astrodome extravaganza to helping fund nonrevenue sports by making the basketball team into a money machine. In later years, Morgan even negotiated the TV contracts for the Notre Dame portion of the annual home-and-home series between the Bruins and Fighting Irish and, in Fischer's estimation, delivered four or five times the money Notre Dame would originally have accepted. Morgan once bargained a better TV deal for the Rose Bowl game than the Rose Bowl itself would have, broadcast executives told Wooden, forcing administrators at opposing schools to reluctantly praise Morgan for making the conference, and therefore UCLA, richer. The visionary with a tireless work ethic, an amazing memory to recall minuscule details of past deals on the spot, and unending loyalty to his school along the way grew into a power broker on a national level.

"I think he was highly respected by all the others in the conference, but not personally liked by many," Wooden said. "I think that was true at UCLA, to be honest with you. I think he was highly respected at UCLA by people in other departments and other areas, but not necessarily well-liked." Wooden for one of the few times may have been too harsh—many, even those put off by Morgan's abrasive style, also saw a compassionate side beneath the sandpaper crust. But in one of the critical developments of the era, Wooden recognized Morgan's many positives and regarded him as an asset despite the opposing temperaments. Neither side ever put the dynasty at risk over a power struggle.

Landing in Houston for the Game of the Century brought the latest contrast, the brilliant business mind of Morgan envisioning an unprecedented promotional moment and Wooden in a losing battle to stand up for what he considered the sanctity of the sport. The TV coverage alone, as the first live national broadcast of a regular-season college basketball game in prime time, would make it worthwhile for the savvy athletic director.

Wooden would likely have been agreeable to playing the Cougars in any typical setting, but the Astrodome, a canyon of a building, a baseball and football stadium, felt all wrong, like "we were playing a game out on a prairie," Alcindor said. They were in a way, with the court centered near second base, some hundred feet from the nearest box seat. The unique setting was just the point, though—it was futuristic, befitting the city's role as a critical part of the Space Race, nine levels, site of the first indoor baseball game, had the first animated scoreboard, and for a night was the center of the hoops universe. That the superstructure in the middle of an open field had also become a meeting place for rats was left unsaid.

Staffers in the Houston athletic department had gone from the initial private projection that they would be pleased with twenty-five thousand fans to struggling to keep up with demand once the teams opened 1-2 and kept winning. Cougars coach Guy V. Lewis and an assistant fielded orders on the phone between their desks in the small office without a secretary, taking turns answering until one got tired and walked out. Some forty thousand tickets ranging from $5 for court level to $2 at the highest level and $1 for students were purchased by mail order alone before in-person sales began in November. The publicity director for Cougar sports programs attached a life-size cutout of Alcindor's head to a wall in his office seven feet, two inches above the ground, plus a little extra, to add to the hyperbole, to capture the interest of media in town for football in previous months.

Founder Eddie Einhorn got his TVS network, for TV Sports, involved after the three major television corporations passed on coverage, then traveled station to station across the country to sell his radical idea of beaming college basketball nationwide in prime time. Riding the same wave of interest that far surpassed even the Cougars' initial expectations, and certainly those of NBC, CBS, and ABC, Einhorn built the idea that the rest of his industry did not want into a 120-station string across forty-nine states. Many did it at the expense of provoking the wrath of network bosses, who did not want affiliates to interrupt regular programming. TVS play-by-play man Dick Enberg would be seated close to the court in a foxhole dug to avoid blocking the view of fans behind him, mostly only heads aboveground, along with writers who would clickety-clack stories out on typewriters and hand pages to a runner to be faxed to offices.

Wooden standing courtside the night before gazed up and around the canyon feeling the floodlights warm his face, recalling in amazement the dinky joints he played in as a back-roads farm kid, not to mention coaching in the unbearable B.O. Barn just three seasons before. He shook his head. "It's hard to imagine that a basketball game would ever be played in surroundings like these." The only connection to the sport he struggled to recognize were the eleven tons of court trucked in from the Los Angeles Sports Arena, USC's home, for the occasion and refitted on the prairie. "We'll be worn-out just from running from the dressing rooms to the court!" one Houston player said, just as Wooden would tell his team a day later during pregame instructions, "Use the restroom now. You won't get back here until halftime. It's too far away."

Three years after the NCAA cited lack of interest around Texas in denying a Houston bid to stage the Final Four in the Astrodome, in a city where the No. 2 team in the country played home games in an off-campus gym with a capacity of 2,500, 52,693 ticketed fans flowed through the turnstiles for the 8:00 p.m. start. Only the Harlem Globetrotters' 1951 exhibition that drew 75,000 in an outdoor stadium in West Berlin topped it for attendance at a basketball game. A vendor who usually sold two or three binoculars for a typical Astros or Oilers game moved eighteen the night of January 20, 1968, which more than doubled initial Houston hopes for crowd size and vindicated Morgan no matter the outcome. "Basketball, as seen from the upper levels of the Domed Stadium, is like an underwater ballet," Edward Walsh reported from the scene for the *Houston Chronicle*. "The players and the ball float back and forth on the court. There is little hint of furious pounding of gym shoes or the sweat and emotions of the players. The view is distant but clear."

Houston exited its locker room to a stunning level of noise from the pro-Cougar crowd and the enormity of the moment with fans now part of the scene, unlike practice in the hollow megastructure. "Slow down," Guy V. Lewis—game inventor, ticket seller, coach—insisted to his players on the trek to the imported court somewhere on the horizon. "I want to enjoy this." Getting unexpected help to continue his basking, Lewis reached the playing surface for the national anthem only to have Einhorn shout orders to wait to play "The Star-Spangled Banner" to allow his TVS to show more commercials. The crowd, puzzled, stood for two minutes before the music started.

Alcindor went to the jump circle with vertical double vision, sometimes even seeing three of the same image stacked on top of each other. His conditioning was just as bad; winded easily after missing two contests and going seven days since his last game or practice, Alcindor couldn't keep up with his team's fast break. Warren raised the possibility of asking Wooden to take the best player in college basketball history out of the biggest game of the regular season—of any regular season, as the Game of the Century—before Shackelford told Warren to not even think about it.

Insanity swirled throughout the cavern. Wooden started Edgar Lacey on Hayes with instructions to play Hayes tight, to force him into awkward spots before even catching the ball, then went to Jim Nielsen when Lacey did not follow directions. Alcindor stayed in the entire 40 minutes and kept missing shots; the volume increased even from the initial pandemonium, until Houston guard Chaney could not hear the ball bounce. The noise spiked again midgame as the Cougars continued to hold a tight lead and the possibility of UCLA losing turned more real. By the second half, advertisers from around the country were calling Einhorn in the foxhole to buy commercial time on the fly, Einhorn was scribbling impromptu scripts in sloppy handwriting and handing them to Enberg, and Enberg dropped in ten-second bits for cars and shaving cream among game action.

Wooden looked down the bench early in the second half to see Lacey at the far end with his head down and not watching the game, dejected to the point that Wooden decided Lacey did not want to go in. Alcindor in the same crucial stretch was fading, struggling with poor conditioning more than the eye injury while missing 14 of 18 attempts. "And some of the press started writing a convenient alibi for UCLA—that Kareem had injured his eye a few games earlier and wasn't at his best, that he was having trouble seeing," Hayes would recall. "If he was having trouble seeing, how come he was [7 of 8] from the free-throw line? They said he had double vision, and my answer to that was the only double vision he was having was Ken Spain and me going up in his face every time he tried a shot." With one Bruin big man unavailable and another laboring, power forward Hayes, Houston's star, seized the opportunity with 39 points and 15 rebounds in what Wooden called "one of the phenomenal games I've ever seen." Fittingly, Hayes had the two free throws with 28 seconds remaining that gave the Cougars a 71–69 victory that ended UCLA's 47-game winning streak and led to fans and cheerleaders storming the court.

Hayes always remembered winning the biggest game in school history, for any sport, as a relief after months of buildup, aware the underdogs could not waste the opportunity or scene that would never be duplicated. He was a twenty-two-year-old with a wife and son, basketball demands, and schoolwork and was unprepared as the product of the relaxed life of small-town central Louisiana to carry so much weight in Houston—"I couldn't get away from the pressure." There were days he would sneak away to a small bayou off campus, lie on the grass, and ask himself, "God, how long can all this last? I can't wait to get away from it all." On the night he vaulted from one of the best players in the country to historic by dominating the Game of the Century, Hayes could at least have the reward of going to the UCLA hotel for casual conversation with Alcindor, before several other Cougars took Alcindor to fraternity parties.

Wooden came across as barely discouraged, believing the Bruins were still the better team, that Houston got a great performance from Hayes, with a college low point for Alcindor and a mostly absent Lacey on the same night and still only won by 2. Wooden also had the benefit of reasoning away the outcome as secondary to the successful money grab, the real point of the trip, and, as always, that only losses in conference and the postseason really hurt. Shackelford saw him enter the locker room with a smile and seeming relieved at the streak ending before it could become another pressure point. Morgan left just as unfazed after the first defeat in one year and eleven months, since Alcindor's freshman season, as his gut instinct for the popularity of the event was confirmed by living the basketball circus. A couple months before four games in the national tournament would net both schools $30,000 (about

$260,000 in 2023 money), the spectacle of nine levels of sight and sound earned the two athletic departments $125,000 each ($1.1 million), more than Houston made the entire previous season as a Final Four participant. In the bigger picture, it would come to be seen as the game that changed college basketball, a forever moment that made national broadcasts of regular-season games common and domed stadiums for championships the norm.

"Why didn't Coach use Lacey?" Allen yelled to no one in particular in the locker room, before continuing the questioning on the bus ride back to the hotel, eventually directly at Wooden. "Coach, why didn't you put our best forward back in the game?" Wooden opted for a private conversation instead of a public debate others could hear. Sensitive Lacey, giving in to the emotions of the moment, sat next to Alcindor on the same drive and decided he would quit. "He knew why he hadn't played," Alcindor later concluded. "Coach Wooden, in spite of his tactical genius for the game, had a serious blind spot when it came to his players and their comportment. Mr. Wooden believed his athletes had to be not only physically and emotionally prepared, but 'morally' ready to play. Lynn Shackelford was his ideal: Shackelford studied hard, belonged to the Fellowship of Christian Athletes, took instruction and advice and criticism beautifully. Edgar was a better ballplayer, but he was his own man who would not alter his personality to suit his coach. He wound up fighting Mike Lynn, another 'moral borderliner,' for the starting spot both should have been awarded. This had been eating at him all season, and getting left on the bench finally cut right through." Wooden, Alcindor explained another time, "had this morality thing going; you had to be 'morally' right to play. From that attitude came a serious inability on his part to get along with 'problem' players. If they didn't go to church every Sunday and study for three hours a night and arrive fifteen minutes early to practice and nod in agreement with every inspiring word the coach said, they were not morally fit to play—and they found themselves on the second team." Alcindor waited several practices the next week for Wooden to explain why his friend had been left at the end of the bench, something as basic as "Lacey was not playing well," but only heard Wooden address Lacey's emotional reaction.

"I've never enjoyed playing for that man," Lacey said, growing angrier with the perception he didn't want to play. "That [Houston game] was the last straw. It all started my sophomore year when he tried to change the mechanics of my shooting. . . . And now I have no one to blame but myself for staying this long. He has sent people by to persuade me to reconsider, but I have nothing to reconsider. I'm glad I'm getting out now while I still have some of my pride, my sanity, and my self-esteem left." When Lacey read Wooden's comment in the *Los Angeles Times* that body language and appearing to be disinterested indicated Lacey did not want to return in the second half, Lacey threw the newspaper down and stormed out of his house.

"You aren't going to print any of this in the paper, are you?" Wooden asked the reporter who visited the Lacey home, Jeff Prugh of the *Times*. Yes, Prugh said. The coach then gave the longer response that he felt bad about the situation, that Lacey was making a mistake and Wooden wished he would come back, but that he would not reach out to help make it happen. "My remark was correct, and I stood behind what I said," Wooden further explained a day later, "but oftentimes, you can be correct but be better off not having said it."

It was, Allen said, "one of the few times that our master psychologist went too far. Edgar had been there for four years. He was one of the guys who had to be treated gently. You should know your people better than that." Beyond the lineup jolt with 12 games remaining in the regular season and in the immediate aftermath of a rare loss, Lacey had more precisely been an important layer to Alcindor's UCLA experience from the beginning, one of the players, along with Warren, who met the Power senior at the airport for the recruiting visit. Lacey took college freshman Alcindor to the It Club in 1965 to hear John Coltrane seduce the crowd with a saxophone, tapping into a mutual interest in jazz that helped build a friendship when Alcindor had few people he could lean on emotionally. On the court, Alcindor considered him a critical part of the success as the Bruins' best frontcourt defender. The decision, the suddenness, and the timing dared a wide-ranging fallout.

"It caused us to do a lot of self-checking, because John Wooden personified goodness, piety, integrity, all those things," Allen said. "If you can't trust John Wooden, who can you trust?" UCLA supporters were just as bewildered, though more by the loss than the Lacey situation, complete with Wooden getting grilled by one of the booster clubs "like the Nuremberg Trials," a member of the Bruin Hoopsters later relayed. "'What have you done for us lately?'" The reaction ten months after a title in an undefeated 1966–67 privately annoyed Wooden, a turning point in his relationship with fans and the first confirmation of fears that Alcindor's arrival would create unrealistic expectations. His world changed forever on the floor of the Astrodome more than anyone, including Wooden himself, could have imagined.

Wooden viewed his postgame comments to reporters as honest, reasonable answers, not an excessive attack and, in fact, felt he made a sincere effort to repair the broken relationship by leaving the door open to a return, until Lacey soon finalized his decision by dropping out of school. Faced with what could have been a major crisis with the loss of an Alcindor favorite and a key contributor, Wooden instead almost immediately turned the departure into a positive. "Some say it was the loss to Houston that made us a better ball club, and some say it was the loss of Lacey," Wooden wrote. "I think it was a combination of things." Not stopping at just saying the Bruins had improved, he saw the new attack of center Alcindor, forwards Shackelford and Lynn, and guards Warren and Allen with the staggering perspective as the best college team in history.

Wooden loved Lynn as the tip of the spear in the 1-2-1-1 zone defense with quick hands that could disrupt as soon as the opponent threw the ball in. He raved about the second season of Warren-Allen as a superb combination, and especially about Warren, an all-time Wooden favorite, as a coach on the floor who "totally understood my philosophy and ran the game the way I wanted it." Shackelford's outside shooting provided a dimension few teams could match. And, obviously, Alcindor, now extra-motivated after seeing the *Sports Illustrated* cover of Hayes releasing a jumper over him in the Astrodome and pasting the picture in his UCLA locker as a reminder of the mission still ahead.

News that Alcindor, Allen, and Warren would skip the Olympic trials, and therefore the Summer Games, came in late February with school officials doing their part by concocting the cover story that the three "regrettably declined" because tryouts in Albuquerque would require missing at least eight days of classes and competing in Mexico City in October could mean losing the entire fall quarter and missing nine NCAA games. Alcindor had so obviously again missed the chance to speak against racial inequality that one of the biggest names from his own campus, football coach Tommy Prothro, picked apart the announcement by noting the three Bruins "would get a heck of a lot more mileage for the boycott cause if they said they were boycotting, but they've never said that. . . . These boys might be in sympathy with the boycott, but they're not really boycotting themselves." Alcindor didn't even put a voice to his anger over treatment of blacks in the very moment of finally making his hard-line Olympic decision permanent.

The attempt to shield the school's image and three of the most visible people on campus held up a couple weeks, before Alcindor, Warren, and Allen said they turned down the invitations to protest the treatment of blacks in America, not because of academics. Louisville's black star, Westley Unseld, cited weariness for withdrawing. Neal Walk of Florida, a white standout, said he would skip Albuquerque and Mexico City to concentrate on school. Hayes accepted the invitation, only to soon give up his amateur status by signing with the San Diego Rockets of the NBA, part of a particularly troubling run of the United States losing its best centers and power forwards, a list that included Bob Lanier of St. Bonaventure.

Another wave of hate mail poured into UCLA, either calling Alcindor ungrateful or using racial slurs, or both. Carl Porter of the *Tucson Daily Citizen* decried the announcement as "Lew Alcindor's first step in the footsteps of a confused Cassius Clay," apparently unaware Alcindor had been walking with Ali for years. "It could be the start of the saddest days in American sports." Not even trying to see Alcindor's stand as a social issue, whether right or wrong, Paul Zimmerman of the *Los Angeles Times* suggested the decision was "probably based on a desire to get at the big package of pro basketball money that awaits him as quickly as possible," even though Alcindor had not so much as hinted at leaving college after his junior season. Arthur Daley wrote in the *New York Times* that Alcindor and track star Tommie Smith were "victimized by those who would use them to promote a boycott that has no chance of serving its purpose," a position Wooden partly shared with the claim of "outside influences trying to use Negro athletes." At least

Alcindor hero Jackie Robinson, though agreeing with skeptics that the action would accomplish little, offered the support that "I feel we've got to use whatever means, except violence, we can to get our rights in this country."

As in the immediate aftermath of the Thanksgiving meeting, no one at UCLA attempted to change Alcindor's mind, support he appreciated when the most prominent person on campus winning gold would have been tremendous positive publicity. Wooden instead remained focused on the end of the regular season, understandable in the moment but also reasonable to anyone who knew his distaste for the selection process since Walt Hazzard made the U.S. squad in 1964 but Gail Goodrich was left off. The disappointment stayed with Wooden through future Summer Games and became severe enough that he saw the Olympics as flawed and dismissed any attempt to equate competing with a sign of patriotism.

The locker room fractured by the Lacey split, the coach permanently changed by the fan reaction to the Houston defeat, and the program facing public outrage from the Olympic decision, at least the Bruins had the stability of closing the regular season with 12 consecutive wins. Rarely in the championship era would stomping through nearly seven weeks of schedule, with 9 of the 12 victories by double digits, be so meaningful. Beating New Mexico State and Santa Clara in the West Regionals in Albuquerque created the matchup UCLA most wanted: Houston, this time in Los Angeles, in the national semifinals.

The Cougars hit town as tourists, with two players appearing on *The Joey Bishop Show*, another trying out for *The Dating Game*, and Coach Guy V. Lewis visiting a hip private nightclub, the Factory. A Cadillac limousine took Hayes and Chaney and their wives on a tour of one of the movie studios and a visit to the set of *Hello, Dolly!* Some teammates, one Cougar said, "seemed more worried about selling their tickets than about the game." Then one of the student managers was arrested outside the Sports Arena before the game on charges of scalping, no great setback to the plan of attack against the Bruins but adding to the feeling that Houston was distracted. Businesslike UCLA in the final hour before tip-off was the contrast in advance of the biggest game of their lives, "bigger,"

Alcindor wrote, "than the previous year's final because we were aware now of what was at stake; the championship had some body to it." They prepared for revenge mostly in silence.

Wooden opening with a diamond-and-one defense for the first time in his career at the suggestion of assistant Jerry Norman—four Bruins in a zone the shape of a diamond, one shadowing a specific Cougar—dramatically upped the stakes with the risky move of Shackelford as the one and Hayes as his man-to-man assignment. That the job would ordinarily have gone to Lacey doubled the stakes on Shackelford, as a shooting specialist who would need the defensive game of his career, and on Wooden, as the coach his team blamed as the cause of Lacey's absence.

The game had barely started when Alcindor came downcourt to set up for an early UCLA possession, posted low, waited for a pass, and felt Hayes, no longer the friendly visitor to the Houston hotel after the Game of the Century, lean against him. "We're gonna beat you," Alcindor heard the defender say. "We're gonna beat you bad." Alcindor had already spent parts of January, February, and March staring at the *Sports Illustrated* cover in his locker several times a week. He didn't need to hear from Hayes to be motivated. When the focused, businesslike attitude of pregame turned into the precision of a 22-point Bruin lead at halftime, Guy V. Lewis spent part of his pep talk to the tourists talking about "pride, not quitting, hanging tough, those good ol' American principles we'll need if we ever fight the Russians or the Chinese or some of those folks." Instead taking on a powerful, focused basketball squad seeking payback, the Cougars sank further behind before UCLA finished a 101–69 victory as vindication for the Norman-Wooden defensive call, for Alcindor with 19 points and 18 rebounds, and for Shackelford after Hayes missed 7 of 10 while playing with an intestinal virus. "That's the greatest exhibition of basketball I've ever seen," Lewis said.

"If they'd thought we'd let them anywhere near us, they were dead wrong," Alcindor wrote, more outwardly excited for the rematch than any game during his college career, so motivated that he felt like he had an elbow above the rim while elevating to finish a basket with a soft touch off the glass. The 78–55 win over North Carolina the next day for the championship and a second consecutive title felt anticlimactic by comparison, even with the praise from Tar Heel coach Dean Smith that UCLA is "the greatest basketball team of all time." The greatest "in the history of intercollegiate basketball," Wooden amended.

Alcindor called Norman at work about a week later, sounding uncomfortable. Norman as the point person on recruiting the Power senior knew Alcindor better than any other adult on campus, the man who took him out for a one-on-one dinner on the Saturday of the campus visit without bothering to invite Wooden because Norman knew Wooden would choose a weekend night with the family instead. In his office days after the triumphant Final Four victory, riding the high of beating Houston, Norman heard, and felt, a strange tone through the line.

Where are you? Norman asked.

Mr. Gilbert's office.

Do me a favor, Norman continued, and come by my office when you have time the next couple days.

When Alcindor followed through as requested, Norman diplomatically conveyed his serious concerns in gentle terms knowing Alcindor could shut down, explaining that many boosters wanted to help the program by hiring players for summer jobs or be supportive in other ways, but after going through the coaches. Norman did not know benefactor Gilbert well, mostly by reputation, but the Wooden assistant of ten years and four championships saw Gilbert choosing the exact opposite approach in excluding the staff to surreptitiously turn himself into an influential figure who dealt directly with players. Someone like that might be interested in more than helping college students, Norman told Alcindor.

Norman quit without a replacement job lined up, certain only that he needed a career that paid more to provide for a wife and two daughters and allowed a better family life than regularly coming home at nine or ten o'clock. While Gilbert's rise to prominence behind the scenes in just one year since befriending Alcindor and Allen played no role in the decision to leave UCLA, Norman left with a similar parting message for his now-former boss, only minus the delicate language used on Alcindor. If I were you guys, Norman told Wooden and new top assistant Denny Crum, I would be really, really careful about Sam Gilbert being around the program.

The rapid ascension of Gilbert, being forced by Morgan into the Game of the Century, Lacey quitting, Norman leaving, a schism with players, and especially the sweltering demands turned 1967–68 into one of the most trying seasons of Wooden's career despite the successful outcome. The man with two championships in a row and four in all and still just fifty-seven years old by early in the offseason was wondering how much longer he wanted the job. The pressure had gotten that bad.

5

CLENCHED FISTS

His junior year complete, his Olympic decision final, the projected victory lap of a final college season still months into the future, Lew Alcindor started the summer of 1968 in his New York City comfort zone that included a return to volunteer work urging kids to get an education and appearing at clinics with other sports stars. While going into the NBC studios July 19 to appear on the *Today* show hardly qualified as comfort zone, the interview with Joe Garagiola and Ed Newman would provide a national platform to speak on racial inequality, even if it meant the discomfort of having to retrace his thinking on the boycott. Better still, the entire segment would be broadcast, unlike a press conference that allowed the media to pluck portions and let other answers fall away.

"Well, I know I'm not going because there's just too many things that point against it," Alcindor said. "I have to go to school and, plus, you know, the atmosphere is that it's wrong to represent this country and then have to come back and, you know, face the music all over again." He knew all too well the story of Ali winning boxing gold in the 1960 Summer Games only to return to Louisville and be denied service at a restaurant in his hometown.

"But you live here," Garagiola reminded his guest.

"Yeah, I live here, but it's not really my country, you know."

"Well, then there's only one solution then," Garagiola decided. "Maybe you should move."

"Well, you see, that would be fine with me, you know, but it all depends on where are we going to move?"

When the segment ended suddenly and awkwardly with a commercial break in midconversation, Alcindor and Garagiola continued the civil but pointed exchange. Off camera but with NBC still capturing the conversation, the host confronted Alcindor with "That's a pretty tough statement you made."

Alcindor: "Well, what I meant was, this is not my country the way it is."

Garagiola: "It's not my country the way it is either, with the riots, the bombings, and all that. But we're trying to get rid of all these situations and this is what we're working for."

Alcindor: "Well, that's what I meant."

Garagiola: "That's not what you said, though."

Back from commercial after Alcindor left the studio, by all indications on good terms despite the acidic tone, Garagiola shared the off-camera conversation that provided additional clarity on Alcindor's controversial position. When *Today* could have piled on and caused Alcindor more grief as a show with influence among viewers likely already among the angered middle class, Garagiola instead offered the support of "I'm in full sympathy with Lew Alcindor in his effort to help his people, and after I understood what he meant. I certainly felt for him." Showing composure and maturity at the suggestion on national television that he move to another country for having a differing view, Alcindor likewise moved forward without hard feelings, calling it a breakdown in communications. Participating in a playground clinic for about one hundred kids a couple weeks later in Long Island City with the press in attendance provided additional beneficial optics, that "I think what I'm doing here now is more important than what I can do in Mexico City," even if he may have been able to do both with the Olympics still two and a half months away.

Having publicly acted on two bold positions, the support of Ali and the Olympic boycott, Alcindor eased into the next major pronouncement of his life, a deeply personal issue but also visible and sure to be equally controversial. Three years of introspection at UCLA led him in the same New York summer of '68 to convert to Islam, after living his first twenty-one years as a

Catholic, attending Catholic schools before college, and extensive readings on Buddhism, Taoism, existentialism, and several Protestant beliefs. The dig for spiritual meaning that started with reading the autobiography of Malcolm X as a freshman became so deep in typical Alcindor fashion that a friend noted the stack of religious books on his desk and said, "Man, just pick one."

Some of the time that would have been spent preparing for the Mexico City Games was instead invested in attending a Sunnite mosque on 125th Street, Alcindor returned whenever possible and was reenergized by each visit "as if at last I had found my place, my people and my path." Alcindor made his decision to become a Muslim final with a ceremony before witnesses and was given a new name by his teacher there. Abdul Kareem told no one except his disappointed parents and a few close friends, still Lew to most.

Their son becoming disillusioned with the Catholic Church and emotionally scarred by Christianity for its role in slavery was particularly hurtful to Cora and Big Al, a reaction he saw coming, deliberately choosing not to inform them until after the ceremony. He shaved his head at the end of the life-changing offseason and went through a second conversion ceremony with a new teacher, who decided the young man again needed a different name. Abdul Kareem was not enough. Another change was made: Kareem for "noble and generous," Abdul for "servant," Jabbar for "powerful."

He returned to Los Angeles for the senior season angrier and more insulated than ever, still put off by artificial Southern California only now with a wider distance between most everyone after the summer of focus on black culture and the conversion to Islam. "I withdrew into an almost impenetrable world," a self-imposed confinement amid a suspicion of strangers that made him more irate in what he saw as a country run by whites for whites. Kareem Abdul-Jabbar, though he would still go by Lew Alcindor the rest of his college career, could not wait to be finished with UCLA basketball, graduate, and live elsewhere. On the other hand, he had also during the same months of life-changing personal development "worked past the age of rage" to shed the racism that so influenced his previous years. "I could still become angered at individual acts of hostility and at the whole pattern of racial hostility. But I could no longer believe that the white man was inherently evil and cruel and black men inherently superior, as some of the other blacks are teaching nowadays."

In basketball terms, "a third straight national title would not be a great triumph, just a lack of failure. Victory after victory we were in a no-win situation." Equally downcast about his relationship with the sport for the first time, after years of considering it an island amid the troubles of the moment in his life, hoops did not merely become a secondary source of satisfaction. It stopped being fun, drowned out by the success that morphed into burden and the same expectations that had ground Wooden down long before. "From the start everybody said we would win three championships," Shackelford said the same season. "That has taken a lot out of the actual accomplishment. I think it's one reason for our businesslike manner on the court. We were only doing what we had been expected to do." Alcindor carried the additional scars of years of hate mail, death threats, bad relations with the media, and disliking the city.

"We'd done the whole thing twice, lost one game in three years and avenged that in a big way, had lots of new talent this year but nothing left to prove," Abdul-Jabbar later wrote. "Every win was expected; every close call, a sign of weakness. We had added Sidney Wicks and Curtis Rowe, who had the size, speed, rebounding ability, and shooting touch of pro caliber forwards. The team was balanced and deep, but the urgency wasn't there all the time."

The gulf grew wider with the May arrest of Lucius Allen for marijuana possession, a second legal issue that pointed Allen to the obvious conclusion that a university discipline would cost him part or all of his senior season. He instead quit school without saying goodbye to Wooden, costing Alcindor one of his few close friends just four months after losing another, Lacey. The dual setbacks, on top of the graduation loss of Mike Warren, left the 1968–69 Bruins with three black players, and the others, Wicks and Rowe, who were two years younger and aggressive in contrast to Alcindor's introverted nature. Warren and Allen may also have been much more outgoing than Alcindor, but in a joyful, welcoming way, in retrospect making Warren the perfect person to meet the Power senior at the airport for the recruiting visit and Allen an ideal first roommate. Alcindor feeling the walls closing in around him early in the senior season couldn't even consider basketball his safe place anymore.

"If I had to do it all over again, I'd have gone to the University of Michigan," he said in the fall in an interview for a magazine article. "Michigan has a campus community—something which I miss at a commuter school like UCLA—and I'd also like being near Detroit and the Black community there." The publication going bankrupt before the story could be published avoided another controversy, but regretting his original UCLA decision and thinking seriously of transferring to Ann Arbor had been confirmed as real, not what he had tried to explain away previously as momentary wanderings of a frustrated teenager. Other times the same season, he said he wished he had picked a school closer to New York and with the community feel on campus of Michigan or Cal, or, when asked about student life at UCLA, that "I try not to think about that at all, man. I don't even go around there *that* much. Those people don't interest me that much." You must be extremely bored, the writer for *West* magazine told him during their interview. "Yeah, well, I'm going to let you make that assessment for yourself," Alcindor replied. "You know? That's a little bit too fiendish to comment on. I can dig where you're coming from, but you can make that assumption for yourself."

Wooden still saw Alcindor as competitive as before in striving to improve, even as it became difficult to find minor flaws in his game by the fourth season in the program. Whatever disinterest simmered inside, the man who knew Alcindor's game best could not detect it. Wooden was likewise encouraged by the addition of junior-college transfer John Vallely, initially thinking the arrival would help the backcourt depth after the exits of Warren and Allen before soon realizing Vallely could step right into the opening lineup. While Wooden considered a proven and dependable lead guard important, maybe even more than most coaches as someone who built his system on small and fast players, he also knew the firepower of a front line with sophomores Rowe and Wicks joining returnees Alcindor and Shackelford would compensate for mistakes that might come in the backcourt.

Perhaps no season of Wooden's entire career, though, made the ongoing conflict with the changing times seem more obvious, even greater than the 1967–68 that pushed him to start considering retirement. "He was fighting a losing battle against the biggest cultural and political changes in American history," Kareem Abdul-Jabbar came to observe. Wooden was born two years after Henry Ford introduced the Model T to the forty-six states and seventeen years before Charles Lindbergh flew the Atlantic solo, and now 1969 would bring a man on the moon and the inaugural flight of the 747 with a hump for a forehead. He had been alive for World War I, World War II, Korea, and at the moment Vietnam.

"He wanted to protect his boys, but he was out of touch with how rapidly the culture was changing," Abdul-Jabbar wrote, noting previous input on the evils of drugs and the potentially dangerous reactions to interracial dating, if threats in phone calls turned into reality. "The Beatles had arrived. Civil rights marches continued. Anti-war protests had begun. Women demanded rights most people didn't realize they had been denied. Rebellion was in the air. Nothing could stop it, not even a well-meaning coach." Wooden, Alcindor observed, "had a faith in the system that was charmingly anachronistic, like a pocket watch or going on Sunday drives in the country. Even when he disagreed with the government, he believed they would ultimately do the right thing because people, even politicians, were basically good." Wooden in 1968–69 became a Benny Goodman man in a Bob Dylan world.

"A lot of people think I'm rather peculiar for a coach," he told a banquet audience early in 1969 as the regular season crawled toward the finish. "Why, just the other day, a man came to me and said, 'You don't like to recruit, is that right?' And I said, 'That's right.'

"'You don't do very much scouting, either? Is that right?'

"'That's right.'

"'And you don't worry much about the other team?'

"'That's right.'

"'Well then, you certainly must be nuts.'

"'That's right. I am.'"

Although able to play his philosophy for laughs, Wooden, beyond the

happy front projected at many speaking engagements, was in reality breaking under the weight of Bruin basketball. The private grumblings of previous seasons had turned increasingly public and common late in the Alcindor
era under the weight of unbearable expectations from ingrate fans. Morgan was more domineering than ever in running the department, and there
were greater demands on his time. (The coach and athletic director at least
agreed on not accepting the offer to return to the Astrodome for a rematch
with Houston, a surprising decision from Morgan considering the payout
would surely have exceeded that of the first meeting. Though usually led by
his business mind, he found a Game of the Century II overkill.) Wooden
was even looking forward to soon being finished with having the dominant
player in the country on the team, to being able to reclaim his past life of
building around six or seven players, fast breaks, and pressing defenses.

"I sometimes wonder if it's all really worth it," his wife, Nell, confessed
one night at dinner at a Westside restaurant.

"Yes, dear," her husband politely replied, "it's like I've told you before: the
good far outweighs the bad."

Still he would wince. "When I have my summer basketball school out
at Palisades High School, they're eager to know how to do things," Wooden
said another time, during an interview in his office. "You don't find that so
much in college players. The college players are more blasé." He got up from
behind the desk to demonstrate how to fake a pass one way and throw it
another. "If you just tell your youngsters that, the college players will say,
'Aw, why do we do this? I'll just throw him the ball.' They must know *why*."
Returning to his chair, he said, "If it hadn't been for the war, I don't think
I'd have left high school coaching. I enjoyed it very much."

Shooting free throws in near-empty Pauley Pavilion prior to practice
became his refuge, even just an occasional five or ten minutes before players began to wander in from the locker room. The stress reliever that started
a season earlier when he asked student manager Bob Marcucci to rebound
seemed to take on greater importance in 1968–69, a rare moment of quiet and
chance to exhale that Marcucci provided. Wooden would ask about Marcucci's
schoolwork and the two exchanged small talk, but mostly the college senior

understood that the boss needed sanctuary and he just watched the fifty-eight-year-old man make about 80 percent of the tries before the court began to fill with players and work called. The repetitions of the ball starting at Wooden's waist, quickly being raised with both arms and released with two hands and a flick of the wrists, as many times as the short window would allow, became therapy sessions. (About three years later, Wooden rebounded for sophomore Keith Wilkes as Wilkes took forty or fifty perimeter shots, one baseline around to the other in a horseshoe path, after practice. Wilkes was stunned at how Wooden, at age sixty-one, delivered every pass in rhythm and with precision.)

Wooden, ordinarily extremely grounded and appreciative of the many blessings in his life, was being chewed through professionally to the point of finding bad in all the good. He latched on to a saying and never let go—"I can honestly say that I received more criticism after we won a championship than I did before we won one. That's why I've always said I wish all my really good friends in coaching would win one national championship. And those I didn't think highly of, I wish they would win several." Wooden more and more openly regretted building the machine, a private disgust gone public, as Bruin fans, not age, shoved him toward retirement. "I don't know whether always winning is good," he would come to say during the championship streak. "It breeds envy and distrust in others, and overconfidence and a lack of apprecia-tion very often in those who enjoy it." Cunningham couldn't help but observe in later years, "I think he was happier before he won championships."

. . .

The Summer Olympics opened October 12 with little, if any, conversation among the U.S. basketball team of Alcindor's absence, and even less worry about whether the hole in the middle made the Americans vulnerable after six consecutive gold medals. "No," said the new star big man, Spencer Hay-wood from the University of Detroit. "Because they had me." Alcindor was fifteen hundred miles away as practice and his senior season began inside Pauley Pavilion three days later with the same certainty of the Bruins as overwhelming favorites for another title. Once tempted by the rare chance to measure his talent against the world and especially the opportunity to mingle with other cultures, he showed no sign of regretting the boycott as his one and only team reconvened in Westwood.

That was especially true October 16, the night American sprinters Tommie Smith and John Carlos entered the track venue for the final of the 200-meter dash with Smith carrying the black gloves he asked his wife to buy a few days before. Smith, wanting a nonverbal statement to transcend language barriers at the global gathering, decided in advance they would become the perfect silent symbol, compact enough to easily carry into Estadio Olímpico yet also an imposing visual once put to use. He wanted to be militant, not violent. Only after Smith won did he reveal the plan to his teammate and third-place finisher to raise a clenched fist in hopes of drawing attention to social inequality and black unity. Smith said he would wear the one for the right hand and offered Carlos the left.

Both alerted silver medalist Peter Norman of Australia of the plan before going out for the medal ceremony. Answering their questions in the intense but quick impromptu conversation, Norman said he believed in human rights and believed strongly in God. "I'll stand with you," Carlos heard him say, yet Carlos still expected to spot fear in Norman's eyes once they mounted the three tiers of the victory stand. Instead, "I saw love." Carlos didn't see him so much as turn his head.

The two Americans approached the victory stand for Smith to accept the gold medal and Carlos the bronze shoeless and with black socks to represent poverty within his race, with Smith wearing a black scarf and Carlos beads to signify lynchings, and grasping the enormity of the moment. "Tommie, if anyone cocks a rifle, you know the sound," Carlos said, referencing their countless times of hearing the starter's pistol as the moment to blast off from the blocks. "Be ready to move." Smith's hand tightened and his right arm rose pointed to the sky as "The Star-Spangled Banner" played. Carlos did the same with his left and a slight bend at the elbow, wanting to be ready to react to any threatening move that might come. He scanned the stadium as the song played for the same reason, while noticing Smith mostly kept his head down.

Carlos's suggestion to Smith was justified—government forces on rooftops in the capital city two weeks earlier, said to be plainclothes members of an elite army unit, opened fire with machine guns into the crowd of thousands of peaceful protesters, soon joined by uniformed law enforcement panicked into believing they were under attack from the college-aged demonstrators. The administration seeking to protect its image on the global Olympic stage initially claimed four were killed and eventually revised the total to twenty-nine, while an American diplomat countered that "nearly two hundred" were massacred. Thousands were beaten and jailed, many never to be seen again. A confidential FBI memo seven days before warned that racial overtones, among other factors, lent credibility to Mexican fears that an attempt would be made to disrupt the Games, and suddenly two American track stars were silently screaming about race and going exactly for disruption in the stadium with sight lines a trained sniper could maximize.

Alcindor found himself "fiercely proud" of Smith and Carlos, aware how much simply choosing to not attend had cost him in hate mail and understanding that taking actual action under the greater spotlight of a victory stand would bring massive consequences. He thought of them as patriots. The worst of it in the moment for both was being banned from further competition by the International Olympic Committee and expelled from the Olympic Village. The Games continued with officials doing their best to pretend nothing happened, including the United States winning basketball gold as nineteen-year-old Haywood averaged a team-best 16.1 points. "I was a freshman in college," he said. "I was the miracle child that happened on the scene, and everybody was like, 'This guy's going to save us.' Yeah, there I was. Saving America."

The UCLA season that soon followed began with a predictable fast start and the additional credibility of consecutive victories over No. 10 Purdue at home and No. 13 Ohio State and No. 5 Notre Dame on the road. Ohio State coach Fred Taylor not only tried the Washington State tactic of practicing with tennis racquets to simulate trying to score on Alcindor, but at times during the week also sent six Buckeyes out for defensive drills to prepare for the suffocating Bruin press, all to no avail once the game started and his team could only go five-on-five without unauthorized sporting goods. Leaving Columbus after the game, heading northwest through the night to South Bend, Indiana, for the first game in Notre Dame's new on-campus arena, UCLA players and their coach began talking religion.

It started mostly with the centers, newly converted Muslim Alcindor and Protestant Steve Patterson, a member of the Fellowship of Christian Athletes. Senior guard Don Saffer, a Jew, and sophomore guard Terry Schofield, a Catholic, were soon involved and Wooden sprinkled comments from his usual spot in the front row but primarily listened. With an awareness to know when to step back, and likely even enjoying seeing his players manage the delicate topic with such maturity, he made no attempt to control the dialogue. If anything, Alcindor assessed, he seemed fascinated. The conversation grew wonderfully spirited and personal and sometimes even loud, necessary to be heard in different directions up and down the aisles, but never argumentative. The passionate hour among the 250 miles as darkness and an occasional rural community flew past outside the windows from central Ohio to northern Indiana, nearing Lake Michigan, felt like a shared experience normally found on the court.

Participants turned instantly quiet when Alcindor broke the news of becoming a Muslim during summer vacation. "Coach Wooden did not look at me cross-eyed," he later wrote. "He seemed to accept it as well as everybody else." Timing made the positive response from teammates and the staff especially important, a genuine emotional embrace, not a fake attempt to soothe a star, in the months of Alcindor distancing himself from the world and finding less comfort than ever from Bruin basketball. The Alcindor personality certainly didn't fit with young guns Wicks and Rowe, but in the surprise bonding moment as December 6 became December 7, one game completed hours before and another ahead later in the new day, "we became a different group of men, much more than just a bunch of jocks traveling around the country bouncing basketballs."

Just as valuable for team chemistry, the midnight ride was also immediate evidence, with the schedule just two games old, of Alcindor following through on the pledge to divorce his racist past. Though long interested in learning about different religions—"Man, just pick one"—the passionate but respectable debate mostly with white people when he might previously have retreated behind a wall of anger proved a new direction. One of them, Patterson, came at him hard ("He thought that everybody should be a Christian"), yet Alcindor rightly took it as an exchange, not a confrontation. In the weeks that followed, a white senior guard, Bill Sweek, and the white head student manager, Bob Marcucci, in particular became good friends with Alcindor, and not just in basketball settings.

The Bruins with a new level of camaraderie pulled into South Bend early on December 7, officially the morning after fourteen hundred people attended the Notre Dame football banquet on the covered floor of the new basketball arena and guest speaker Joe Garagiola said from the podium, "It's nice to look out here and see a group of college students with neat and well-kept haircuts." Garagiola did not, apparently, suggest anyone who did not fit his ideals move out of the country. While the bonding bus ride likely made no difference in basketball terms—UCLA was so far ahead of the chase pack in talent that a splintered locker room could have won the championship in three and a half months—the 250 miles since Columbus had been so dramatic that Sweek stepped off the bus immediately feeling the program had just moved forward. The overnight hours, Heitz said, were "deeply special" and the most memorable moment of his four Westwood years.

Beating Notre Dame later the same day made the trip complete, especially for reserve senior guard Don Saffer with 11 points and commendable defense against Fighting Irish star Austin Carr. Saffer so didn't want the night to end after his finest game as a Bruin that he skipped the bus to the hotel and walked the two miles in the snow with nothing heavier than a blazer, arriving freezing but euphoric. In all, the Bruins of early 1968–69 went from playing in Los Angeles, then Ohio and Indiana, going back to Pauley for two home contests, and U-turning east again to New York for three. "Well, Curtis, how does it feel playing in a big-time place like Madison Square Garden?" a radio announcer asked Rowe on sacred hoops ground, the original Alcindor basketball classroom. "My idea of big-time basketball," Rowe shot back, "is L.A."

Rowe and Wicks before the midpoint of their first varsity tour were already messengers for the heights of Southern California hoops as recruits from Los Angeles positioned to make immediate valuable contributions on the roster of a Los Angeles school drenched in seniors. Both were also star prospects, the latest successful outcome for assistant coach Jerry Norman as the point man on recruiting, but especially after Wicks needed a freshman year at Santa Monica City College to improve his grades. Norman had to land him twice, and Wicks had to be deeply set on Westwood to pick the Bruins as a high school senior, not switch to one of the many schools where he could have qualified academically, go through a second round of dozens of universities chasing him as a JC transfer, and then select the Bruins again. In time, the unique double commitment from Wicks would become one of the important recruiting outcomes in program history.

In the moment, though, with Alcindor overshadowing everyone else and especially varsity rookies, Wicks was a reserve forward with an undisciplined game that kept him on the bench behind Shackelford despite more talent, superior athleticism, and early signs of stardom. Shackelford, the perimeter scoring threat with high-arcing moon shots, better understood how to play off Alcindor, giving him a critical advantage Wicks could not counter, and Shackelford grasped the team concept central to Wooden teachings and made far fewer mistakes.

"I need to know the players I put on the floor don't make mistakes," Wooden said when Wicks went to the coach's office for an explanation midway through the season. "Any other questions?"

"I guess not," Wicks replied.

He left still frustrated, unable to grasp how the better talent could not have the better role, an inconceivable concept to Wicks with the additional contrast of Rowe having already gained Wooden's trust with steady play to win the starting job at the other forward. Wooden would always choose dependable over dazzle. While Willie Naulls, instrumental in Alcindor and Allen remaining at UCLA two years earlier, said he talked Wicks out of quitting in 1968–69, Wicks contended he resigned himself to the unhappy situation and to working to a future in Westwood. Just as important as the player's endless determination to stick with the original recruiting commitment, Wooden did not see the resentment come through and, if anything, saw that Wicks maintained a sense of humor and kept working. The emotional victories—the conversion giving Alcindor a new inner peace, putting his racial animus in the past, the bonding bus ride to Notre Dame, Saffer's snowy walk filled with pride, Wicks's resolve—were more significant than the actual wins in the first weeks of the season. The Bruins and their coach feeling the strain had shown themselves to be resilient. More importantly with a final push ahead for the Alcindor class, they had shown the ability to move forward.

6

IN CASE OF ATTACK

Army lieutenant Freddie Goss had been stationed at the Pentagon two months when UCLA's flight from Los Angeles landed in Newark the afternoon of December 26, 1968, and a chartered bus took the Bruins into Manhattan, first to the Hotel New Yorker for check-in and then Xavier High School for practice. "This is where we won our forty-ninth game in a row in high school," Lew Alcindor, in gray herringbone slacks and a double-breasted navy blue blazer, said quietly to a teammate as they walked downstairs to a locker room to change, happily embracing the role of tour guide. Power Memorial Academy was about a mile away with his No. 33 Panthers jersey in a glass showcase alongside a scrapbook of his exploits, because Alcindor "was always looked upon as a kid from Inwood who went to Power who went to UCLA," JV coach Brendan Malone said. "But he was always considered a New Yorker."

"To those who have been following Alcindor since his high school days at Power Memorial, Lew seemed more at ease, more confident than ever," Phil Pepe reported in the *New York Daily News*, likely tapping into his own history with the subject. "He signed autographs in the hotel lobby, something he shied away from when he was here last year. He greeted old friends cordially, spoke easily with reporters and kidded with teammates." Wooden credited the transformation to maturing, while Alcindor chose "I can see the light at the end of the tunnel" as the cause of being strangely social. Practically everything as a senior, down to the simple good times of renewing acquaintances, went through the prism of the escape from UCLA.

Goss's going the 225 miles to watch the Bruins against Providence the next day at Madison Square Garden as part of the Holiday Festival tournament constituted the greatest return to normalcy possible after thirteen months in Vietnam. The other starter in the Gail Goodrich backcourt on the 1965 title team not only had the soft landing of being transferred from misery to the Pentagon to oversee inner-city youth programs in Washington, but in time to attend the third and last of the annual Alcindor college homecomings. Twenty-five years old and watching in uniform from a section of UCLA fans, or at least New York City Alcindor fans backing the team a final time, Goss the afternoon of December 27 completed the circle from Wooden recruit to 'Nam combat vet to stateside army officer cheering the victory.

Goss had been military since joining the campus ROTC as a sophomore at the suggestion of a former roommate who transferred to West Point and wrote Goss from inside the military culture with the warning America was becoming more entangled in Southeast Asia than most realized. Thousands of college-aged men may be drafted. Sign up for ROTC to enter the service as an officer and choose a specialty rather than getting drafted and sent to the front lines as a grunt if it comes to that, former Bruin football walk-on Carl Peterson told Goss in the letter that arrived November 22, 1963. Peterson in the same note recommended the advice be shared with mutual friend Arthur Ashe.

The basketball player and the tennis standout took the direction and spent three years getting heckled by passing students shouting weekly reminders of military service as voluntary, Wednesday after Wednesday, endlessly, being laughed at while marching on the intramural field. The UCLA ROTC was impossible to miss in fatigues in the heart of campus, near Pauley Pavilion once it opened Goss's senior season and Bruin Walk, a main foot thoroughfare. Right shoulder arms. Parade rest. Left shoulder arms. More marching.

But they did set their own path. Second Lieutenant Ashe entered the army as a systems analyst and assistant tennis coach at West Point able to play tournaments and stay in the United States giving clinics for officers' kids on bases. Goss at the same rank and with the same assurances he would not see Southeast Asia, went to Fort Lewis, Washington, as a personnel officer also preparing to tour installations in America for basketball clinics. Processing troops heading overseas, ensuring soldiers had the proper shots for jungle life, checking the volumes of paperwork had been completed, that a next of kin had been listed, were the closest Goss would come to the war zone.

So being sent to Vietnam came as a shock. The conflict turned severe, as Peterson predicted in writing, and soldiers, not administrators, were the urgent need. And Goss would be a convoy commander instead, charged with meeting air force C-141s ferrying in fresh troops, boarding and briefing them on the next steps of being driven to their unit in the field and what to do in case of attack en route. Bunkers were along the main road, Highway 1, Goss told the men. Evacuate the bus or truck and seek shelter. This was after some jets, depending on the location and the week, landed with a sharp downward slash on final approach, not a gentle finishing glide, to dodge potential ground fire from beyond the base.

Goss as the officer in charge rode shotgun in a jeep at the front of the convoy, a driver to his left and a man and a machine gun behind for possible retaliation. Over the months he made use of the bunkers several times as the enemy aimed rockets and set mortars on the road. Another jeep pulled up the rear, behind the last large transport. The lieutenant fifteen months removed from the graduation ceremony inside Pauley would complete the delivery and turn back with his team to drive into danger again another day with a fresh group. After all the broken promises—he would remain in the United States, he would be given leave to return to try out for the 1968 Olympic team—he finally got the Pentagon transfer in October 1968.

Alcindor's former Power teammate Danny Nee had joined the Marines in April 1966, completed boot camp at Parris Island, and went through infantry training at Camp Pendleton, a hundred miles down the coast from Westwood, without contact with Alcindor, just as Nee never talked of his connection to the famous athlete after arriving in Vietnam in September 1967. Keep your cigarettes dry, keep your toilet paper dry, and don't get your ass shot off—those were Nee's concerns during ten months of intelligence for a helicopter squadron, charting on maps where choppers took fire, and as a helicopter gunner. Ten months of combat, rats, monsoons, and heat, nighttime especially scary, mountains and mud, weeks without showers and uniforms so wretched that khakis were burned once a replacement set arrived. He didn't think much about the UCLA center enduring the hardship of the dunk being banned.

Bruin guard Don Saffer in the months before Nee's departure for Parris reported as ordered to a drab-green high-rise in downtown Los Angeles midway through his sophomore season for a military physical. He had asthma bad enough to require an inhaler puff or adrenaline shot from trainer Ducky Drake four or five times a season, practices and games, just not bad enough to keep him from the superb condition Wooden demanded. Flunking and still playing elite-level college sports would feel wrong to the introspective Saffer, even if it couldn't beat a bad right knee keeping New York Jets quarterback Joe Namath from serving yet being fine for the NFL stampede. "Sure I play football, but I play pretty carefully, as carefully as I can," Namath said, grasping for an explanation amid a public debate on his status. "But, man, I couldn't run those obstacle courses." The threat of the draft gone, Namath would brag six months later of planning to scramble more in the upcoming 1966 season, his second as a pro. Also, he said from the safety of being blocked from service, "I'd rather fight those Reds in Vietnam than get married. There are too many pretty girls in the world."

Saffer in the downtown government building shivered slightly among the hundreds who received the same ghastly notice by mail in the first days of 1966, partly from the cold while stripped to his boxers but mostly from the fear of what being stamped as a young man of good health could mean. Some around him in lines of mass testing bent forward, some turned their head and coughed on demand. Although scared he might be taking the first steps into jungle hell, and dreading the waiting to learn the outcome, Saffer more than anything carried the guilt of living a better life than most his age, part of a glamour team in a glamour town, getting a free education on a beautiful campus, enjoying himself socially while another guy about the same age coveted dry toilet paper.

He couldn't help but feel sorrow at his good fortune. Even passing the physical to qualify for the draft, and saying he would have gone if called, gave way to the relief of receiving a lottery number that made being plucked from gilded life unlikely. The college years passed, the shivering day in the very public exam room remained the closest Saffer ever got to military duty, and still he would visit the war memorial near his Westchester High School in Los Angeles during college and see the names of several former classmates who didn't come back from Vietnam. The guilt never stopped.

Six days after Goss attended UCLA-Providence, Ohio State football coach Woody Hayes left on his fourth goodwill tour to Vietnam with such enthusiasm that he departed from the West Coast the morning of January 2, hours after his Buckeyes beat USC in the Rose Bowl rather than return home triumphantly with the team. The visits had come to mean as much to Hayes as the troops he would meet, ever since he prepared for the first in July 1966 by buying fatigues before leaving Columbus—"I thought that they might not have any big enough over there"—and studied maps and read recent books on the country. He brought the 1965 Big Ten highlight reel and one from OSU's 1961 season, to be played on projectors in the days after arriving in Saigon. That grew into a twenty-three-day swing in June 1968 from the Mekong Delta on the southern edge of the peninsula up to the demilitarized zone separating North and South Vietnam.

Troops loved seeing fresh clips of O. J. Simpson in the Rose Bowl during the 1969 trip Hayes considered the high point of his tours in what had to also rank as one of the best periods of his entire life. His friend Richard Nixon would be inaugurated president on January 20 with the Ohio State band scheduled to perform amid the festivities. To then go from California to Southeast Asia as a newly minted national champion was celebratory enough, but the fourth visit brought the additional thrill of meeting Colonel George Patton, the son of one of Woody's biggest heroes. Not merely an admirer of the general, Hayes loaded his Ohio State office with shelves of Patton books and promoted him into Buckeye lexicon: quarterbacks were taught to shout "Patton!" at the line of scrimmage to call an audible for a running play, in homage to Patton's success with ground forces during

World War II in particular. "LeMay!" would be yelled in the same situation for a pass, a tribute to the success of air force general Curtis LeMay in the sky. Colonel Patton parted stunned at Hayes's knowledge of his father.

As in previous visits, he ignored the advice of officials and insisted on being choppered into hot spots to meet troops in danger zones as well, ate in mess halls with the troops, and asked the men for phone numbers to call their parents once he got back to Ohio. At home before and after January 1969, Hayes scheduled outdoor practices on days of freezing temperatures in Columbus to prepare for the upcoming game in a cold-weather location and barked at the Buckeyes, "If you're going to fight in the North Atlantic, you have to train in the North Atlantic." He knew it firsthand—Wayne Woodrow Hayes enlisted in the navy six months before Pearl Harbor, served in Pacific and Atlantic operations, commanded 450 tons of submarine chaser during 1944 U.S. offensives in the South Pacific, and reached lieutenant commander before an honorable discharge. In what he saw as battles of Midwest Saturday afternoons, light-years from true combat or the glorified image of German U-boats hunting a convoy of Allied merchant ships, his different careers and different times collided to use kill zones to inspire.

No one among the UCLA athletic department celebrated war the same way, and certainly not the head basketball coach forever proud of his navy duty except with better perspective. Wooden had the viewpoint of a man who prioritized weekend family time over recruiting and considered championship seasons teaching moments rather than a way to get rich, but especially as the father of a marine. Jim Wooden in Los Angeles since leaving the Marines in 1959 stood as John's daily up-close reminder of the stakes of battle as Vietnam intensified through the next decade. One of the Bruin student managers, George Morgan, the son of a tank commander who won a Silver Star on Iwo Jima, would proudly volunteer in 1971 for the same life, down to eventually becoming a tank officer himself, with such conviction that George went directly to Headquarters Marine Corps to enlist while home in Virginia. He went to them. Peterson, with one older brother in the army and another in the navy, was disappointed to flunk his physical because of a bad right knee and miss his chance to serve. Two of Pete Newell's sons were in the navy, a great distance from danger, based in Honolulu at different times from the middle to the end of the sixties, but both had the grim task of processing the body bags that came back full from Vietnam.

Dentists around Los Angeles were getting $1,000 to $2,000 to fit potential draftees with unnecessary orthodontics that would disqualify them from serving, and others facing the possibility of meeting Goss at the end of a trans-Pacific flight gamed the system. Dragging out graduation as long as possible, six years in some cases, became an art to keep the shelter of a student deferment. The nonathlete at UCLA who accidentally accumulated enough credits for a diploma without realizing it stayed in his fraternity house anyway in another dodge attempt. When the dreaded government letter showed up, he moved to San Francisco with the claim he could not report to a Los Angeles draft board, before Uncle Sam found him in Northern California, before he U-turned to L.A., before he decided to try to reason with the military, before he was eventually spotted in uniform and talking about boot camp at Fort Ord. Football star Gary Beban got the scare his freshman year of having to go home to the Bay Area to show proof he was still a college student after dropping a single class set off alarm bells with the draft board.

The threat in most cases was not as severe for basketball because of height restrictions, but some Bruins just in case heard the reach of Sam Gilbert and other connected boosters could make the Vietnam problem go away. Gilbert got Lucius Allen, for one, tucked away in the relative safety of the National Guard after he quit school and the government was, Alcindor later wrote, "warming up a spot for him in Danang." Senior guard Bill Sweek, a major contributor to UCLA at 14-0 through late January, would in months decline an invitation to Phoenix Suns training camp as a seventh-round pick to take a job he did not want, teaching high school in Connecticut, because male instructors were in such demand that they received deferments as well. He instead worked a classroom in New Haven and played in the semipro Eastern League with players doing heroin and bringing guns to games in equipment bags, going from John Wooden teaching socks straight into a gangster operation.

Sweek's current team in Westwood, already an obvious No. 1, had the additional emotional boost of remaining undefeated and mostly unchallenged despite three trips to the Midwest and beyond. Don Saffer quitting rather than continuing to be frustrated with a reserve role made no noticeable impact in the standings, either. Performing with the focus of a program digging for its first championship and the talent and confidence of a roster that already had two, they were up to 83 wins in 84 varsity games for the senior class and finding jovial moments while trudging through the usual boredom while waiting to peak for the tournament. Even Alcindor broke from detached life for an attempt at playful at the Seattle airport upon ducking through the doorway to enter the cabin for the flight home wearing a trench coat and dark glasses and announcing, "This plane is going to Cuba!"

Alcindor at the same time was dealing with the double agony of his chosen isolated existence joined by an increasing number of migraine headaches, bad enough by late in the season that one night a doctor would not allow him to warm up for a home game until fifteen minutes prior to tip-off. "It's got to be the constant pressure he's under right now," Wooden said. "He can't even talk to a friend or anybody else and not have to answer questions about what he's going to do about pro basketball." Alcindor had also been secretly playing through a painful right knee that required shots to reduce pain and inflammation and, Wooden relayed, caused the team physician to wonder about his durability once the assumed No. 1 draft pick joined the NBA or ABA and the schedule jumped from about 30 games a season in college to 82 in the regular season at the next level. The 1968–69 woes soon also included the scare of Alcindor learning his father spent a night in a hospital after an auto accident that demolished the car, although Big Al escaped serious injury.

The fates had so ganged up against him as a senior—multiple physical pains, the mental distance from most of the college experience, the scare with his dad—that his final regular-season home game ended in a 46–44 defeat when USC successfully pulled off the stall tactic Wooden hated. The second loss for the senior class and the first ever in Pauley for the home team was mostly meaningless in setting—UCLA would open the tournament in the same place five days later—yet almost surreal in the building freshman Lewis Alcindor helped unveil in 1965. Given the chance for a proper exit in 1969, the Bruins beat New Mexico State in the first round and Santa Clara in the second with sixteen-year-old high school junior Bill Walton in attendance, capped by thunderous applause for Alcindor, heading to the bench for the last time at home with about 8 minutes remaining. The ovation continued as he slipped into a warm-up jacket, until Wooden finally motioned him to stand and acknowledge the send-off. Alcindor pulled fellow senior Kenny Heitz up with him, and both raised index fingers to signify No. 1 heading into the Final Four in Louisville. The school band played "My Old Kentucky Home."

The Bruins were in Louisville and a day away from the semifinals against Drake when the four-way conference call that would change Alcindor's life forever began with NBA commissioner J. Walter Kennedy in New York City, Bucks chairman Wes Pavalon and general manager John Erickson in Milwaukee, Suns president Richard Bloch in Beverly Hills, and Suns general manager Jerry Colangelo and coach Johnny Kerr in Phoenix. Kennedy, behind a polished brown desk, explained he would use a 1964 John F. Kennedy half-dollar to determine which team about to finish with the worst record in each conference would get the No. 1 choice in the most anticipated draft ever. He went through the tossing procedure, how he would use his right hand for the throw and the catch and turn the half-dollar over onto the back of his left, going for clarity but also building tension.

Alcindor had yet to decide between the NBA and ABA, but he did know he wanted to be with the Knicks in New York, the Warriors in San Francisco ("a swinging town"), the Lakers in Los Angeles, or the Celtics in Boston ("where the winners live") if he chose the established league he grew up watching. None were options, though, as Kennedy prepared for the toss, just the Bucks and Suns at the bottom of each conference. Faced with two disappointing possibilities, he leaned to Phoenix with better weather, a preference that would have increased once friend Connie Hawkins arrived in Arizona in June as a free agent.

Colangelo at twenty-nine was young for a personnel boss, even a personnel boss who ran a first-year team in a cactus-land outpost with no other major-league franchise. It was only three years after the commissioner, upon learning of the city's interest, graded Phoenix "too hot, too small and too far away" to be a successful market, though he never specified the same location concerns with the oceanfront Lakers and Warriors farther still and San Diego and Seattle about to be added a year before the Suns. But Colangelo prepared with the vision and action of an experienced executive. He had been scouting the Bruins in person since the Holy Cross and Boston College games in Madison Square Garden in 1967 and in the meantime making roster decisions specifically with Alcindor in mind long before knowing if the Suns would get him or even whether the NBA would get him. Colangelo passed on experienced players in the 1968 expansion draft who could have brought quicker credibility in a new market and instead went for three twenty-five-year-old perimeter players who could shoot from the outside to complement Alcindor's inside game, just as Wooden programmed with Shackelford. Colangelo wanted the nucleus to grow up together, not pass into retirement as Alcindor reached stardom, and had watched UCLA close enough to consider the long-distance plotting a worthwhile gamble. Colangelo had "dreamed long and hard about that. To me, that was always the end of the rainbow." If it blew up in his face, Phoenix would still have decent young players and a choice near the top in the '69 college draft, just not the very top.

Colangelo had never talked to Wooden, but knew from being a scout and assistant to the president in Chicago when Keith Erickson played for the Bulls and from similar conversations with Goodrich in Phoenix that the Wooden reputation for teaching fundamentals and emphasizing character was fact. It made him more certain of Alcindor's limitless future. Colangelo was so confident of the payoff with Alcindor that he worried when the Suns started 1968–69 with a 4-3 record, threatening to doom the big-picture plan by getting too good too soon. He needed them at the bottom of the Western Conference in the second season, not respectable. The nosedive from there was good news to the general manager waiting with outstretched arms at rainbow's end.

Colangelo plotted out March (the coin toss) and April (the draft) of 1969, deciding in advance the Suns would go with the results of fan balloting in a local newspaper if they were the ones to decide between heads and tails. Kennedy in his office on the twenty-third floor of 2 Pennsylvania Plaza in midtown Manhattan could watch the Hudson River flow far below in the late-morning sun as Phoenix accepted the option to make the call or defer to the Bucks. From Beverly Hills, Bloch, an Arizona businessman relocated to Southern California, carried the Phoenix voice by declaring heads, the poll winner with 54 percent of the vote.

"I'm going to put the phone down because I can't do it with my feet," Kennedy said.

He placed his eyeglasses on and tossed at 11:10 a.m.

"The coin has come up tails," the commissioner announced, before setting a hand over the mouthpiece and telling others in his office, "You should hear the cheering, it sounds like election night."

Pavalon and John Erickson danced in a joint bear hug and other Bucks officials joined the embrace for a mob celebration before Erickson met the media and kept a straight face while tossing out, "We will get together soon with Coach Larry Costello and his assistant, Tom Nissalke, and see what our needs are and who is available for the draft." It may have been lingering trauma from Pavalon's lit cigarette stabbing into one of his ears during the initial hug. "We would have called tails anyway," Pavalon said. "Or we would have deferred to Phoenix because of their contest."

In downtown Phoenix, Colangelo slumped into his chair and an *Arizona Republic* writer noted him aging a dozen years on the spot. Adding to the body blow, the Suns contingent could hear the Milwaukee celebration through the speakerphone box on his desk. Kerr, standing next to the sitting Colangelo, hands clasped in front at the waist, dropped his head forward at the body blow that the team would instead be choosing from among Jo Jo White of Kansas, Neal Walk of Florida, Simmie Hill of West Texas State, and Larry Cannon of La Salle at No. 2. Colangelo, forlorn and with a frozen look of disbelief, waited for his office to clear out, then decided he needed to drive, just to process the setback. He steered through the Valley for three hours, miles of seeing everything in town and seeing nothing, stopping at one point to look back at the city and ache.

The commissioner in New York flipped again for late-arriving NBA staff members wanting to be at least a delayed part of history and to allow TV cameras ushered in on the blue plush rug to create a reenactment. Kennedy tossed several times. Tails kept winning.

Alcindor in Louisville offered no public reaction to the result, mostly because Wooden placed a gag order on all players until after the tournament. "Maybe I am overprotective," he admitted. "But the last three years haven't been easy. I think these boys are taut. We've got just a couple of days left. I don't want some little thing spoiling it all." Shackelford and Heitz escaped the bubble to look for frogs along a creek under the hot Kentucky sun, but Alcindor, wanting the media attention for one of the few times in his life, was frustrated at not getting to clarify comments in the *West* magazine article earlier in the season he thought made him look foolish and illiterate for condemning campus life and telling the writer to make assumptions. Kentucky coach Adolph Rupp in the same hours pushed for him to be barred from the National Association of Basketball Coaches' All-America team as payback for the Olympic boycott, an effort that failed. And Alcindor had a championship to win. The NBA draft order was far down his list of concerns, beyond plans to fly to New York after the Final Four to meet with both leagues while the rest of the Bruins returned to Los Angeles.

The challenges on the court, meanwhile, remained rare, even with a 3-point victory over Drake in the semifinals that prompted Alcindor to rank the Bulldogs as one of the three toughest opponents of his college career, along with Houston of 1967–68, likely the victorious Game of the Century Cougars rather than the pushover Final Four opponent, and, strangely, Colorado State of 1966–67. The home game as a freshman against a relative unknown that permanently bonded him to Wooden still stood out that much, long after Colorado State finished 13-10. Individually, "There weren't that many good centers in college. I wasn't forced to compete that hard. I had to develop more or less on my own."

Drake had already gone from 10-4 with 3 losses in 5 games to rescuing the season with 12 consecutive victories and finally, most shockingly of all, standing up to the Bruins from the great distance of No. 11 in the country. Not only that, the Bulldogs, with a small, fast lineup, used a pressing defense to fluster a Wooden team, exactly as undersized Wooden squads did to win the 1964 and '65 titles. In the flipped 1969 version, panicky UCLA scrambled just to get into an offensive rhythm, and Wooden, on his heels, shuffled lineups at an unusual rate as turnovers mounted. Rowe, a forward, was pressed into a lead role in bringing the ball upcourt.

Sweek got pulled in the first half for a missed assignment and smoldered through an extended stay on the bench, certain he did not need to be taught a risky and embarrassing lesson this late in his career, as a fifth-year senior, with one guard, Saffer, already gone and another, Vallely, in foul trouble. Wooden had come down hard on Sweek before, but for antics, most notably not playing him three straight games for going off a diving board at the hotel pool in Oakland while wearing a UCLA blazer. Sweek did escape discipline for lead roles in instigating water fights or rigging buckets with water to tip on teammates who opened the wrong hotel door at the wrong time. Any mistakes against Drake, though, were game errors, the same anyone could make and did make during the night of 20 turnovers, in addition to the uncounted defensive flaws.

When Vallely fouled out with about 90 seconds remaining after his 29 points kept the Bruins in front, a starring role for the junior-college transfer in his first Final Four, Wooden had no choice but to summon Sweek from exile. Determined to make a point on the way in, Sweek drew out removing his warm-up jacket and casually strolled down the sideline and toward the court, a saunter with the Bruins playing for their championship lives and needing focus, not a silent protest.

If you don't want to play, Wooden told him, go sit down.

Sweek spun around, walked toward the end of the bench, and kept walking. Remembering it was almost Easter break for UCLA, he decided on the spot to head to the locker room, change clothes, leave Freedom Hall before the end of the game, and hitchhike to California for a pit stop on his way to vacation in Mexico. Drastic emotions overruled the chance to win a third title until Sweek found the dressing room locked. The game continued out of sight, he couldn't gauge developments from the noise, and finally someone from the arena opened the door in the late moments of the 85–82 Bruin escape capped by Shackelford's two insurance free throws in the final second.

The initial act of the exaggerated slow walk angered Wooden. Sweek leaving the court and abandoning the team, though, turned the coach irate and more emotional than being in a tight semifinal with the title defense at surprising risk. The most experienced Bruin, a key player never more key than when UCLA needed guards to handle the ball against a difficult defense, had in a single act shown up the coach and abandoned his team. The victory secured and a spot in the championship game against Purdue set, Wooden struggled to maintain his composure as he headed to the locker room with a wrath different from the predictable passion of screaming at officials and demanding precision at practice.

Sweek, alone in the shower, had never seen anything like the Wooden who suddenly appeared at the entrance and quickly became the unforgettable image of a prim sports legend in a suit, tie, and dress shoes needing to be restrained by assistant coaches from going into the spray to attack a naked player. "Coach looked like he was going to launch at him with both fists," Alcindor remembered. Sweek was concerned Wooden would punch him or knock him down, and with the awareness that a highly conditioned college athlete could not swing a response at a fifty-nine-year-old superior except to do as little as possible to defend himself. Plus, although it didn't flash into his mind amid the volatility and water, brawling nude with St. John Wooden at the Final Four could have damaged his hopes of being drafted by the NBA in about two weeks. The only thing he knew for sure in the surreal instant was that he was scared and astonished at the level of anger being sent in his direction, complete with staring at veins bulging from Wooden's head.

"You wanna fight me, old man?" Alcindor heard Sweek say. "You've been messing with my mind for five years!" A lot of players laughed, others followed along in silent disbelief, mouths open, as Sweek continued to verbally take on Wooden.

You're right, Coach, Sweek said sarcastically. In fact, he continued after just the right pause for effect, you're always right. Edgar Lacey quit the team, Coach. But you were right. Don Saffer quit the team, Coach. But you were right.

Wooden standing close enough for his dress shoes to be getting wet grew more incensed when it didn't seem possible, before the assistants pulled the boss away. Sweek wrapped a towel around his waist and walked

into the main part of the locker room filled with teammates understand-
ably baffled by the bizarre events, dressed, and returned to the hotel with
the rest of the Bruins. The Mexican vacation would wait.

Wooden, whether misremembering the scene or attempting to down-
play the strange night of March 20, 1969, later described it as "a little trouble." It was, more accurately, a confrontation, the ugliest encounter with a
player in the championship era, maybe the worst of his entire UCLA career
and perhaps the most volatile Wooden became under any circumstances
in Westwood. He had always been fiery, as most referees could attest, but
never seeming to be out of control to the point of turning physical. That
it happened a month after he scolded student manager Marcucci for not
turning in the players who snuck girls into their hotel rooms in Seattle,
and Marcucci arguing back in front of the team with a list of built-up
grievances, added to the perception of an exasperated Wooden struggling
to find footing inside his hurricane of changing times.

Having not been told anything since leaving the locker room, but
knowing chances were good he would be sent home during the off day
before the title game Saturday against Purdue, Sweek stuck to the schedule and reported to the team breakfast on Friday. The Wooden who always took pride in being able to admit when he was wrong may never
have shown it more than in the Louisville hotel while extending the olive
branch of admitting he overreacted and saying he never suggested Sweek
had played his last game as a Bruin, while other coaches might have dismissed a player for insubordination. Not merely apologetic in return and
appreciative of the chance to finish his career the next night on the court
rather than with a banishment, Sweek saw a level of empathy and patience
that stuck with him forever. Both put the ugly moment in the past.

. . .

The Bruins felt the title game as the end of a tedious line, so desperate for
motivation that Alcindor held on to the slight that "we were picked to lose"
by the press, as if the chance to become the first program to ever win three
championships in a row were not inspiration enough. Players who spent

years grousing about being expected to win every game were suddenly annoyed that Dave Kindred of the *Louisville Times* predicted a Purdue win, and Alcindor exaggerated it into practically a consensus national opinion. Facing an All-American who scored 33 points against them in November in Pauley, Rick Mount, may have been additional inspiration, along with the additional boost of Juilliard grad Ferdinand Lewis Alcindor Sr. sitting in with the school band on trombone.

UCLA took the court to boos before the younger Alcindor got the same villain treatment in pregame introductions. He went out as he came in, the bad guy in most settings beyond Los Angeles' Westside, the reason for the early suggestion that baskets be raised and, he believed, the cause of the dunk being outlawed. Late afternoon on March 22 inside Freedom Hall didn't help the imaging. Alcindor dominated in a way that overshadowed John Vallely making the all-tournament team and the game-changing defense by Heitz on Mount, a fitting exit for Heitz as well as a key contributor to the same three titles without much spotlight. The latest, and best, reminder came with Harvard Law School a few months away, while Bruin-to-the-end Sweek made all three of his attempts as part of an overpowering offense.

Alcindor's UCLA career ended at 5:57 p.m. on March 22, 1969, and with 1:19 remaining in the coronation, after 37 points and 20 rebounds, after 88 victories in 90 varsity games, with his father blowing brass, in the hometown of idol Ali and the city of the first title for the feel of coming full circle. Three seasons, with all but 16 of the contests while No. 1, ended with more national championships than losses and Wooden beating his alma mater to become the first coach to win five titles. The wide smile on the walk to the bench upon being replaced by Steve Patterson was the rare display of emotions on the court that underlined the happiness of the hour and relief at the end of the four years, before Alcindor and Wicks, sitting on the bench, raised both arms and extended index fingers to proclaim No. 1. Wooden walked over to quietly ask them to stop. The 92–72 victory finalized, Alcindor stood on a chair to take the net off one of the baskets and kept it around his neck as a trophy, while Heitz got the other.

The only regrets were Lucius Allen not showing for any of the postgame parties, after Alcindor hoped for a reunion, and being replaced before the chance for a late illegal dunk as a farewell to the rules committee.

"I'll just say it feels nice," Alcindor said while stretched on the bed in his room after the Bruins returned to the hotel and before heading back out for an alumni party and a team dinner. "Everything was up in my throat all week. I could see ahead to the end, but there was apprehension and fear. Fear of losing. I don't know why, but it was there. Before the other two tournaments, it didn't feel that way. This one did. But, wow, today after I came to the bench, I was yelling. Wow, I was excited. We just had to bring this thing down in front again where it belongs." The din and darkness of the restaurant became a place of a celebration that turned public amid Alcindor signing autographs, the sound of players reminiscing, and a band that at one point offered the melancholy "Days of Wine and Roses" with perfect timing as an ode to past moments of carefree youth on the last night these Bruins would be together as players.

The NBA could not have imagined it began the race, once the UCLA season ended and Alcindor could turn his full attention to life after college, in second place. The preference to sign with the Nets had clearly but secretly emerged, though, by the time he reached New York with Sam Gilbert along as one adviser and Los Angeles stockbroker Ralph Shapiro as another. Giving Alcindor more to consider, two former Globetrotters, Wilt Chamberlain and Connie Hawkins, encouraged him to see the barnstorming jesters as a serious option. "The experience of playing almost every day, the extensive travel and learning the fine points of the game with the Trotters, who for all their clowning, are fine players, is a great help in maturing a player," Hawkins said.

Except Alcindor had arrived in Westwood with the maturity and talent of a successful pro, needing only to gain strength and stamina to keep up with adults logging about three times as many games a season. As much as he would have appreciated the chance to experience other cultures and unique settings—the touring Globies played royal ballrooms in England, visited Nikita Khrushchev in the Kremlin, had audiences with three popes—Alcindor since his youth had dreamed of real games, not exhibitions for laughs. That was especially true of real NBA games. He could still easily remember learning by watching Russell and the Celtics, Wilt and the Warriors, and others at Madison Square Garden. He'd met the NBA guys, Jerry West and Red Auerbach and others, and couldn't easily turn away from the chance to face the best.

The NBA had the Knicks drawing an average of 15,383 fans per game to the sport's mecca, Madison Square Garden; the ABA had the Nets at 1,108 in Commack Arena on Long Island, including 249 one game and 384 another. The ABA as a whole averaged 2,981. Two ABA referees resigned early in the season to return to working college games, saying conditions were better there. The owner of the Minnesota Pipers fired his coach at the banquet for the All-Star game. The ball was red, white, and blue and refs wore uniforms of red shirts, royal blue pants, and white shoes. The minimum salary for 1968–69 was $7,500, compared to the NBA floor of $10,000 for rookies and $12,500 for veterans. The Pipers spent their first season in Pittsburgh, moved to Minneapolis for 1968–69, then back to Pittsburgh, before a name change to the Pioneers, before another name change to the Condors. When Alcindor attended a game between the same vagabond Pipers and home Colonels the off night at the Final Four, he found the play "wasn't the quality of the NBA, but it was good basketball," hardly an enthusiastic endorsement from someone who wanted to measure himself against the best.

But the ABA had the one lure the NBA could not match: New York City. The Nets were his secret hope based on location as Alcindor headed from Louisville to his hometown for the final decision without either side aware he would be "almost as happy" to play with the Nets as the Knicks. The upstart league with a red, white, and blue ball in its second season opened talks on the verge of a historic victory. The ABA, for its part, spent months preparing wisely for the showdown with the NBA with the belief that the coup acquisition could force a merger or, truly dreaming big, make it a permanent competitor. Trying everything included two Indiana Pacers executives, general manager Mike Storen and legal counsel Dick Tinkham, approaching billionaire Howard Hughes to give $1 million to sign Alcindor in exchange for putting Alcindor on a new franchise in

Los Angeles and giving Hughes Television Sports Network the broadcast rights built around a big name in a big city. Storen and Tinkham spent three days at the Desert Inn as Hughes's guests and appeared to sell a top aide on the idea, but never got an answer from Hughes himself.

Undeterred, the league invested about $10,000 on a study of Alcindor to gain any insight that would sell him on the ABA, hiring psychiatrists and industrial psychologists, talking to people who knew him from UCLA and New York, and employing a private detective to dig into his California life. Team executives, realistic if uneasy at the fact that a college student could be the difference between long-term life or eventually going under, "wanted to know who we had to get to in order to help Alcindor make the decision we wanted," Storen said.

Calling the research Operation Kingfish added a comical espionage tint to the smart, proactive approach that returned two key points. First, Alcindor—not his parents, not Gilbert, not Wooden or any UCLA influence—would make the choice. Alcindor at twenty-one had that much confidence. And, he would stick with the initial call. Alcindor told both sides he did not want a protracted negotiation, just one offer from each before reaching a conclusion, making a public announcement, and ending talks. A bidding war would be disrespectful to all involved, he said, as someone who prioritized the simple and straightforward over fawning. The Operation Kingfish dossier said so, just as J. D. Morgan had four years earlier—"If we ever used a soft sell, it was on Alcindor." The same player at the end of his college career still just wanted to make an informed decision, not a scene. The 1948 John Wooden who stuck with UCLA even after Minnesota officials got through on the repaired phone lines with the job he wanted more would have been proud.

Alcindor, his father, Gilbert, and Shapiro and his brother met with Kennedy and the Bucks on Monday and received an offer of $1.4 million over five years, a good proposal to Alcindor, without any sign of Kennedy ever pressuring Milwaukee to trade the pick to a team on Alcindor's NBA wish list. The Knicks, Lakers, Warriors, or Celtics with the No. 1 pick could have ended the chase on the spot. Instead, Alcindor and his advisers spent part of Tuesday with Nets owner Arthur Brown, Brown's attorney and tax consultant, and Commissioner George Mikan in Brown's apartment. Brown set a $1 million certified check on the table for five seasons and followed with details that Alcindor would receive 5 percent of the Nets if the team went public, plus an annuity of $12,000 a year for ten years in a mutual fund as deferred compensation. The package was worth $2 million, Brown claimed.

The Alcindor group left stunned the ABA would build the most important business deal in league history on the *perhaps* of the Nets going public, when no one could say they would be in business in a couple years, and the *maybe* of future earnings of a mutual fund with numbers based on past returns. Gilbert had been led to believe from previous conversations the ABA offer would be concrete, but Brown changed the plan on his own to what they saw as $1.12 million guaranteed for five seasons, the check on the table plus the $12,000 for ten years, and a lot of speculation. It took little conversation after leaving the apartment for all to agree the NBA, clearly the better league, also easily had the better offer.

Alcindor had done well to not let the massive decision affect his mindset late in his college career, as evidenced by the frustration in March at the *West* magazine story. He still cared about the perception of Bruin basketball even in the final weekend of the season he could not wait to end. He was just as committed to staying true to his word (as Operation Kingfish predicted) and followed through with a quick and final decision (as Alcindor promised). Never appearing to be rattled by the magnitude of the moment, and more seasoned CEO weighing dual offers than newcomer to million-dollar deals, he phoned Kennedy later Tuesday with the good news for the Bucks and the NBA. Alcindor still preferred New York, just not at that price difference.

"He doesn't want to play in Milwaukee," Mikan insisted the next day, pounding his fist on a desk and raising his voice, correct about that point but wrong at any volume in also claiming, "The door was never locked." Alcindor and his father agreed Lew had given his word and it would have made "me feel like a flesh peddler" if he reopened negotiations. He would have made much more money by allowing a bidding war and could have had the ultimate outcome of a bigger contract and a New York homecoming, yet kept to his principles. Brown diverting from the planned ABA pitch of guarantees and Mikan backing the offer after Gilbert signaled a problem by asking for confirmation this was the Nets' best offer became the malpractice that cost the ABA everything—the rebel league never recovered from the ineptitude of the final days of March 1969 before the partial life raft of four of the six remaining teams merging with the NBA in 1976.

Alcindor ascended into his new professional world as the greatest college player ever in the eyes of most. The 1965 new arrival had become the 1969 senior that proved skeptical Wooden wrong four years in a row. The Bruins could build on the foundation of a single superstar after all, and a seven-footer of a single superstar at that, resoundingly answering the initial worries that almost led them to pass on the Power senior without trying. In the final judgment, "He was as easy to coach as any player I've ever had. He never gave me one ounce of trouble. He was totally unselfish, a team player." Anything less might have derailed the championship run years early and impacted future decisions in recruiting. The problems that did come—jealousy among teammates, the public reaction to stands on racial issues, enough fear on occasion that security had to be increased—were not Alcindor's doing, Wooden concluded. A mental path had been cleared for Wooden in case the Bruins grew interested in a prodigy center in the future.

Though easy to instantly conclude the Alcindor era of predicted dominance come to life had changed college basketball in showing how much publicity and money one man could bring to amateur sports, the true legacy of the three varsity seasons and 1968–69 in particular would not be known for many years. Individually, the skyhook Alcindor perfected with co-mechanic Wooden their final two seasons together grew into Kareem Abdul-Jabbar's signature move and helped him retire as the leading scorer in NBA history. But on a larger scale, the Game of the Century became a groundbreaking moment as the first step in contests in domed stadiums, events that eventually became common, and the upstart ABA never recovered from the botched pursuit of Alcindor. He had been imposing enough to greatly impact the NCAA, NBA, and ABA at nearly the same time.

Still, Wooden said on the flight home from Louisville with a fifth title in six years, "I always felt a well-disciplined little man could do better than a big man," as though the same three seasons had done little to change Wooden in a basketball sense. TWA Flight 443 heading southwest at sixteen thousand feet with sleepy young men in navy blue blazers reclined in their seats and their coach sipping a cup of steaming coffee eased toward Los Angeles with Alcindor quickly distanced in more ways than location. "With Lewis gone next year, this team will be faster," Wooden said. "We'll be fast-breaking again like the UCLA teams of the past, and hopefully, we'll be able to use our pressure defenses to greater advantage." A full day had not passed since the championship, and he already could not contain the excitement at the chance for a reset.

Alcindor was in New York, eventually to sign with the Bucks four days before the draft in April, while Wooden headed into an offseason with his annual youth basketball camp at a nearby high school, with some of the one hundred participants traveling from the East Coast and the South, and having John R. Wooden Drive dedicated in his native Martinsville, Indiana. He fastened his seat belt on final descent, looked out the window at the Los Angeles skyline, a contradiction of exhausted and revitalized, removed his glasses, and rubbed his eyes. "Yes sir," he said softly, "it will be a pleasure next year, coaching to win instead of coaching not to lose."

7

BB

John Wooden's dream of a return to the speed game with smaller players and a life free of drama didn't even last to the opening practice before sophomore guard Andy Hill and junior forward John Ecker arrived at his office the morning of October 15, 1969, with a request: cancel the workout hours away, the first for the defending champions, in support of the Vietnam Moratorium as a national day of protest. While Ecker went along mostly as moral support for his friend on a suicide mission, Hill thought the suggestion made perfect sense and felt he offered sound reasoning that UCLA basketball collectively joining the antiwar movement would boost the cause, that the Bruins would be representing the majority opinion on their campus in condemning U.S. involvement in Southeast Asia, and that players believed strongly in the one-day strike. Wooden had spent six and a half months since the end of the Alcindor era looking forward to getting his previous world back only to be slapped across the face with conflict the very day of the restart.

"Andy, you don't have to come to practice," he answered in a scathing tone. "You don't *ever* have to come to practice."

Hill's being stunned and saddened by the blunt-force trauma of the reply was the reminder of Wooden's ability to disembowel his opposition without raising his voice or coming closer to cursing than a stern "Goodness gracious." Extending to "Goodness gracious sakes alive" was peak fury and a siren to seek shelter. (He confessed to cussing once, as a kid at older brother

Maurice for flinging manure at John's face during work on the family farm in Indiana, prompting their devoutly Christian father to take a switch to John.) "I wish just once he'd swear at me—use *all* the words," one Bruin said. "He puts more venom into his 'Goodness gracious sakes alive' than any marine drill sergeant or hippie protester I ever heard." Pointed and precise words were his weapons of choice for overheated commentary, not the high-volume brawling verbal takedowns of most in his profession, just as Wooden would covertly berate referees from behind a rolled-up program without being detected by the thousands in attendance. "He had a great way of saying what he wanted to say in a manner that was very deceiving to the public, let's put it that way," one top official, Hank Nichols, said. Wooden even did the same with opposing players, usually to their great shock, reasoning it as a competitor doing anything within the rules to gain an advantage.

The moratorium Hill wanted to support on the first day of the 1969–70 season, before quickly backing down and remaining on the team, had become enough of an issue for the White House that the West Wing political machine roared into action. Deputizing retired University of Oklahoma football coach Bud Wilkinson as the face of the counteroffensive to student protests may have seemed a curious choice by domestic policy chief John Ehrlichman amid the concerning public divide over Vietnam, but it also underlined Nixon's relationship with sports and its personalities. He built such a friendship with Ohio State football coach Woody Hayes that the president would cut short a budget meeting in November to watch part of the annual rivalry game against Michigan before heading to a dental appointment, then had a TV hooked up in the dentist's office to continue watching. When candidate Nixon needed a replacement speaker at a 1968 Milwaukee event ahead of the Wisconsin Republican primary, he got Packers quarterback Bart Starr, the biggest name from the biggest team in the state, to step in. Arnold Palmer appeared unexpectedly at Nixon's hotel suite in Atlanta a couple months later and was escorted right in. Incumbent Nixon even paused election night '72 to call Redskins coach George Allen to hear about the upcoming opponent, as if it were a quiet night at home. While Nixon could afford to be somewhat relaxed with a landslide victory projected, and soon completed, it was still the final hours of balloting to be the leader of the Free World, yet he made time to talk New York Giants.

The president as a former tough, scrappy, untalented reserve offensive lineman with leadership skills at Whittier College in the suburbs east of Los Angeles felt a connection and genuinely appreciated athletes and coaches on his side, not just as props for the conveyer belt of obligatory photo ops. He had built a particularly strong bond with Wilkinson through the years and listened to the advice that Wilkinson be brought in to help X-and-O the response to campus unrest despite a lack of experience in high-stakes real-world matters. Tell students they were being exploited by organizers for political purposes without a true concern for young Americans, the ex-coach advised. "It's easy to manipulate kids," Chief of Staff H. R. Haldeman agreed as his boss's disapproval ratings over Vietnam grew dramatically, "because they love to get excited. You can foment them up for a panty raid, or in the old days, goldfish swallowing." Wilkinson's attempts to scold the underwear pranksters into changing their mind about schoolmates dying in Southeast Asia went nowhere, though. (It was almost as patronizing as the 1968 suggestion from Lyndon Johnson's white-haired press secretary that the LBJ reelection campaign should "organize one of the electric guitar 'musical' groups to travel around to meetings. It is not too difficult to get some kids with long hair and fancy clothes and give them a title such as 'The Black Beards' or 'The White Beards' and turn them loose. They don't have to be very good musically to get by as long as they have rhythm and make enough noise.")

Wooden seemed the most obvious Nixon match, given all they had in common. Both built national profiles as Californians and each overcame setbacks to reach the highest levels of their professions, Nixon after losing the presidential election in 1960 and the race for California governor in 1962 and Wooden as someone who did not win a national title until his sixteenth season in Westwood. The Nixon administration counted three former UCLA students in high positions, Ehrlichman and Alexander Butterfield as well as Haldeman. And, Wooden was a Nixon man, albeit quietly in his preference to keep political talk private. Having the respected, popular coach stumping for the president under fire would have been exactly the public counterpunch the White House wanted to the panty thieves and fish swallowers, even if it would have made little difference locally as Nixon carried California in 1968 and '72. With Wilkinson six years removed from Oklahoma and Allen, Starr, and all the Packers among the pros, the popularity of Wooden and Hayes on campus would have been particularly welcome support for Nixon as the highest levels of government lobbed threats toward college protesters.

Nothing, though, compared to Haldeman, who was at the center of Nixon's orbit while also a Wooden friend, the head of the fundraising drive to build Pauley Pavilion, and a season-ticket holder since the early 1950s, even while living in Washington. The package with the same four seats—center court across from the benches, in the first row of the second level to avoid the view being blocked by lower railings—arrived at the family home in the Hancock Park section of Los Angeles to start Haldeman's annual ritual with the rectangular calendar kept by the phone in the kitchen. *BB*, he would write on the date of every home game, shorthand for *basketball*, finishing one month on one page and flipping to the next to ensure every effort would be made to keep the night free. When that wasn't possible, especially once Nixon took office in 1969, Haldeman followed the Bruins via newspaper and radio. Harry Robbins Haldeman—Bob—may have been a sports fan in general, but BB was the clear favorite, with the additional pride of cheering in the arena he helped get financed.

While Haldeman would have backed the Bruins no matter what, "I don't think Bob would have established any particular rapport with any other coach," Jo, his wife, said. "It was just who [Wooden] was." The coach likewise appreciated the relationship and considered Haldeman a friend, remaining loyal and caring even in the ensuing years when Haldeman was jailed for his role in the Watergate cover-up. The Bruins, and Wooden in particular, were in the West Wing during the Nixon presidency.

Yet there is no indication of the administration approaching Wooden to join the sports circle Nixon cherished personally and valued professionally. Whether he would have accepted an outreach is unclear—Wooden backed the president but had little interest in campaigns and even less in participating in a Washington food fight no matter who was at the top of the ticket. Dealing with Andy Hill's politics was anxiety enough.

Only months before Hill's ill-fated suggestion to Wooden, seven student leaders went to the White House on behalf of hundreds of other students who had signed a pledge of draft resistance, to be met by Ehrlichman and National Security Advisor Henry Kissinger in the Situation Room. "If you guys think you can break laws just because you don't like them, you're going to have to force us to up the ante to the point where we have to give out death sentences for traffic violations." Nixon stayed away from similar attempts at intimidation, but did call campus dissenters "ideological criminals" and "new barbarians" in a play to his conservative base gulping down the law-and-order message the administration leveraged so well. Vice President Spiro Agnew stepped in as the attack dog: "The young, at the zenith of physical power and sensitivity, overwhelm themselves with drugs and artificial stimulants" and today's student "now goes to college to proclaim rather than to learn," because a "spirit of national masochism prevails."

California's top elected official likewise revved his take-no-prisoners message again the same year, Reagan responding to strife at San Francisco State with "Those who want to get an education, those who want to teach, should be protected in that at the point of a bayonet if necessary." He spun the chambers again in April with an appearance in Yosemite that included responding to a question about campus demonstrators with "If it takes a bloodbath, let's get it over with," before saying a day later he didn't know he said it and, besides, it was a figure of speech if he did. It helped that he had the backing of a loud national media voice, *Time* magazine, with the severe editorial in April that "when extremists halt classes, they kill the spirit of a university in somewhat the same way that the Nazis did in the 1930s." To make sure its position was clear, *Time* followed the next month with the megaphone of "If there was one word that summarized the feelings of much of the U.S. toward the radicals last week, it was: 'Enough!'"

Thankfully left to focus on basketball as his campus remained calm by comparison, Wooden quickly and gladly distanced himself from the riches of the Alcindor era with the declaration at the dawn of 1969–70 that "I am looking forward to this season more than I have the seasons of the last three or four years. We are not on the spot like we were before. The problems are fewer. I don't have to play nursemaid to so many hurt feelings." The front-court would still be a Bruin strength, he insisted, only now it would be the entire unit, forwards Sidney Wicks and Curtis Rowe and center Steve Patterson in the unenviable role of succeeding the greatest collegian ever. Including top reserve John Ecker, with the imposing presence of a football tight end, Wooden rated it the most physically powerful unit he ever had. He felt just as good about the starting backcourt, with John Vallely as the senior leader and sophomore Henry Bibby replacing Shackelford as the shooting specialist.

"It'll be nice to know," Wooden told the media in what would become a common refrain, "that I'll again be doing my best to win rather than to keep from losing." He happily called the new group minus a single pillar the Team Without and counted the days living under the strain of Alcindor's varsity seasons—1,095—the way a prisoner marked time on a sentence. Without a superstar dominating the offense, without the resulting jealousies, and without being anointed champions before the season, Wooden sounded like a man who had survived an ordeal, not reached a pinnacle.

Sharing a table with Freddie Goss among several coaches at a luncheon of area basketball writers, an emotionally exhausted Wooden, a regular attendee at the weekly gatherings each season, told his former Bruin guard turned UC Riverside boss in a near whisper to get out of the business. "You ought to be like Jerry and get into something else," Wooden said, referring to Jerry Norman, on his way to becoming a financial success since leaving the bench for the private sector. It felt to Goss that Wooden was relieved to share his distress at what the job had become, as if sitting at the table with an open chair between them morphed into therapy. Wooden was fifty-nine and in his twenty-second season coming off a $17,000 salary in 1968–69 but Goss as a rookie in the profession could still save himself.

Wooden could not have found many better sounding boards, whether he had decided in advance to advise Goss to find a job with more stability and money or turned impromptu career counselor. Wooden had, after all, recruited Goss from nearby Compton, relied on him as a key part of the 1965 championship team with Gail Goodrich and Keith Erickson in starring roles, and had recommended Goss when Riverside called Wooden in 1969 for suggestions. Goss after leaving the army hadn't planned to get into the business until the confidence boost of hearing Wooden nominated him without prompting.

Freddie, Wooden told him at the table in their new relationship as peers, this is no life. "When I went to UCLA to play," Goss said years later, "the team had just gone fourteen and twelve, but he never acted like 'I gotta win or they're gonna fire me.' He looked at coaching basketball as a way to teach ethics. At some point, it became this fast-moving train, and he didn't know how to get off."

Using money to illustrate a point indicated the depth of his frustration. Wooden as the rarity of the Depression victim who did not become insecure about finances, despite enduring severe setbacks, had never been motivated by finances, a personality trait J. D. Morgan and the administration exploited through many years of underpaying their hugely successful coach, who contributed to the problem by refusing to ask for a big raise. The time John the family bookkeeper got mad at his wife for forgetting to enter a payment in the checkbook, one of the few times anyone could remember him taking an angry tone to Nell, was more the same attention to detail as Coach Wooden in practice than stressing over dollars. He received a Mercedes-Benz as a retirement gift years later, but eventually traded it in for the Ford Taurus he wanted. To make salary part of the conversation with Goss was out of character.

. . .

Wicks as the quickest and fastest of any Wooden big man to that time was at the core of the coach's believing the Bruins would remain national contenders at a time others circled overhead in anticipation of the post-Alcindor payback. It didn't matter that Wicks was the opposite of the ideal Wooden player the season before, too much of an individual in a program that required even superstars to fit in, which led to Wicks logging fewer minutes than Rowe and Shackelford despite greater talent than both. Wooden considered the sophomore Wicks undisciplined, though not selfish, in trying to assert himself at the cost of team ball by driving to the basket and straight into defenses sagging on Alcindor inside. Rowe, by comparison, was so consistent and dependable in an eventual three-year run as a starter that Wooden would come to say he never had a bad game, just some that were better than others.

The same determination that cost Wicks big minutes had, a season later, in 1969–70, been channeled into improved shooting range, better defense, and, most of all, buying into the system. "I was so much better," he said. "I didn't get it at first, then it was like it all clicked in. I wasn't making the same mistakes. You know that phrase Coach Wooden always used, 'Be quick, but don't hurry'? Well, I finally understand it. I knew I had to cut down on my mistakes if I wanted to be starting, so instead of forcing things, I began to let the game come to me." Wooden was impressed to the point of believing Wicks could go from reserve to next UCLA superstar within months. When it happened, the transformation was the basketball version of the speed of light, a dramatic step forward in approach and play.

"Not immediately, but dramatically, as the season progressed," Wooden said. "Now our style was cut for a power driver like him." Indeed, timing helped—having Patterson at the high post, near the free-throw line, opened a lane to the basket for Wicks that didn't exist with Alcindor anchored inside. As if moving past the expectations and center-dominated format of previous years wasn't relief enough, the strides by Wicks added to Wooden's excitement at moving ahead.

The October 27 issue of *Sports Illustrated* became the reminder of how difficult that would be. Dated twelve days after his former team opened practice at Pauley Pavilion, Alcindor's first-person retrospective with coauthor Jack Olsen was journalism background joined with anger in three installments laced with friction. "I'm going to tell you my life story from as far back as I can remember, and if you think that it takes a lot of conceit for a 22-year-old basketball player to tell his life story, then that's your hang-up," they wrote, confrontational from the first paragraph of part one. "The way things are in America today—and have been for 200 years—the story of any black man has meaning, even if he's a shoeshine 'boy' or a porter or your friendly neighborhood Uncle Tom. Maybe you won't read about them; maybe you will read about me because you're interested in basketball. That's fine. A long time ago I learned to accept the idea that people have no interest in me except as a jock. But I'm also a person, a human being, just like those other black men who walk about invisible to many of their fellows." The article filled most or all of ten pages, not counting a relaxed, smiling Alcindor on the cover in a Bucks uniform or the inside shot of Alcindor staring seriously at the camera straight ahead while wearing a dashiki.

Alcindor had given every indication of moving forward peacefully since joining the Bucks with much of the same oversize interest that once accompanied his arrival at UCLA. Milwaukee's season-ticket sales tripled and team officials capitalized by bumping the price of the top seat at individual home games from $5.25 to $7. He settled into a two-bedroom, thirteenth-floor corner unit with a view of downtown where women strolled in front of the apartment complex and sometimes tried to secure his unlisted phone number. To use the second *Sports Illustrated* installment to unload on Los Angeles, his relationship with the media, his lonely Westwood existence, friendships being relegated mostly to black students, various games, and the decision with Allen to nearly transfer after their sophomore season was a shocking pivot complete with a scorched-earth headline.

UCLA WAS A MISTAKE

Alcindor's assertions later in life that he never regretted attending UCLA were revisionist history. Part three on November 10 focused on the Olympic boycott, the senior campaign, his conversion to Islam, and the early days of the transition into the NBA. At least he had the positive of the 1968–69 conclusion that "I could no longer hate anybody. I could no longer afford to be a racist. If racism messed up a lot of people who had to take it, then it must also mess up those who had to dish it out. I did not want to be that kind of narrow man."

"Well," Wooden answered when asked about the series, "he doesn't sound like a very happy young man, does he?" In moments of greater reflection, the coach said he was "very, very sorry to find out that he seemed to be as unhappy as he indicated" and "If Lewis felt there were some problems at UCLA, I honestly believe he would have been ten times more miserable at many other places he could have gone." The postmortem hurt Wooden. Another time, Wooden said he was "distressed to learn that he felt I had held myself too far from my players. But he was a young man who would not let you get too close to him." The former pupil chose to occasionally call Wooden anyway in his first several NBA seasons and visited when the Bucks were in Los Angeles, indicating a stronger connection than Lewis realized, especially during his rookie campaign of 1969–70. There were times Alcindor to himself thanked Wooden for pushing him so hard in college that it made for a smoother transition to the NBA.

The program he left behind opened with the strange designation of No. 4 in the country in the Associated Press media voting, though while also still the familiar No. 1 in the United Press International balloting of coaches. Wooden, likely going for psychology more than honest analysis, played to the ominous mood of life after Alcindor by noting, "Any game films we might have of teams which played us in the last three years are useless" and "We're operating blind, in effect" because of it, as if he cared about breaking down opponents' tendencies. If Wooden had no interest in scouting the other side in any ongoing season, he had less than zero in what another coach might have done in past years. In reality, he remained dedicated to routine, built on the three-by-five cards and notebooks of what previous UCLA teams did the same date for the 1969 preseason sessions that began at 3:00 p.m. and briskly snapped from drill to drill. Three-on-two conditioning from 3:40 to 3:50, shooting by position from 3:50 to 4:00, one-on-one and three-on-three defense from 4:00 to 4:10, strong-side defense from 4:10 to 4:20, attacking zone defenses from 4:30 to 4:35, down the list through five-on-five fast break from 5:05 to 5:10 and finally zone defense from 5:10 to 5:30.

Wooden made it a point to not let the Bruins think they were starting over. Alcindor's assessment of successor Patterson late the previous season didn't help—"Oh. He's a white boy from Santa Maria, that's all"—but underestimating Patterson became symbolic for the new roster wanting to prove it still belonged in the championship conversation. Patterson, in addition to his skin color and his roots 150 miles north of Westwood, had already shown potential on offense, just far behind the scenes, and with no chance of winning the perception game with the media as 1969–70 dawned. Practicing against Alcindor had destroyed Patterson's confidence, adding to the challenge of stepping into the starting lineup, but he was mature and would have been held up as a dream center in most any other program, with enough talent that he would later play five NBA seasons and another in Italy.

At least he had the credentials of a top prospect. Bibby was another example of an unknown moved from the freshman to the varsity team and was the most unlikely of Bruins. A farm kid from Franklinton, North Carolina, who would wake at 4:00 a.m., dress in the dark, pound a breakfast of fatback meat, eggs, molasses, and biscuits. He tended to the pigs and cows before and after school and only then, usually around 7:00 p.m., crossed a dirt yard to dribble and shoot at the rim on a shed, under the only bulb on the outside of the home with a leaky roof. Wooden only got interested after Bibby's high school coach, also the principal, wrote the required introduction letter and because the Bruins badly needed guards. Bibby after minimal interest from colleges close to home, North Carolina State and less from Duke and North Carolina, still almost chose Guilford College in the familiar territory of Greensboro over the shimmering basketball kingdom in Westwood.

He stepped into a time warp and came out on the other side in radical 1968 Los Angeles. Unfazed, Bibby averaged 26 points a game on the freshman team, was a hard worker and accepting of coaching, and immediately contributed an average of 17.1 points his first eight varsity games as the starter next to Vallely in the backcourt. "Even Lynn didn't get the ball away like Henry can, or shoot with such range," Wooden said. "I don't believe I've ever had a player with more range than Bibby." It took one month of varsity games for Bibby to be cleared to shoot whenever open.

• • •

LSU's Pete Maravich was the known—the successor to Alcindor as an offensive tsunami, the subject of more attention than any other amateur in the sport and most pros, already an all-time college great by early in 1969–70 as the Tigers reached Pauley Pavilion. He had played, and thrived, in a similar role at different levels since his early teens, an incomparable and willing showman in scoring, passing, and dribbling with flair at six foot five. "Pete Maravich," Wooden said, "could do more with a basketball than anybody I had ever seen." Maravich once won a $5 bet by spinning a ball for an hour, shifting among all ten fingers and many knuckles, and other times dribbled from an aisle seat in a theater as a movie played on the big screen ahead, before switching to the other aisle about halfway through the feature to make sure both hands developed. Everyone in Clemson, South Carolina, knew in the dark if young Maravich was at the same show. Eleven-year-old Pete taught himself to dribble while pedaling his bike two miles into town. His father, Press, Wooden's friend and onetime sounding board on Alcindor strategy, also had Pete lean out the passenger-side window of the car and dribble as Press drove neighborhoods and open highways, slowing down and accelerating at different stages to challenge the boy to maintain control. Pete would often entertain guests at home with exhibitions in the living room, sometimes dribbling with gloves to make it harder to feel the ball and sometimes while blindfolded, going behind his back and between his legs. When it snowed, he shot outside in the carport with an overcoat and gloves.

Wooden first saw him at the Campbell Basketball School, a summer camp in Buies Creek, North Carolina, and a favorite offseason stop as a place of teaching and a village setting that spoke to the gentle pace of his rural youth. Buies Creek, between Raleigh and Fayetteville, fed his soul in a way Los Angeles never could during eleven annual June visits in his nirvana of cafeteria meals, evening softball games, instruction on sock techniques, and the importance of double-knotting shoelaces. It didn't matter that the clinics were run in gyms without air-conditioning amid the satanic potion of Southern summer temperatures and humidity, melding with the smell of worn basketballs and sweaty participants to create a wretched odor of burning rubber that stayed with campers for decades. The large fans brought in mostly just created a loud blowing noise and redistributed the heat. Plus, he got the bonus of rooming with his friend and contrast, the cussing, beer-drinking Press Maravich.

While some tutorials were in the main facility, Carter Gym at Campbell College, no Pauley Pavilion to begin with, Wooden with more success than anyone else in the history of his profession regularly volunteered to teach defense, a less glamorous subject, across the street at the high school, an even less glamorous site. Pete Maravich making the impossible with the ball seem casual turned hundreds of middle school boys delirious with excitement and disbelief, but Wooden generated a reverence even among preteens and early teens too young to have a true grasp of his accomplishments. The dignified way he carried himself, the rarity of a legend coming to small-town Carolina, and how adults in basketball-crazed ACC country spoke of him, created the feel of an average-size man who didn't bark being able to command the court. The rowdies turned instantly quiet and attentive for Wooden's group addresses amid the mechanical racket and swelter of Carter.

Maravich the same years was the rare high schooler allowed in the counselor games filled with college players, beating older athletes in shooting contests for Pepsis and prompting visiting Boston College coach Bob Cousy, the former Celtics star, to demand a time-out one day to learn the identity of the kid magician who just delivered the precision half-court pass with a ridiculous amount of spin. Pete wasn't even in college when Wooden rated him more talented as a ball handler than Harlem Globetrotters tricksters Goose Tatum and Marques Haynes, in addition to the time Wooden passed a ball to the eighteen-year-old at the top of the key and announced to campers, "Mr. Maravich will now demonstrate the one-handed jump shot." Pete drained 20 in a row.

"That, gentlemen," Wooden said, "is the one-handed jump shot."

Wooden, of course, had no interest in recruiting a player who overdribbled, preferred the tricky play, and took wild shots, even with a proper out-of-stater's letter of introduction. Wooden dreaded the thought of ever having the leading scorer in the country on one of his rosters. Besides, Pete said all along he only wanted to play for his dad upon graduating from high school in 1966, taking Wooden off the hook before a fireworks of dollar signs went off in J. D. Morgan's head followed by another Alcindor-like recruiting edict.

LSU senior Pete Maravich—and LSU coach Press Maravich—entered

Pauley on December 23, 1969, with a 6-1 record and with the unique distinction of an opponent being the main draw for a UCLA home game. The new most celebrated NCAA star in the nation played for the other team and was the anti-Alcindor—an extrovert wanting to put on a show, complete with the flamboyant nickname Pistol Pete. He also knew his father in Deep South football country had "taken such a terrible beating down here for what he's let me do" by dominating the ball. Maravich the performer had a signature mop of brown hair and droopy gray socks, a fashion fad that started when teenage Pete stayed with a friend during summers in North Carolina, needed a pair before leaving for another marathon basketball session at the Raleigh YMCA, sometimes ten hours a day, and reached into a dresser. Out came socks colored by use and time and so big they fell over to cover half his shoes, a strange sight but an instant boost after years of large feet at the end of skinny legs making him appear slow. "Two broomsticks in sneakers," an observer once said. He just felt faster.

The Westwood stop was the fourth game in four states, part of a six-day brutal schedule meant to boost the LSU profile for recruiting and showcase the basketball theatrics that Press encouraged, really more barnstorming tour than college itinerary. The coach said of the player, "It just kills him to throw a simple chest pass!" and the father said of the son when Wooden suggested Pete learn proper footwork for defense, "You don't understand. He's going to be the first million-dollar pro."

The Tigers played at Oregon State the night before, bused eighty-five miles north to Portland for the flight to L.A., faced the best team in the country with heavy legs, predictably lost bad, and moved on to the next booking, two games in Honolulu. The largest crowd in Pauley Pavilion history, with so many fans standing behind the baskets that folding chairs had to be hustled out, watched Maravich score 38 points, but while missing 28 of 42 shots and committing 18 turnovers, a ridiculous number even for someone living off high-risk plays. That Bibby shined on defense this time as the primary Maravich defender with regular double-team help from Vallely, another step forward in Bibby's early progression, made it an especially satisfying 133–84 win for Wooden. At the very least, "It was a game that was very special to us—which very few games were," Patterson said. "We were somewhat jaded, blasé. He electrified things. He brought a sense of humor and a sense of style that probably put gray hairs on coaches."

A high school senior from La Mesa, ten miles east of San Diego, watched from the section behind the UCLA bench. Six-foot-eleven redhead Bill Walton had already made his college choice, but not a public announcement, and attended several home games in 1969–70 as a very interested observer, none bigger to him than the carnival of Maravich at Pauley. Walton fell in love with the constant movement of basketball at age eight and the chance to impact every possession, offense and defense, and not needing to wait for action as required in football, the sport older brother Bruce excelled in, or baseball. Bill still remembered being a sixth-grader attending a Wooden clinic at the University of San Diego, how Wooden made the details come alive, and being "in absolute awe of this man who treated the game with such reverence and respect." Watching on TV as the Bruins beat bigger Michigan in the title game about two years later was the evidence that speed and the system with skinny players like himself could defeat the perception that size meant everything. The success of a previous big man in Westwood further cemented hopes of his own future there in some of the same years of wearing Alcindor's No. 33 for Helix High.

"Basketball was my religion and the gym was my church," Walton said, and in later years he spun the story of being the easiest Westwood recruit ever, practically a Bruin since that day in sixth grade if they would have him and certainly once a letter from UCLA assistant coach Denny Crum in Walton's sophomore season made them the first college to make official contact. Walton was unsure enough to at least visit Stanford the same weekend as a guard from Los Angeles, Greg Lee, and a forward who grew up in Ventura before moving to Santa Barbara for his senior season, Keith Wilkes. But it also became the trip where the three huddled in a quiet moment alone and decided on enemy ground to join forces in Westwood as a package deal, the best UCLA outcome ever in Palo Alto.

Wooden, hesitant as always to travel to chase high school prospects, even mega-prospects within the state, went to San Diego only because Crum insisted. Crum took the extra step of telling Nell her husband would miss dinner on a certain night, to make sure John had no reason to decline the trip. The winter evening in 1970 was more kidnapping than recruiting run. Crum drove his skeptical boss to the airport, they flew about thirty minutes to San Diego, hopped a car to La Mesa, and watched through Wooden being besieged in the stands for autographs. Helix players were so flustered by his presence, taking bad shots in an apparent attempt to impress, that their coach called time-out, brought the Highlanders to the bench, and didn't say anything for thirty seconds to allow them to breathe and regain composure. "Well," Wooden finally said to Crum near the end of the game, "he is pretty good, isn't he," a stellar review in Woodenspeak.

Walton was, more precisely, generally rated the second-best recruit in the country, behind center Tom McMillen from Mansfield, Pennsylvania, although Crum went with instincts, not proximity, in urging the Bruins to target Walton. "He is as good a prospect at this stage of development as I have ever seen," Crum said after Helix finished 1969–70 with a 33-0 record and 49 consecutive wins in all. San Diego State coach Dick Davis, after watching about fifteen Walton games, called the hometown product "the best high school player I've ever seen" with the particularly valuable comp for UCLA fans that "he's like Alcindor and he's probably a better shot blocker at this stage than Alcindor was. He's a good shooter, he runs hard, he jumps . . . he just does everything." Including being smart and loving school.

The only issues were medical, starting with congenital defects in his feet that would not be diagnosed until well into adulthood and knee surgery at fourteen after taking a cheap-shot hit in a pickup game. While not an issue on the court, as the Bruins would come to learn, a lifelong stuttering problem caused endless embarrassment and turned Walton painfully shy. Eventually, "I grew up thinking that everybody's feet hurt all the time and that only the lucky ones were able to talk." Basketball and academics, writing in particular, were ways to express himself.

For all the obvious contrasts—different color, different coast—he and Power senior Lewis Alcindor were remarkably similar as unselfish players who didn't want the spotlight, teenagers uncomfortable in social settings, students who loved school, dominant centers drawn to a coach who didn't want dominant centers, and counterculture products of the sixties who were strangely captivated by the structure of gentleman John Wooden. Social worker Ted and librarian Gloria in La Mesa fell for Wooden as hard as Big Al and Cora four years before overnight in New York, especially once Wooden visited the Walton home, promised their son nothing beyond an education and the chance to earn a starting spot, and asked for seconds of Gloria's potatoes served with the roast beef.

Walton never bothered with an official campus visit, just to Stanford, because he had been making so many informal trips to Pauley Pavilion since the previous season, usually based around the basketball schedule. He came several times, for Alcindor's final home game among others, the tournament win over Santa Clara, and would certainly not miss the Maravich light show while also feeling sorry for Pistol Pete living a schedule without mercy. Walton's trips were more nonchalant, a drive north with friends or hitchhiking, then the game, then often crashing on a couch in whatever dorm lobby had availability and furniture that was long enough. If none were handy and the weather stayed dry, he happily claimed a patch of grass on the quad, a busy pedestrian area in daylight, maybe with the luxury of sleeping under a tree for slight privacy. Wooden finally assigned Andy Hill to arrange accommodations and food for future visits.

The current Bruins, meanwhile, rode a schedule loaded with home games and weak opponents to a 21-0 start that doused opponents' hopes of vengeance. The Team Without had emerged exactly as Wooden projected, resilient and fast and with Wicks suddenly the best pro prospect in the country at forward in the eyes of Lakers general manager Fred Schaus, among others. "In many ways," Wooden said, "he has as much physical ability as anyone I've ever seen at his position." Wicks by late February was UCLA's leading scorer, leading rebounder, and primary shot blocker. He had the responsibility of manning the back row in the zone press as the final barricade before the rim, sometimes brought the ball upcourt, and usually defended the opponent's best frontcourt player regardless of position. The six-foot-two, 150-pound toothpick who grew up wanting to play football at USC had turned into the six-eight, 220-pound best player on the best basketball team in the land.

The close of the regular season brought the warning signs of 2 losses in 5 games along with a 2-point win, all in the final month, but also a feeling of shared responsibility and credit the Bruins could not have imagined the previous three seasons of orbiting around a seven-one, three-eighths sun. "This team is so tremendously balanced," New Mexico State coach Lou Henson said. "It's just as good as the Alcindor teams—possibly better." UCLA heading into the tournament at 24-2 beat Princeton in December with Kenny Booker's defense to slow Tigers star Geoff Petrie, edged Oregon State in January when John Ecker floated in a driving hook with 6 seconds remaining and five players averaged double figures in scoring. Four players—Wicks, Vallely, Bibby, and Rowe—averaged between 15 and 19 points a game, an even distribution especially noteworthy with Wicks at an All-America level. His growth had come to include trusting teammates and not feeling a need to dominate the ball, and when Ecker hit the shot to beat Oregon State, Wicks raced to get to the hero and lift him in the air.

"Not everyone gets to play with Lew Alcindor in their life," Vallely said. "But this year it seems like we're playing real basketball, the way we grew up playing it. It's difficult to make comparisons because Lew was such a great player. We all know this, though: it's a lot more fun now. I mean, we must be more fun to watch. With Lew, the way he is, once you've seen him hook two or three times, it's over. He used to hook it in a few times and we'd win by thirty. What a drag, huh? Now we're running and pressing and all of us are getting into the act—you know, just like regular basketball."

"I'm like any fan, I guess," Wooden said. "It's more fun, sure, and I'm even enjoying the tight games. It used to be that in close ones, well, we'd be okay. Lewis was there, and we'd work things out. There didn't seem to be much to it. Now I feel like I have something to *do*. I feel more alive. It's been a long time."

What Patterson called improved esprit de corps—"We're so much more together this year"—Arizona coach Bruce Larson simplified to "UCLA has five men doing something now, not just one." Opening the postseason in Seattle with an easy victory over Long Beach State, a Southern California neighbor hoping, wrongly, to stay with a national power, added to the Bruins' confidence heading into the regional final against Utah State. Aggies assistant coach Dale Brown deviously peeking around a curtain to catch the end of the Bruin practice just before his underdogs began their workout yielded the intel of UCLA the day before the biggest game of the season fine-tuning a running dribble into a jump stop and pass.

"Now, Curtis," Brown heard Wooden say to Rowe, "you don't have your elbows out."

"Cut hard" was another time, Wooden drilling fundamentals as if in the first practice of a new season.

Brown at thirty-four had been trying to soak up Wooden's teachings since taking a job coaching the seventh- and eighth-grade teams at Garfield Junior High in Berkeley in 1964, after packing his wife and daughter into the family Oldsmobile 442 for the trip from his native Minot, North Dakota. He saw tanks driving the streets of the Bay Area going mad and hippies protesting at Cal in the building across from the office of Athletic Director Pete Newell. Finally getting close, with only a curtain of separation, Brown, though realizing he had stolen only a minuscule portion of practice, couldn't believe what passed for tournament prep. These are drills teams do in fifth grade, he thought to himself.

Brown was hardly the first to be struck by UCLA's simplicity on practice days, before bursting from elementary school for drills to college bullies for games, in his case the 101–79 victory that sent the Bruins to the Final Four at the University of Maryland. H. R. Haldeman marked *BB* on the calendar for March 21, 1970, to attend the championship game ten miles from the White House, his favorite club advanced to face Jacksonville by beating New Mexico State in the semifinals, and his friend John Wooden arranged a three-hour team tour of Washington earlier in the week to get the capital experience. Players could remain on the bus during sightseeing stops, but had to at least come along for the drive.

Free-spirited Jacksonville coach Joe Williams ran a program where the roster had input on where to play road games, were able to help plan pregame warm-ups and out-of-bounds plays, and, at the moment, had freedom to tour the White House without team restrictions. "They do what they want," Williams in his thirty-sixth year of life said before facing Wooden in his twenty-fourth year of college coaching. Williams wore a white double-breasted sport coat for luck, or, a friend suggested, because he could step into the crowd and blend in as a peanut vendor if the Dolphins were having a bad night. There could not have been a greater contrast, down to practice the day before—Jacksonville straggled in late and spent part of the allotted hour in a Globetrotters-like warm-up routine devised by players, while UCLA began at 4:00 p.m. sharp and snapped through drills organized by Wooden. Beyond the personality differences, the Dolphins had one of the few front lines that could trouble UCLA, with seven-two Artis Gilmore as an elite center alongside seven-foot Pembrook Burrows III and six-ten Rod McIntyre. ("That name," Pembrook Burrows III explained, "isn't unusual—my father was named that and so was my grandfather.")

Wooden the next day waited until just before tip-off to inform Wicks he would be defending Gilmore, what seemed to be an impossible task for Wicks, a great talent but giving away six inches to a skilled, powerful mountain of an opponent. The glare Wicks shot at previous opponents as a declaration of war was defused this time by going into Gilmore's neck. Even "the most intimidating man in basketball," in the words of a coach not involved in the final, was surprised by the assignment, followed by early confirmation Wicks wouldn't be able to muscle Gilmore away from the basket. Attaching himself to his man's hips, the exact side to be determined by the ball movement, resulted in three quick baskets from close range as Jacksonville broke to an 8-point lead.

The adjustment to playing behind Gilmore, with other defenders ready to drop down to help, enabled Wicks to push him out a few feet and use superior quickness and jumping ability from there to shift the matchup back in his favor. Wicks blocked 4 of his shots and outrebounded Gilmore 18–16 despite the size difference. "I think Gilmore was surprised to see a six-eight guy go up and block his shot, but I've never seen anybody better than Sidney this year," said Patterson, an Alcindor teammate a season earlier. The afternoon that began with easy scores finished with Gilmore missing 20 of 29 attempts in all and an 11-point win over Williams and his double-breasted white.

"Everybody was looking forward to playing without Lew," Rowe said amid the celebration in the crowded locker room. "Right now, if Alcindor was on the team, who would the reporters be talking to? Look around the room—the reporters are with five people and that's beautiful." He said it on the evening four Bruins had scored at least 15 points, no one had more than Rowe's 19, and Wicks, Rowe, and Vallely made the all-tournament team.

It felt different to fans at home, too, that about two thousand people greeted the team on its return to Los Angeles International Airport a day later, an increase players noted with pride. Among its many feats, UCLA 1969–70 had done the unlikely by making Bruin backers seem appreciative again after years of growing to take winning for granted. For proof, the flight attendant encouraged passengers over the loudspeaker to deplane as soon as possible to avoid the scrum that would form once the team, waiting patiently to be considerate, went from the first-class section into the terminal. Patterson, among others, spent about thirty minutes signing autographs in the gate area alone, before the crowd followed players and coaches to baggage claim, and upon next driving away created a traffic jam on a Sunday afternoon that rivaled a freeway rush hour.

In what would forever stand as one of his top accomplishments, Wooden had gone from two titles with guards in the lead role to three built around a center to winning with stars at forward. Heeding Norman's advice on the pressing defense led into encouraging input on incorporating sophomore Lew Alcindor and then in the 1969–70 of great uncertainty a return to his comfort zone of the high-post offense and speed. The coach who never considered himself a strategist had, at the very least, done exceptionally well adjusting to changing rosters.

The decision Bill Walton always said had been made years before became official seventeen days after the airport party when he called coaches from USC, San Diego State, Cal, and Duke to give the runners-up the bad news. The public disclosure of the news came two days later in word being sent to the media, without a press conference, without the *ding-ding-ding* of newsroom teletype machines startled awake and without the days of coast-to-coast analysis that followed Alcindor on his lonely island in the Power cafeteria. The 1970 version didn't involve media behemoth New York City, for one thing, but perception was the more likely cause of the interest gap. Walton was not seen as otherworldly, the way NBA teams in 1965 were already talking about losing games on purpose in four seasons to be first in line for Alcindor at draft time. Walton merely projected as a superstar.

His future having come into better focus, Wooden in the wake of a fourth consecutive title and a sixth overall seemed content, an ease he projected as he took hundred-yard strolls on spring afternoons from his office to a deli in the Student Union for lunch. On the days he spotted the familiar faces of the *Daily Bruin* reporters who covered basketball, Wooden happily joined the students for light conversation that inevitably included, to his delight, baseball and the Dodgers in particular. Not only had the first season after Alcindor gone as well as he could have hoped, but four of the five starters, everyone except guard Vallely, and all the top reserves would be returning next season. The Walton-Wilkes–Lee–Tommy Curtis recruiting haul was arriving within months.

On other college campuses, however, bad news kept coming. In the northeast Ohio town of Kent, though, the national mood turned especially dark when members of the National Guard called out by the governor to protect the Kent State campus against further destruction by violent activists fired haphazardly on peaceful protesters. Thirteen seconds of shooting just after noon on May 4 resulted in four unarmed students being killed, three others going to the hospital in critical condition before surviving, and another seven suffering lesser wounds.

"The Kent State Four!" local residents chanted while protesting memorial services. "Should have studied more!" The conservative community blamed the victims and spread horrible rumors to smear their character, and a Gallup poll soon determined 58 percent of Americans faulted the dead and hospitalized.

"Anyone who appears on the streets of a city like Kent with long hair, dirty clothes, or barefooted deserves to be shot," said one resident, among the many to decide the students had it coming.

ABOVE: High school senior Lew Alcindor announces his decision to attend UCLA on May 4, 1965, the day that changed college basketball forever.

RIGHT: John Wooden in front of the UCLA bench in the national semifinals in March 1968.

OPPOSITE: Lew Alcindor dominates inside against USC, as he did against everyone.

LEFT: John Wooden with freshmen players (from left) Lew Alcindor, Lynn Shackelford, Kenny Heitz, and Lucius Allen.

BELOW: Bill Russell (left), Muhammad Ali (middle), and 20-year-old Lew Alcindor (right) at the Cleveland Summit in June 1967.

ABOVE: The court as an island as UCLA plays Houston in the Game of the Century on January 20, 1968.

RIGHT: Lew Alcindor celebrates after UCLA wins the 1969 championship in his final college game.

Sports Illustrate

MARCH 31, 1969   50

THE MILLION DOLLAR FINISH

UCLA'S HAPPY G
LEW ALCIN

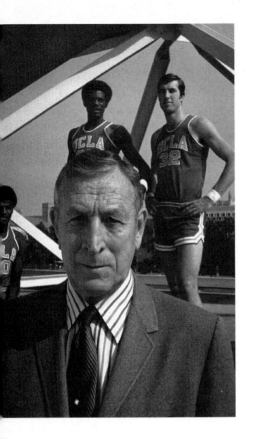

ABOVE LEFT: John Wooden stands in front of three key 1970-71 Bruins: Curtis Rowe (left), Sidney Wicks (middle), and Steve Patterson (right).

ABOVE: Sam Gilbert, a father figure to many UCLA players and a troubling presence to the coaching staff and administration.

LEFT: Athletic Director J. D. Morgan had an integral role in elevating UCLA into a power in college sports.

OPPOSITE: Bill Walton had few peers in college basketball history, especially on defense.

ABOVE: Nineteen-year-old Bill Walton protests U.S. involvement in the Vietnam war in May 1972.

LEFT: Notre Dame coach Digger Phelps runs his Fighting Irish through practice in January 1974, days before facing UCLA.

John Wooden exits a winner after UCLA beat Kentucky for the 1975 title in his final game as coach.

"Have I your permission to quote that?" a researcher asked.

"You sure do. It would have been better if the Guard had shot the whole lot of them that morning."

"But you had three sons there."

"If they didn't do what the Guards told them, they should have been mowed down."

The UCLA basketball banquet that night at the Hilton in Beverly Hills had the unfortunate timing of celebrating within hours of the tragedy at Kent State. Two thousand people within days demonstrated on the grounds of the national champions, leading to approximately seventy arrests. Three shots were fired into the home of the ROTC commander at Stanford. Fires were set in ROTC buildings at UC Davis near Sacramento, Oregon State, Princeton, and other spots. The dinner program at the swanky hotel a few miles from Pauley Pavilion continued on schedule with Wicks being named MVP and Most Improved, Rowe being honored for excellence in the tournament, and Patterson as outstanding team player, Bibby top newcomer and best in free throws, Vallely for academics, and Larry Farmer for outstanding freshman.

Bill Seibert, a seldom-used forward planning to leave the program despite another year of eligibility, used his farewell address at the podium to tear into Wooden for double standards in treatment of players and poor communication. The eight hundred attendees were initially stunned into silence, before some in the crowd booed or tried to shout Seibert off the stage—his own father yelled at him to shut up—and his mother cried watching the very public revenge mission. When he finished with the claim that coaches lacked sensitivity, teammates on the dais tellingly backed him with a standing ovation, while others in the audience approached in a rage. One guest threatened to punch him. Wooden, noticeably not using Seibert's name, later called it "just an unfortunate incident in which a young man who didn't get to play much complained publicly about it and stirred up others who weren't getting to play. All coaches have to deal with this sometimes. We did not recruit the player, [did] not bring him in on scholarship, but we did give him a scholarship later, and we did not take it away from him, even when he embarrassed us as he did."

Wooden had suddenly been plunged back into a world of constant tension six weeks after the latest title, even more once players met three days after the banquet and spent hours on a one-page typed letter to be sent to Haldeman and, they hoped, forwarded to the Oval Office. Addressing the demands to "President Richard Nixon" as opposed to less respectful names used most other times was a wise attempt at professionalism to be taken seriously. Playing directly to the target audience, the chief of staff, the Bruins included their thirteen names and the sign-off at the bottom to catch Haldeman's eye: "U.C.L.A. 1970 N.C.A.A. Basketball Champions." They weren't going for subtle.

> We, the undersigned, are thirteen U.C.L.A. students who wish
> to express our grave concern and disapproval over the President's
> policy of expansion of the immoral, genocidal and imperialistic
> war the United States is now waging in Southeast Asia. We support
> the meaningful and peaceful demonstrations held throughout this
> country. We deplore the tactics of violence of both students and
> law enforcement agencies that are suppressing the intentions of
> those who are truly concerned with peace on earth. We further
> wish to clarify that we are not "bums" as we college students have
> been so wrongly accused.

The statement went on to denounce Nixon for ignoring demonstrators and for sending troops to Cambodia, followed by proposing the immediate withdrawal of U.S. personnel and arms in Cambodia, setting a goal of being out of Vietnam by January 1, requesting a public investigation into the Kent State killings, and an end to local, state, and federal authorities hassling the youth of America. Whether the letter reached Haldeman, let alone Nixon, was never determined, but Wooden reacted with anger at the attempt and especially at the man he held responsible for most of the writing. Correctly reading it as mostly the work of Andy Hill, with some players suspecting an informant among them had gone to Wooden, led to another icy conversation in the coach's office in a repeat of the one-sided October Moratorium exchange. That Wooden again pummeled away without vulgarity or raised voice made Hill feel even worse. He would rather have been yelled at or cussed out. The biting, measured comments cut deeper.

Deciding, wrongly this time, that Hill, Ecker, and Schofield put Seibert up to the blindside banquet speech pushed Wooden over the edge. Pick your new school and I will help arrange it, he told Hill after pulling him from class for an impromptu meeting with the staff. Wooden wouldn't dismiss them from the team—past Bruins had walked off during games, had been arrested, and had blasted away at the coach himself without having scholarships pulled—but inviting them to leave was almost as bad. Each either enjoyed the school or teammates or still loved the area after attending nearby high schools and declined the offer.

Enough concern existed about the strained relationship with coaches that players discussed renting a hotel room to invite Wooden to hear their grievances. Wooden beat them to it by calling a meeting in Morgan's office that turned into the unexpected development of the staff and the athletic director wrongly thinking players would ask Wooden to resign. Suspicion again turned to a mole on the roster. The Bruins had no such intention and, if anything, were stunned the topic came up when they simply wanted to talk through the issues that went public at the banquet. Most did feel a double standard existed where the top players got away with more, and there were communication problems, mostly the reserves at the end of the bench feeling ignored. But the idea of a coaching change was never discussed.

The tension was palpable, with Morgan noticeably angry, when Wicks stood up and changed the mood by telling Wooden he should not feel threatened by the group wanting to clear the air. If anything, the star forward said, Wooden should be proud players came together to support each other with a mature approach, just as Wooden had always encouraged. Even Wooden had to smile a little at the logic. Wicks, Hill later wrote, "had made us closer as a team than we had been during our recent championship season."

Wooden in the end was able to head into summer on a good note after the championship followed by Walton's decision, the banquet, Nixon's letter, and finally the meeting in Morgan's office that finished upbeat to set a positive tone heading into 1970–71. "There's no limit to what we could do next year," Patterson said. "We were a very green team going into this season and we were learning a new system." Getting beyond the learning curve in 1970–71 and adding Walton, he decided, "Well, the end is not nearly in sight."

8

ORANGE CRATES IN THE ALLEY

The influential San Francisco Sound had reached such psychedelic heights by the start of the new decade that the Grateful Dead, Jefferson Airplane, Santana, and Crosby, Stills, Nash & Young were all recording at the studio Wally Heider's in the fall and winter of 1970, sometimes with three of the supergroups simultaneously filling each of the separated rooms. The Dead tour the same months included a stop at Queens College in New York City that led the school paper to wonder in review, "Are the Grateful Dead devils or angels?" considering its "ability to drive people to peculiar heights of ecstatic frenzy . . . their whole being absorbed, taken over." "Last night was a free zone," the paper at the University of Pennsylvania reported after the concert there, "reality suspended, the law flagrantly violated. The Grateful Dead was the cause of it all." The eclectic rockers played Fillmore East in Manhattan the night Jimi Hendrix died in September and the Winterland Ballroom with the Airplane back home in San Francisco the night Janis Joplin died in October.

The Bay Area had been ground zero for the counterculture movement since Berkeley overflowed with activism in the mid-1960s and especially once the Summer of Love in 1967 took over San Francisco's Haight-Ashbury district. The Gray Line bus company started the Hippieland daytime sightseeing excursion, billed it as "the only foreign tour within the continental limits of the United States," and included a stop at the home several Dead members shared at 710 Ashbury Street. The guided expeditions were an immediate hit with visitors wanting to experience the alternate universe, just safely and briefly inside a moving vehicle, to witness the one hundred thousand transplants attempting to build a utopian society or to protest the war or for the abundance of drugs, free love, and artists. The gawkers in the rolling bubble made it feel like rolling through a human zoo. George Harrison visited and decided the Haight crowds were "bums," but the migration had been so overwhelming that the zoo effect remained in 1970.

Los Angeles, already a world entertainment capital through movies and television, was catching up musically with a migration that tracked with its overall growth. Neil Young, Graham Nash, Stephen Stills, and Gram Parsons all arrived in recent years, finding record companies hunting for new talent and each other as communal support. (Nash originally came from England to visit love interest Joni Mitchell, entered her home in Laurel Canyon, found David Crosby and Stills there on a summer day, and soon fell into a three-part harmony so ridiculously right that Nash began laughing in the middle of singing.) Linda Ronstadt came in 1965, formed the Stone Poneys, and traveled to outskirt clubs in Hermosa Beach near the airport, to Huntington Beach about forty-five miles south of L.A., to Santa Barbara a hundred miles north, and to pizza parlors anywhere if the Poneys could get a gig. Glenn Frey and Don Henley joined Ronstadt's show as backup singers and talked about forming a band, eventually to be known as the Eagles. Agent Irving Azoff called the scene "like the gold rush," an explosion of talent mixed with opportunity unlike anything in entertainment.

The wave turned the bungalow homes of Laurel Canyon into a colony of actors and musicians changing the entertainment industry ten miles from Westwood. The small streets winding above the landmark Beverly Hills Hotel on a main drag, Sunset Boulevard, bloomed camaraderie, talent, drugs, and sex in house parties of artists trying out new songs. Other nights were spent in community at the Troubadour, the Whisky a Go Go, or the Roxy once it opened in 1973 with Neil Young, Graham Nash, and Cheech & Chong onstage and Elton John and Carole King in the audience. (A couple former UCLA students, Ray Manzarek and Jim Morrison, spent part of 1966 with their young group the Doors as the Whisky house band opening for featured acts.) The Ash Grove was hot with folk tunes, while a cowboy vibe flowed in the Palomino in North Hollywood, a couple hours' drive from the honky-tonks of the Central Valley and the Bakersfield sound of Merle Haggard and Buck Owens. But especially the Troubadour, where John, Young, Mitchell, James Taylor, and Kris Kristofferson played for spectators Jack Nicholson, Peter Fonda, and Johnny Cash, among the many, and Warren Beatty romanced Carly Simon. Led Zeppelin played the Forum in 1970 and afterward went to the Troubadour for almost three more hours of jamming.

Music lover Bill Walton happened into the perfect place at a perfect time. Assigned the same ground-floor room in Dykstra Hall as freshman Lew Alcindor five years earlier, likely because the oversize bed remained, he arrived in September and moved in with new teammate Greg Lee with so few items that it took Walton five minutes to unpack. Pauley Pavilion was one flight of stairs down and a short walk away, Lee's Volkswagen Bug available for greater escapes. "I was more than ready to get started," Walton later wrote. "I was ecstatic about the freedom of getting away from my parents. There was the energy and activity of all the politics, the classes, professors, lectures, and books in the library; great new people to meet including so many beautiful, extremely friendly, and warmhearted coeds. And there were the Grateful Dead and all the other bands to go hear on campus and all around L.A. any night of the week—endless possibilities and opportunities for plenty of high-altitude training."

Skimming the *Daily Bruin* one afternoon while sitting on their beds, Lee spotted an announcement of Neil Young playing that night in Royce Hall, a campus landmark as one of the university's four original buildings. The roommates hurried on foot, arrived before most any other customers, and without paying the $2.50 admission were waved in by security, who recognized the latest basketball stars. Lee and Walton claimed spots in the second row, gladly waited for the show, and were soon carried along by the waves of the Young classic "Old Man" as well as "Cowgirl in the Sand," "A Man Needs a Maid," "Tell Me Why," and others. Of particular relevance early in the first school year after the massacre at Kent State resulted in the death of two female and two male students, the set list also included "Ohio," a declaration of what had become of American campuses, originally delivered with Crosby, Stills & Nash but a Young solo in Royce.

Walton at seventeen had already turned against Richard Nixon and American involvement in Vietnam, even if his public protests were still in the future, a strong antiwar sentiment shared by much of the student body and another reason he considered UCLA a good fit in atmosphere as well as basketball. Far into retirement, he would look back on early life in Westwood as "so much better than I could have ever imagined," but newcomer Walton offered the harsher assessment that "because I was a basketball star and not just another college student in the seventies, I was very weird. And very lonely. I didn't have a lot of friends. There were times when I had none. I used to walk to games wearing a T-shirt and sandals, and people thought that was weird. I lived a half mile from Pauley, so I walked, and people used to yell at me and say I was crazy. I really took it personally that people didn't like me. So I started riding my bike, because that was the only way I could get around without people stopping me, and they thought, 'Wow, that guy is *weird*!'"

He entered the B.O. Barn during volleyball practice in the fall, walked to coach Al Scates, and announced he and Lee would like to join the team after basketball season. Great, Scates said, aware Lee was a talented beach player and figuring Walton could quickly learn to rule the net at six foot eleven with athleticism and timing, before Walton limped back to Scates in March and begged off his commitment with the explanation of being too beat up. UCLA won the men's volleyball NCAA title at Pauley Pavilion anyway, with a postmatch celebration that included a player slipping Scates two large joints in the handshake. Walton made the same unfulfilled verbal commitment the next year, then gave up all pretense his body could handle the double duty. Had he waited a little longer and followed through, Walton might have practiced against Wilt Chamberlain, working out with the third and fourth teams as part of rehabilitating a knee injury after his Laker career.

Walton and Lee soon became two of the many Bruins of the era to make the mile journey to the house on Bentley Circle. Like the others, they would go to talk to the doctor who lived there, a pediatrician at the UCLA

Medical Center but well respected for his expertise on adult athletes, or simply to enjoy the warmth of the home and the family that lived there. The front door stayed unlocked to allow visitors to enter on their own, just as everyone from friends of the kids' to Lakers stars walked in to be counseled or fed. Walton would occasionally go from a late-afternoon practice to the team meal in the Student Union on to Bentley Circle, enter unannounced, walk to the kitchen for second dinner, and without a word or hint of regret commandeer the food being eaten by one of the Vandeweghe sons, twelve-year-old Kiki. Miss America 1952, Kiki's mom, would return the stolen portion and fix Walton his own full plate.

Freshman Walton away from the court regularly chose silence, especially early in the school year before building the kind of trust he needed with most on campus to push past the extreme shyness caused by his stutter. Lee quickly became not only his roommate and friend, but a security blanket as a teenager of great intelligence who often ran interference by carrying conversations in social settings. The day he and Lee walked into the apartment of a mutual friend in Santa Monica, though, and Walton spotted a *Sports Illustrated* from the previous season with Tom McMillen on the cover under the headline "The Best High School Player in America," Walton bent down, picked the magazine up from a table, and looked it over.

"I'm better than this guy," he said. Behind closed doors or not, bashful Walton quickly established himself as a ferocious competitor of great pride.

• • •

Jerry West had always been a taut rope emotionally, the aftershock of growing up with a physically abusive father in a West Virginia home so absent of warmth that one of his sisters named it "the ice house." It got worse when an older brother he looked up to was killed in combat in the Korean War when Jerry was thirteen. The constant emotional anguish of early life turned him into a future superstar. A kid who would stay outside shooting baskets even in the worst winter weather to avoid being home, until he turned himself into an all-time great with a smoldering, haunted soul. West became the brilliant Lakers guard with a career others would dream about and to himself the player who was never good enough, scorched by the times he did not win, especially the 6 losses to the Celtics in the Finals during the 1960s. Even being named MVP of the '69 series wasn't good enough—L.A. lost to Boston despite his heroics. Decades later as arguably the greatest general manager in NBA history, coworkers in the front office still knew not to playfully jab the boss about Boston the same way they might fire devilish locker-room digs at others.

The usual stress overdose turned particularly dark as the late 1960s faded into the '70s. The avalanche of boyhood trauma turned him inward and uncomfortable in public; he played for a team unable to climb higher than best in the Western Conference, in a town where a college team had a greater following and his marriage continued while irreversibly broken. Late in the summer of 1969, West had the strange sensation of being followed in his white Ferrari, and not the same way kids would tail him as long as possible on drives home from the Forum after games. Reading *Helter Skelter* years later, the book detailing the murder spree by Charles Manson, Linda Kasabian, and other members of the Manson Family over three nights in August, West came to page 357: "Observing a white sports car ahead of them, Manson told Linda, 'At the next red light, pull up beside. I'm going to kill the driver.'" West often wondered if he could have been that driver.

The Westwood Drug Store and especially Hollis Johnson's, the cozy 1950s-style diner in back, became an island of calm in a Jerry West world spinning off its axis. One of the biggest names in town may have appeared in Hollywood with expensive clothes and high-end Italian sports cars, but part of him longed for the West Virginia life of good, understated people and the outdoors, even if he wished the emotional demons that chased him from home would disappear. He met fellow Mar Vista resident Hollis Johnson, discovered a mutual love of fishing, and became a regular at the luncheonette with a fading Formica counter, eight or ten upholstered swivel stools bolted into the ground. Best of all, it had a back room that made the public dining area seem glamorous, a little space where West turned empty delivery milk crates into a table and chairs.

Wooden and his assistants for years loved Hollis Johnson's for the same reasons, with the bonus of it being a few blocks from the athletic department. Lunchtime walks down the gentle hill were common, until the staff was visiting so often that the namesake owner became a friend giving hoops advice to the men with multiple national championships. The actual experts nodded along in mock agreement, smiling through bad suggestions because Hollis was that great to be around, a latitude few others enjoyed in a time of Wooden frustrated by know-it-all fans. Many students knew Hollis's kindness in slipping an extra burger or sandwich in the bag of food at the register, on the house and without mentioning it. Gary Cunningham became a fishing buddy, working Crowley Lake for trout at sixty-eight hundred feet in the Eastern Sierra, and West hit the same spot with Johnson other times. West Virginia University and senior guard Jerry West beat John Wooden and the Bruins in the Los Angeles Classic on December 29, 1959, but they didn't get to know each other until an introduction by Johnson after West joined the Lakers in 1960. Countless breakfasts and lunches followed in the back of the diner, beyond view of most customers, "two small-town, everyday guys shooting the breeze, not quite believing our good fortune, always knowing it could end tomorrow," as West put it. "I have always loved hanging out in places where I can just be Jerry, and this place . . . became very important to me."

Wooden, likely picking up on the tortured soul West never hid, became an immediate counselor. "Jerry," Wooden said one day early in what became a friendship that lasted decades, "when your team won, did you take all the credit?"

"No, Coach, of course not," West replied in his twang.

"Well, then, Jerry, when your team lost, there is no reason for you to take all the blame."

West understood, but did not change.

Assistant coach Jerry Norman occasionally took recruits to Hollis Johnson's as part of campus visits in hopes of giving a true indication of daily life at UCLA, as opposed to a fancy restaurant the way many schools would in an attempt to impress. Sitting in the back also allowed more privacy and made for easier conversation than sitting shoulder to shoulder to shoulder in a row at the counter. Wooden, Norman, and the prospect instead circled a pair of orange crates pushed together for a table in the alley outside the back door and Johnson draped a tablecloth over the wood slats of the boxes. If West happened to be there, he would oblige Norman's request to stop by, an all-time great player and an all-time great coach, just a couple everyday guys, pitching a high school kid in an alley.

Walton came into West's life in a similar way, through Hollis Johnson's, but as the most unlikely dining companion compared to Wooden, Pat Riley, Gail Goodrich, and others. West was fourteen years older as Walton entered UCLA, one a proven superstar and the other a very promising but unproven freshman, one an adult who took pride in dressing well and the other a teenager so unkempt, to the point of slobbish, that West wanted to tell him to take a bath. The Walton parents were a constant support to Bill and his three siblings despite no interest in sports themselves, while West's father and mother created a scary and cold home. Walton already showed signs of turning activist while West was far from a social crusader, a role on the Lakers that belonged to forward Elgin Baylor, who had greater self-confidence and a life of growing up black in inner-city Washington.

But Walton was a basketball sponge, and West, like Wooden, appreciated dedication above all, even talent. It just so happened Walton had a lot of both, and as far as he was concerned, West had been an important part of his life for about eight years, since Bill with a $9.95 transistor radio in San Diego dialed across Chick Hearn broadcasting Lakers games as the most exciting and interesting thing he'd ever heard. Getting hooked on Hearn's machine-gun delivery led to the Lakers becoming his favorite team. To then be able to walk from his dorm to the diner behind the Westwood Drug Store, enter the back door that saved the freshman with a stutter from unnecessary banter with customers, and often find Jerry West made Hollis Johnson's a safe zone for Walton as well. While West enjoyed the diner as a place to escape his celebrity life, he did not notice the speech impediment as much as Walton craving anything hoops, morning after morning of conversation and Johnson delivering rounds of overstuffed omelets and stacks of pancakes to a turned-over milk crate in the room out of sight.

"I would be wolfing down this food," Walton said. "Jerry would be there eating. He'd be on his way to practice. He would tell me about the NBA. It was just the greatest time." West found him to be a character, fun and smart and bursting with energy, and West liked characters for being true to themselves. Plus, Walton "almost reminded me of someone from West Virginia"—a compliment—"the way he dressed. Shaggy looking." Strangely, the adult mentor living a Ferrari existence but longing for fishing-hole moments gained as much or more from the friendship.

Walton, joined by Lee, Keith Wilkes, and Tommy Curtis among the eight members of the freshman team, charged into the first day of practice with the same zeal that would come to mark each of his first three years. A Bruin in his mind since sixth grade, he could barely contain himself as Wooden called the first-year players together on the court, walked them into the locker room, sat on a stool, and began to instruct the newest charges, certain, Walton said, "he was about to give us the key to heaven on earth, show us the path, guide us to become the next great team in history." They got doused by the talk on shoes and socks instead, to be followed by pointers on how to tuck in their jerseys, tie the drawstring on their shorts, and dry themselves after showers, especially their hair. The audience, full of eye rolls, struggled to keep from laughing out loud. Wooden removing his own shoes and socks for a demonstration, revealing varicose veins from lower leg to foot along with hammertoes, killed the remainder of the excitement.

Leaving the close quarters, the Bruin understudies were directed to the stands to watch the varsity workout unfolding with precision from the first day, nonstop chatter from players on the court and a brisk tempo that reignited Walton. Pay attention, Wooden told the newcomers, because you are expected to now know the practice routine. "We thought at the time that a lot of the stuff Coach Wooden was selling . . . were the stupidest things ever," Walton later wrote. "But we never doubted the honesty, righteousness, dedication, preparation, commitment, and excellence that was behind it all."

It felt different than the Alcindor unveiling from the start, whether because San Diego didn't seem as foreign as New York and Walton therefore didn't seem as much of a curiosity, or because Lewis set gawking standards with his race, size, and talent. Then the varsity-freshman exhibition featuring newcomer Walton went off minus an arena christening or a tribute night to Wooden, the events that added to the aura of the contest five years earlier. The anticlimactic 1970 version was Walton playing about 13 minutes in the first half and none in the second while struggling through his third day with a bad stomach. He did block 3 shots in limited action November 29 in his first game in a Bruin uniform, a glimpse of his future brilliant defense, as the varsity rolled to a 93–59 win with guard Kenny Booker replacing the graduated John Vallely in the starting lineup alongside returnees Curtis Rowe, Sidney Wicks, Steve Patterson, and Henry Bibby.

As in the days of Alcindor, Allen, Shackelford, and Heitz, the freshman schedule brought little competition and so little challenge for the prodigy center that Wooden reached back to the memory of Jay Carty muscling Alcindor. This time, Wooden chose Jim Nielsen, a 1969 graduate after three titles as a six-seven reserve forward entrusted to use experience and strength to make Walton work despite the size difference. Just as importantly, Nielsen aware of the injury concerns surrounding Walton found the proper balance of being aggressive without risking the future of the program.

Walton by early in 1970–71 was so obviously a supreme talent that Wooden cleared him to practice with the varsity several times a week, a promotion Alcindor never received at the same stage. Walton showed the same skill level against the upgraded competition, dominating the inside on defense with several blocks, sometimes in a row, and, just as importantly, the same mindset. He offered no hint of being intimidated by upperclassmen, not even Wicks, who intimidated practically everybody and tried to put Walton in his place one practice by finishing a drive to the basket with a ferocious dunk on Walton. "Sidney!" Wooden screamed down as he watched from the concourse between the first and second levels of Pauley Pavilion, hating slams in drills as much as in games. Walton may have been victimized in the moment, but remained the same effervescent rookie who saw being on the court as a spiritual experience. His confidence could not be broken.

The same compliment of occasional promotions to varsity practices, sometimes moving back and forth the same day with Walton, became especially meaningful to Wilkes, struggling with the transition from small-town Ventura to Los Angeles and still just seventeen years old. Pickup games in the B.O. Barn and Pauley Pavilion and then official practices in Pauley were his comfort spots, not the campus that felt as big as Ventura and into the rest of the city that overwhelmed him. Basketball was the stability. Showing he had talent well beyond most freshman, while remaining eternally easygoing and likable, led to the important development of quickly being accepted by older players, even on the days when Rowe grew angry with Wilkes for hitting shot after shot in his face.

Wilkes looked at varsity practices as an inexperienced stage actor getting a Broadway audition, particularly as a forward when the two established stars were forwards, seniors Wicks and Rowe. Some days, Wilkes would sit in the stands to watch portions of the varsity workout and dream about the day his chance would come to uphold the tradition of UCLA basketball, mostly confident he would handle the challenge starting the next season but also humbled by the skill level on the court in front of him.

A thirty-four-year-old UCLA assistant football coach made a point to attend as many of the practices as possible, captivated by the ways the organization and urgent energy inside mostly empty Pauley Pavilion translated to his sport. Dick Vermeil in his first season as offensive coordinator already had the benefit of working under Tommy Prothro, a brilliant football mind and a Wooden-level practice genius. The chance to learn from Prothro was exactly the point of leaving the Los Angeles Rams for Westwood, so he could see for himself, up close, why the Bruins kept beating opponents with more talent. He just didn't expect to become entranced by Wooden as well.

The afternoon basketball sessions became a personal study hall for the up-and-coming football man with aspirations of becoming a head coach at a major college or in the NFL. Wooden behind closed doors nearly daily put on a clinic of preparation turning into precision execution, as any Bruin since 1948 and several Midwest schools before that could attest. The day Wooden reached up to jab an index finger toward Wicks's chest after a bad play stayed with Vermeil as proof of being able to demand excellence without an accompanying thunderstorm of verbal abuse. Vermeil considered himself just as fortunate that Wooden also gladly answered questions on coaching principles after the workouts or later in conversation, whenever Wooden's schedule allowed.

Vermeil as a California lifer and Los Angeles resident for a little more than a year understood the popularity of his new friend, especially locally, and turned UCLA basketball into a football benefit. He already had the connection of Bruce Walton, Bill's older brother, starting at tackle in what would become a three-year run with the first-string offensive line. The Wooden name, though, transcended anything on campus and most anything in Southern California sports after four titles in a row and six in seven years, a sixty-year-old with star power to high school seniors.

Anything you'd like to do? Vermeil routinely asked prospects as part of arranging upcoming campus recruiting visits.

I'd like to meet Coach Wooden, many football players responded.

Wooden never turned Vermeil down when the schedule allowed. Wooden spoke with the football players the same as highly regarded basketball prospects for his own program, never pushing UCLA with a hard sell but spotlighting the quality education they would receive and, in this case, praising Prothro. The upperclassmen serving as hosts seemed just as excited to be in Wooden's office. On the weekends that visits aligned with the basketball schedule, coaches were sure to take the recruits to basketball games in Pauley to experience the highest level of school spirit, likely with a large contingent of the current football roster on hand. When Vermeil returned to Westwood in 1974 as head coach, he made a point to have the first meeting of the new staff include a visit from Wooden, and football coaches for months made a point to leave early for practice at Spaulding Field about a hundred yards away and walk through, rather than around, Pauley Pavilion, to spend a few minutes watching the latest work of an orchestra conductor on the court.

. . .

Wooden learned after the victory over Rice in the second game of the season that J. D. Morgan approached an assistant coach at halftime with orders to be delivered to Wooden to keep Rowe and Wicks on the court after the usual starting forwards spent the opening 10:14 on the bench for arriving late to warm-ups. The aide, following established procedure for Morgan trying to interject in basketball matters, passed along nothing. Wooden could understand Morgan wanting information in advance on every prospect brought to campus and then meeting the recruit alone during the visit, realizing players in the high-profile program might face unique scrutiny, but drew the line at game input. If you want to do that, Wooden told him two days later on Monday, the first day back in the office, get another coach. Morgan had so obviously broken their arrangement of Wooden handling the team and Morgan the business that Morgan immediately backed down with "Well, I was out of line," and that he simply got caught up in the moment of Wicks and Rowe on the bench with twelve thousand customers wanting stars. Wooden for one of the few times saw his boss could be reasonable and admit a mistake, "So it was forgotten."

Twelve straight wins followed the first two, most by wide margins, before a loss at Notre Dame behind 46 points from Austin Carr. Bill Bertka, still running his scouting service as in the days of tracking Alcindor in the freshman-varsity game, found himself getting fewer requests for Westwood intel than most any team in the country anyway, despite the obvious need for opponents to unearth any weakness. It didn't take an independent report for other schools to realize the Bruins were predictable in using the same cuts, screens, and passing angles as always and winning with repetition. "They execute so well that they know exactly how to counteract anything you might do defensively," Bertka said. "It's amazing that teams know exactly what they're gonna do—but they still can't stop them." There could be few greater compliments for Wooden. Beyond the discipline, quickness, and finesse brought together by nonstop drilling in practice, Wicks, Rowe, and Patterson delivered a starting frontcourt that for a second season provided muscle to complement the precision. "It will take a combination of the New York Knickerbockers and the Milwaukee Bucks to dethrone them," Baylor coach Bill Menefee said, including the latter for obvious reasons but also because Alcindor's team had built on the encouraging 1969–70 to start 20-4 in his second NBA season.

Wicks in particular had become so imposing by his senior season at six foot eight and 225 pounds, with an attitude to match, that the NFL took him seriously as a prospect. The Dallas Cowboys, among others, scouted basketball games in the long-shot hope of uncovering a convert and would soon dispatch three members of the front office to the Final Four as well as hosting a hospitality suite at the Marriott to entertain coaches. Houston in March would mark the fifth year in a row with the Cowboys at championship weekend as the last step in an annual process that started with sending about three hundred letters to NCAA basketball coaches in a blanket inquiry scouring for candidates for Sunday football. The Cowboys already had the payoff of Utah State forward Cornell Green becoming All-Pro safety Cornell Green. Though realistic Wicks the major NBA prospect would stick with basketball, the Dallas scout in charge of tracking amateur hoops decided, "He's probably too tall to be a defensive back, but he'd be an excellent tight end. Heck, he's a real man—he could be a linebacker."

Wicks, Missouri coach Norm Stewart said early in 1970–71, is "a complete basketball player. On defense, he intimidates you, on offense he's got all the range." Wooden thought Wicks had the potential to be the best forward in NBA history if his focus continued to match his physical skills. The three-year transformation had already been one of the most impressive of the championship era—frustrated sophomore to flourishing with new responsibilities as a junior to national Player of the Year candidate as a senior—by the time his final regular season neared an end with the Bruins back at No. 1 after dropping to third following the Notre Dame loss.

Wooden took winning 4 games by a total of 13 points in one stretch as a sign of poise, not vulnerability, even if Washington coach Tex Winter opted for "Damn! How can those people continue to be so lucky?" If anything, the flight home from Seattle after one of the near misses caused greater anxiety once Wooden spotted Wicks exposing his butt crack while standing in the aisle in drooping jeans and leaning forward. "Isn't that disgraceful," Wooden told the *Los Angeles Times*' Dwight Chapin in conversation. Wooden appeared unfazed by the close calls, though, a confidence his Bruins would repay by entering the tournament with a 25-1 mark and a finishing victory over No. 3 USC.

Learning his team would be on the same flight as UCLA from Los Angeles to Salt Lake City to open the tournament prompted Long Beach State coach Jerry Tarkanian to change the itinerary, before his 49ers could be forced to deal with the visual of jamming into economy while the regal Bruins glided among the clouds in first class. He knew of J. D. Morgan's generous travel policy just as he knew Long Beach was already buried in the imagery of little brother desperately trying to catch up to the premier program. USC, though annually absent from the postseason as conference runner-up, at least was a top-3 team nationally much of the season and could stay with the Bruins on the court and win a recruiting showdown. USC and UCLA lived on the cover of Sports in the two major metro dailies, the *Times* and the *Herald Examiner*, Long Beach mostly inside among the tire ads. UCLA was a member of the nationally regarded University of California system, Long Beach the lesser California State University chain. Imperious Morgan refused to schedule the 49ers while looking down on them as a pirate program at a school offering inferior education. To the many seeing through the hypocrisy of Morgan wagging a morality finger while Sam Gilbert bankrolled Bruins, the real reason was the fear of losing to Tark.

Flying to the same city on the same day, and on the same plane until Long Beach balked, made a collision seem inevitable, then impossible to avoid once Tarkanian had the travel plans changed and still got hit with the perception he wanted to avoid: the 49ers waiting for their bags at the luggage carousel and Wicks and Rowe suddenly walking to the same area among the Bruins in what Tarkanian's wife detailed as cashmere coats, alligator shoes, and felt hats. "We look like the Salvation Army next to them," Jerry told Loel Schrader of the *Long Beach Press-Telegram* as they waited in baggage claim, still conscious of his players feeling inferior. They simply could not avoid each other. When Tarkanian recounted the scene for a reporter and the story made it into *Sports Illustrated*, Gilbert confronted him a year later—"You shouldn't talk so much"—but also boasted of the spending spree and even informing Morgan of the purchases.

The strong-arm tactics that shook others, Morgan most of all among Gilbert's UCLA interests, had no chance of working on Tarkanian, who was tough, smart, and well acquainted with the gritty side of basketball. He made no apologies for having his own interpretations of rules on recruiting and eligibility. Tarkanian was, however, forced to contemplate Gilbert's Bruin investments at length once Tark settled on UCLA as the source of complaints that prompted NCAA investigators to put Long Beach under a microscope. He could handle the deep scrutiny and didn't even particularly hold a grudge against the school he was sure turned him in, but deep scrutiny as UCLA got a pass during several years of violations, and bragging about them, was maddening.

Tarkanian still regularly complimented the Bruins when swearing revenge would have been understandable. He spoke of Wooden in particular with the highest praise and an appreciation of how kind Wooden had been to him as a relative unknown working the junior colleges. Tarkanian saw Morgan as lighting the fuse of NCAA interest, not UCLA basketball and certainly not Wooden individually. Long Beach had grown into a threat thirty miles from Pauley Pavilion with George Trapp and Ed Ratleff, along with Glenn McDonald waiting out his freshman season and, Tark was sure, made him an enemy to Morgan protecting the Westwood empire that counted on basketball to fund much of the athletic department.

Wooden in turn respected Tarkanian despite the obvious contrasts—"I don't always agree with his methods, but I don't think there is any doubt about his ability to coach the game." Much the way Wooden had great fondness for Press Maravich despite their differences, Wooden and Tarkanian were dissimilar personalities but a basketball match that grew into a warm relationship. Tarkanian considered being invited to UCLA to dissect the zone defense he ran with great success at Riverside City College, after Jerry Norman, scouting JC games, watched the 1-2-2 work in suffocating ways, the ultimate compliment.

"John Wooden and I have always gotten along very well," Tarkanian wrote. "He was great to me, and a man in his position didn't have to be. He didn't have to take time with a young coach at Long Beach State when he had a great program going at UCLA. When I first took the Long Beach job,

I was attending a sportswriters' luncheon in Los Angeles and John Wooden was there. I didn't know him well, but he went out of his way to take a few minutes to tell everyone that Long Beach had made a good choice in hiring me. I couldn't begin to say what a thrill it was for me to hear that coming from a man such as John Wooden. It meant so much to a guy who was still in junior college and getting ready to take his first four-year job."

In Salt Lake City on March 19, 1971, a day after UCLA beat BYU and Long Beach defeated the University of the Pacific to set up the highly anticipated Bruin-49er collision, the two coaches attended a 10:00 a.m. coaches' meeting with plans to next go to their hotel and return for a noon press conference to promote the West Regional final about twenty-four hours away. Let's stay and talk, Wooden suggested to Tarkanian, rather than leaving and coming back in an hour. They found a quiet spot, just the two of them, where Wooden passed along the secret that Indiana University tried to hire him. He declined without hesitation, despite the obvious lure, so easily that Wooden didn't bother trying to leverage the approach into a well-deserved raise from UCLA. As much as John and Nell missed their home state and never felt fully comfortable in Los Angeles, nothing could coax them away from the children and grandchildren in Southern California.

Instead, Wooden continued, he recommended Tarkanian, and the IU athletic director was interested. Call him, Wooden encouraged. Tarkanian couldn't wait to return to the hotel to tell his wife of the exciting news that just fell from the sky, a dizzying opportunity to climb from No. 3 in L.A. to one of the best in the entire state passionate about hoops. Wooden had gone from friendly to life-changing helpful the day before the showdown with a trip to the Final Four in Houston at stake. Even if some regarded the move as Wooden motivated by the chance to get a rising forty-year-old coach out of the West, not the desire to help someone who had earned the promotion, years of positive comments, before and after the Salt Lake City moment, indicated Wooden genuinely held Tarkanian in high regard, regardless of the unique relationship between the schools.

UCLA and Long Beach had met fifty-one weeks earlier in the tournament in Seattle, but with the 49ers unranked and future pro Ratleff relegated to the freshman roster. The Bruins won by 23. This time, with Ratleff already a star as a sophomore and better stability throughout the program with Tarkanian in his second season, they began ranked eighteenth, struggled through the opening month, and recovered to finish the regular season with a 14-game winning streak and at No. 17 in the Associated Press poll. Wooden considered them the best defensive team UCLA faced in 1970–71. The Bruins had never seen these 49ers, a reality underlined when Long Beach held a 44–33 lead with 14 minutes remaining.

Wooden in the moment thought, of all things, how he and Nell might be able to enjoy Houston as spectators, not an unpleasant option after four consecutive years of working the weekend, and Tarkanian believed, "We had 'em." The competitive side kicked in as Wooden began smacking the rolled-up program into each hand and a vein in his forehead bulged to the surface while he chastised his team on the ledge with "You're nothing but a bunch of All-American women chasers and hopheads!" The dynasty teetered with the Bruins unable to hit outside shots and Wicks on the bench with 4 fouls, one from disqualification, as Morgan at the scorer's table along one sideline screamed at the referees, demanding closer inspection of Ratleff's defense. "Watch number forty-three!" he yelled several times from the first row.

Then number forty-three fouled out with 5:23 to play. UCLA finally generated offense with Wicks playing again, Long Beach took a bad shot to end one late possession and another time had no choice but to throw up a low-percentage attempt under pressure with the clock expiring, the last gasp of the upset bid that fell short 57–55. The finish with a 24–11 run by the Bruins "was a screw job," Schrader, the reporter with a good relationship with both coaches, said. "They just took it from Long Beach." Tarkanian crossed paths with one of the referees years afterward, the one Tark held most responsible for the game turning against the 49ers, and could not stop himself, still, from pointing out the poor officiating he believed kept the Bruins alive.

Seeing several hundred fans waiting at the airport when the team returned home the next day in defeat stunned Tarkanian into reconsidering the Indiana job that two days ago seemed like a dream. While the 24-5 season was the tangible of Long Beach building into national prominence, and with several key players set to return in 1971–72, the emotional surprise welcome convinced him the program had finally connected with the crowded Los Angeles basketball market in just his second season at the school. A bad showing against UCLA that proved the 49ers were far from the lead pack would have prompted Tarkanian to call the Hoosiers and schedule an interview, but the actual outcome of playing the best team in the country into the final seconds and the heartfelt airport scene meant he couldn't walk away now. Indiana instead hired away the thirty-year-old coach at Army, Bob Knight.

The chain reaction Wooden started by turning down Indiana's approach would have a fallout that lasted for decades as Knight demanded the Hoosiers into a power and Tarkanian was available and willing to take the UNLV job in 1973, but it had no impact in Westwood at the time on the eve of another Final Four. A return to Houston and the Astrodome grew as the bigger storyline three years and two months after the Game of the Century, with a different roster by March 1971 but the same concern that such a massive facility means terrible depth perception for shooting. "You're out there alone," Wooden said in the days between the return from Salt Lake City and the departure to Texas. It makes the background a lot different for the shooters. But it certainly won't affect us more than the other teams." He paused. "Well, maybe it can't affect us too much, because we haven't been shooting well anyway."

Houston went from being dismissed as a Final Four site to hosting the sport's showcase event in six years thanks to January 20, 1968. Organizers, responding to the feedback from Wooden and others, placed the court closer to the stands and added seven thousand portable seats around the playing area in an attempt, however impossible, to create some intimacy and a backdrop for shooters compared to the thirty or thirty-five yards from courtside to the nearest fans at the Game of the Century. Plus, placing the court four feet higher led to the fresh problem of some among the closest seven thousand in the new seats standing in exciting moments and blocking the view of many in back. Tempers flared repeatedly among spectators, and others focused their wrath on threatening to decapitate press photographers sitting cross-legged along both baselines.

Wicks a year after dominating Artis Gilmore and Jacksonville in the championship game in College Park had moved to toying with the opponent in Houston, a brazen act for anyone else but the only sensible way for him to go out. The career that began in setbacks and disappointment, first needing an extra year to enter UCLA and then struggling through a frustrating sophomore season, was nearing the end with Wicks as the best forward and second-best big man in school history. The case could be made for second best at any position, pending a debate with the ghosts of college guards Goodrich and Hazzard, by the time Wicks, swinging his confidence like a club, was emotionally battering Kansas in the Astrodome. "Look out, here I come," he hollered at Dave Robisch on a night of 21 points and handling the ball against full-court pressure. "Halt," he commanded on another possession as Robisch moved in, and Robisch complied.

Wooden and Crum had their one true moment of tension—"I'm the coach of this team, and don't tell me how to coach my team," Wooden snapped at his No. 1 assistant when Crum persisted on a strategy debate, a topic he had no chance of winning but continued anyway. Wooden encouraged input from his staff, dissenting opinions as well to make a fully informed decision, but Crum somehow pushed him to an unusual place. They squabbled briefly but publicly, the stakes of the Final Four amplifying everything, before Henry Bibby moved to a chair between them to create a buffer.

Even with the strange sight, easily handling the No. 4 team in a national semifinal became secondary in Wooden's mind once the Bruins showered, trickled from the locker room to the team bus, and a custodian found Wooden folding towels. The janitor, who initially paused to congratulate Wooden on the important victory, was instead moved to comment on the area being nearly as clean as at the start of the day. Few comments about his team could mean more to the coach who bragged in his 1972 autobiography, surely with the 1971 semifinal in mind, "Many building custodians across the country will tell you that UCLA leaves the shower and dressing room the cleanest of any team. We pick up all the tape, never throw soap on the shower floor for someone to slip on, make sure all the showers are turned off, and all towels are accounted for. The towels are always deposited in a receptacle if there is one or stacked neatly near the door." Student managers are part of the team, he emphasized to players every season, not servants.

Wooden would recount the postgame Astrodome exchange with great pride well into his nineties, beaming at the memory in a sign the feedback had stayed with him as much, and maybe more, than the previous hours on the court. Another time, he bragged about hotel waitresses saying the Bruins were the best-behaved group of athletes they had encountered and that the workers were shocked to hear compliments on their fine job serving. A manager complaining about select rooms being left a mess, conversely, prompted Wooden to stress to his team to treat hotels as their own homes. Being sloppy off the court leads to playing sloppy, he believed, a continuation of his approach that basketball should be used to teach life lessons, not just win games. "I teach homely values," Wooden said, and "I still believe in old-fashioned virtue. But then I was brought up that way and we cannot alter what we believe in. Nor would I wish to, because I believe sincerely in virtue. Players may resent my speaking of this, but, if I keep speaking, perhaps some of it will sink in."

Their world turned more unconventional two nights later as Wicks and Rowe labored on offense while Patterson, the placeholder, the bridge center between the exit of Alcindor and the entrance of Walton, found a shooting rhythm from long range to score 20 points in the first half. He had averaged 12.4 in the regular season and previously in the tournament remained deep in the background, offering no hint of the performance to come that would secure a place in Bruin history, and suddenly transformed into "the sword that chopped our heads off," as Villanova's Clarence Smith described. As if to underline UCLA had stepped into an alternate universe, Wooden made the rare move to stall, a tactic he hated, in hopes of forcing the Wildcats out of a zone defense and also making the rules committee realize it should adopt a shot clock. He wanted Villanova more aggressive in man-to-man, not lying back, feeling the team with an obvious advantage in talent could better attack one-on-one. "You're the national champions!" Villanova players yelled at the team that refused to attack, and "Play ball!" "Bruins are bush!" the Wildcats rooting section chanted.

Wooden held his ground early in the second half even as the lead dwindled, walking the ball up, passing around the perimeter and waiting and passing again, rarely shooting, risking a national championship to prove a point to the NCAA, until Villanova accepted it needed to start chasing before all the time had expired. UCLA, resilient to the end, regained control and finished the 68–62 victory as the toughest title game yet with Rowe contributing 8 points, Wicks 7, and Patterson 29 before declaring, "I might as well die tonight."

Wicks approached Wooden on the court, before the celebration continued in the locker room. "It's been a nice three years," Wicks said, even if, actually, it hadn't always been. Wicks started to walk away, then came back with an addendum.

"You're really something."

Wooden would come to consider the 1970–71 squad among his five favorites ever, the only one among the seven champions in a row to make the list, forever appreciating the composure in close games and continuing the winning tradition without a superstar center. The collapse many predicted and hoped for never came. He then solidified his future by turning down a chance to coach the Lakers, offering the financial security UCLA never did, soon after waving off Indiana. Wooden in the process sent a statement as meaningful as the just-crowned Bruins: turning down his ideal location and a huge raise meant he only saw a future in Westwood, a future about to include varsity center Bill Walton.

9

A MOST UNUSUAL YOUNG MAN

"**I**t has been a long time since I have looked forward so eagerly to a coming basketball season and I hope that you share this enthusiasm," Wooden began his annual offseason letter to the team, despite the graduation of four-fifths of the opening lineup. "The 1971–72 Bruins will be short on experience in comparison with most of our recent teams, but it will not be short on talent, and I would much rather have talent without experience than experience without talent." He was optimistic to the point of predicting a 24-2 regular season in conversation with Nell, even while bracing for the inevitable growing pains of a young squad.

For a coach so against boasting that he chastised players for the minimal celebration of raising a finger in celebration near the end of the 1969 title game, Wooden in internal correspondence was practically ordering the food for the victory dinner seven and a half months in the future. Sophomores Bill Walton, Keith Wilkes, Greg Lee, and Tommy Curtis, juniors Larry Farmer and Larry Hollyfield, and senior Henry Bibby as the lone returning starter would be that easy to work with, Wooden decided, a belief that made sense in the moment even if it would later prove woefully misguided. He loved their intelligence, not only on the court but as the best academically of any of his previous UCLA rosters. They also had good camaraderie.

Walton in particular was a joy, exuding constant happiness on the court and in uniform instantly taking control with a torrent of words that was a contrast to the painfully withdrawn student off the court. Speech problem or not, no Wooden player had ever talked more in games or called out more advice in directing traffic around him than Walton, both to tremendous benefit. The early indications that Walton would be a star as projected combined with proof that a center-oriented system worked with the proper personnel allowed Wooden to again move away from his preferred small lineup without the same worry he had Alcindor's sophomore season.

"Every expert sees something else of great import in Walton's talent," Wooden detailed. "In my mind, next to his tremendous ability and unselfish team play, his foremost offensive skill was on the outlet pass. Never have I coached a player who was more skilled at outletting the ball to initiate a fast break. He always had the ball ready to throw even before he came down with the rebound. In fact, there were times when the ball was nearly at mid-court before Bill's feet hit the floor. On defense, his intimidating shot-blocking was his greatest asset." Wooden considered Walton all-seeing as both a passer able to spot an open teammate and a defender with the innate ability to anticipate the opponent's next move.

Publicly declaring, "Only a lamebrain would pick us for national honors, with a completely new team," and insisting USC had a better roster for Paul Westphal's senior season, may have been Wooden trying to lower expectations or specifically reduce the pressure on Walton. Either way, it took eight games, eight easy home victories against a soft nonconference schedule, to convince Wooden the potential he gauged behind closed doors before the season was a true "superclub." His mood had shifted that dramatically from the same first steps with Alcindor, when he had cringed in November and December of 1966 as the Bruins were anointed champions for the next three years. This time, Wooden himself stoked expectations, from the team letter to the private forecast to his wife to saying in the early stretch that the Bruins were progressing ahead of schedule as "one of the most exciting and interesting teams I've had." The 1971 Wooden likewise did not show the same worry over modifying the playbook to fit a star center, perhaps because Walton as faster and a better passer than Alcindor made him an ideal fit for the offense, requiring less adjustment.

Responding in kind, students camped outside Pauley Pavilion for two or three days before big games to get tickets—general admission: twenty-five cents—sometimes typewriter in lap for homework, sometimes playing cards and scarfing pizza and playing Frisbee, and often backed by rock music piped in from campus radio station KLA. Inside, tip-off became "kindred to a religious experience," a graduate student said, or maybe exactly the opposite of godly with song girls in hot pants wriggling to "Jesus Christ Superstar," "Lucretia Mac Evil," and "American Pie" during time-outs and a male student stripping as the school band played the *1812 Overture* to cheers from the crowd. "Pour it on! Pour it on!" fans often yelled with the Bruins already up big, another two victories per week taken for granted. Wooden family members seated near courtside could be heard shouting, "Gracious sakes, ref!" Season tickets had, after just five seasons in the arena, become points in wills and divorce settlements.

"It gives the students a bond they wouldn't ordinarily have," an undergrad said. "It isn't just because the team is a winner. It is Wooden, the model man, a father image the students are all proud of. It is UCLA as a school—the only time a commuter school of twenty-seven thousand with myriad interests can have a common experience. That's the key."

Walton loved the spirit of the new, renovated, cohesive varsity in contrast to the divided group he practiced with the season before. "I wouldn't have been happy if I had to play with that team," he said, "but I'm happy with this team; with these guys it's great fun." He and Lee had a strong friendship that carried over as a connection on the court, playmaker to No. 1 scoring option. Laid-back Wilkes was universally liked and the perfect complement to Walton's inside game as a feared perimeter weapon, much like Shackelford with Alcindor, while also an underrated defender and passer. Juniors Larry Farmer and Larry Hollyfield would have expanded roles as two of the forwards needed to replace the summer departures of Wicks to the Portland Trail Blazers as the second pick in the draft and Rowe to the Detroit Pistons as the eleventh, along with center Patterson to the Cleveland Cavaliers as the No. 18 selection and guard Booker to the Phoenix Suns as No. 213 in a year of 237 choices. More than accepting continued life as a role player when others might have pushed for a larger role as a returning senior who had waited his turn, Bibby flourished as a mature leader and additional shooter from the outside and became important for the mood and the offense.

Farmer arrived from Denver a year before the Walton-Wilkes-Lee-Curtis recruiting class only because another prospect turned Wooden down, creating an opening for Farmer after his high school coach sent 8 mm game films to UCLA for a sales pitch. Farmer just knew he belonged since watching the Game of the Century at home with his dad and being struck that playing for the Bruins meant being part of an event, not just games like everyone else played. The recruiting visit included Crum and Cunningham taking him to the cement footprints of Hollywood stars at Grauman's Chinese Theater, a typical tourist stop, without either assistant being aware that Farmer was a film buff who watched black-and-white classics with his mom and admired Spencer Tracy and Clark Gable. Los Angeles felt meant to be to Farmer. Once he saw girls in hot pants there on a warm Friday night for the first time, No. 2 choice Drake, in Des Moines, Iowa, or any fallback, flew out of his teenage-boy consciousness. Spending much of the next day at Disneyland and the night watching Ray Charles own the room in theater-in-the-round in Anaheim made the long weekend complete.

Farmer in May 1969 didn't talk to a single possible future teammate and so much as saw only one, Henry Bibby, as Bibby jogged at the UCLA baseball stadium. The head coach at every other recruiting visit either picked Farmer up at the airport or dropped him off for the flight home, but he didn't meet Wooden until Sunday, the third day in Los Angeles, and only in Wooden's office in one-on-one conversation about family, poetry, education, and work ethic. No basketball, and no subsequent ride to the airport from the head coach.

Nothing could sway him from UCLA even though the program didn't seriously recruit him until late, had a campus with players unavailable to meet during his visit, and where he'd be among a student body strongly antigovernment. Even being proudly pro-military in a time of its peak unpopularity at colleges didn't faze him. The son of a staff sergeant, the younger brother of a solider serving in Europe, the highest-ranking student officer at Manual High School after three years of Army ROTC, Farmer loved order and the polished brass. The same battalion commander Farmer chose to register for the draft on a Wednesday in Denver, because Wednesdays were Uniform Day at Manual, and he could proudly return to classes with a look to match his beaming mood. It was just after he watched other signees limp into the office with fake injuries as dodge attempts, doctor's notes at the ready. Larry Farmer, a guy who loved James Brown, the Temptations, most anything Motown . . . and John Philip Sousa patriotic marches.

Walton was so immediately impressive that comparisons to Alcindor began almost as soon as he transformed himself from the curly, thick red hair draped around his shoulders to the Wooden-approved groomed look in time for team photos the day before practice opened. That Walton was also the instant equal of Alcindor in wanting to dodge the spotlight added to the similarities, complete with Walton declining a request for a solo photo. He would pose with teammates or not at all. "It really hurts me to look at the guys and know that no matter how much I want it to be the UCLA team, it will be the Walton Gang," he said. "You can't change that." The public relations staff in the athletic department were just as realistic in understanding that attempting to promote the Bruins as the Bibby Bunch in a nod to seniority would be pointless. The Walton Gang it was.

Being weighed against the proven greatness of Alcindor at a time Walton had no credibility beyond an encouraging start was just as maddening. He may have been brash enough to sneer back at inanimate Pennsylvania high school star Tom McMillen on the *Sports Illustrated* cover the year before, but Walton's worship of all things basketball included an appreciation of the Russells, Chamberlains, and Alcindors who big-footed before him, a genuine reverence that never left even when he did have a legitimate claim in later years. Wooden saw Walton resenting such talk as an early factor in bad relations with the press that would continue all four seasons, and the comparison would later turn Walton hostile. Being placed on Mt. Olympus as a sophomore was excessive to him and, more than anything, ridiculous.

That he was already a better leader as a freshman than Alcindor ever would be, certainly in college and maybe through the brilliant NBA career that followed, was indisputable. Walton may eventually have become a superstar defender and arguably the best passing center in NCAA history, capable of winning games on both ends of the court, but the passion that set the tone for teammates was his greatest asset, Harshman said. "He's better than Alcindor because he plays with more enthusiasm," Tarkanian would say. Unexpressive Alcindor came off as not playing hard all the time, sophomore Walton as so jubilant in basketball that his spirit alone could boost a roster.

"He is a young man of many varying moods," Wooden said. "His attitudes change from day to day. He is not unlike Lewis in that he is a very private person who does not let people get too close to him, and who has strong convictions about life. People wonder about him because he's so outspoken. When he speaks, he speaks with conviction. He lets you know where he stands at any given time. We do not stand on the same side on every issue, but that is no reason we cannot respect one another. For instance, Bill and I disagree on a number of things, but we have no disagreements. Like Lewis, he is extremely coachable and cooperative on [the] court and a completely unselfish player."

Walton, his coach came to conclude, "is a most unusual young man," and not in a bad way. "It bothers Bill to be in the limelight all the time" was how older brother Bruce put it. "He doesn't like to talk about himself and thinks whatever he accomplishes is a team thing. There's a lot of pressure on him and I don't think he likes that." When reporters tried to praise him as the next great center, as a worthy descendant in the lineage of Bill Russell to Wilt Chamberlain to Lew Alcindor—now Kareem Abdul-Jabbar as his name change became official in 1971—Walton insisted they only said it because he is white.

"I'm just starting in sports and already I'm being called a superstar. It's just not right," he said. "I don't like it when everyone wants to interview me and no one pays any attention to my teammates. Without them, I'd be nothing. This is a team game, and I'm just one of the guys on our team. I think I've gotten twice as much publicity as I deserve because I'm the Great White Hope in a game that has been dominated by blacks. If I were black, I would just be another center who plays well. In basketball, I want to be judged by my play, not my color. I'm white, and I wouldn't blame the blacks if they took up arms and went into outright revolt. If a black man drove by and gunned me down right now, I'd figure it was all right because of what whites have done to blacks."

The longer the 1971–72 season went, the greater the upward trajectory from promising varsity newcomer to instantly dominant the less chance Walton had of getting his wish of a spotlight for the entire team. "He's the best college basketball player I've ever seen," Santa Clara coach Carroll Williams said. "He's better at both ends of the court than Lew Alcindor was—he dominates like no college player in the history of the game. And that includes Bill Russell, who I played against." "That kid, Bill Walton— he destroys you," Stanford coach Howie Dallmar said. "He's better than Bill Russell at their competitive age and development."

"Are you saying that Walton is the most impressive center—inside—that you've ever seen?" a reporter followed up.

Dallmar paused. "Yeah." He at least allowed, "Of course, there was Alcindor, too." Some of Dallmar's players came to see their coach among several in the profession who privately considered Wooden hypocritical, but nothing would get him to tone down praise for Walton.

By the time Walton blocked his man's first 3 shots, rejected 5 other Washington attempts after that, scored 27 points, and grabbed 24 rebounds in an easy home win over the Huskies, his last best hope for slowing the trend was gone. "Well," Wooden said, "Lewis was an overwhelming player, but so is Bill. It's hard to imagine anybody playing a better game than Bill did." The same Harshman who while at Washington State poked Wooden about forfeiting the three years of Alcindor on varsity, this time, as Washington coach, wondered, "Alcindor? I kinda wish he was back; that Walton was fantastic."

Not only that, Harshman said, this had already proven to be the best of all Wooden teams, even before the NCAA tournament as the ultimate proving ground. The group that jetted from Los Angeles to Portland easily won the first eight games, sometimes doubling the opponent's scoring total. The supposed test of No. 6 Ohio State coming to Pauley ended in a 26-point difference. Notre Dame and new coach Digger Phelps, in his sixth game at his dream job, were sent home with a 114–56 scorching as the Bruins pressed and played their starters late into the second half, so much unnecessary bloodshed to Phelps that he crouched in front of his bench late in the avalanche, looked down the sideline, caught the eye of Gary Cunningham, and mouthed two words.

Fuck you.

Phelps saw the respected and well-liked assistant coach, an enemy to no one, do a double take, then stayed locked on Cunningham while motioning to Wooden as if to say, "And the guy next to you, too!" When Wooden sought Phelps out after the postgame media sessions to explain the Bruins were trying to sharpen for the conference schedule just after final exams ate up most of their usual practice time, Phelps grew more irate. He was sure Wooden was lying about running up the score to avenge the Notre Dame win eleven months earlier in South Bend, the lone UCLA blemish in a championship season.

"John," Phelps responded, "you do anything you have to do to beat me, because someday I am going to kick your ass." Phelps may have been, even at twenty-nine, a showman and a master motivator seizing any opening to inspire his capsized program to success, and as a younger coach he studied and admired Wooden's work on the 1964 and '65 championships in particular, but the slow burn ignited on December 22, 1971, was real and lasting. Turning and walking away without allowing for further Wooden explanation emphasized the anger created by the previous hours, a seething that stayed with Phelps for years.

. . .

What would have been an impressive 8-0 start for any UCLA team held special significance for the young team handling the transition to varsity life with ease amid national expectations and while second only to the Dodgers in fan interest among Los Angeles teams. Even in the regular season of a record 33-game winning streak, the Lakers without a championship since arriving from Minneapolis in 1960 "had very few fans, and when they showed up for the game, they were rooting for the other team,"

Jerry West said. "We were trying to make our own way. We were like explorers, to be honest, in the town." "They far overshadowed us and they overshadowed a lot of professional teams because of their excellence," West said, to the point that the Lakers even with a roster with greats West and Elgin Baylor felt like the little brother in L.A. hoops.

The boisterous support that carried from the Alcindor era to the Wicks-Rowe-Bibby generation gained a fresh level of excitement with Walton, who was a lit sparkler on the court. Not merely an injection of emotions that would have been trigger enough, he gave the fast break Wooden demanded and fans loved a dimension never seen before as a center who got a rebound and whipped the first long throw. The dual act of controlling the loose ball and firing the pass would sometimes come before he even touched the ground. Demoralizing opponents with blocked shots had a similar effect on crowds as Walton needed less than half a season to become one of the best Bruin defenders ever at any position, and maybe already ahead of senior Lew Alcindor among big men. Customers thirsting for blood became such a factor that visiting coaches began game-planning for the crowd, not just the team, and opting to go minutes at a time without taking a shot to dull the ravenous Pauley faithful into boredom. At home, players noted, their same overmatched roster might be given different instructions.

"When we were up by twenty points, we kept pouring it on," backup center Swen Nater wrote. "When we were down by ten points, we raised our game and made the comeback to win. Nothing could rattle us, no fan, score or official. Nothing could cause us to think it was hopeless or in the bag. We were tough, as tough as nails." Players might have decided Wooden was a lost cause as a square, but, Nater continued, "UCLA players were mentally tough because our coach was. Nothing rattled John Wooden. Nothing affected his concentration. He was a tough son of a gun."

Going on the road after eight home contests and five weeks of schedule became an important test, even without, again, the curiosity factor to match that of varsity rookie Alcindor in Pullman. The sophomores of 1971–72 heading to Oregon the first week of January, Corvallis on Friday and Eugene on Saturday in typical back-to-back conference scheduling, would also get the introduction to away-game John Wooden, a bigger threat than most opponents. The Bruins had flown from Los Angeles to Portland, bused two overcast hours south through the Willamette Valley to their Corvallis hotel on a chilly afternoon, and prepared to step into the lobby when Wooden rose from his seat near the front. "We didn't have a meeting about this before we left," he said, "but because this is our first road trip, I hope you will act as gentlemanly as you do in your homes. You're always to be on your special best behavior with those you come in contact. And I want to impress upon you to keep your rooms neat—even after you check out. This is directed at two of you—and you know who you are—who had to be called back to your rooms about this last year." He did not identify the culprits by name. Otherwise, wanting players to be in at least pairs, for safety, is one of the few rules he insisted on during travels. Wooden previously even relaxed his policy that anyone caught smoking would be kicked off the team, "but I hope I don't find out about it."

The same basic routines that were repetitive for previous teams became, in the opening week of 1972 in western Oregon, important insights into how the young roster would handle the first attempt at special best behavior and hostile crowds. The Bruins practiced for an hour in Corvallis and returned to the motel well ahead of the ten thirty curfew Wooden had used for years, home and road, with the understanding players could keep the lights on for homework and stay up after Pauley games to watch the 11:00 p.m. tape-delay broadcast popular around town. Trainer Ducky Drake, outwardly the tough cop but more softy with a big heart, was Wooden's enforcer with eyes and ears everywhere to catch truants who dared the clock. A Bruin on a trip years before walked into his hotel room to find Drake sitting on the bed as the grim reaper and offering only to let the guilty party choose whether to be sent home that night or the next day, before the player needed a couple minutes to beg his way to freedom without apparently Wooden being informed.

All Bruins were accounted for in Corvallis to stick to the routine: 10:30 breakfast, 3:30 supper, a pregame nap, and a bus to Gill Coliseum for the 8:00 p.m. tip-off and victory over the Beavers. Another win the night in Eugene included a national-television broadcast that was a larger showcase for the new Bruins. An expanded audience that witnessed Oregon center Al Carlson elevate to release a hook and Walton simply take the ball out of his shooting hand just before release.

Going back on the road later in January for more than a regional release, seven players arrived for the Midwest trip with identical jackets, the obvious result of a spending spree by someone outside the program that Morgan and Wooden either did not detect or chose to ignore. They likewise did not say anything when numerous players got drunk at O'Hare Airport before boarding the 747 for the ride home in first class after beating Loyola and Notre Dame, though given Wooden's history of blocking attempted drink orders on other occasions, he may simply have missed the signs in Chicago. Alcohol in public would likely have been too much for the coach who understood what Bruin basketball meant for the image of the entire university.

The same concerns from the Alcindor years of defenses resorting to rough play to counter a star center who could not be countered with normal strategy increased in 1971–72 as the nimble Walton outraced, outjumped, and outsmarted most every man given the impossible assignment to slow him down. While Jim Nielsen knew to back off in freshman practices, after all, varsity opponents would not be as considerate of Walton's injury history. Being smacked in the mouth on a hook shot against USC ("That was the cheapest shot I've ever seen," Walton said) led to a tooth being knocked out and Wooden demanding Trojan Ron Riley be ejected, even though officials did not call a foul. Walton said he got elbowed five or six other times in a game so physical that Wooden considered taking out all his starters earlier than planned to avoid potential injuries. Walton later in the season had to personally call time-out to gather himself after being hit in the ribs against Cal State, Long Beach, a move that sent Wooden to meet with 49er assistant coach Dwight Jones in front of the scorer's table to declare Long Beach's tactics disgraceful and unethical.

"Every year we play Long Beach," Bibby said, "we get slugged."

"That little squirt was mouthing off all day," Long Beach forward Leonard Gray said back. "But I couldn't do anything because he's small and I'm supposed to be bad guy. If I'd have done anything, I'd have gotten run out of the country to Cuba." Walton, Gray added, is "a crybaby," a reputation built in one varsity season that would follow the rest of his college career. "Walton is strong, but you can't touch him," Louisville center Al Vilcheck said another time in 1971–72. "The officials put him in a cage. He cries a lot. I just don't feel a man of his ability should cry so much."

The college game had been growing more violent anyway, from crowds around the country turning especially nasty and scuffles in games seeming to increase in frequency and severity. The issue became unavoidable after an Ohio State–Minnesota street brawl in January in Minneapolis, setting new standards for ugliness, resulted in two Buckeyes with concussions, two hospitalized overnight, and multiple sightings of players being kicked in the head and groin while on the ground. "I never saw anything closer to the jungle than last night at Williams Arena," said Vern Mikkelsen, retired after a ten-year career with the Lakers. "The guys I felt sorry for were the cops. They looked just like a little platoon trying to hold off Napoléon's army. There must have been hundreds of fans who spilled on the court. I actually expected to hear the public address announcer put out a call for the state Civil Defense." A rarely used Minnesota junior forward, Dave Winfield, "leaped on top of [Ohio State's Mark] Wagar when he was down and hit him five times with his right fist on the face and head," *Sports Illustrated* reported. "When the stunned Wagar managed to slip away, a fan pushed him to the floor and another caught him on the chin with a hard punch from the side."

"I believe crowds may have been as mean and severe and critical in the 1950s as they are now," one of the top administrators for high school sports in California said, "but the black-white aspect has changed things." The portion of the state federation that covered much of Los Angeles made it policy to send one white referee and one black referee to games involving black schools. Never two white officials anymore. Unrelated to race, but speaking to the new rage, Wooden walked on the court to a USC fan holding up a baby-blue stuffed Bruin nailed to a cross with the sign THIS IS FOR SAINT JOHN. Someone flung a knife that landed at Perry Wallace's feet as the first black player in the Southeastern Conference lined up for a free throw in Alabama. At least some humor was attached to fans showering the cocky Villanova guard Chris Ford with dozens of hot dogs launched from the stands during pregame introductions in Philadelphia. Schools upgrading from tight quarters that turned into claustrophobic pressure cookers of heat and noise, as UCLA did in moving from the B.O. Barn to Pauley Pavilion, did little to ease tensions.

Well, Wooden said, "Students are quick to rebel at anything now," and it creates a chain reaction, one basic game moment leading to a larger second retaliation rather than players keeping their composure as before. "The principal turmoil among youngsters is not the fault of the youngsters but of those who have sired them," Wooden decided. "We have examples of the permissiveness of the coaches and we have examples of the permissiveness of parents. As coaches, how can we preach self-control, one of the great values of basketball, and then act like maniacs ourselves at times?" Student sections early in the 1970s, the chairman of the NCAA basketball rules committee seconded, are "relatively undisciplined compared with previous generations. I think people are more permissive now. They do a lot of things they didn't do ten years ago." At least it got no worse at Pauley than a generic two-man fight between Bruin Swen Nater and John Stege of Santa Clara in January.

"In past years you might get four or five boos a half," Ernie Filiberti, a senior Pacific-8 Conference referee, said, "and most were justified because you probably blew that many calls. Now they're booing you before the game starts. It's a sign—tear down all authority figures."

. . .

Utah State assistant turned Washington State assistant Dale Brown had the welcome assignment of picking up John Wooden at the Bruins' Pullman hotel several hours before tip-off in dreaded Bohler Gym where a live Cougar mascot was caged outside with fans taunting visiting teams with "Feed 'em to Butch! Feed 'em to Butch!" The WSU booster club went easier on Wooden in the banquet hall of middle-aged men in business suits, women in nice dresses, and kids taking advantage of the Washington's birthday holiday on a Monday. The Cougar Club may have presented him with a pair of red earmuffs in playful promise of the noise to come that night, drawing a smile from Wooden, but was also a rapt audience eager for his views on the

ABA, the current hoops scene, and campus turmoil. Pom-pom girls in scarlet and gray, the school colors, even led a cheer for the enemy: "W! . . . O! . . . O! . . . D! . . . E! . . . N!" hours before thousands would try to scream him deaf.

Leaving the shoebox with a 30-point victory and his hearing helped drive Wooden to drop all pretense and, skipping over merely outing himself as a lamebrain from the beginning, declare, "I'd have to say at this stage this team certainly is as good as any I've had at UCLA. If we go on to win the title, I'd have to rank this team as stronger than any I've ever coached." While the conclusion could not have been a shock as the Bruins showed themselves more talented and deeper than any Alcindor roster and just as energetic as the swarming, aggressive Goodrich-Hazzard squad, the level of honesty outside the Wooden home or the coaches' office was unexpected. The calendar showed February, after all, with two weeks and three road games still remaining before just the start of the tournament and needing four more wins after that before a champion would be crowned in Los Angeles. Even more surprising, the coach previously and often angered by outsiders raising expectations with premature praise had inexplicably invited more grief on himself in two sentences than any columnist with a dozen barrels of ink. John Wooden with a roster loaded with sophomores unwittingly set himself up for another two seasons of needing to improve on the best club in school history, and probably in college basketball history.

His friend Marv Harshman agreed that people were watching the best of all Bruin squads, thanks most of all to the talented second unit, and Cal coach Jim Padgett said, "I'm not sure there is a way to beat this team." Not stopping there, Wooden made life tougher for Walton in particular with the view that "it's inconceivable to me that anyone has even come close to dominating games like Bill has this season," all the more impressive as Walton silently played through near-constant pain in both knees, not just the left that required surgery in high school. The congenital foot defects diagnosed in later years had already started to cause the chain reaction of repetitive awkward movements and aches up the legs, into the hips and pelvis and the spine.

By the time the regular season ended with a 26-0 record, the offense was averaging the third-most points in the country, the defense was allowing the seventh fewest, and the average margin of victory of 32 points set an NCAA mark. For all his hidden preseason excitement, Wooden had actually undersold the Walton Gang, the ultimate indication of how well the first three months had gone. They were overwhelming to the point of boring, play-by-play man Dick Enberg said in admitting previous Bruins were more exciting to chronicle and that ratings "have to be down this year. The wins are too one-sided. It's such a great team there's no real competition." Wooden turned icy toward Enberg upon learning of the comments, taking it to mean the voice of UCLA basketball and football had defected into rooting for opponents. Wooden, usually accommodating to the media, made his displeasure clear by declining a request for a postgame interview, before Enberg eventually had the chance to explain and the two returned to good terms.

"The NCAA tournament? You mean the UCLA Invitational," Loyola coach George Ireland said as the postseason began, and no one seemed fazed in the 90–58 victory over Weber State that Wooden called a miserable showing. Wooden, though disappointed, retracted nothing, while the chance to play on the springy floor at BYU helped Walton's tender lower body, the reason Provo and Stanford with a similar bounce were his favorite college courts. The victory over Long Beach State two days later was a return to dominating, after the Bruin band, staying in the same hotel as the 49ers, decided it needed to rehearse at 3:00 a.m. on game day and again at 9:00 a.m. Tarkanian finally gave up on sleep and took his team outside to run plays in the parking lot.

The Final Four brought the Bruins full circle, to the Sports Arena and a semifinal against Louisville and Coach Denny Crum. "Where's all that money you promised to pay me under the table last season?" Walton jokingly asked him as the teams stood close in the corridor outside the locker rooms before taking the court as North Carolina and Florida State went into overtime in the first game. Crum in less than a full season had already become a great hire, and his decision to leave rather than wait for Wooden to retire to claim his dream job would prove to be just as wise. But UCLA players, loose and supremely confident in the last moments, still called out in the corridor crowd for Crum to leave the dark side and return to Westwood, just before easily eliminating the Cardinals.

Being a mouthy Bruin came easily to many, certainly more than previous Wooden rosters, especially once the projected success proved accurate and their coach who hated expectations grabbed a megaphone as well. Walton, painfully shy in social situations, could also be quick to talk down to fellow students, adult fans, the media, and others and spent part of the day before the championship game watching Florida State practice while standing close enough to make sure Seminoles center Lawrence McCray spotted him already on patrol. McCray missed several layups during the drills and kept looking over his shoulder to check if Walton saw. Lee needed one varsity game to anger Wooden with a breath of sportsmanship calling the Citadel a very good junior college team after the 56-point win in the season opener. Curtis would have been the boldest of the trash-talkers anyway and walked into the Sports Arena with the added emotional jolt of a Tallahassee native facing his hometown team and several players he had known for years. He then became the backup guard who sparked the 81–76 victory as the finish to a 30-0 season.

"Now I've got a nice gold watch to wear where they live," Curtis said, taunting away.

He considered getting a rare challenge "beautiful" and "freaked out it was so much fun." Lee and Larry Hollyfield, though, were dejected on the bench during the trophy presentation, as if on the losing team, and Bibby was so disappointed by the slim victory that he described winning a third crown as "It gets to be old after a while." He, at least, had the excuse of two previous crowns. But when first-timer Walton came to the pressroom and reporters in back shouted to him to raise the microphone and speak louder, he snapped back, "There are a lot of empty seats up front." Also, he said after the dream of winning a championship as a Bruin had finally come true, "I felt like we lost it."

Wooden for once did not have to remind players to remain humble in victory, not with his morose lot as a final and fitting image of a three-day event that turned additionally sour with opposing coaches wondering if the Wooden machine had become bad for the sport. "They didn't mean it personally," Pepperdine's Gary Colson said, but many "said they thought the fact UCLA keeps on winning is hurting college basketball." One Bruin had already asked Wooden if he'd get off their backs if they lost a game, believing the winning streak at 45 games had become a focus of the coach. If anything, Wooden countered, he planned to be more demanding in 1972–73. Six consecutive titles, eight in nine years, and fourteen months without a loss did not feel like a time of celebration.

. . ᵧ .

Former East Coaster Wilt Chamberlain, relocated to Los Angeles since being traded from the 76ers to the Lakers in 1968, unveiled his custom home in March 1972 after two years and $1.5 million of construction with two hundred tons of stone and enough redwood to build seventeen standard residences. He christened 15216 Antelo Place, ten miles up the 405 from Pauley Pavilion, as Ursa Major in honor of the constellation comprising some of the stars of the Big Dipper, one of Chamberlain's nicknames. The front door was fourteen feet high and two thousand pounds, the cathedral ceiling in the great room was forty-five feet in the air, the mirror over the bed in the master bedroom retracted for open skies, a wall-to-wall waterbed dominated what he called the playroom, views on clear days could reach Catalina Island, twenty-six miles off the coast, and the swimming pool outside was big enough to later be carved into three pools. The project manager heading the transformation from Cold War antiaircraft missile spot in Bel Air to galactical compound called the finished look "Wilt-style," as if needing no further explanation.

The ten thousand square feet of bachelor pad on nearly three acres on a point in the Santa Monica Mountains could have accommodated the 350 guests for the housewarming, but Chamberlain opted for split parties, an easygoing early session followed by an unrestrained gathering for visitors less inhibited. Jerry West saw the breakdown that would become common for Ursa Major bashes as more specific, married couples first and singles preferring late-night activities later. John and Nell Wooden made the drive up the steep, winding private road near Mulholland Drive with the early crowd, surely feeling out of place in such an ostentatious setting with O. J. Simpson, Sugar Ray Robinson, Chick Hearn, and Joe Louis also among the hundreds who passed through at various times.

The season had arguably been Wooden's most successful ever, as former Bruin player and assistant Crum claimed at the Final Four from a position of great credibility. Yet it had also been several months of the same feeling of not fitting in. Wooden was misquoted in an Associated Press report about the Atlantic Coast Conference a month before practice opened and wrote individual letters of clarification to angry readers despite having actually done nothing wrong. The coach, with a good relationship with the media, regardless of holding reporters partly responsible for the unreasonable expectations, in December lashed out at *Los Angeles Herald Examiner* beat writer Doug Krikorian for mocking UCLA's soft early schedule, even though it had been a swipe at Morgan as the man responsible for lining up opponents, not Wooden. "I guess I should apologize for our record over the past eight years," Wooden said, getting defensive when he could have let the snark pass as the rare disappointing comment among tens of thousands of words of positive press each year. "Nothing seems to please people anymore." He called Krikorian at the office the next day to express regret at what for Wooden constituted an outburst and soon made a public mea culpa. And then fellow coaches at the end of 1971–72 blamed his program for hurting college basketball.

Walton's contempt at meeting the media after the championship game continued into the offseason, when Lyle Spencer of the *Santa Monica Evening Outlook*, a friend beyond their working relationship, wrote that the just-completed sophomore season showed Walton had the potential to become the greatest player in basketball history. Even being aware how much Walton hated the Alcindor comparisons as heresy could not prepare Spencer for Walton storming at him inside Lee's apartment when they next saw each other a few days later.

How could you say such a thing? Walton demanded to know. It felt to Spencer more confrontation than conversation.

How could you disrespect Kareem and Chamberlain and Russell?

Spencer was stunned at getting berated for being complimentary.

Wooden's enthusiasm at the start of the season and Walton as an electrical current of joy on the court had so obviously disappeared as the team gathered in the locker room for a final meeting that Wooden "feared" for his star and teammates. The concern seemed to be based on the players' emotional direction, not harm coming to Walton as he grew more outspoken on controversial social issues. "Fellows," Wooden told them, "I'm very proud of you and next year you're going to be even better. We'll know more about each other and what to expect from one another. The Bruins will be a much superior team because of it." Wooden always remembered looking around the room to see smiles and heads shaking in agreement. "But by the time you are seniors," he added solemnly in a quick and unexpected mood shift, "you'll very likely become intolerable."

He left the room without another word.

10

NIXON'S TRAP

Bill Walton may have prided himself on being a nonconformist, or in conforming on the correct side of issues while misguided opponents failed to properly fall in line, but he was the ultimate basketball traditionalist, a contradiction that confounded Wooden for decades to come, concluding, "He seemed to lead two separate lives." Walton by his 1972 offseason had proudly joined the national wave of students railing against U.S. involvement in Southeast Asia and declared no one older than thirty-five should be allowed to become president. Wooden was eventually heard to say he had never seen a better leader on the court or a bigger follower off it, a personality zigzag that took on larger importance as the Bruins began the offseason with a string of six consecutive championships.

Wooden worried about Walton in a way he never did Alcindor during the activism of the 1960s, aware Alcindor thought his decisions through before public stands, while Walton, though also highly intelligent, led with his emotions. The same jet pack of passion that propelled him to become a transcendent player made him a reactionary and even vulnerable in the eyes of the most prominent adults on campus. High-profile Walton is being used by the antiwar faction for publicity, Wooden allowed to Temple assistant coach Don Casey during a quiet moment at one of the several summer basketball clinics Wooden liked to attend to tap into his love of teaching.

Chancellor Charles Young agreed all the way to fingering a specific culprit: Greg Lee, point guard, Walton confidant, and, Young was sure, the real problem behind UCLA basketball's new image predicament.

Concern escalated again on May 9, 1972, with Walton, Lee, Keith Wilkes, and Larry Farmer among the estimated one thousand students who gathered for a noon rally in the heart of campus to protest the White House decision to mine Haiphong Harbor in North Vietnam. The American and state flags were cut down from poles before the group, many familiar to Walton, passed through several buildings while chanting slogans, confronted Young with demands classes be halted, and headed down Westwood Boulevard, the main north-south artery to the school. Phones began ringing in the basketball offices, calls alerting coaches that the linchpin of the program was part of the mobile crowd and perhaps in harm's way. Passing through Westwood Village, the commercial center of the university, the pack reached Wilshire Boulevard after a mile on foot, made a sharp right turn at the major thoroughfare with an eye on the ultimate beachhead, Interstate 405, a half mile in the distance. Taking a major Los Angeles freeway would be a publicity jackpot.

It took only marching into a waiting line of police in riot gear, adorned with shields and billy clubs cocked in hand, the first real sign of resistance, to stop the protesters. The rebels wanted to make a statement, just not at the cost of bodily harm or arrest, and officials estimated their passions had so quickly evaporated that only half of the original one thousand remained. Fifty to one hundred, including Walton, sat in the road and stalled traffic in the normally crowded intersection of Wilshire and Veteran Avenue, shouted opposition to the war, then obediently dissolved a half mile from the finish line, the 405, upon being ordered to withdraw. "They told us we had fifteen minutes to disperse—I told them I only needed one," Farmer said. "I'm a six-six black guy. I didn't want to give them a chance to look past the cute girls in the front row and get to me." Though among the compliant in peaceful retreat, Walton remained defiant enough to later chastise students he knew who did not participate, asking, "Don't you care enough?"

"There's no in-between with Bill," Cunningham said. "Either he did or he didn't. He was either turned off or he was turned on. And if he's turned on, it's a hundred percent. That's the way he is."

The *Daily Bruin*, the school paper, ran an editorial May 10 that led with "Today is the day to strike. Today is not the day for 'business as usual.' Today is not the day to go to class. Today is the day to rally, to march, to close down the university. Because today is the day to end the war." Some students returned to Wilshire and Veteran, some went building to building on campus to shout encouragement to join the new protest, and others, including arguably the best college athlete in the country in any sport, entered the headquarters of the school administration, Murphy Hall. Walton was among the group that fortified overnight positions with most anything heavy and movable, from tables and chairs to trash cans and fire hoses, before leaving the next morning voluntarily and with nothing accomplished.

Contrary to national perceptions of the city, the state, and the UC system as unhinged hotbeds of mobocracy drowning in vice, civil disobedience had for years mostly been the worst of it in Westwood. The deadly shootings of two students in Campbell Hall in 1969 was a dispute over leadership of a Black Studies program, not a protest incident. Elsewhere the same week in May 1972, with the United States in its seventh year of official involvement in Vietnam, police sent tear gas into a crowd of two thousand University of Minnesota students who had attacked with rocks and bottles and burned a car; a gathering of five thousand demonstrators turned violent at the University of Florida as law enforcement was assaulted and protesters in turn clubbed in a melee that stretched sixteen blocks; and students tried to burn down an armory in College Park, Maryland. A rally of nearly three thousand people at the University of Wisconsin resulted in trash fires and Molotov cocktails being hurled at police and campus buildings amid widespread clubbing, a little less than two years after a car bomb there killed a thirty-three-year-old innocent bystander. (Two brothers involved in packing the Ford Econoline van and parking it next to the target building in 1970, one a student pilot, had previously stolen a two-seat Cessna from an airport and dropped three jars of flammable liquid on an army ammunition plant thirty-five miles from campus, although none of the glasses detonated on impact.) In California, antiwar protesters and law enforcement with batons fought at Stanford at night, Berkeley marchers pelted police with rocks and bottles, and UC Santa Barbara students shut down their local airport with a mass turnout.

Los Angeles' two biggest universities experienced no such volatility, no matter what opponents' recruiters claimed to boil parents of high school seniors into a panic. A plan to snarl traffic at Los Angeles International Airport that had circulated among several colleges in the region, leading organizers to hope for one thousand cars and three thousand students to create a disruption to feed the nightly news, essentially ended when authorities pulled drivers over for going too slow around the horseshoe road. Most sagging demonstrators got frustrated and departed, leaving approximately two hundred who survived the brutal police tactic of pen and paper. End of protest. Cops, beyond campus law enforcement, hadn't even been called to UCLA for an uprising in two years by the time Walton spotted a fresh gathering of fellow nonconformists midday on May 11, a few hours after exiting the uneventful Murphy Hall takeover.

Chancellor Young even then initially called for reinforcements only because the fire department, considering troubling scenarios as protests continued around them, insisted it would not handle a gas spill without better protection in case the mood turned violent. The gas had been splashed upon the ground, after all, when demonstrators overturned three-wheeled carts that janitors drove around campus. Police did keep order for the firemen, but when two hundred students soon sat in the street and refused to disperse, campus officers in the lead and city cops at their backs advanced. Rocks and bottles flew their way, before protesters gave ground and entered the building, where students inside turned a commandeered fire hose on the lawmen in pursuit.

Furniture began to rain from windows freshly broken on the second floor of Royce Hall, tables and lecterns and chairs, some meeting a splintery end on the grass below. Police with helmets and nightclubs formed a skirmish line. Many students got the message: Retreat. Others didn't. Walton, among the few dozen didn'ts, described his role as nonviolent and nondestructive, and others spotted nothing worse than removing wood barricades in some spots outside the administration building and placing obstacles at other points. But he ignored commands to evacuate. The helmets and nightclubs, reading a different tenor compared to the peaceful and brief sit-in on Wilshire a couple days before, were in no mood to be patient. Arrests were made.

Six weeks after winning his first national championship and six and a half months before opening the 1972–73 schedule with the possibility of breaking the NCAA record of 61 consecutive wins, the overwhelming preseason favorite for Player of the Year was loaded on a bus in handcuffs one hundred yards from where the John Wooden Center would open in 1983. "The whole world is watching!" Walton yelled while being taken away. Four other detainees about to be loaded in, three wearing the same bracelets and one being escorted toward the vehicle with the assistance of two officers, one on each arm bent hand to clavicle behind his back, came up to Walton's chest at best. The white helmets and black visors of a couple of the cops may have reached his shoulders just before Walton ascended the few steps at the front passenger side with a snowcap of bushy red hair and still in conversation with a lawman to his right.

Walton, sitting handcuffed on the bus with LOS ANGELES POLICE DEPARTMENT painted across the side and L.A.P.D. across the width above the front windshield, spotted Young surveying the grounds from the main quad with a mix of sadness and anger.

"Fuck you, Chuck!" Walton shouted out the window.

He held up a middle finger for Young as well. In the middle of the mayhem unfolding on his campus, Young internally laughed off both personal attacks, the spoken and the nonverbal message, as the stupid but harmless acts of a college kid caught up in a moment.

The chancellor should actually have been regarded as an ally as Walton came to realize in later years, often apologizing to Young in the decades to come. Young was practically one of them, a UC Riverside undergrad, a UCLA master's and PhD, still only forty after three and a half years on the job, liked by students and respected within the athletic department. He attended most home games for basketball and football, was well-known as a vocal supporter of both, and often stood near coaches on the sideline at the

Coliseum. He enjoyed Wooden personally and grasped what the dynasty in motion meant for the university in money and national branding. Young, a member of the Air National Guard at sixteen after lying about his age to enlist, grew up a Democrat, was against American involvement in Southeast Asia and in favor of advancing civil rights. He was known to buy pizzas while chatting with students during peaceful demonstrations in a time of campus leaders elsewhere needing security. Walton had no reason to dislike Young other than the job title that automatically branded him as Establishment.

By the evening of May 11, Young was even personally working to get Walton released from jail in Van Nuys soon after watching the long-repurposed school bus lumber away from the middle of campus. The chancellor's office became the command center for phone calls, mostly with the LAPD, and Walton was out on bail before nightfall after what he called "a few unpleasant and boring hours," thanks in part to the man he had just treated as an enemy. Walton remained intentionally vague into his seventies on who bailed him out—some reports said brother Bruce Walton along with Sam Gilbert, others claimed Wooden—but insisted Wooden drove him back to campus with a stern lecture before Walton soon faced criminal charges and a possible university suspension that could cost him games.

"He got special treatment," Young said. "We weren't fools. We didn't want to ruin the basketball program over that incident. The other silly kinds of things that he did, like the beard and one thing or another, they were stupid, but they didn't hurt anybody. They didn't create problems for the campus. They created problems for him that could have knocked him off course, but it didn't. You have to say bravo to John for how he handled that. But you also have to say bravo to Bill. He dealt with it." Young always considered Walton a good person, just misguided in youthful exuberance and too easily used by others.

Wooden a day after the arrest of the "emotional youngster" said the school, not the basketball program, would handle the discipline for an incident out of season. The court case resulted in Walton pleading no contest and paying a $50 fine. The university, meanwhile, maintained it would leave the school penalty to Dean of Students Byron Atkinson, but with a certainty *Sports Illustrated* made a bad guess in reporting, "The chancellor, some feared, considered throwing Bill Walton right out of school." The chancellor considered no such thing and, if anything, practically laughed at the possibility of the dean handing out a serious punishment. Atkinson was a close Morgan friend, Young had already sent the message that Walton should receive delicate treatment, and the basketball program would not be put in harm's way. Walton got put on two-year probation.

Now a certified rebel with a rap sheet and everything, Walton boasted, "I plan to continue my actions . . . and do everything I can to close this school down." Not only did he never come close, the strife accomplished little if anything—fifty-two were arrested for failure to disperse and one for assault on a police officer, but Walton being taken into custody wasn't mentioned until the eighteenth paragraph in the *Los Angeles Times*' main story. Photographer Jim Ober returned to the *Los Angeles Herald Examiner* office downtown with an exclusive picture of one of the most famous athletes in the country about to step into a police bus, yet no one in the newsroom reacted with much enthusiasm even after realizing that, yes, that really is Bill Walton in cuffs. The horrible day for UCLA was quickly washed away beyond the immediate area as one in an endless string of national campus conflicts, complete with Los Angeles mayor Sam Yorty failing badly at trying to smear Walton as "a Communist dupe."

At least one proud former marine sergeant considered confronting Walton for the serious lapse in judgment while representing Bruin basketball, but the ex-jarhead's father accurately read the angry reaction and instructed Jim Wooden to stand down. "Don't," John told him. "Please don't. I've got this handled." Jim—with a crew cut or closely cropped hair since high school, the captain's personal guard on the aircraft carrier *Bon Homme Richard*, later in charge of a machine-gun platoon in the Third Marine Division based in Japan, out of the service since 1959, a Pauley regular in seasons after—followed instructions. Marine second lieutenant George Morgan, the former basketball manager, the son of a retired marine colonel and Silver Star winner at Iwo Jima, heard of Walton's actions after returning stateside from his Okinawa base weeks later. He was not surprised, knowing Walton, and had no issue with peaceful protests, but was frustrated and disappointed to learn Walton had even a minor role in destruction.

Worst of all for Walton, he had just unwittingly aided the Richard Nixon reelection express. The president at various times referred to his student enemies as "mindless rioters," "professional malcontents," and "these bums, you know, blowing up the campuses" because he believed it and also to stoke the longhairs into protesting in greater numbers. Just as gubernatorial candidate Ronald Reagan had successfully turned occasional mayhem on California campuses into political gains in 1966, the White House of 1972 embraced any chance to frame Nixon as the law-and-order candidate needed to get tough on the unappreciative anarchists riding an education in many cases paid by taxpayers and on the grounds of state schools. He received a briefing paper earlier in the presidency to prepare for increased violence on campuses within months and wrote across the front, "Good!" "The student radicals were always despised," Nixon speechwriter Pat Buchanan said. "They were considered brats who had privileges that none of the working folks had. Here they were, drinking, smoking pot, demonstrating, hanging out at Woodstock. We capitalized on that."

Nixon's trap, Berkeley mayor Warren Widener called it.

Handed six feet eleven inches of example with even more privileges than most, there was no hint of Walton being turned into political fodder by the West Wing, and Jo Haldeman never heard her husband mention the arrest of the best player on his favorite team, either in gloating or disappointment. H. R. Haldeman had lived enough actual political showdowns to not be personally affected by a repeat of the chants Nixon and his senior staff had been hearing for years. If anything, the White House six months before the election would have sent Walton a thank-you card for aiding the landslide win to come. He had stepped right into the trap.

. . .

Wooden, of all people, had an image problem as the Olympic basketball trials began with Walton and Wilkes both declining invitations. Like the Alcindor-Allen-Warren decision four years before, a superstar UCLA center brushing aside the chance to play for the national team came wrapped in a disjointed explanation, this time the NCAA claim that doctors advised against offseason competition to spare the troublesome knees, before Walton copped to "I just don't want to play." Given his medical history and feelings about the Establishment, and nothing in sports screamed Establishment like the self-aggrandizing International Olympic Committee, both may have been true. At least he and the school mostly avoided a repeat of the Alcindor '68 public hell storm, whether because the 1972 version felt less shocking or because of the difference in skin color, but it passed Walton as such a mild breeze that in the future he could not remember if he got hate mail.

The Wilkes decision was barely mentioned in comparison, yet said more: he would probably have accepted an invitation if Wooden had pushed, as the U.S. Olympic Committee requested, but the coach never did. Wooden's distaste for the global sports festival had become that permanent. The 1964 disappointment of Gail Goodrich being cut and four years later supporting his players' Mexico City boycott had by 1972 grown to Wooden speaking out against the selection process and the political nature of the Games as a whole. Plus, the backroom politics Wooden believed harmed the American rosters through the years had grown especially personal as the NCAA proposed Wooden or Dean Smith of North Carolina head the team in Munich, West Germany, while voters from the NAIA, representing smaller universities, the Amateur Athletic Union, junior colleges, and the armed forces gathered behind Adolph Rupp, seventy years old and ailing. The retired Henry Iba, after guiding the United States to gold in 1964 and '68 with a combined 18-0 record, became the compromise choice.

Wooden was wrong that the power struggle among groups vying to control amateur basketball in the United States cost the country much of its top talent—stars remained interested, and the decision by the biggest star two Olympics in a row had nothing to do with organizational infighting. He may have recalled decades later being open to coaching in the summer of 1972, but Wooden at the time indicated only disinterest and may, in fact, have seen more value in working his basketball camps for additional income while being woefully underpaid by his primary employer. The emotional side of Walton came to wish he had participated, "But under the circumstances, it was best that I didn't play. Had I gone through that incredibly demanding schedule all spring and all summer long—the training, the exhibition games, the travel—I wouldn't have been ready for UCLA's next season. The U.S.A. was my country, but UCLA was my team." Nothing, though, could change the perception that a lack of Bruin representation again created the sense among others of "This environment, we're above all this," George Karl, participating as a guard from North Carolina, said many years later, the feel of being lorded over still fresh.

Worse, UCLA basketball was being viewed as unpatriotic. "Of course, when you talk about great college coaches you have to include John Wooden," Celtics legendary General Manager Red Auerbach wrote. "John's a good friend of mine, and I respect him as perhaps the greatest college coach who ever lived. I mean that.

"But I've always had an axe to grind with UCLA: *Why didn't any of those great ballplayers represent this country in Olympic basketball?*

"Stop and think about it. Why? Was it because John wasn't named the Olympic coach? Was it because they didn't care? Was it because he didn't have that kind of control over them? Why? Where was Jabbar, or Alcindor as he was known then? Where was Walton? Where were the great UCLA stars when their country was putting its reputation on the line? Where the hell were those guys?

"I don't hold John accountable for that, but I *do* hold the school accountable. I think UCLA's record in that regard is disgraceful.

"And please don't give me any of that crap about the school being located in a very radical political atmosphere. Bull. The school's located in America, and that should be enough.

"Kentucky kids played. Indiana kids played. Dean Smith's kids [from North Carolina] played. From Michigan, Ohio, all over the place, the great players played and made their country proud. All except the kids from UCLA. Where the hell were they?"

Auerbach's 1985 assessment of being good friends with Wooden overstated their relationship, before the 2004 recasting, more accurate to those who knew, of the men sharing a mutual respect but Auerbach always finding Wooden "a little standoffish. I think it was the Midwesterner in him."

Brooklyn native Auerbach was closer to Dean Smith, Adolph Rupp, and Indiana coach and Wooden critic Bob Knight among prominent college coaches. His appraisal on the Olympic controversy did not change, though: Bruin stars were spoiled, lacked patriotism, and ducked the honor of playing in the Olympics. To Karl, "We, the plebes of basketball, felt they were treating us like an arrogant part of society because of their championships." Walton "not playing for his country left a sour taste in my mouth, and in many others," Knight said, especially since the selection committee appeared willing to let Walton bypass the tryouts and advance directly to the final roster in deference to proven greatness and knee problems.

The lone Bruin who did try out at the Air Force Academy arrived as the antithesis of the image of entitled UCLA. Swen Nater likely had the smallest role on his team of any of the sixty-six candidates for Munich, such an invisible basketball life as a reserve that he rationalized his time in Westwood as "Practices are games to me. I pretend there are two starting lineups. It's the only time I get to show what I can do." His career had been adversity, not privilege, from the incomprehensible rise of a six-seven junior getting cut from the high school team to two years in junior college to being recruited by Wooden with the warning that backing up Bill Walton would mean few opportunities to impact a game. But, the coach added with the same accuracy, working against Walton for two seasons would prepare Nater for the pros better than the fifty or sixty games as a starter at another school. Then, when Nater agreed with the logic and stepped into the massive shadow, rarely to be seen again in blue and gold, "He was kind of pitiful at first," Wooden said.

His personal path was even steeper—born in the Netherlands, from a divorced home, three years in an orphanage, relocated to Southern California with his adoptive parents, and didn't hear about basketball until nine years old. Nater from there was kicked out of junior high for frequent fights, grew disappointed when Wooden's gloomy prediction on playing time came true, then wondered if he should have transferred or turned pro after the first season at UCLA. Nater still became the upbeat teammate known for keeping the Bruins loose, a challenging role as the mood turned humorless. More to the point in summer 1972 on the eastern base of the Rocky Mountains, pitiful had turned into one of the best big men in the country without anyone realizing it, even while not close to the best on his own campus. Not merely the chance to make the Olympic team, the trials would be the first and likely, barring a Walton injury in 1972–73, the only public college showcase Nater would ever have.

He already had the private credibility of pro scouts, unable to learn much from limited game action, watching the backup impress against Walton in UCLA practices, just as Wooden had imagined in the unusual recruiting pitch. Nater as a mobile center who could shoot better than most big men had quietly and quickly turned into a serious prospect in the closed Pauley Pavilion workouts as part of the trajectory that would lead Wooden to eventually say no other Bruin had ever improved as much as Swen Nater. In the reveal among hundreds of coaches, organization executives, and fellow players in Colorado Springs, Nater "was like a superstar," to Jack Herron, representing the armed forces among the many factions of U.S. amateur basketball. "He cleaned up on all those guys." Herron, wanting to spotlight candidates from his group, arranged to have a former air force guard placed on the same team as Nater when the sixty-six players were broken into eight squads, certain that delivering the ball to an offensive talent at center would make Gregg Popovich look good. Knight as their coach rode the referees from the first game and relied so heavily on the relative unknown that Nater in later years often thanked Knight for the spotlight while also finding Knight "to be an exceptional teacher" with a knowledge of the game "in the same league" as Wooden's.

Herron was partly vindicated. Popovich got close to making the team until he was cut despite the roster maneuvers, but Nater in the life-changing two weeks reached the previously unimaginable height of leading vote getter for Munich. "All the other players and coaches trying out for the team kept coming to me and asking how in the world do you ever stop this guy," said USC coach Bob Boyd, an opponent twice the previous season, before laughing and reminding that it's possible the Bruins presented other problems more pressing than how to counter the backup center. Maryland's Tom McMillen, with a much higher profile coming in, got cut, not Nater, as his NBA and ABA draft stock soared by the time the reduced roster left Colorado for a more focused and intense training camp in Honolulu.

The exact location—barracks on the submarine base at Pearl Harbor—was an Iba statement as much as itinerary. The older barracks had been vacated when events in Vietnam changed navy priorities and housing plans. Coaches and officials stayed in officers' quarters. Iba, sixty-eight years old and four years into retirement, wanted a military mindset with a snarling taste for victory, complete with two-a-day practices and difficult living conditions. Two of the potential issues that prompted Walton to decline to play had come true long before the Americans got close to the Olympics. In Nater's case, that meant meals only after the dual workouts, exactly when he and others felt least up to eating. The options became a big lunch following the morning session and a big dinner following the afternoon practice or no full dining.

Unable to get food when hungry, feeling weak and dehydrated, and pushing himself through challenging practices, Nater finally went to Iba to report filthy barrack conditions and, most urgently, a drop from 250 to 230 pounds. When Iba denied Nater's request to eat in the navy mess at other times, Nater, physically spent and coming to grips with the whiplash of the career highlight of Colorado Springs turning into an ordeal in Hawaii, quit. "Now isn't that a hell of a note," Iba said after Nater returned to Southern California and the image of the Bruins of first-class flights reemerged. "That guy has got to be a little squirrelly." Former teammates and other staff members piled on in unusually harsh tones, with one assistant coach, Don Haskins, noting, "Nater wouldn't have liked two-a-days if they'd have been at the Waldorf Astoria," and another, John Bach, calling it "a case of intensity. Instead of getting out here and working two hours and getting the job done, he just wanted to go at his own pace and do it his way. That's why he was a second stringer at UCLA and that's why he was a second stringer on this team."

Bach rushing to condemn conveniently overlooked the real reason Nater didn't start in Westwood—one of the greatest players ever did—and that anyone who improved as much and as fast as Nater did not flinch from work. Plus, a successful 1971–72 in the Wooden system of demanding practices and relentless conditioning drills, albeit in single sessions, indicated Olympic-level fortitude, as any Bruin since 1948 would attest. He wasn't even the only Pearl Harbor camper dismayed at the conditions, just the only one to speak up, and it didn't matter that speaking publicly after returning to Southern California resulted in players being moved to better quarters. In the personal bottom line, Nater had walked away from a good shot at a gold medal in a country that neighbored his birthplace, from the chance to next test himself against some of the best on a global level, and from the rare chance to play meaningful minutes in games, an opportunity that would not come in two UCLA seasons.

Stopping in Los Angeles en route from Honolulu to West Germany sparked chatter among players that Walton might join the team now that the worst of it, the tryouts and especially the two-a-days, had passed. As proof the rumor mill had no credibility, teammates also said they were told Wooden would have agreed to coach if he could take his UCLA roster (not true), that Walton declined to go to the Air Force Academy because the invitation was sent to the school rather than home (not true), and that most coaches turned down the chance to head the team in 1972 out of fear of replacing two-time winner Iba (not true). But just the possibility of Walton as a late arrival generated interest given his standing as the best amateur in the country plus an opening at center, even if the dramatic entrance was never a realistic outcome.

Maryland's McMillen replaced Nater instead on the team that reached Munich as the gold-medal favorite despite the absence of two top centers and North Carolina State star forward David Thompson, who declined an invitation in part to rest a knee injury, in part because he didn't know anyone other than Wolfpack teammate Tom Burleson, and in part because he didn't think he would have a big role. The skill of the twelve-man roster and especially the talent gap compared to most challengers overcame Iba's preference for a slow-drip offense that frustrated players and became additional confirmation that Walton, with a love for speed, had made the right decision to stay home. It would likewise not go unnoticed by the end of the tournament that fast-break proponent Wooden had the playbook the Americans needed, with or without Walton whipping outlet passes or Thompson as an unstoppable scoring option. Even the presence of several future NBA guards, including Doug Collins of Illinois State emerging as a U.S. star and an Iba favorite, could not convince the coach to move into the fast lane, insisting defense would carry the Americans.

Pool play ended September 3 with a 99–33 victory over Japan and a 7-0 record, followed by four days off to prepare for the start of the single-elimination medal round. North Carolina State center Tom Burleson, a success story similar to Nater who had worked himself from project to difference maker, returned from a day of sightseeing on September 5. Seeing an unusually long line at the checkpoint to enter the Olympic Village, which was rare after weeks of flimsy security, Burleson spotted an opening in the parking garage many had used before as a shortcut to U.S. housing. He and a couple Italians on the same route brushed past a German guard with a rifle who spoke no English, then another.

A third sentry, with an obvious command of the language, stopped them.

"Son," he told Burleson, "you're in the wrong place at the wrong time." The player followed the order to put his hands on the wall, all seven feet two inches of him frightened, as the guard put a gun to his back.

Nine Israeli athletes, coaches, and officials taken hostage by Palestinian terrorists in Village dorms before dawn were being marched blindfolded through the garage to buses for a ride to helicopters and then a hop to a suburban airport for a 727 to Cairo. Burleson looked left to see the two Italians on the ground, guns also at their backs. Burleson glancing at one of the eight kidnappers about sixty feet away prompted the guard to move the weapon to the back of Burleson's head. Burleson, praying to God to allow him to get to his room, staring so intently at the wall that small blemishes seared into his memory, could hear the hostages shuffling toward the vehicles. He could hear them crying.

Burleson learned with everyone else that an incompetent rescue attempt at the airport by West German authorities in the first hours of September 6 resulted in the death of all nine hostages, a West German police officer, and five terrorists, in addition to the two Israelis killed during the initial takeover. Walton watched on TV from California in horror. Competition halted for a day, before the U.S. basketball team beat Italy to earn a trip to the gold-medal game against the Soviet Union.

The Americans had mostly gone unchallenged the first eight games, but the Soviets had talent and, more importantly, experience playing together, an advantage against a young roster in its first tournament. The most controversial ending in Olympic basketball history followed, with Doug Collins making two free throws to give the United States a 50–49 lead, the USSR throwing the ball in for a final possession, then a second inbounds play when that failed, and then a third the Soviets finally turned into a last-second layup for a stunning victory. The officiating had been so blatantly one-sided to deliver a Soviet victory and the rules so poorly interpreted that the United States refused to accept the silver medal they insisted they did not deserve.

Iba had also badly mismanaged his roster by keeping one of the generation's best defenders, Bobby Jones, on the bench for the final USSR possessions, while also refusing to put in seven-two Burleson to block the vision and maybe even the pass of the Soviet player needing to throw the ball far downcourt. "If he plays," forward Jim Forbes said of Walton, "all of this becomes academic." Nater could have been enough to push the Americans over the top as well, to get far enough ahead that a final play would not have mattered.

Richard Nixon finished his landslide reelection victory on November 7, about three weeks after UCLA returned to practice in advance of a season Wooden was secretly anticipating more than most realized. Adding to the intrigue, Walton was growing more outspoken than ever, with no sign of retreat.

11

FORCE DU JOUR

John Wooden took bites from a slice of the cake brought to celebrate the start of practice for his silver-anniversary season and pronounced himself ready at age sixty-three to be on the job at least two more years and maybe longer, health willing. The previous five months of the superstar center being arrested, two Bruins skipping the Olympic trials, and a third quitting after seemingly making the team left him so unfazed, in fact, that Wooden for the first and only time forecast a perfect record. "Some people enjoy doing crossword puzzles; I liked predicting the outcomes of a season's worth of games." He wrongly projected at least one loss in 1963–64, 1966–67, and 1971–72, but ahead of 1972–73 saw the potential for a historically good team and allowed himself to join the expectations game and imagine grand possibilities.

Matching Wooden's mood in advance of the milestone season, customers three weeks later began lining up on a Monday at 3:00 p.m. for student tickets that would go on sale on Wednesday at 9:00 p.m. The queue soon stretched to include approximately one hundred hopefuls spending Tuesday night through Wednesday morning outside Pauley Pavilion in the rain. The rivalry football game the same week generated such little campus interest by comparison that few UCLA BEAT USC T-shirts sold for $3.95 in the bookstore display next to the ARCHIE BUNKER FOR PRESIDENt and LOVE THY NEIGHBOR (BUT DON'T GET CAUGHT) shirts.

The Bunker candidacy did have promise—America's favorite TV bigot received votes at the 1972 Democratic convention to be the nominee for vice president, as did Mao Tse-tung and the wife of the former *Republican* U.S. attorney general, while a senator from Alaska both nominated and seconded himself to be George McGovern's running mate. In Westwood, though, "Most people look at football players as ordinary students," explained John Sandbrook, a *Daily Bruin* writer. "Basketball players are super celebrities." It was an unfair fight, of course, a football team near the end of an 8-3 season being measured against Wooden's program in an era when fans made Final Four hotel reservations at the start of seasons. Plus, enough apathy existed in other areas, not just football, that the traditional balloting for homecoming queen had been scrapped in 1970 and replaced, in buffoonery that would make Democrat delegates proud, by a pet contest. Boa constrictor Pussy Galore, named for a James Bond *Goldfinger* character, beat out a fruit fly, a rabbit endorsed by the school paper, a fat beagle in sunglasses and a scarf, and a borzoi hunting dog.

Administrators hoping to nudge the campus away from an atmosphere of protest and disinterest rolled out Bruin Week in mid-November—they brought in comedian Joan Rivers, who drew fifteen hundred to two thousand to a Student Union ballroom, an improv group, and multiple dance events to stress an upbeat atmosphere. Wooden's troupe did its part with the Varsity Preview game, the preseason exhibition that replaced the varsity-freshman game once the ban on first-year basketball and football players competing at the top level was lifted earlier in 1972. The new format was mostly a glorified scrimmage of players switching between the Blues and the Golds, but also the important assessment of Walton appearing as focused as ever on the court in his first public basketball setting since the arrest, the Olympics decision, and a summer vacation of hitchhiking and backpacking through the western United States and Canada.

Walton and Keith Wilkes as juniors, the contrasting styles of Greg Lee and Tommy Curtis as options to replace Henry Bibby at point guard, Walton's brilliant passing making him a third distributor, the valuable if understated contributions from Larry Farmer and Larry Hollyfield, the lightning development of Swen Nater, and the promise of sophomores Dave Meyers and Pete Trgovich had the potential to surpass 1971–72 as the greatest of all Wooden teams. Walton, the most super of the celebrities, returned sure it would happen. Wooden, the center of it all, embraced the potential with the constant energy of pushing the Bruins practice after practice to punch the accelerator.

"Okay, that's starting to become acceptable," he told players. "Now let's see you do it again. But FASTER this time."

The emphasis on speed delighted Walton as someone who shared the love of constant movement on offense. But the massive long-term implications of his happiness being tied to the point-guard decision could not be known at the time in the absence of the slightest hint of the storm forming, and especially not with the chance to touch immortality—Greatest Wooden Team Ever—right in front of them; even Wooden himself, a preparation savant, a genius at visualizing lineup combinations, could not have been able to understand the stakes as he weighed Lee against Curtis.

Lee brought the disciplined ballhandling Wooden desired, the dependability of passing to the right spot at the right time, feeding Walton and Wilkes through sound decisions, as well as a feel for the game that he had as the son of a high school coach. At six-four, he also had a five-inch height advantage over Curtis. Being a smart-ass willing to show it publicly guaranteed Lee would not be a personal favorite, but he was a Wooden-type point guard and had the respect of teammates to step into the vacated Bibby leadership role. And as critical as anything early in their third season together, Walton preferred Lee, by a lot.

The two were close friends from the beginning, the freshman sensation from San Diego and the fellow rookie from Los Angeles' San Fernando Valley who would get him the ball. Lee lobbed to Walton at the rim with such precision that the early days of alley-oop passes turned into an unstoppable offensive weapon, only with Walton prohibited from finishing with a dunk for an exclamation point. They were equally in sync off the court, with Lee happy to carry conversations when the stutter made Walton want to melt into the walls. While Lee came from inland Reseda, he had talent on the sand to later become a beach volleyball star and shared an outdoorsy vibe with the big man, who despite the famous ocean swells of his hometown was drawn more to biking and backpacking.

Together, Walton and Lee became the emotional center of the locker room, Walton as the franchise player constantly promoting team play with a fountain of energy and Lee his most trusted partner. As had become obvious to no less than the university chancellor and would become apparent again in the future, their voice, usually one and the same, carried.

The most valuable player in the country had also by the start of 1972–73 turned as anti-Curtis as he was pro-Lee, pushing the lineup debate to a place of friction. To Walton, believing the issue went beyond standing up for his friend, Curtis was selfish and wanted to show off, a ball stopper who killed the flowing offense Walton and, supposedly, Wooden wanted. "Whatever playing time Tommy Curtis got—ever—was way too much," Walton eventually wrote. Walton for years publicly bashed Curtis more than any other teammate at any level and probably more than any dozen of his other least favorite teammates combined.

Walton was not alone in his assessment of Curtis as practically the opposite of the Wooden ideal in style of play and personality, but Curtis had an advantage in speed and was better in the pressing defense for a coach who prioritized fleet athletes and squeezing opponents. Wooden also remembered several occasions the previous season of teammates appreciating boisterous Curtis as an energy boost, an emotional injection becoming increasingly necessary as constant easy wins lulled the Bruins to boredom. No jolt was more important, of course, than against Florida State for the 1972 title, particularly good timing for Curtis as the most recent game as Wooden considered the fifth starter to go with Walton, Wilkes, Farmer, and Hollyfield.

"Wooden inhibits the individual," Curtis said. "We're all different, but he punches out copies. My game is inhibited now, and I'm not the player I was. But I'm the player he wants. He wants to win. So do I. He knows the best way. He's proven it. So I have to go his way. But it's no fun to play as a machine instead of as a person. I'm small, but I hope to play pro ball just to see if I can still play my old way." In the bottom line, Curtis rationalized, "I've bent to his way. Everyone does. You do or you don't play and we all want to play. I have moves I haven't used yet, but he won't let me use them. I passed behind my back one game and he pulled me right out of the game."

Going with Curtis as the opening-night starter created the first real tension between Walton and Wooden. The irreplaceable coach and the irreplaceable center had a good working relationship from the outset, but without the deep personal bond that came in later decades, similar to the Wooden-Alcindor path. Whatever conflicts previously existed were either minor issues blown into something larger (Walton unhappy at needing his hair cut to the standards of Bruin basketball) or ruled beyond Wooden's scope (Walton being arrested). But disliking the point guard assigned to get him the ball was a serious hoops matter with the potential to damage play with Greatest Wooden Team Ever barely underway.

Plus, Walton was growing bored with the lack of competition, usually seeing backup Ralph Drollinger as a greater challenge than opposing starters. (Drollinger eventually realized his best moments were mostly in early practices, as Walton worked back into prime shape after summers mostly distanced from the game. Once Walton reacquired his game rhythm and conditioning, Drollinger became any other chalk outline on the ground.) Indicating a general discontent and not merely a restlessness on the court, Walton began to openly regret his decision to attend UCLA, where "there is no togetherness among the students. The school is in a wealthy area and most of the students come from well-to-do homes. They are not hungry and they do not feel for the hunger of others. Many go to their fancy homes at day's end. They don't really live together. They're not typical of young people today. I think sometimes I should have gone to Berkeley. The students are much more together there. They're aware of the wrongs in our world and they act to try to correct them. A university is supposed to be a place for young people, and I think it's right young people should have a say in how things are run, as they do there."

Most concerning of all, the basketball joy of the first two seasons, one on varsity, was already giving way to the cynicism of a hardened older man. Walton and other returnees rolled their eyes when Wooden went back to one of his favorite superstitions of *coincidentally* finding a penny on the ground during the final talk before the season opener and declaring it a good omen before following the worn script of tucking the coin into one of his loafers. While he retained great respect for his coach, Walton in a time of shifting emotions found many Woodenisms "ridiculous." On the court, he groaned seeing opponents give up pursuing offensive rebounds in favor of quick retreat on defense to get back before the Bruins could outsprint them to the other end for an easy basket.

The University of the Pacific took the drastic measure of customizing an offense specifically for the visit to Pauley Pavilion. Stan Morrison may have been thirty-three years old and in his second game as a college head coach, but he knew the Bruins well after spending the previous two seasons as an assistant at USC, the four before that in the same role three hundred miles away at San Jose State and one on the staff at Cal. He hosted high school senior Gary Cunningham on Cunningham's campus visit for recruiting, played for Newell in Berkeley in the years the Bears owned UCLA and the West, and had stayed in touch with his mentor as Newell fumed about the open secret of Gilbert laughing at NCAA rules. Unlike Newell, though, Morrison liked Wooden personally, ever since Morrison as a high school coach attended several days of Wooden presentations at a 1964 clinic in Reno and Wooden invited him to continue the conversation over several subsequent lunches and dinners. Morrison furiously scribbled away, amazed at his good fortune, kept the notes forever as a prized possession, and came to call Wooden a friend despite the icy Cal-UCLA relationship.

Morrison heading into his first season grew particularly concerned over Walton's potential for destruction on defense, worried Walton could humiliate severely enough to injure some Tigers the rest of 1972–73. Walton's brilliance on that side of the ball, elite quickness mixed with the instincts of an NBA veteran mixed with size, could damage psyches and force opponents into wild shots that came down on the top of the backboard. Morrison, unlike other coaches who dared to dream, did not embrace the illusion Pacific had a chance. A competitor but also a realist wanting his players in one emotional piece for the fair fights ahead on the schedule, he designed a new portion of the playbook that eliminated risking a regrettable outcome in the paint. The name Bend Back came from the constant of players curling around to receive a pass for short-range shots or longer jumpers. Anything but the interior under one-man patrol, Walton having convinced opponents by the start of his junior season that lower-percentage shots had a better chance of success.

The 1-2-2 set, with the point guard on top initiating the offense, with double low posts and double wings near the free-throw line, worked well in theory as the huge underdogs got the open perimeter shots they wanted. Pacific just missed most of them in a squandered what-might-have-been and eventual 81–48 loss, before Wooden, whether sincere or straining for kind words in the name of sportsmanship, met Morrison for the postgame handshake on the sideline with "I love what you ran against us." Don't get discouraged, he added, being as encouraging as he had been eight years earlier in Reno. Morrison declared UCLA "the finest amateur basketball team I have ever seen, and I include the USF teams of Bill Russell," but in the blizzard of misses and the rush of his first road game as a head coach he did not notice anything unusual with Wooden's appearance.

. . .

Given what had become regular comments from Wooden about his job stress, Wooden showing physical wear as he turned sixty-two could hardly be considered unusual. He was a trim five-eleven and approximately 180 pounds, but loved red meat and sweets, often had trouble sleeping after games, and remained slightly stooped over from a ruptured disc in his back, still lingering from a hard tumble in a pickup game in the 1940s. Lunch at Hollis Johnson's might be chili and an ice-cream sundae, among many favorites, and a night out with Nell lately often meant Lawry's, famous for thick cuts of prime rib and roast beef. Wooden did not drink, but smoked for decades, since the navy days, although he stopped the first day of practice until the last game to set an example for players. He had quit completely in recent years. When he collapsed getting out of bed one night in the offseason of 1967, Wooden believed rest in the hospital and at home sufficiently addressed the exhaustion diagnosis.

The decline had become so obvious, though, that Wooden concluded early in the 1972–73 schedule he looked "like death warmed over" in the photo on his driver's license. Signs of serious trouble grew bad enough the night of December 10, eight days after the Pacific game, that he checked into St. John's Hospital in Santa Monica, an irony not likely lost on the critical peers who had for years sarcastically used the name St. John to mock Wooden behind his back. Doctors diagnosed a gastrointestinal ailment, a minor malady.

With a campus-wide sigh of relief offsetting the ominous note that the head coach still had no timeline to be released, assistants Gary Cunningham and Frank Arnold ran practices, until more definitive, more concerning word came December 13: cardiologists determined arteries—plural—leading to the heart were 65 percent blocked. John Wooden had heart trouble. He would remain in St. John's, albeit with the encouraging news that doctors envisioned him being able to resume normal activities, even the stressful normal of life on the fast-moving train.

Cunningham as interim coach allowed for an easy transition, however long the new role lasted. He ran practice according to the Wooden script, of course, no surprise given the abrupt handoff that left no time for an individual imprint but especially given Cunningham's history as a Bruin forward until graduating in 1962 and with seven seasons on staff. Cunningham was more like his mentor in personality than any Wooden assistant of the championship era, and, son Jim Wooden would come to say, more like Wooden than anyone in any role. They even had a similar career swing, the way Cunningham once looked forward to life as a college professor and Wooden imagined decades as a high school English teacher, before each landed someplace far different. Of more immediate concern with the routine being disrupted, and with both nearly religious on the value of routine, Cunningham had the respect of players as well as the experience to be a reassuring hand in an abnormal time.

Cunningham in the third week of the schedule moved forward without deviating from their index-card world and with the same crisp, focused bursts of activity, spending as many as fifteen minutes on some drills and as few as five on others. When Wooden eventually entered December 11–16 in his notebook, he added a cursive note stacked in six lines, one per word, in the margin on the left side: "In Hospital Coach Cunningham in charge," as if Wooden might someday forget his only extended absence ever. His need for organization apparently demanded it.

Wooden remained under observation for a seventh day as UCLA hosted UC Santa Barbara and a thirty-three-year-old assistant coach with a doctorate in educational administration looked up to find himself in charge of the top-ranked team in the country riding a 48-game win streak. Cunningham may have had 116 games as freshman head coach running Wooden's system, but this was not sending Lew Alcindor out to step on MiraCosta College. While Santa Barbara arrived with little chance, so much as a close game would have been noted nationally and riled the fan base that assumed championships and blowout wins. Cunningham might be needed for longer than Wooden's first missed contest since taking over in 1948, after making 679 in a row, and struggling to dismiss UCSB would be no way to build confidence.

Cunningham visiting St. John's the day of the Santa Barbara game and finding the patient with a lot of color in his face would have been reassuring enough, but the 98–67 victory at night that included long stretches of peak Bruins combined for several hours of soothing medical and hoops bulletins. "I have never seen a team employ the basic skills of basketball—passing, dribbling, rebounding. and shooting—better than this UCLA team," Gaucho coach Ralph Barkey said in review, additional comfort in an uncertain time. "I don't believe," he added, "the Bruins showed a negative effect" from Wooden's absence.

Wooden was released the next day, December 17, with permission from doctors to immediately resume work in moderation. Chairs would be placed on the sideline near midcourt so the coach, ordinarily a fountain of energy in practice, his happy place, could rest while still tracking his team. Wooden might step away to briefly lie down in the locker room. No lengthy interviews. He began a daily walking routine, on the track adjacent to Pauley Pavilion when on campus, that would eventually build to five miles of quiet time he enjoyed as the chance to shut out the world. He began to eat more fish, never a favorite, and "no more chili sizes or banana splits after games for me. The doctors have ruled those goodies out, but I can still eat plenty of fruit and I like that." Assistant coaches and others were assigned to handle his mail and additional office work as the athletic department unleashed an administrative version of the swarming UCLA zone press of the midsixties. In New Orleans at the end of the month for the Sugar Bowl Tournament, Cunningham stood in at social functions.

Wooden's bosses had always been good about recognizing the unique challenge of herding the monster, starting with the pledge new athletic director J. D. Morgan made shortly after taking over in 1963 to handle budgets and scheduling. They were fine with never offering a raise to reflect his central role in the cash machine, and never needing to agree to a big bump since Wooden refused to request a larger salary, but the administration had a genuine concern for his well-being. For all Morgan's bluster—slamming a fist on his desk and barking at coaches and staffers in his deep voice among the constant attempts to intimidate—he could also show great compassion. In December 1972, that included conversations with Young that the university should consider ways to support Wooden in a tough time.

Remarkably, considering the health scare centered on a sixty-two-year-old longtime smoker with a heart problem and a high-stress job, no serious conversations took place during the week about replacing Wooden for health reasons, or even informal internal discussions to be prepared if it turned out the optimistic view from doctors had been overstated. Nor did Wooden ever appear to consider retirement during 1972–73 once the cardiologist cleared his return. J. D. Morgan had long kept a list of coaching candidates for most sports in his empire, to be prepared to react quickly in an emergency or simply if a change was needed, yet never discussed possible replacements with the chancellor or told Cunningham to stay ready for a permanent promotion. Morgan did have the calendar to consider, knowing Cunningham would be the option to finish 1972–73 if needed, before conducting a full search in the offseason, possibly starting with trying to grab Denny Crum back from Louisville.

Wooden entered a near-empty Pauley Pavilion on December 21 wearing a blue UCLA windbreaker covering his shirt, brown slacks, and basketball shoes, as if it were any Thursday and not the significant benchmark of his first practice back. His walk seemed uneasy and his face pale, reporters and photographers noted after being allowed rare access to watch courtside in a nod to the occasion. "I've always told my players to be quick, but don't hurry," he said, smiling, "but my doctors have told me that I can't follow my own advice. I can't be quick or hurry."

The few Bruins warming up showed no emotion, until the full roster reached the court and players one by one approached Wooden in a courtside chair one by one with handshakes, smiles, and pats. He met with the team in the middle of the floor, telling them in a soft voice that he felt fine but would need to go slow for a few days, then returned to sit while Cunningham and Arnold directed drills. Wooden occasionally walked to watch from a different vantage point or talked to a player individually and also found the energy to shake a finger and chastise Farmer for the unnecessary flair of a reverse layup without a Santa Barbara defender close. Wooden watched and remembered.

"We didn't really pay too much attention to this developing saga," Walton later wrote. "We were so young, naïve, and supremely confident in our own invincibility. And Coach was so old. Looking back later, we should have noticed the rapid deterioration of his health that was taking place right in front of us.

"When we had arrived at UCLA three years earlier, Coach, at [sixty] was still spry, vibrant and dynamic, with a real spring and bounce to his step. And he went from this dashing, upright, statuesque force du jour to someone who was now stooped, pale, hesitant, gaunt, and outwardly broken. Over the years, we have all learned ourselves to never discount the effects of stress on one's health. But I can see how I wore him down and out." Walton cared enough that he bicycled five miles each way to visit Wooden in the hospital and later, after Wooden returned to the bench, reminded him during an excitable moment in a time-out to stay calm—"Hey, hey. Easy, easy."

The personal test of the first game back resulted in a standing ovation from the limited crowd inside Pauley Pavilion a half hour before tip-off against Pitt, then another when the Bruins returned to the locker room after warm-ups, and again just before the start from what had become the latest home sellout. Simply having his name called out over the public-address system during team introductions led to a fourth salute, before another as he accepted a Grecian urn during a halftime ceremony at center court for being named *Sports Illustrated* Sportsman of the Year. Wooden waved his right hand, bashfully hung his head, and released the slight smile of an appreciative man who disliked the spotlight.

What Wooden later referred to as "a little heart problem" remained at the forefront of the season, even as the team carried on unfazed by beating Pitt and Notre Dame with ease within twenty-four hours to push the winning streak to 51. Proving his competitive side was as strong as ever, he sent Christmas cards with a flurry of ho-ho-hos on the cover, sixty-one in all—the number that would break the record for consecutive victories set by the University of San Francisco in the Bill Russell–K. C. Jones days. Though possibly an amazing coincidence, it was more likely Wooden's sneaky sense of humor.

The Bruins constantly downplayed the pursuit of history, no one more so than the coach, who felt it as another boulder dropped on already-weary shoulders. It wasn't enough that an ungrateful, unrealistic fan base expected him to win every title, he also had to win every regular-season game, too. But at least the countdown to 61 hyped by UCLA faithful and the media inserted rare heightened stakes for one of the few times in place of the usual yawning early months. There hadn't been a November and December like it since 1969 and the national glee at awaiting the implosion sure to come with the departure of Abdul-Jabbar, and, before that, 1966 and the varsity arrival of the Alcindor-Allen-Shackelford-Heitz class. While chasing ghosts had never been a priority—not Wooden trying to live up to a past success, not Walton wanting to be regarded as the best center from Westwood—USF of the 1950s did offer a challenge in a time when few existed.

"We count on the championship," one player said, wisely speaking with anonymity to avoid the wrath of Wooden. "As far as we're concerned, the other clubs can send in their games. Why take the trouble to play them? They'll just lose them. They know it and we know it. Coach wouldn't like to hear us say that, but he knows it, too. He would never say it, but he knows it. He doesn't always say what he means. He says what he feels he's supposed to say. I tell it as it is." Wooden allowed only that the chance for 60 and 61 on the annual Midwest swing would motivate the Bruins to a peak usually reserved for March.

"It's so easy for us to win, it's not fun for us anymore," the player said. "There's no competition, no challenge. It's just something we're committed to, like a job. We're workmen, doing piecework. We take 'em to pieces. We take 'em apart one at a time. We laugh at them. That's the only fun we get. That and things like the playoffs and setting the record. We need something special to stir us up. The record is special, so these games coming up are special. We'll laugh through them, but at least they mean something, so they'll be fun to play. Winning isn't fun anymore. Because we never lose. And we ain't gonna lose these games, either."

TWA Flight 24 from Los Angeles to Chicago prepared for a morning takeoff with the winning streak at 59, the Bruins in first class, two UCLA pennants at the front of the cabin, and the flight attendants, all women, costumed in UCLA T-shirts. As if players being pampered wasn't enough of the image Morgan wanted to project, he scored the additional marketing boon of reporters briefly being allowed on board to chronicle the mood of the team with the record so close. Cameras and floodlights turned the 747 into an impromptu Hollywood set, before the bubble-nose plane surged into the sky and pointed toward Illinois with eggs Benedict and toasted banana bread served for breakfast. There is, Wooden said en route, "no sense trying to soft-pedal it. The players are well aware of the record and they'd like to have it."

Beating Loyola to tie USF brought little outward reaction, before boarding a chartered Greyhound for a late-night ride to South Bend and the chance at the record almost exactly two years after the loss to the Austin Carr Irish. "We'll win," Lee said. "After all, we always win." The Notre Dame band screamed away at UCLA players—"Hollyfield, you suck!" "Hollyfield, you ain't shit!"—Larry Hollyfield having grown into a favorite target as a returnee from the 1971 squad. Finding an opening to respond, he threw a pass in after a made free throw and, with all eyes following the play to the opposite end, hocked a loogie at a drummer. "That was fun, them wanting to kill me," he said later of facing down an arena full of enemies.

Walton would always remember South Bend games as especially difficult, facing fans so hostile that some threw coins at Bruins on the court, occasionally metal warmed by cigarette lighters in a repeat of a favorite trick among rabid spectators in some European arenas. Walton saw the Phelps game plan of slowing the pace in the visit the year before as "boring, frustrating, embarrassing, and no fun at all—all of which pretty much describes Digger," and then January 1973 in the same Joyce Center felt "excessively violent" as hard hits went in both directions.

Wooden finally walked toward midcourt during play to complain to Phelps about the rough tactics from Fighting Irish forward John Shumate on Walton with a promise to retaliate by sending in six-eleven, 240-pound Swen Nater, and "you know what he'll do." The physical play that bothered him all season, as well as in the Alcindor years, had reached a climax. Wooden as the unlikely source of threats seemed to startle Phelps, before Digger returned fire with "It's a two-way street" with the comfort of having three football players at the end of his bench as basketball subs.

The Bruins in the aftermath of the 82–63 victory for the record returned to their subdued selves, without carryover from the heightened emotions of the game or the achievement of more consecutive wins than anyone in history. Farmer and Hollyfield slapped hands and shared a moment of older players feeling they made up for the loss two years earlier. But in the end the record they privately wanted created so little sense of accomplishment that Walton was asked afterward if he would remember the game for a long time and replied he would not. "This isn't the greatest thing that's happened on this day," Wooden said. "It's my granddaughter's birthday," and also his father's birthday. He smiled. "But the most important thing is that this was cease-fire day in Vietnam. That's much more important than this." The peace treaty agreed to by the United States and North Vietnam ended fighting in the conflict that had become a large part of Walton's life, and therefore the program's.

Wooden wrote Phelps a note in cursive on UCLA letterhead four days later that quickly ended up in the hands of *Philadelphia Inquirer* columnist Frank Dolson, a Phelps media pal.

Dear "Digger"—

I owe you and John Shumate an apology and hope you will accept it in the spirit in which it is offered.

I acted hastily without thinking clearly and taking all things into consideration and, as usual, actions from emotions are seldom with reason.

Best wishes.

Sincerely,
John Wooden

P.S. Please convey my feeling to John [Shumate]. He is a fine young man and an outstanding basketball player and I did him an injustice.

• • •

The multiple minor health issues that ganged up on Lee to ruin the opening weeks of his junior season led into an emotional drain that had him talking about giving up, without clarifying whether that meant quitting basketball or transferring or remaining but caring less. Not having fun, he was ready to "bag it," just as Wooden, unhappy with the offense, made him the starter again. A former roommate sent a mock certificate from the Curtis Fan Club anyway, urging Lee to "be loud and obnoxious" and to "strive always for soul," inserting levity into a challenging time. Curtis getting a bad case of the flu then solidified Lee's role, stability he especially needed in the weeks of often feeling disconnected.

For all the issues—Wooden's health, the point-guard reshuffle, physical play, turmoil in society, the potential NBA distraction for Walton of the

Philadelphia 76ers winning the coin toss March 20 for the No. 1 pick in the draft—the Bruins had built into a twice-a-week clinic on disciplined basketball meshed with playing fast and fun. The regular season ending at 26-0 followed by tournament wins over Arizona State, San Francisco in the regional at Pauley Pavilion, and Indiana in a national semifinal in St. Louis finally pushed Wooden to the strange land of impromptu practice plans. He turned the Bruins loose for the final workout of the season, the night before the championship game against Memphis State, by allowing joking and even an alternate universe with dunking in reaction to feeling they were tense against Indiana. Madman Wooden operated without the safety net of a three-by-five index card approved by history, at the Final Four of all places, with everything on the line.

Whether carryover or coincidence, his center arrived at St. Louis Arena the next night unlike any Walton in nearly three full seasons of moods on open display. The Walton as tip-off approached, especially motivated by what Walton considered a poor performance in beating Florida State for the crown a year earlier, struck Wooden as "the only time this season I've seen him so emotionally ready to play." Aki Hill, a coach who moved from Japan to spend 1972–73 learning from the Bruins, attending most every home workout and game with Wooden granting behind-the-scenes access, saw Walton turn pale with focus, so much intensity that it caused a change in complexion. "He was the best practice player," Hill said. "Always focused. But that day was very, very special." Walton's "bony chin was set hard" when the Bruins came out for warm-ups, Dwight Chapin wrote the next day in the *Los Angeles Times*. "His eyes seemed to fight the crowd. He hopped and pumped his hands back and forth."

"We're almost ready to go," Memphis State radioman Jack Eaton told his audience back home over the crowd noise and the school bands, "and I thought of a lot of things I could say but I am so nervous I forgot what they were."

"Half his game is passing off," Tigers coach Gene Bartow told Eaton on the pregame show, explaining the strategy to not double-team Walton. "We'd like to make a shooter out of him tonight." Larry Kenon, a talent listed as two inches shorter than Walton, opened playing behind UCLA's star center. Walton kept swooping around him for easy baskets and Kenon picked up 3 early fouls, forcing Bartow to switch from man-to-man defense to zone. UCLA kept throwing lobs to the rim from every direction, especially Lee and some Larry Hollyfield, and Walton kept converting, usually easy baskets but also soaring to backhand a pass in with his right hand.

Impossible enough to counter on normal nights, peak Walton turned into the spectacular basketball sight of the best player in the country synced with his best-friend point guard on the biggest stage. The pregame mindset carried into an unstoppable performance on the court. Sitting about ten rows up near midcourt in a section set aside for coaches from around the country, previous Walton victim Stan Morrison watched Memphis State stay close in the first half and was still sure the game was over with Walton working hard to get open and Lee finding him at the rim. Morrison, a player since the 1950s, a major-college coach since 1966, had never seen a better performance. Former Bruins Terry Schofield and John Ecker, watching on TV in Los Angeles, sprang from their chairs several times to cheer.

J. D. Morgan tracked every foul in the first half, this time with his usual rage at officials compounded by the knowledge that most of the calls against UCLA were made by a Missouri Valley Conference referee working a game involving a Missouri Valley Conference team. The flame under Morgan turned up higher yet when Walton was called for his third personal with 4:14 remaining in the first half, forcing Wooden to take him out. "Wiles," Morgan said at the start of halftime after charging to Pacific-8 executive director Wiles Hallock, sitting courtside, "if you don't go into the locker room and do something about this officiating, I'm not going to be responsible for my actions. This game may be under protest." Hallock paid little attention, aware of Morgan's personality and a history with officials that Hallock believed reached paranoia. He understood the furious athletic director just needed to scream at someone.

A sprained ankle ultimately forced Walton from the game with 2:51 remaining and victory secure, not fouls despite playing his final 9 minutes 27 seconds with 4 personals. Heading to the locker room after the buzzer at one point required help from Kenon, an opponent, and the portion of walking on his own near a free-throw line came with his left shoe and sock off, showing the taped ankle he'd twisted, and bandages hugging both knees as always. It was not the picture of a conquering hero moments after receiving a minute-long standing ovation from fans upon being replaced and the architect of one of the great performances in NCAA history, even if Wooden would rank Gail Goodrich's 42 points in the 1965 title game the best individual showing of his coaching career. Walton delivered "as great a game as I've ever seen played," said 76ers coach Kevin Loughery, in attendance to scout for the draft. "A perfect game, so perfect that I know he could take any team in the NBA and make it a winner."

Bartow's desire to turn Walton into a shooter ended with 21 baskets in 22 attempts, everything except for a lob in the first half, and 44 points. Walton, Bartow declared, is "the best collegiate player I've ever seen. We played him wrong. We tried three or four things, but I guess we didn't try the right one. If you let him have the ball, he'll kill you." The 14 assists by Lee were the difference, Walton insisted, and a satisfying close to a difficult personal season that both had to believe locked Lee into the starting job next season.

Bill, Drollinger told his teammate and friend in the postgame locker room, do you realize you went 21 for 22 tonight?

Walton did not say anything. But Drollinger saw in his face the reaction of a humbled man that bordered on embarrassment, Walton's humility showing in private in a way like never before.

Maybe because the finish was that dominant, maybe because he had decided before but wanted to wait until the finish to answer the question that kept coming up, maybe because he was beginning to place more moments in a historical context as the end of his career drew closer, Wooden broke previous policy of refusing to pick the best UCLA team and anointed the second varsity season of the Walton Gang as No. 1. He highlighted the center's greatness, of course, but in true Wooden fashion emphasized the group's constant poise, a topic about to become a major storyline without his realizing it in the celebration of a ninth crown in ten years. Beyond that, though, "The seventh straight meant nothing," he said. "All coaches want to have the first one. When I got that, I said I'd like to get the second in a row because that had only been done two or three times previously. Now we got the second, I said, 'Well, if we can win three, then we'd be second to [Kentucky's Adolph] Rupp, who'd won four. Then we get to the next year, and we win and tie Rupp. That was important. Then we get to five, well, nobody had gotten to five. And it would have been three in a row. No one had done that. But what's next after that? The sixth? The seventh? After the fifth championship and third in a row, everything else was just icing on the cake. The rest didn't have an impact in any way."

Walton agreeing to meet with 76ers representatives that night was more courtesy than interest in turning pro a year early, even with the NBA able to hold up the previous hours as a sign that no challenges remained on college courts. He loved most teammates, several to become lifelong friends, respected his coach, enjoyed student life, and had never so much as hinted at declaring for the 1973 draft. Walton at times wasn't even sure he wanted a basketball career, a position that continued late into the senior season, but he would play in Westwood if he played anywhere in 1973–74. Yet he politely sat through forty-five minutes of the owner and general manager trying to tempt him with contract possibilities that could have topped $2 million for four or five years and Loughery handling the basketball angle when Walton would rather have been at victory parties with players and cheerleaders.

The 76ers found additional hope when the conversation ended without a definite no, enough encouragement that the same two executives followed the Bruins back to Los Angeles as the deadline to enter the draft approached. Walton and his father went hiking in the Sierra Nevada while owner Irv Kosloff and General Manager Don DeJardin waited a couple hundred miles south in a hotel in the city to be prepared if they got the chance to continue the pursuit. "Maybe if we fly over California and drop hardship forms throughout the state," Loughery said from the East, "one will get to him."

Nothing from the pros moved him, not even the stunning ABA sales pitch the same night in a hotel room that Walton could choose his team—placing an expansion club in L.A. would be a possibility if he didn't like the existing San Diego Conquistadors—and even his roster. Alcindor didn't get that level of bowing down. Anyone but Julius Erving, league executives told him, because Dr. J needed to be on the other coast for competitive and marketing balance. The vision was Erving in New York, a move that became official within months in a trade from the Virginia Squires to the Nets, and Walton in Los Angeles, though apparently without a 1973 version of Operation Kingfish. Walton could have surrounded himself with George Gervin, Connie Hawkins, Dan Issel, or George McGinnis at forward. Or Artis Gilmore or Mel Daniels would play center and Walton power forward. Greg Lee, lightly regarded by the NBA, would be one of the guards. Maybe owners could have found enough money to lure Wilkes, another Walton favorite, a year early as well. Jerry West would be hired as coach or general manager. They had added a hardship draft three months earlier, in case a valued player chose to leave school early, and awarded San Diego the first pick.

Stanford center Rich Kelley followed developments one night as an interested observer, working his way through bottles of Lucky beer with roommates in Branner Hall. Loosened mightily by cheap brew with screw tops that had riddles on the underside of the cap, hoping to avoid two more head-to-heads with Walton next season, Kelley found a piece of paper. Please turn pro, he wrote by hand, turning more tongue-in-cheek amid the flow of jokes with friends and Lucky. Go to the ABA. Go to the NBA. Here's $12.16, or a similar oddball amount Kelley scribbled, to clinch the decision. You can have all my used basketball socks as well if you want. Kelley riffed off the top of his head for one page, included the cash and coins, and mailed the letter to Walton care of the UCLA athletic department, but never learned if it got to the intended target.

Walton never wavered. Not only would he return as a senior along with most of the best team in school history, except for graduating forwards Farmer and Hollyfield and center Nater, but Wooden also stayed despite Nell's hopes he would retire. It was a month after a letter to the editor in the *Los Angeles Times*, with UCLA at 22-0, began, "Maybe we should reevaluate that title, 'The Wizard of Westwood.' With men like Lew Alcindor, Bill Walton and the fantastic supporting cast, even Mrs. John Wooden could come up with seven national championships." The chance to escape the madness did appeal to Mr. John Wooden, but not right now, with so many possibilities still ahead.

12

THE CROSS IN THE POCKET

Fan in Chief H. R. Haldeman handed his alma mater the chance to be part of history by providing White House backing to the idea of his Bruins touring China in the summer of 1973 for games against local clubs. Haldeman's role in inserting UCLA as the latest and largest move of using sports to build a diplomatic bridge between the distrusting political adversaries would give the school a role in global affairs, to the understandable delight of university officials and the athletic department headed by publicity maven J. D. Morgan. The Game of the Century in the Astrodome that excited his marketing side in 1968 boosted the program's profile within college basketball; this was high-visibility participation in the most delicate of East-West relations.

Even Wooden, grasping the historical significance as well as the promotional benefits of Morgan potentially hyperventilating about the Bruins into ambassadors' ears, was on board at the personal cost of losing a large part of his offseason. The level of certainty over whether international envoy Bill Walton would mute himself was less clear—if he cussed at innocent Chancellor Charles Young while being arrested, what verbal hell would Walton rain down to embarrass Nixon with the world watching? It was also irrelevant. Morgan was barely into the team meeting in his office to lay out the details when Walton raised a hand in mid-explanation to say he would not go. Summers were for beaches and hiking and long red hair flowing in the wind on extended bike rides, he reasoned, not being a political prop under scrutiny in the Ping-Pong diplomacy that would boost Nixon's standing.

Wooden decided either the Bruins go as a team or they don't go at all. Walton immediately felt anger and disappointment aimed in his direction by the voters who wanted the unique experience and would in later years come to regret the veto that cost him a trip unavailable to most Americans. In an instant, he went from claiming a passionate interest in world issues to passing on the opportunity to live the pressing topic of U.S.-China relations sixteen months after Nixon's historic visit to Peking. Far into adulthood, he wished Wooden or Morgan or Ernie Vandeweghe, anyone, would have tried to change his mind, a lobbying that never happened. In the moment, "I was a twenty-year-old college student fleeing from everyone who was trying to make me into anything other than a twenty-year-old college student."

The all-star team cobbled together to replace the Bruins included Walton pen pal Rich Kelley, George Karl of North Carolina, Indiana's Quinn Buckner, Alvan Adams from Oklahoma, and coach Gene Bartow, coming off the title-game thrashing, without a hint of potential international incident among them. In Canton, already steaming in humidity in mid-June, locals waved enthusiastically at passing buses ferrying the delegation through town. In Peking, several thousand spectators came to the beautiful arena for practice alone, watching mostly in silence, as if studying, except for hushed *aaaahhhhh*s anytime an American went vertical and finished a dunk. The eighteen-thousand-seat gym had been sold out far in advance for the first game in the capital city—the equivalent of ten cents for the best seats, five for the others—a level of obvious excitement that prompted one member of the party to jokingly ask whether tickets would be scalped outside. "Of course not," a Chinese official responded briskly, finding no humor in the question. "It is against the law."

As a reminder they were in a land of great suspicion toward outsiders, especially American outsiders, one player tossed his sneakers out the hotel window in a moment of youthful indiscretion, then found the shoes waiting atop the front desk the next day upon arriving in the new city, to the spooky amazement of all who realized how much their movements were being tracked. (Sneakers became a thing. Kelley threw his worn pair of size 16s in the trash can in his room when packing for the trip home, only to have a maid run from the hotel to the bus out front about to depart for the airport, apparently concerned the owner had forgotten them.) The U.S. team chosen with high character in mind easily won in each of eight stops against eight different opponents, layered among visits to numerous tourist spots, VIP treatment, and banquets flowing with food, drink, and toasts, and the olive branch of apple pie à la mode for dessert one day. Ultimately, when three members of the Politburo and the very influential wife of Chairman Mao Tse-tung attended one of the games, the White House had the desired signal that China was pleased at the direction of the relationship. UCLA officials could only grit their teeth at the missed global opportunity.

The mood for 1973–74 had been set in the process: increasing disinterest even when given the chance for a unique opportunity—Wilkes and Lee were also against going—and a team dulled by success. The Bruins were suffering from Bruin fatigue. "This group of UCLA players has, more or less, old-timers," Oregon State coach Ralph Miller said. "They're not as enthusiastic, perhaps, as they were as sophomores and juniors. They've won so many games and championships that it's easy for them to say, 'What the hell— what else do we have to do?'" Wooden diagnosed the problem as senioritis, but also a team needing to be challenged once it became apparent the lure of a third championship wouldn't be motivation enough. Before long, he was wondering out loud about the stars being more focused on their professional futures than the current season, a surprising development after three years of Walton, Wilkes, and Lee who had been the definition of selfless.

Back under basketball's magical spell after an offseason of long rural bike rides and classes at Sonoma State in Northern California's wine country, but not any Chinese banquets, a recharged Walton returned for his senior season with the excitement of a newcomer. Not only pronouncing himself in top physical shape—maybe for the last time in his life—Walton considered 1973–74 "by far" the most talented Bruin team in any of his four years, with good reason. Lee and Wilkes were back as two of his all-time favorite teammates, in college or the pros, along with Meyers, Curtis, and Trgovich, along with varsity newcomers Marques Johnson, Richard Washington, Ralph Drollinger, and Andre McCarter. ("Sadly," Walton wrote later, "we still had Tommy Curtis on the roster.") It would turn out as arguably the most talented and deepest frontcourt in NCAA history, even with the graduation loss of forward Farmer and center Nater: Walton and Wilkes became Hall of Famers, Meyers played four seasons in the NBA while missing another with a back injury, Washington six plus one lost to a knee injury, Johnson eleven while missing two because of a neck injury, and Drollinger one.

Others, in turn, noted an encouraging new level of maturity in Walton, which was perhaps a response to costing the entire team an experience in China or a further sign of his excitement for the season ahead. "Sometimes with Bill, I feel like I'm handling a piece of glass," Wooden said. "At times he is an enigma . . . inconsistent, changeable, impatient. But his true nature, the one few people see, is extroverted, open, and sincere. He definitely ranks up there in the unusual-person category. Even though we differ, I like him. I like him a lot." To Cunningham, "He's a complex person who has to feel he's being treated as more than a basketball player before he'll open up. He's very shy in groups and is uncomfortable around people he doesn't know. For whatever reason, he thinks people are out to exploit him. There's a basic lack of trust. But I can see that slowly changing as he's grown up. Remember, he's not grown up yet." When he won the 1973 Sullivan Award in February as the outstanding U.S. amateur in any sport, Walton in his first solo press conference of the season came across as gracious, honest, and introspective.

"I would say that I'm a much better human being than when I came to school here," Walton concluded later in the season. "I'm much more well-rounded. I'm just a stronger person. . . . I'm much happier now, much more relaxed and much more self-confident. . . . I don't try to prove myself to anybody and I don't try to please anybody. I just try to do what is right. . . . If it comes out all right, fine." He was to the point of being open to working relationships with the media, dining out with Doug Krikorian and Bud Furillo of the *Los Angeles Herald Examiner*, and then with Dwight Chapin of the *Los Angeles Times*, and even giving an extended interview to Ted Green of the *Times* that included driving Green and Lee to dinner in his gray Toyota with the front seat removed and Walton driving from the back seat for extra legroom.

The head coach understood Walton and felt upbeat about their relationship. He allowed Walton to use his office to meditate, usually after practice as a stop en route to the training table in the Student Union. "We had to bring two pieces of fruit and a handkerchief," Marques Johnson said of one of the team sessions. "Why, I have no idea." An assistant coach from NSULA spending a week around the Bruins in the early days of practice, one of many times through the years that Wooden opened his program to young coaches hoping to learn from a behind-the-scenes look at the machine, left practice with Wooden, walked a minute to the office, and opened the door to find Walton and several nonplayers relaxing on the floor.

It was still a senior season in which the unwanted spotlight prompted the projected No. 1 draft pick to daydream about quitting basketball to become a teacher or a lawyer or to fight forest fires. His love for the game, and for Wooden and UCLA hoops in particular, remained impenetrable as the NBA and ABA learned the previous March in the St. Louis hotel. Walton upbeat about life as a Bruin as 1973–74 started, if not the attention that went with it, came with the medical bulletin that he was in the best shape of his life. While it would have been a noteworthy update no matter what, the topic took on particular relevance with Walton aware opponents in the coming months would play him more physical than ever, as with Alcindor once every other attempt at a countermove had failed. Walton could not have been more primed for a crescendo finish to college as part of the attempt at an eighth consecutive title.

Sports Illustrated, the ultimate national media voice on sports, had grown so desperate for new ways to preview the inevitable next Westwood celebration that its preseason Top 20 spotlighted the student managers. The rest of the country, the chase pack, got the typical of roster breakdowns, injury issues, and schedule analysis, but for No. 1 UCLA, it was "Bob Marcucci, who did the honors during the tenure of Lewis Kareem [*sic*], was fast with a towel, but could not handle warmup jackets. He always took them one at a time. George Morgan, now a Marine based at nearby Camp Pendleton, accomplished chores for the Wicks-Rowe teams and never missed a play or a pun. Les Friedman, who toiled during Bill Walton's first two years and is now in law school, was quick to the chairs but had no left hand. Now Friedman's brother Len, a junior and the new head manager, shows the most potential of the bunch. All he has to do is eat his greens and keep his proper silence." The uncredited writer did provide the scouting report that Lee had sold some teammates on the benefits of being a vegetarian and that Wooden and Walton disagreed over hair length. "When you're under a dictatorship, you do what the boss wants," Walton said. "I even had to cut it twice. I may be an anarchist, but I'm no dummy."

The Bruin universe was upbeat: Walton playfully jabbing his coach, Wooden bending to accommodate players and national publicity for managers, and the early benefit of the rule change in Walton's second season that allowed freshmen to join the varsity. Even that broke right for UCLA— Johnson arrived capable of immediately making a significant contribution and Washington had similar star potential and in the moment the ability to play in most games despite the frontcourt riches. In talent, experience, and atmosphere, it was impossible to be set up better for success.

"UCLA may be the greatest team in basketball," Maryland coach Lefty Driesell said as the Terrapins' visit to Pauley Pavilion approached. "Not just college basketball, all basketball. If we could break their streak, the consequences would be greater than if we won the national championship. It would be remembered longer, because sometimes I don't think they're human."

The good vibes of the buildup to 1973–74 got the Bruins only through the early days of practice, but ultimately only until the moments it took Walton to notice Wooden striding with determination, as if angry, toward Lee warming up. Walton could not hear the conversation, but from the other side of the court read the tone as contentious, then could see Wooden headed in his direction.

"Bill," Wooden said, "it has come to my attention that you have been smoking marijuana."

Walton, caught off guard, struggled to keep a straight face at Wooden coming to him with this now, after smoking each of the previous three seasons on campus, barely containing his laughter at Wooden either just learning the breaking news or for whatever reason finally being moved to confront Walton.

"Coach," Walton replied after quickly composing himself and locating a sincere tone, "I have no idea what you're talking about."

Wooden took a deep breath. "Good," he said. Whether he naïvely believed Walton or not, Wooden got the answer he wanted, quickly turned, and started practice before Walton had a chance to change his mind and opt for the truth that would have presented Wooden with a major dilemma.

Lee chose honesty—and was replaced in the opening lineup. Walton losing his closest teammate, his dependable distributing point guard who knew exactly where and when to deliver the pass, the player Walton credited for the historic night against Memphis State, would have been bad enough. Curtis as the replacement made it worse. He went to Wooden's office several times in the coming weeks, "begging, pleading, trying to explain why Tommy Curtis was not right for our team, our style, our psyche, our game, our life, our fun."

What Wooden would have done if Walton admitted smoking pot would never be known. Wooden almost certainly realized he had to be consistent in disciplining two players with similar personal histories at the school, and if anything, Walton would have to face a harsher penalty. Lee, after all, had not been arrested or put on school probation. The likely outcome in that scenario was Lee keeping his job and facing a lesser discipline, unless Wooden was prepared to demote arguably the greatest player in NCAA history to a reserve role for being a typical college student in 1973. Walton protecting himself also unintentionally saved Wooden.

A *New York Times Magazine* deep dive on the Bruins hit the stands with either the best or worst possible timing, fifty-four hundred words dated December 3 that included the eighteen of "John Wooden comes as close to an embodiment of Jesus Christ as anyone on the current sporting scene." As easy as it would have been to imagine Wooden gasping at the analogy, if not outright hating the compliment, he had always been open about his strong Christian faith. (Even if the many opposing coaches who found him a sanctimonious hypocrite for preaching values while Sam Gilbert ran wild were not so open when mocking him as St. John.) Indeed, when freshman Drollinger said he wanted to start a team Bible study class, Wooden got excited and told players they were expected to attend. Two or three showed, none named Walton or Lee. Wooden appeared on an hour-long TV special hosted by televangelist Oral Roberts, one of the country's most recognizable preachers, five weeks after the 1970 title, going against *Ironside*, a Jim Nabors variety show, and *Bewitched* on the networks in the 8:30 p.m. slot in Los Angeles. Another time, Cora Alcindor observed after Wooden's 1965 overnight home visit to meet Lewis's parents, "He's more like a minister than a coach," and a rival coach said after losing a different recruit to UCLA, "We thought we had one kid sewed up, but then Jesus Christ walked in. The kid's parents about fell over. How can you recruit against Jesus Christ?" To Cora's son, Wooden's occasionally watching practices from the top rows of Pauley was where "he would look down on us like a benevolent God."

Wooden, actually all mortal, was a deacon at the First Christian Church of Santa Monica, kept the Good Book close at home and on his travels and for decades kept the same silver steel cross either tucked out of sight into his left palm, wedged between his index and middle fingers, or in a left-side pocket during games as a source of serenity without most anyone aware it was there. Eventually worn smooth from constant rubbing, though with the alpha and omega from the Greek alphabet still visible, signifying beginning and end, the gift from his minister in 1942 just before entering the navy remained a constant companion during speeches well into retirement. When other coaches socialized at local drinking holes after hours at the summer hoops camp Temple's Harry Litwack held in the Poconos, Wooden chose to stay behind to do the dishes in the shared cabin. Never before, though, had his morality so crashed into his career as when benching Greg Lee helped set a course to Bruin self-destruction.

For all Alcindor's 1968 claims that Wooden preferred Lynn Shackelford over Edgar Lacey, the 1974 evidence of virtue factoring into the fate of the Bruins was far more damning. Lacey refused to enter a game, one of the biggest transgressions an athlete can make. Lee's previous outing was 14 assists with a national championship on the line. Nothing new had happened on the court, no laws or university rules were known to have been broken, no recent injuries played into the decision.

Walton's instincts that the change at point guard had turned the Bruins inconsistent did not come through in the box scores. Beating Driesell and Maryland only 65–64 in the second game may have caused concern inside Pauley Pavilion, but could be explained away as a good showing by the visitors, the No. 4 team in the country with talent and experience in John Lucas, Tom McMillen, and Len Elmore. Unlike Wooden, who could look at the matchup as one of many nonconference tests through the years, Driesell had put so much focus on the game that he had his team practice at 10:30 p.m. in College Park so players could get their bodies adjusted and not feel they were pulling an all-nighter when tip-off came in California.

Drollinger aggressive in sharing his Christian faith at nineteen years old—suggesting the team Bible study, often appearing at Wooden's office announced to discuss religion, giving Wooden books on spirituality—contrasted his basketball personality. Being at UCLA said as much, that he went there rather than accept another among some two hundred other scholarship offers in large part because Walton's presence guaranteed Drollinger would be the backup center. His career had gone this far because everyone told him tall guys should play hoops, not because he loved it, never more obvious than when Walton arrived before a game talking about how he spent the morning imagining a turnaround bank shot to use that night, rehearsing the move in his mind over and over. Drollinger knew he could never come close to matching such passion for the game.

One of his talents, and he did have basketball skill despite his minimal role, was realizing early that he could parlay the sport into the chance to build a future that did not involve playing. Drollinger didn't deceive himself. He wanted the UCLA education, appreciated the chance to be part of the No. 1 program in the country, and liked being just 150 miles from home. But expectations and pressure in basketball made him nervous, even after he grew to seven-two and dominated high school contests around San Diego.

The unease was so obvious that in the midcourt circle just before sopho-more Drollinger and Grossmont tipped off against senior Walton and Helix, Walton told his alleged opponent to take any shot without fear of it being blocked, to do anything he wanted to score. Make the game about building your confidence, Walton told him. Drollinger instantly wondered about the psychological ploy underway, yet Walton kept his word, laying off to allow Drollinger a big offensive night while making sure Helix still won easily, an extraordinary gesture that stayed with Drollinger for decades.

Now the second week of December 1973 had become particularly try-ing with a showdown against No. 2 North Carolina State in St. Louis days away and his mother in UCLA Medical Center for an operation to ease a nerve issue causing hot, stabbing pains in her face. Drollinger could at least take comfort in knowing Walton was in good health heading into the individual battle with Tom Burleson, at seven-two able to dwarf the best player in the country by three inches, and a skilled seven-two despite the image of an awkward thin man on stilts who contributed little beyond height. One layer of solace came the day Carolyn Drollinger had surgery a mile from Pauley Pavilion. Wooden received word during practice the procedure had been a success, stopped the session, walked to Ralph on the court, and delivered the good news through tears of joy.

The encouraging prognosis allowed a relieved Drollinger to fade back into his familiar and preferred role of invisible seven-footer as the Bru-ins left for the neutral-site game against North Carolina State. Though it would not match the buildup for the Game of the Century in the As-trodome, or the eventual perspective of UCLA-Houston as the night that changed college basketball forever, facing the Wolfpack did have the J. D. Morgan seal of marketing approval. Wooden even surprised Morgan by immediately accepting the invitation, because this was a game in a tradi-tional setting, not the same extravaganza as Houston in 1968, which was built on the novelty of the site, the island court, and the record attendance.

The hype centered entirely on the teams this time, with UCLA as the defending champion returning to the scene of Walton and Lee overwhelm-ing Memphis State, and with North Carolina State as the program certain it would have been in the 1973 title game if not for the recruiting violations that led to an NCAA ban after a 27-0 season. Walton and Wilkes from the West and electric forward David Thompson, Burleson, and point guard Monte Towe from the Southeast were all back. The current Bruins had won 78 in a row, the Wolfpack 29. Wooden only asked that the game not be played in Raleigh, just as the Wolfpack said they would not go to Pauley.

Middle America as the compromise still provided the cash register Morgan wanted with an arena of 18,431 seats and plenty of experience hosting large hoops events. ABC would handle the national broadcast for the matchup, originally proposed by the man handling television packages for the Atlantic Coast Conference and backed by the UCLA athletic director with an expertise in TV deals. Digger Phelps did color commentary on the broadcast, giving him the chance to scout the Bruins while having his expenses paid. Tickets that went for $5, $4, and $3 in the Astrodome were priced at $10 and $8 six years later in St. Louis Arena and immediately sold out. The eventual $100,000 take for each side from the gate and broadcast was more than either would have received from meeting in the title game still under debate in the Carolinas. "Win *or* lose, it's no mistake," Morgan, his face hardening, his tone turning full bully, thundered before tip-off at the suggestion that facing such a skilled opponent early in the season would be an error.

The Bruins stepped off the bus and into the Chase Park Plaza hotel for check-in the snowy Missouri night of December 13 aiming, as always, for later conference play and the postseason tournament, not victory streaks or peaking in December. "Imagine," Lee told reserve guard Gavin Smith at practice the next day, scanning the arena's empty seats. "Tomorrow there will be eighteen thousand people up there who will have paid ten bucks a ticket and who have nine-to-five jobs and nothing better to do than getting it on by watching ten guys run up and down a court chasing a ball." Lee shook his head in retelling the story the same night. "If we win, great. If we lose, life goes on. We've got too many other things to look forward to in life. Next week. Next month. Next summer, at the beach." They were equally nonchalant that only one Bruin, Curtis, had actually seen the Wolfpack, on TV the year before while home sick as UCLA teammates played.

Early afternoon of game day with a 4:15 p.m. start arrived with the North Carolina State band playing in the lobby, Thompson and Burleson signing autographs, and jubilant middle-aged men in red blazers singing the school fight song. Eight floors up, the Bruins gathered near the elevators for their departure unfazed in chanting, "Wolf . . . Wolf . . . Wolfpack!" At 78 wins in a row, they were somewhere between daring an opponent to pose a threat and privately laughing at anyone believing they actually had a chance. Not so privately, the original message of PACK POWER scrawled in soap on a hallway mirror by a State backer had been altered with a simple adjustment to PAC 8 POWER.

When the game started, though, and Walton picked up 4 fouls in the first 9 minutes, one personal away from disqualification, the Wolfpack, down 15–10, had an unexpected opening. Morgan, sitting across from the benches, yelled at referees until he almost lost his voice.

"Watch 'em pushing away," Wooden chimed in as part of his steady stream of jockeying the officials, often from behind the rolled-up program and most directed at the ACC ref working with the Pac-8 representative.

"That's an offensive foul. You called that offensive foul on us."

"Oh, for crying out loud! Bad call. Bad call."

"Feeling good?" he scolded after Thompson was awarded a two-shot foul. "You should be."

"John Wooden—despite what those who worship him like to believe—is not so terribly different from dozens of other college basketball coaches," Frank Dolson of the *Philadelphia Inquirer* wrote after sitting a few yards away, within hearing distance. "He has great material, and he makes the most of it, which is surely the mark of an outstanding coach. But he is not a saint. He is not impervious to the pressures of winning basketball games. And he is certainly not above intimidating officials." Wooden always saw it as sticking up for his Bruins and looking for any edge within the rules to win, just as he would clandestinely ride opposing players.

Drollinger went from rarely playing in a meaningful situation to seeing Wooden point to him on the bench to replace Walton 9 minutes into the biggest regular-season college game in six years. Encouraging his teammate and friend as if they were still at midcourt for tip-off before Helix at Grossmont, Walton told Drollinger to look into Wooden's eyes from the court whenever he felt nervous and see how much the coach believed in him. Sophomore Drollinger heard senior Wilkes exhorting "You can do this!" and "You're ready for this!" their first few trips up and down the court in another attempt to boost Drollinger, swimming in his usual basketball anxiety, calling him "Young Ralph" as always in a term of endearment.

Drollinger amid the self-inflicted stress and the startling role change couldn't help but also embrace the rare opportunity to contribute to the dynasty. He took Walton's advice to look to Wooden for unspoken encouragement, got additional boosts from Wilkes's in-game pep rallies, and fell back on his own faith to know everything would work out with Jesus Christ, until Young Ralph had played well through the end of the first half and halfway into the second. The 5-point UCLA lead when he came in was only down to 2 when Walton returned with 9:52 remaining, a better barometer of Drollinger's impact than the 8 points and 5 rebounds in 19 minutes. Walton sparked the dominating final stretch that led to an 18-point victory without adding a fifth foul, then returned to the hotel to circulate a petition among friends and strangers in the lobby urging the impeachment of Richard Nixon.

Their attempt to relitigate the 1973 championship foiled, the gift of Walton spending 21 of the 40 minutes on the bench wasted, messages in soap on hallway mirrors invalidated, devastated Wolfpack players took the rare step of closing the locker room to reporters, in contrast to openness after victories. "I'd like to be in the finals against them," Towe said upon emerging, "but after the jolt we've had we're going to have to take a look at ourselves, talk it out, pull back a little, and pick up the pieces." They had within hours gone from 29-0 and No. 2 in the country to being jarred to introspection, even before Towe spent the flight back to Raleigh lying across two seats with his face turned into the cushions and refusing to speak to anyone. A rematch three months later in the 1974 tournament appeared to be the only hope for redemption.

"We'll have one," NC State forward Tim Stoddard insisted.

. . .

The NCAA leveled Long Beach State on January 6 with an indefinite ban on postseason play and most television appearances in basketball and football, for at least three years, as part of what the national governing body called among the most serious infractions it had ever seen. Someone in the 49er athletic department cut out a picture of Walter Byers, the NCAA's executive director, and placed it over a dartboard in an office, quickly to be riddled with holes. "Wanna take a shot?" an assistant sports information director asked a visitor in between his own throws that created a thumping loud enough to be heard in the hallway. "Everybody else around here has."

That Tarkanian went to Nevada Las Vegas the previous summer, that Tark successor Lute Olson had no link to the previous staff, that the athletic director and school president were seen as part of a new administration determined to correct past misdeeds, and that the football coach resigned the month before slightly eased the penalties. Tarkanian pronounced himself "absolutely shocked," denied wrongdoing, and expressed sympathy his former program would suffer under such an injustice, but never noted how a high-profile school thirty-five miles away had yet to be so much as investigated despite obvious evidence of misconduct. "Hey, Tark," Pan American University coach Abe Lemons, smart-aleck Oklahoma good ol' boy, shouted at him a few months later, "I understand the NCAA's gonna reopen Devil's Island for ya. They're gonna give ya thirty days in the 'lectric chair. Don't fret, Tark. I'll send ya magazines and cigarettes in the pen.

"Reminds me," Lemons continued, "of the guy drivin' down the road doin' sixty and everybody else is passin' him goin' eighty. And the cop stops the guy and he says, 'Why me?' And the cop says, ''Cause you're easier to catch.'" No one needed to ask Lemons to explain.

Washington State coach George Raveling, with his own Bruin problems to consider, slumped in a chair in his hillside home in Pullman overlooking campus hours after the NCAA announced the Long Beach penalties, sipped a beer, and chatted with friends while Sunday night faded into early Monday. He appeared exhausted after going over film of UCLA-Maryland at Pauley Pavilion, taping his weekly TV show, writing his column loaded with quotes and anecdotes of sports personalities for six Washington newspapers, and fielding calls. Driesell among them phoned his former Maryland assistant to wish Raveling luck the next day against the Bruins in the Performing Arts Coliseum, the replacement for Bohler Gym, of the famed Alcindor visit. Win and your picture should be on the cover of *Time*, Driesell told him. Raveling's eyes glistened at the thought.

Raveling at thirty-six and in his second season as a head coach admired his next counterpart enough to keep a large file on anything written about Wooden, even if wouldn't rank with the greatest document Raveling owned, the pages Martin Luther King Jr. used at the podium of the "I Have a Dream" speech. But he also planned to dramatically slow the pace by holding the ball for minutes at a time, a tactic Wooden hated when it had been used since the Alcindor days in desperate attempts to knock the Bruins out of rhythm, and because nothing else worked. This time, it allowed the 5-8 Cougars to stay within 30–27 at halftime, before Wilkes and Curtis scored 9 points early in the second half and Wooden countered with his own stall the final 12 minutes in a message to the rules committee that a shot clock should be added to outlaw boringball. He also vowed after the 55–45 victory to respond in kind if future opponents tried the same crawling strategy, just not at Pauley—he did not want to deprive his own of the fast break life they paid to see. "Who am I to question God?" Raveling said with a shrug when told of Wooden's reasoning.

Walton crash-landing under the basket in the second half, after coming down on the shoulders of Washington State defender Rich Steele, was the real UCLA concern anyway, what Walton saw as a "despicable act of intentional violence and dirty play." The crowd that booed during pregame introductions went silent as he lay sprawled on the court in obvious pain, then delivered a standing ovation when he got up, and another when the brief attempt to continue playing proved unbearable and he asked to be removed with 10:23 remaining. Walton, though, had merely bruised a muscle above the right hip, the school announced a day later after the return to Los Angeles, not something more serious, an upbeat prognosis considering the original fear of a serious back injury. He would undergo therapy, including whirlpool baths, and should be ready to face Cal later in the week, the Bruins announced.

Although no one at the time could have realized the frightful implications or even what it meant in the short term, the night of January 7, 1974, in Pullman and what was later found to be two broken bones in his spine would become one of the worst moments of Walton's life. Well into retirement, the misdiagnosed injury became the root of such constant agony that Walton, seeing no way to end the pain, considered suicide. In the middle of the senior season, he was expected to play on.

He did not suit up against Cal, though, and also missed the Stanford game the next day. Ten days after the injury, Walton went through a solo workout at a downtown Chicago health club in hopes of facing Iowa that night in a neutral-site contest and still felt considerable pain anytime he quickly went left. Drollinger, his confidence growing, started a third time in a row instead, again hearing a river of encouragement from Wilkes, as Digger Phelps scouted the Bruins in the Midwest for the second time in a month. No one could say if Walton would miss the next game as well, only that the season had turned more tenuous than a 13-0 record would indicate, that the record win streak had grown to 88 in a row, and that Notre Dame was waiting in South Bend.

13

THE LOST SEASON

Richard Phelps—Digger to most as the son of a New York under-taker, "the devil himself" to Bill Walton—had officially been waiting for UCLA once his soaring Fighting Irish beat Georgetown on January 15, 1974, to improve to 8-0 and hold at No. 2 in the Associated Press rankings. But it really had been since December 22, 1971, and the searing 114–56 loss at Pauley Pavilion with the Bruins playing their starters late and sticking with a pressing defense, the night he swore revenge on Wooden in the terse postgame interaction.

John, you do anything you have to do to beat me, because someday I am going to kick your ass.

Phelps didn't have to tell anyone during the week since Georgetown of his certainty that January 19 would be that someday. In reality, he had been simmering since being hired in 1971 as a twenty-nine-year-old with one season of experience as a head coach, at Fordham, and the obligatory boilerplate promises to drive the program from badly broken to greatness. He was the son of the former Margaret Sullivan, Maggie, great-granddaughter of immigrants from Ireland, green clover to the core, an Irish Catholic lass with a caring heart who for much of her life attended mass and received Communion daily. Troubling news was often greeted with "Jesus, Mary, and Joseph!" and positive developments with "Glory be to God." Coach Digger Phelps at St. Gabriel's High School in

Hazleton, Pennsylvania, had a shamrock put on uniform shorts despite purple being St. Gabe's primary color and in October 1965 wrote Notre Dame football coach Ara Parseghian to share his dream of getting the hoops job in South Bend one heavenly day. Phelps saw it as destiny.

When he did get hired five and a half years later, Phelps arrived with visions of national championships and assumptions every top high school prospect likewise saw it as the ultimate destination, then got hit by the reality of a 6-20 first season and a country full of recruits who didn't bleed green. Kevin Grevey had a nun for an aunt, so coaches at the university with Father Theodore Hesburgh as president and Father Edmund P. Joyce overseeing the athletic department reasoned Grevey a done deal, before he chose Kentucky. Pete Trgovich, from seventy-five miles away in East Chicago, Indiana, turned away, for UCLA at that. Attempts to pry Walton out of California went nowhere.

The Irish at No. 2 after beating Georgetown had John Shumate and Gary Brokaw as first-round NBA draft picks four and a half months in the future, freshman Adrian Dantley emerging as a star, and freshmen Bill Paterno and Ray Martin as recruits with national profiles. They also had a coach who saw the benefits of in-person scouting. Phelps after watching the Bruins beat North Carolina State in St. Louis was among the first outsiders, and among the first anywhere beyond Walton, pressing Wooden to reverse the decision at point guard, to diagnose UCLA as a vulnerable team. It took only the early close call against Maryland for Phelps to see the demise of the dynasty coming from "the surprisingly poor caliber of the Bruins' performance. This was not the same UCLA team I have seen in the past. Walton and Wilkes are still great, of course, but the other starters—Dave Meyers, Pete Trgovich, and Tommy Curtis—don't seem to have the same ability as some of their predecessors." Contrary to celebrating the demise taking shape, Phelps was pleased at their Maryland escape and hoped the Bruins would continue to win to push the record streak to 88 in a row. He wanted to be the one to break it.

The chance now directly in front of him, Phelps the hard-driving master motivator delivered practices supercharged with ploys designed to turn his Fighting Irish into true believers as well. "Digger lived and died for

these games—to be in the spotlight, to create media hype," forward Paterno said. By Friday, the Day Before, Phelps seemed to have spent the
week focusing more on psychology than on strategy to slow Wilkes, the
understated star he considered the true key to stopping the Bruins, because Walton playing well was a given. He made sure his team knew he
would have the baskets switched to the opposite end from the current
location to mess with the visitors' offense, as if there were a difference
and both teams wouldn't get the exact same time aiming at each basket,
but no one questioned the strange plot development. The conclusion of
practice on two of the three days between Georgetown and UCLA were
devoted to cutting down the nets to be prepared for *when* the time came
Saturday to celebrate, and, he alerted them, "Someday you will tell your
grandchildren about this." Phelps was confident to the point of allowing a
Sports Illustrated photographer to capture the moment for the next edition.

He had tried the same sales job a year earlier, telling friends for weeks,
"You've got to come out," and how UCLA will have just tied the record
against Loyola and underdog Notre Dame will stop the streak with all
eyes on South Bend before the Bruins could claim full ownership. After
all, Phelps said, contender George Foreman destroyed undefeated champ
Joe Frazier just five days before in Jamaica to take the heavyweight boxing crown, so it must be a time for shocking outcomes. So many out-of-
towners followed the advice that the Phelps home had visitors in the guest
room, the living room. and the TV room, and his blue-and-gold Thunder-
bird turned into a shuttle service from his house to the game. But those
Fighting Irish were 5-8 at tip-off and would finish 17-12.

With the hype of an 8-0 start and a No. 2 ranking by January 1974,
some three thousand of the faithful, mostly locals, trudged through snow
and fog for a pep rally on Friday, the Night Before. The turnout and level
of passion rivaled any football rah-rah assembly except for visits by rival
USC. Featured speaker Sid Catlett, a starter from the last Notre Dame
basketball team to beat UCLA, in 1971 behind Dwight Clay's heroics,
read a fictional note from Walton to Fighting Irish star Shumate:

Dear John,

*Sorry I won't be at the game on Saturday. There seems to be a yellow streak
running up my back.*

The crowd roared in delight.

Shumate the same Friday night answered a knock on his dormitory
door to find approximately fifty college-aged people with a request in a
tone that sounded more like a demand. Declare a Black Power protest
just before tip-off, the militants suggested. Turn South Bend, Indiana, in
1974 into Mexico City in 1968, they encouraged, take advantage of the
national-television cameras just as John Carlos and Tommie Smith had
done by stabbing fists into the sky. It was the same campus where five
years before fans booed coach Johnny Dee for using an all-black lineup
against Michigan State, some of the spectators counting off the five as if
not believing the sight and needing confirmation, before Dee quickly sent
in two replacements of lighter complexions.

When you're announced, Shumate heard from the crowded hallway outside Fisher Hall 113, we want you to sit down in a circle with your head down
and your hands together. Stunned into near silence and trying to process the
strange cold call, Shumate could only imagine protesters approached him as
a team emotional leader and best-known player. It certainly wasn't Shumate's
background. He lived through the 1967 Newark riots, close enough to danger
that he and five friends coming back from playing pickup ball in New York
City were stopped and ordered out of the car by National Guardsmen. But he
was entirely apolitical, a religious college senior who regularly called his father,
a Pentecostal minister in New Jersey, to share prayers over the phone. John
Shumate personified the ideal Wooden charge, in play and personality.

Shumate gathered himself and in absolute terms declined to protest,
worried the activism could end his career, and the fifty visitors departed
in anger, some calling out, "Uncle Tom," in retreat. He phoned Phelps
to report the interaction, stopped by several parties in the dorm to ask to
keep the noise down in consideration of the several players in the building,

and assigned monitors on different floors to police the decibels. Everyone gladly complied, wanting to do their part to repel the invaders from Los Angeles. Finally, he called his parents at the end of the night, typical in their relationship.

Barely able to sleep during the night as tension built for the noon tip-off, he awoke for good at 6:30 a.m. as pressure continued to build on Shumate as the star understanding the significance of the day ahead for the entire program. He called his father the minister again.

Dad, John asked, would you pray for me?

The request was not unusual. They often shared in devotionals, ad-libbed rather than Bible readings, John always asking for God to direct him, keep both teams safe, and for him to play with strength and confidence. Neither ever asked nor offered invocations for victory. The Morning Of, though, John went further, admitting being pinned under the stress as days of Phelps psych jobs backfired into the most important of the Fighting Irish overwhelmed by the drama and implications of the day. In his uniform and warm-up jacket hours later, a photo of Shumate staring into the distance with a blank face before tip-off titled MR. COOL on the next cover of the *Sporting News* was actually the opposite of Shumate working to corral his emotions ricocheting off every seat in the arena. On the call with his father before heading out, on his knees, leaning forward with his hands pressing together on the lone bed for the single occupant in Fisher 113, minister and congregant prayed for John to have confidence, stay healthy, and play his best.

The team gathering at 8:00 a.m. in a crypt below the basilica on campus for a mass by the university's senior vice president veered from scriptures to full-Phelps saying, "The chances are good that years from now you will look back on this day as one of the most memorable of your life. Is this melodramatic? I don't think so." Shumate, after the group walked to the locker room, turned ministerial without prompting.

"I had a dream," he said. Phelps continued to write on a chalkboard. The room inside the Athletic and Convocation Center felt church-like to Shumate as he gained momentum, turning gospel preacher on the spot and suddenly showing no sign of pressure as players continued to get ready around him, several appearing nervous in the final moments of preparation with less pregame chatter than usual.

I had a dream there was a bear—a bruin—in the forest, Shumate continued. A leprechaun appeared. "Mr. Bruin, come here," it said.

The bear suddenly vanished.

What happened? a teammate asked as an ideal straight man in shared enthusiasm.

The leprechaun was wearing a bear rug! Shumate responded.

The room ignited.

"We are! ND! We are! ND!"

Phelps stared at his team leader with a smile, an expert at motivating players admiring the work of another and most of all appreciating the frenzy before him. When Phelps winked to acknowledge a job well done, Shumate got goose bumps.

Phelps had everything in place for one glorious thunderclap of a day—his players frothing at the mouth, their minds dancing with secret basket switches and leprechauns, UCLA still unbeaten as desired, Walton playing in a corset to stabilize his back, Wooden not only lined up for payback but the prey in the very town he spent nine seasons coaching at South Bend Central High. The student section was always energized, but the rest of the crowd felt just as invested this time. Twenty days after Notre Dame football beat No. 1 Alabama in the Sugar Bowl and one day after Notre Dame hockey beat No. 1 Michigan Tech, Maggie Sullivan's son was certain the same defining hour had come for Fighting Irish basketball, flamboyant coach marking his territory against gentleman counterpart. "I know in my three years there, he was more prepared for UCLA than he was for any other team," Dantley came to say. "I know that."

In case doubt remained whether the underdogs were truly prepared to stand up to 88 in a row, Dantley drove inside at Walton protecting the rim and bashed Walton in the nose 57 seconds into the game. Though an accidental collision, Dantley's message of refusing to be intimidated was intentional, and his drawing blood turned the crowd of 11,343 more rabid. Walton had cotton stuffed in his nostrils to go with the corset and greeted

Dantley for decades to come, through NBA careers and retirement, with some version of "Hey, I remember you gave me that elbow."

Dantley's determination only grew in his first experience in the rivalry as he found UCLA to be a cocky team "with some of the worst filthy mouths you could ever think," spewing comments about mothers, in contrast to the portrayal of respectful champions in the image of Wooden. He heard Curtis, the worst of all, "talking all the time. All that bad-mouthing stuff at me. If this had been a playground game, I would have busted his head. I tried to keep my composure."

Still, the Irish were down 70–59 when Phelps called time-out with 3:22 remaining, his dreams about to be ruined decades before grandchildren could be told. He remained defiant in the huddle anyway, as insistent as at any practice during the week, so adamant that players saw the passion in his eyes as their coach snarled at the huddled parishioners to have faith as well. "If you don't believe that we can do this, then leave and go to the locker room right now," Phelps told his flock. "If you stay here and believe, then we can do this."

Notre Dame roared to life with the adjustment to a smaller lineup and orders to throw a man-to-man press at the Bruins, leprechauns chasing bears in the forest. UCLA wilted in ways unimaginable for an experienced roster steeled by tournament pressure and constant life as the hunted. Three turnovers that led to Irish baskets closed the gap. Phelps the master motivator, in the most important moment of the most important game of his life, suddenly also had the defining strategy move in the huddle, proving himself to be capable of more than psych jobs. Even better for him, it came at the expense of Wooden, a colleague Phelps greatly respected—Fordham coach Phelps used the UCLA press made famous by the 1964 and '65 titles—but saw as *the* competition.

Wooden hated calling time-outs, as Phelps and other opponents knew well, regarding stopping action a sign of weakness and stopping early an especially bad sign of an unprepared team. "Never did I want to call the first time-out during a game," he said. "Never. It was almost a fetish with me because I stressed conditioning to such a degree. I wanted UCLA to come out and run our opponents so hard that they would be forced to call the first time-out just to catch their breath. I wanted them to have to stop the running before we did." Phelps gained the insight from the 1972 Wooden memoir *They Call Me Coach*, although the memory didn't flash into Digger's memory during the game. In the Alcindor days, TV crews in the production truck slightly beyond the court would scream through a headset at Tom Hansen, the Pacific-8 Conference executive sitting at the scorer's table, to find a way to call time-out, because Wooden wouldn't and stations had commercials to air. The Wooden policy was bad for business. In South Bend in 1974, deep into the game that could end the record winning streak, his team wobbling and unable to score, he remained as adamant.

Wooden would not relent and did not gather his team on the sideline until 21 seconds remained, and then only after the 12–0 run by the Fighting Irish and after Dwight Clay's corner jumper with 29 seconds to play provided the final points in Notre Dame's 71–70 victory. Phelps's belief his opponent would stay the course rather than regroup paid off. Twice Tommy Curtis looked to the bench to catch Wooden's eye, anticipating a stoppage that never came and instead seeing only his coach sitting stoically with legs crossed. The time-out Wooden finally did call was too late and did no good, such a poor response to the momentum shift that he would say after the season, "I personally lost the Notre Dame game through my own complacency." Even Walton playing all 40 minutes with the corset and contributing 24 points and 9 rebounds couldn't help as UCLA uncharacteristically lost its poise with 6 consecutive missed shots and 4 turnovers the final three and a half minutes. "I know I was guilty," Wooden said.

Euphoric home fans "came out of the stands like bumblebees," said one of the referees, Rich Weiler, who ran for the nearest basket and took high ground on the stanchion to avoid being run over. Revelers charged the court from every direction with so little concern that reporters either tucked under sideline worktables stretched baseline to baseline across from the team benches or risked being trampled. Not even six feet, nine inches of flashing bright light in gold pants and gold jersey impossible to miss slowed the stampede. Shumate in the lane after grabbing the final rebound and flinging the ball in the air saw a wave of humanity storming toward him, then tripped while being mobbed and fell over a body. He landed nose first. Unable to get up as fans piled on in celebration, groggy from the exhaustion of the previous hours, coupled with the fresh blow to his face, struggling to breathe after the fresh injury, Shumate fading in and out of consciousness was rescued from the demolition derby by his uncle and a couple ushers. He didn't remember anything between trying to extricate himself from the pile of revelers and being jarred from the daze in the locker room by doctors with uncorked smelling salts. The first thing Shumate saw was Phelps snapping fingers in front of Mr. Cool's face and saying, "I love you."

The nets were cut down according to plan. When Phelps recognized a man entering the locker room as a representative of the Hall of Fame, intent on a new collectible, he told a student manager to hide the game ball and find a spare to hand over. The fake ended up in a display case in the basketball museum, and Digger could laugh nearly fifty years later while looking at the actual souvenir above the TV in his home.

Phelps shouted "Intensity!" to open his address to the team as an assessment of the day and what he loved during the game, especially aware, as always, of emotions. Also, he said in the locker room, players could attend victory parties, but no calls at three or four in the morning asking for help getting out of jail. "UCLA came to play—they were a good team," Phelps added before, softly, "I love you all. You're the greatest," a joy the Bruins almost never showed even in the biggest wins. Then the Irish knelt and prayed.

J. D. Morgan quickly hunted the referees escaping the hysteria, enraged after recognizing Weiler as part of the crew when Iowa beat UCLA in football four months earlier, as if the coincidence had to be a plot. Morgan's standing as master of instant recall of minuscule details had been affirmed, even if the search appeared to end without a capture. His coach, by contrast, understood the historical significance but with the anesthesia of knowing the loss didn't cost the Bruins in the conference race or, worse, the tournament, his primary concerns. Walton left the visitors' locker room with his head drooping from a hooded sweatshirt, the sadness obvious before he passed Dantley's aunt in the hallway with a final blow: Hey, don't worry about it, big fella, you can get another streak going.

Many players stepping on the team bus to Chicago for the flight back to Los Angeles, about the same time a group of Notre Dame conquering heroes entered a campus cafeteria for dinner to a standing ovation, found Wooden just inside the entrance with encouraging words. Life goes on. Keep your head up. Be proud of everything you have accomplished. Wooden was so at ease with the first defeat in two years, eleven months, and three weeks that he had no problem allowing Dick Enberg and Rod Hundley, the play-by-play man and analyst for the TVS broadcast, to hitch a ride for the 110 miles to the airport and their air connections. Enberg as the voice of the Bruins on radio and TV in Los Angeles, in addition to calling the Game of the Century from the Astrodome foxhole, already knew Wooden well. Relative newcomer Hundley sitting in a row about halfway back, though, had never seen anything like the coach's deft touch in turning a gloomy day more upbeat before the bus even left the arena.

The *South Bend Tribune* broke into the evening edition to report the outcome as a bulletin at the top of page 1, with only enough time to provide one paragraph of detail before full coverage the next day, and plans went into action to proclaim Digger Phelps Week with a city council resolution in his hometown of Beacon, New York. A day apparently would not be sufficient. In the years to come, the children of adult Bill Walton would try to hurt their dad during arguments by threatening to attend Notre Dame, and a high school senior from near Pittsburgh attending as part of his football recruiting weekend, Joe Montana, decided he'd witnessed "a pretty good game," before eventually signing with the Irish. Phelps upon being told he would be inducted in the athletic department Ring of Honor during the 2013–14 basketball season insisted the ceremony be held January 19, just as he would use a photo of the scoreboard showing the 71–70 final score at the top of the cover of one of his memoirs. The night of January 19, 1974, at the home of Richard and Teresa Phelps, three-quarters of a mile from the Athletic and Convocation Center in a usually quiet middle-class neighborhood, became a carnival of a couple hundred revelers. Kids zoomed around. Grown-ups who came to town, some longtime backers from previous career stops so determined to attend on tight schedules that they used private planes. The governor of Indiana. White House aides. Media friends.

Guests packed the living room of the two-story brick house with a bay window that looked to more guests gathered in the snowy front yard in the neighborhood jokingly known as the faculty ghetto because so many Notre Dame teachers lived in the immediate area. It was actually more middle and upper-middle class, and also close enough that Phelps's son often walked to watch afternoon practice and neighbors could pull one of Digger's daughters to a game in a toboggan when she broke a leg and couldn't fight through a snowstorm on her own. Knute Rockne's former house was around the corner. With the party roaring practically down the street from the arena, Phelps in his dream moment, surrounded by success and attention, told the story over and over of force-feeding his players confidence by cutting down the nets at practice, before the Irish did it for real amid the postgame stampede that carried Dantley and others on their shoulders.

Unattached Phelps assistant Frank McLaughlin spotted a pretty lady among the crush of humanity and asked if she would like to join a group splitting off to find dinner. In conversation at the restaurant, she explained she worked as an aide at the White House and that her father was a connected Notre Dame grad. Her job in January 1974 as Watergate crashed down, eight months after H. R. Haldeman dutifully followed Nixon orders to take the hit and resign as chief of staff, included putting the previous day's good news on a three-by-five index card for the president to read each morning. The summary saved Nixon, under emotional siege and desperately needing sunny developments, the time of scouring clippings from the staff.

Oh, proud smart-ass, proud liberal McLaughlin told the beauty in from Washington, there must be days you give Nixon blank cards.

She got up from the table with "Why don't you respect the president of the United States?" and walked out without waiting for an answer.

UCLA in two days would be stripped of the top spot in the Associated Press poll after the strange development of a loss. The Bruins at 13-1 and No. 2 in the country had a coach who had steered from showdown losses to national-championship recoveries before, yet they were also more susceptible than at any time since the early days of 1969–70 and the proving ground of the post-Alcindor era. Wooden soon began speaking of a team that didn't play with the same drive of the previous two seasons, and Wilkes, among many, later saw a group beaten down by years of expectation, how "every time we didn't blow somebody out, it was a moral loss. We had to win a certain way. That wore on us." The Alcindor Bruins fought through the same burden. The current super-team, as started to become evident on January 19, 1974, could not.

"These should have been the best years of our lives, but they haven't been," Nell Wooden said. "Nine national championships in ten years is great. So are the winning streaks. But the fans are so greedy. They've reached the point where they are unhappy if John wins a championship game by only five points. If he loses a game, they're going to say that he's too old and he's lost his touch. You learn to prepare yourself for the [worst] and then hope it doesn't happen. They can stretch the rules and let him stay until he's sixty-seven, but I wonder if it would be worth it. What more does my husband have to prove?" John was hardly sleeping after games, replaying the previous hours in his mind over and over, mentally mining for anything the Bruins could have done different.

Even a six-day break to regroup after South Bend followed by a 42-point win over Santa Clara and Notre Dame coming to Los Angeles barely generated a spark. The Bruins won the rematch that would ordinarily have been an energy injection to push through the final six weeks of the regular season, and still UCLA continued to deflate, going through the motions. Dantley privately and accurately predicted a Bruin victory, figuring the Walton Gang would be locked in to avoid a repeat embarrassment at home, but also noticed the telling personality change that the Bruins did not have it in them to trash-talk even during a successful revenge mission. The most emotional it got was Wooden visiting the Fighting Irish locker room afterward to put an arm around Shumate's waist and say not recruiting him was a mistake and good luck in the future, a particularly touching moment to the former New Jersey high school player who once wrote Wooden about his desire to come to Westwood. "What did he want?" Phelps in a sneering voice asked Shumate after Wooden left.

Notre Dame within a single week in January 1974, one Saturday on the road and the next at home, became the way to graph the third season of the Walton-Wilkes era. Supported by home fans, the Bruins could beat

No. 1 to retake the top spot. Lacking poise and on hostile ground, they were a slow leak, fatigued by expectations and rolling their eyes at folksy Woodenisms. What appeared to be good humor when Walton doused Wooden's opening-night ritual of "finding" a penny on the floor during the pregame locker-room talk turned darker as 1973–74 bled out. Players were heard to privately call Wooden at sixty-three "Prune" behind his back in a mean-spirited tone. "Walking Antique" was another. They ignored instructions from the bench one game to switch the defense, with the Wooden explanation that "they listen but don't hear." So done with the spotlight and the morality plays and the country-Indiana slogans, "We thought everything he said was crazy," Walton said.

At least the Bruin mystique remained, so they arrived at Oregon State with an 18-1 record, No. 1 for 110 of the previous 127 weeks, and Beavers forward Paul Miller saying, "It kind of made you wonder. Did you even belong on the same court with them?" Facing the UCLA brand could still feel like starting a game "and they're ten points ahead, just because of the intimidation factor," center Doug Oxsen said with similar wonder. Miller and Oxsen didn't realize the rapid descent had reached the stage where even being psyched out didn't matter—Oregon State won with Oxsen playing a large role in Walton being limited to 9 shots. The 50-game conference win streak was over, too, and Wooden some fourteen months removed from being hospitalized with a heart problem was hit in the chest by an apple thrown hard from about fifteen feet away.

McArthur Court at the University of Oregon seventeen hours and fifty miles later rocked so hard at the arrival of a staggering champion that the overhead scoreboard bounced on its moorings from the vibrations of fans stomping the ground. Eugene had always been a tough stop for opponents in the same way as Bohler Gym in Pullman, the facility often being more challenging than the home team, and the crowd this time screamed so long and so loud that the Ducks could not hear instructions from coach Dick Harter during a huddle in the second half. Blood was in the water. A month after being in South Bend to support his friend and former Penn assistant coach Phelps, Harter moved toward adding to the UCLA downfall with special appreciation of his team's determination on display. Few coaches, after all, made guts the core of the program the same way, with practices that could last four hours, rope climbs, players holding a brick in both hands during slide drills to improve defense, and reps of absorbing charges from an incoming teammate. Placing five-gallon buckets under each basket saved cleaning up the vomit.

The defeat to the Ducks and the dual spiritless showings that became known as the Lost Weekend sounded alarm bells as the first time UCLA either failed or refused to show up two games in a row at least since the downpour of championships began with the Hazzard-Goodrich teams. It may have been the first in any era in Westwood for Wooden, who didn't always have success in his early years yet constantly praised the effort and attitude. (He said the rest of his life that no Bruin team provided more satisfaction than the 1948–49 squad that defied low expectations to finish 22-7 and none maximized potential more than the 1961–62 roster that finished 18-11.) To learn of Lee's indifference, then, with the statement "When you got nothing, you got nothing to lose," quoting Bob Dylan's "Like a Rolling Stone," in a postgame interview in Mac Court turned Wooden livid.

Players had already taken to singing along to the Jimi Hendrix version of the hit played on a tape recorder during bus rides. Practically laughing at their downward spiral, the Bruins hit the refrain "How does it feel?" hard.

In one week, the Walton Gang went from crushing Oregon by 18 points in L.A. to losing to the Ducks by 5 and from beating Oregon State by 5 at Pauley to losing to the Beavers by 4. Never was the implosion of what could have been the best team in school history and maybe even the best in college basketball history more obvious than in the inability of the far superior roster to match the effort of an Oregon team that would finish 15-11 and Oregon State en route to 13-13. That was the worst part for the coach who never sweated wins and losses as long as the Bruins played with maximum effort and focus. Worse than going from 88 wins in a row to 5-3, more damning than dropping to No. 3 in the polls, harder to accept than back-to-back losses for the first time in almost exactly eight years, since Alcindor's freshman season, the Bruins were disinterested.

"He's got to be scared now," Harter said. "They don't have the hunger to win. I don't think you can blame Wooden for that—or the players. But I think that's the case." USC is the best team in the country, Harter added, despite UCLA having beaten its crosstown rival by 11 points two weeks earlier. Resuscitating his team in a malaise at this late stage, with 6 games left in the regular season, "will be Wooden's final challenge. If he can rally these guys, if he can get them to come back and win the NCAA, the way they are right now, that would be some coaching job."

Wooden's view that the Bruins were "just too sure of themselves, going through the motions, flirting with complacency," was only partly accurate. Complacency and going through the motions were the entire problem, not caring enough about winning anymore as the downfall of a group running out the clock. They didn't assume victory as much as they didn't care about victory. "A coach needs to take care of this," theirs later wrote, "and I couldn't figure out how to do it, how to snap them out of it." His prediction in the final team gathering after the 1971–72 title that the sophomores in the room would be intolerable and uncoachable as seniors had come true.

"The 1974 Bruins may have taken it away from themselves when they stopped striving to find out how good they could be," Wooden eventually concluded. "And I wasn't a smart enough coach to prevent it from happening."

The search for solutions prompted the rare step of ending the first practice since the Lost Weekend early to convene a team meeting in the locker room. Lee would replace Curtis in the starting lineup, Wooden announced to Walton's great delight. Also, Bob "Die-lyn" quotes in the press will no longer be tolerated. The three easy wins that followed with better offensive flow indicated newfound energy, and then even the close call of a 2-point win over Stanford was washed away by beating No. 7 USC by 30 in the regular-season finale.

The program that since the mid-1960s had been mostly known as a constant show of force had slowly but clearly entered a world of drastic momentum swings since being exposed in South Bend. What Phelps detected as early as December against Maryland had become obvious as the Bruins wandered through February and March and into the first round of the tournament with a first-round matchup with Dayton as the greatest example of inconsistency. This time, with the 36-game postseason win streak still alive, they went from leading by 17 points in the first half to falling behind in the second to nearly losing in regulation when a good Dayton shot, a 15-footer with 4 seconds remaining to break an 80–80 tie, bounced away. UCLA was down to escape acts to stay alive in the first round against the No. 20 team in the country.

Never during the championship streak had the Bruins required overtime in the tournament to advance, and now they needed three in Tucson. Their first extra periods at any stage of the schedule since 1969 ended with a 111–100 victory, thanks in large part to Lee's leadership and offense in the tensest moments down the stretch, and Flyers coach Don Donoher empowered even in defeat: "I think the fact they lost three times during the season and the fact that a club like us carried them into three overtimes will help the other teams that play them" and "They know they can be beaten."

. . .

North Carolina State, the top-ranked team as the beneficiary of Notre Dame losing at Pauley Pavilion and UCLA's double pratfall in Oregon, the same night in the same first round eliminated Providence in Raleigh as another step in the redemption season. Recovering from losing to the Bruins in December would have been enough given the emotional toll of St. Louis, as Towe's flight home with his face buried in the cushions would indicate. Except the response would continue with beating No. 4 North Carolina in the next-to-last game of the regular season, No. 4 Maryland in the ACC tournament, and No. 5 Providence. No longer one of many challengers, the Wolfpack, with 22 wins in a row, experience, and a talented starting lineup beyond the second-best player in the country had a credible claim to being the tournament favorite ahead of the worn-out Bruins. No one had been able to say that since Houston in 1969 with the Game of the Century as proof.

A drinking problem did nothing to keep Thompson from turning into one of the ten greatest players in college history, maybe the five greatest, with a game played walking on clouds. The seventeen-year-old succumbing to peer pressure attending beer parties as a freshman had become the senior imbibing every day, enjoying fraternity bashes and the hero's life of a well-liked small-town kid who stayed close to home to lift State to No. 1. The night he consumed, drove a back road home with the Isley Brothers and Stevie Wonder blasting from the tape deck, and slammed his Pontiac Grand Prix nose first into a tree, somehow avoiding injury or worse, made Thompson realize he had a serious issue and needed to quit drinking. He stopped for two days.

The Thompson of late 1973–74 was without equal in the country among noncenters anyway, the same mix of talent, work ethic, and physical gifts as Walton, except with Walton an elite athlete for his position and Thompson superhuman. His nickname, Skywalker, even at six-four, was both fun and close to literal in giving North Carolina State a dimension no one could counter, especially once coach Norm Sloan responded to opponents sagging on Thompson to deny him the ball by telling Thompson to break for the basket and jump. From there, Sloan said, "Really, all you've got to do is keep the pass in the gym and David will get it." At the heights Thompson reaches, Pitt coach Buzz Ridl said in advance of facing the Wolfpack in Raleigh, there's not much a defense can do.

Thompson got so high attempting to block a shot near the free-throw line in the first half of the East final, though, that his feet clipped a shoulder of teammate Phil Spence. Thompson somersaulted back to earth and landed on his head with a thud someone later described to him as the sound of a bowling ball dropped from the top of the backboard. "My teammates feared I was dead," he wrote. "My eyes were rolled back in my head, and I was totally out. The sight sickened Coach Sloan, who later remembered, "I was numb. I wished I wasn't even associated with this team or this game." Spence said he cried at the sight and prayed, and Burleson called it the worst accident he'd ever seen. Towe thought Thompson broke his neck. The crowd in Reynolds Coliseum, State's regular-season home as well, went silent as Thompson left on a stretcher and went to the hospital.

Thompson returning to the bench late in the game as an observer with a bandaged forehead, before going back to the hospital for overnight observation once State beat Pitt, brought relief about the same time UCLA tipped off against San Francisco in Tucson to secure an eighth consecutive Final Four.

Whether he would be available to face the Bruins in the semifinals seventy-five miles away in Greensboro remained a mystery through two days of people calling with offers to pay the medical bills, security guards being posted outside his room to protect against overzealous fans, and Walter Cronkite and O. J. Simpson calling to check in. On the third day, Thompson rejoined the team for a light practice and felt the Wolfpack so uptight over his condition during a locker-room meeting that he suddenly dropped his head, jerked it to one side and then the other, widened his eyes and rolled them back, stiffened his body, and shook in spasms. Then Thompson started to laugh at the prank intended to loosen the mood, a scene he learned from watching *The Exorcist*. Actually, he had no lingering issues other than a mild headache.

UCLA had faced State just three months earlier and didn't need additional scouting, or any scouting in the Wooden approach, to be aware of Thompson as an aerodynamic marvel. Wooden even delivered the rare compliment of mentioning Thompson in the pregame instructions, something he never did for stars Elvin Hayes, Pete Maravich, or Artis Gilmore among previous opponents capable of single-handed destruction, even Hayes and Gilmore in the higher stakes of the Final Four. The last break from tradition anyone could remember was Austin Carr days before the visit to South Bend in January 1971.

Yet the Bruins were still unprepared. They didn't think Towe could shoot so well from the outside. Playing too far off forward Tim Stoddard on the wing allowed time and clear lanes for easy passes to Thompson at any elevation. And Wilkes may have been an underrated defender, overshadowed by his All-America skills on offense, but was not close to a match for Thompson's pyrotechnics. Though beyond the scouting report, Burleson took the court accepting the personal challenge of the center matchup as the chance to show himself as more than a moving seven-foot-two wall, that he had worked himself into a basketball talent through years of juggling to improve his coordination and running with ankle weights on the family farm in the mountains of western North Carolina to get stronger. The cliché request to pose alongside five-seven Towe for photos, tall next to small, made Burleson angry. What others would have seen as the death sentence of facing Walton in a national semifinal he regarded as an opportunity.

Thompson "stunned us with his athleticism," Wilkes said, as if it were a sudden development, but UCLA still led by 11 with 10 minutes left in regulation. Then Greensboro Coliseum as a virtual home game for the Wolfpack turned into South Bend, Corvallis, Eugene, and, even in defeating Dayton, Tucson. The lack of discipline with poor shot selections not only handed over the big advantage, the Bruins nearly lost in the final seconds before Stoddard's corner jumper for the win didn't fall, and then they survived the first overtime when Burleson missed a short bank against Walton. Given two reprieves, UCLA capitalized by going up 7 points with 3:27 to play, only to give that away, too, by playing without poise, making more bad decisions on offense, with a decisive turnover of a charge by Tommy Curtis, a call that irritated Wooden the rest of his life. J. D. Morgan surely noticed Rich Weiler, his postgame target at Notre Dame, as one of the referees.

The dynasty ended with two blown late leads, an 80–77 double-overtime victory for North Carolina State with 28 points and 10 rebounds from Thompson, 20 points and 10 rebounds from Burleson, his statement made, and Walton carrying a chair into the shower to sit under steaming water for twenty minutes. Later asked if he was glad his college career had ended, Walton smiled and shrugged his shoulders. Asked about his emotions as the final seconds ticked off the clock, he smiled and shrugged again. "We got careless," Lee said. "We did a number of things we shouldn't have done. We were taking twenty-foot jump shots with an eleven-point lead. That's asking for trouble, that's helping the other guy." A solemn bus ride to the hotel and what Gary Cunningham called the quietest Bruin postgame team dinner ever followed as a sense of finality set in, of the season and the championship streak but also essentially at the end of the Walton Gang that got bored with the chance to be considered the greatest team in college history.

It was a moment years in coming—finding no joy in winning the 1972 title, Wooden's gloomy long-term prediction days later, passing on the shared adventure of the China trip, the lineup decision that ruined Walton's good mood at the start of his senior season, early warning signs from the Maryland game, tuning out Wooden, and months of poor focus and an inability to close out reeling opponents. Road defeats to Notre

Dame and a North Carolina State roster that would have been deserving champions any season were explainable, but not the Lost Weekend. The Bruins ultimately needed five or six good minutes at the end of regulation in Greensboro with a championship on the line, or even three good minutes to close the first overtime, and couldn't muster either.

Being required to return to the arena two days later for a meaningless game against Kansas to determine third place in the tournament added to the sorrow. Even Wooden in the privacy of the locker room after North Carolina State railed against the tradition of a consolation-prize contest between two programs that would prefer to slink out of town, while publicly finding the right tone between supporting a final stand by the group and understanding tickets had already been sold for four games over three days. The Bruins, the seniors in particular, could threaten all they want to not show up for the undercard before NC State–Marquette, but top NCAA executives were confident Charles Young and J. D. Morgan would flex university muscle if necessary to make sure UCLA-Kansas happened. That made the Bruins' 78–61 victory the final, fitting symbolism: Bill Walton, who started his Westwood career with endless enthusiasm, who considered the sport his religion and the court his church, who dreamed of getting his chance to uphold the school's hoops tradition, in the end had to be talked into taking the court.

"For the first time in my career, I believe I became complacent this season," Wooden said the next day on the flight home to Los Angeles, self-reflection that seemed more emotional release than basketball analysis. Walton's back injury against Washington State had made him extra-cautious, the coach also decided in retrospect, and relaxing the dress code and eliminating the training table to avoid menu conflicts for his vegetarians was part of the lost discipline on the court. Wooden miles in the air in the early days of healing used the disclaimer "If I'm back" for 1974–75, although with no indication retirement was a serious option. The greater likelihood was that he would return post-Walton with the same excitement as in the first season after Alcindor.

"I enjoyed working with this group," he ultimately decided, contrary to the months of evidence. "Bill Walton and I had great rapport, I felt, despite some disagreements. You couldn't ask for a nicer player than

Keith Wilkes. I understood Tommy Curtis and Greg Lee. Curtis was very outgoing. Lee sometimes spoke too soon and too much. But there were no major problems with either of them."

Upon landing in LAX, Walton "got out of there as quick as I could. I was so ashamed and embarrassed" while "in the ultimate fog of breaking Coach Wooden's most urgent plea to us, which was, 'Do your best. Your best will be good enough. But whatever it is you do, don't beat yourself, don't cheat yourself, don't shortchange yourself, because that's the worst kind of defeat you'll ever suffer and you'll never get over it.'" In the years to come, he would forget what he did the rest of the day or even where he went from the airport, remembering only the short exchange with Wooden just after stepping off the plane. "I'm sorry, Coach," former UCLA center Bill Walton eventually told him, "for ruining it all." The only relief was that the summer at Sonoma State allowed him to graduate a quarter early, saving Walton from having to return to campus for classes.

Though hardly solely Walton's fault, the Bruins had permanently broken a Wooden core principle several times within two months, wasting big leads against Notre Dame and the eventual champion North Carolina State and losing to inferior Oregon and Oregon State. Competitive Greatness was, after all, at the pinnacle of the fifteen blocks of the Pyramid of Success, and Poise, also greatly lacking, shared the second row with Confidence. The timing made it worse, at the end of the season and the end of the Walton Gang, with no room on the calendar for redemption.

Walton left as arguably the greatest player in college basketball history, and humbled. As someone who was both a challenge for coaches in personality, though someone Wooden liked despite the conflicts, and a dream player until the gasping end, he played at an extraordinary level, often through immense pain, lived team basketball, and radiated so much joy on the court that opponents considered it an extra UCLA weapon. In the bottom-line assessment of their three varsity seasons together, "if you took all the centers who ever played basketball, selected ten fundamentals you'd like a center to have, and graded each one on a scale from one to ten, I believe Bill Walton, when healthy, would be number one," Wooden came to write. "It would be difficult to select anyone over him." Walton, in turn, about six weeks before the end of his college career offered the perspective that "I mean, we hardly agree on anything. But I respect him as a man, not for what he believes but for having the stomach to stand behind it, to live the way he thinks people should." They had ended on good terms.

Walton had already made his thoughts on the future clear before the afternoon of March 27, the day after the flight back from Los Angeles, as NBA commissioner J. Walter Kennedy prepared for the coin flip to decide whether Philadelphia or Portland got the No. 1 pick in the draft. Unlike the 1969 Alcindor pursuit, Walton in 1974 had no interest in the ABA, which was weaker than ever, even though it had a franchise coached by Wilt Chamberlain in San Diego and told Walton a team would be put in L.A. if he preferred. He still had the option to pick the coach and the roster, anyone but Julius Erving, the same as the year before. Walton was, however, willing to use the dying league as leverage: if the 76ers won the toss, he would take California and the ABA. "I'm no longer a basketball player, I'm a sun lover," he said. "I won't play in any city where the weather is inclement." Philadelphia missed out the year before because Walton wanted to stay in college and a second time because he confused Portland with Honolulu. Mentor Jerry West praising Portland as a fine city clinched it.

The participating teams were in person this time, at the Beverly Hills Hotel for a meeting of league owners, as Kennedy held another half-dollar, this time a 1946 minting.

"Heads," 76ers owner Irv Kosloff called, just as the Phoenix Suns had in the Alcindor flip conducted over the phone.

Kennedy tossed. "It's tails," he said, the fifth year in a row with the same outcome.

Trail Blazers president Herman Sarkowsky immediately ruled out a trade to the first-place Lakers that would give Walton his dream outcome of his preferred league and preferred city. Questions about drafting a player who didn't want to be there kept coming, a reflection of Walton's desire to play in a warm-weather location and his obvious love of Southern California, and of the Lakers, who had been talking openly for six months about wanting to make a trade. What would you do if he refused to sign with Portland after the draft? a reporter asked Sarkowsky in Beverly Hills. "Cut my throat and let the blood flow," Sarkowsky replied. Actually, the appeal of outdoorsy Oregon, a region Walton had visited three years in a row, and the endorsement from West, had Walton looking forward to joining the Trail Blazers, not diagramming an escape route. Walton didn't even send his agent, Sam Gilbert, into contract negotiations with salary demands. There was just one thing: no one could tell him what clothes to wear, when to shave, and certainly not when to cut his hair.

14

EPILOGUE

"**A**re the ladies beating down your door now that you're a pro?" a reporter asked Portland Trail Blazers rookie Bill Walton at a Forum press conference hours before Walton's preseason debut, the first time the No. 1 pick in the draft would be in uniform since the third-place game against Kansas.

"Let's go on to the next question," he responded.

Walton arrived with red hair to his shoulders, a folded blue scarf across his forehead tied behind his head to corral the locks, a scraggly beard, and twenty or so media members interpreting the look as a declaration of independence the instant he escaped Wooden's grooming clutches. Even being back in Southern California to play the Lakers ten miles from Westwood fed the storyline of quick rebellion. "I kind of anticipated that when I left UCLA that sort of thing wouldn't be important anymore," Walton said. "I've done a lot of thinking about the importance that's placed on the length of one's hair. It's not my trip." His love of backpacking and rambling country bike rides fit in Portland, even if it meant a pro career within 110 miles of the tandem scene of the Lost Weekend that would haunt him forever. Plus, in a few hours, Sidney Wicks would be a Blazers teammate and Jerry West an opponent, with Keith Wilkes and the Golden State Warriors facing Tom Burleson and the Seattle SuperSonics in the other game of the exhibition doubleheader.

John Wooden was preparing to open practice eighteen days later with the same optimism of his post-Alcindor world in 1969, certain the Bruins under renovation again had at least the potential for success despite the loss of a great center and four key players in all. It helped on a personal level that two of his all-time favorites, the very nonmilitant David Meyers and Ralph Drollinger, were back and that Meyers had grown into such an exemplary leader that Wooden delivered the high compliment of appointing him the captain for the entire season. Wooden, who preferred a simple and stable point guard, knew Andre McCarter remained too flashy, but the front line of Marques Johnson, Richard Washington, Meyers, and Drollinger was reason alone for optimism.

Planning for 1974–75 included, in true Wooden fashion, nearly a page of notes on lined paper with holes for a three-ring binder, a cursive numbered list, one through fourteen, of X-and-O matters and nonstrategy issues. Build Trgovich's and Drollinger's confidence. Be patient developing the zone press. Organize time-outs better, possibly a reaction to what he considered the personal failure of the loss at Notre Dame in January. Prepare Washington to play both the high and low posts. The coach who regarded stalling a disease on the sport also included the surprise that the Bruins should consider using the Four Corners slowdown offense to protect leads, either because the roster would not be as good as 1973–74 or as another direct response to recent events.

Placing two of the most telling items far down the order indicated Wooden did not rank the list in order of importance.

12. Forget the last season and concentrate on each day of practice. Don't take anything for granted, analyze, plan, work, evaluate, prepare.
14. Be patient with players on floor, but be firm on discipline both on and off the floor.

Reclaiming a foundation of structure and discipline became paramount, perhaps for his own sanity as well as the best interests of the program facing the latest dramatic roster shift. Wooden, in the bottom line, wanted to turn the regret expressed on the flight home from Greensboro into action and reestablished a program heading toward a bright future—Meyers was the lone senior and an impressive recruiting haul of David Greenwood, Roy Hamilton, and Brad Holland was underway, even if the Bruins got involved too late to turn Larry Bird away from Indiana. On the schedule, the 8-0 start with wins over opponents ranked tenth, eleventh, and fifth were especially encouraging progress reports, and even losing to Stanford and Notre Dame at midseason gave way to a quick recovery as a sign of resiliency.

Wooden quietly began informing trusted allies he would retire at the end of the season. Gary Cunningham was quickly informed. Wooden was sitting alone at a UCLA women's game in Pauley Pavilion in early February when John Sandbrook approached for what Sandbrook thought would be casual conversation. Instead, Wooden told the *Daily Bruin* sportswriter of the 1960s who had become special assistant to Chancellor Charles Young, he was the third person to know. Fred Hessler, the team's radio play-by-play man, received word, as did a few opposing coaches, greatly increasing the possibility the news would become public.

J. D. Morgan was told and began to consider potential replacements. "What about Tarkanian?" Byron Atkinson, the dean of students who kept Walton from being suspended after the arrest, asked for laughs, just for the theater of coaxing his good friend into a rant. Morgan found no humor in the suggestion. He had locked on Gene Bartow, the Illinois coach who two years earlier, while at Memphis State, was buried under the avalanche of Lee-to-Walton precision passes. Morgan topped Wooden's secrecy by bringing Bartow to Southern California for a job interview in February without Wooden being aware of the succession plan taking shape.

The news broke when, strangely, Washington State coach George Raveling reported March 9 in his column as a contributor in the *Seattle Post-Intelligencer*, "The public announcement won't come until mid-April, but John Wooden won't return as head coach at UCLA next year.

"Several sources up and down the coast have told me of Wooden's pending retirement. The reported top candidates to replace the Wizard of Westwood are current Bruin assistant Gary Cunningham and Ex-UCLA assistant Denny Crum, currently the head coach at Louisville."

Most connected to UCLA basketball and fans either missed the item that went national on the Associated Press wire or disregarded it, despite being printed in multiple Southern California papers. Few within the program reacted when Lyle Spencer of the *Los Angeles Herald Examiner* reported the morning of the national semifinal against Louisville that Wooden had decided to retire, or at the *Los Angeles Times'* non-bylined item the same day citing an unnamed UCLA alum that Wooden will quit. While Meyers and Trgovich said they knew earlier in the week, and Wooden was reading one of the newspaper reports an hour before tip-off, the postgame locker room in San Diego went silent once Wooden told the team. Most reporters had a similar stunned reaction when Wooden repeated the announcement in the press conference after the Bruins beat Denny Crum and Louisville to advance to the championship game.

Why Wooden devised the fake story of an impromptu decision after the semifinal never became clear. The truth that he decided long before but wanted to keep the focus on the games would have been understandable, yet Wooden retold the lie the rest of his life. Nell Wooden said her husband actually made up his mind in December, and John had been telling reporters for several days. He was even Spencer's source for the *Herald Examiner* story.

The reasons were more straightforward. "Perhaps it was Nell's health, which had increasingly concerned me," Wooden later wrote. "I was very good when it came to not worrying about those things that I could not control—Dad had taught me that. But Nell's health was different. I just couldn't stop worrying about it. How much it got to me I can't say, but it may have been why my energy, vitality, and spirits had gone down through the year. I wasn't really the same person anymore." Plus, he was sixty-four, though feeling good and past the health scares of 1972, and fed up with the expectations of ungrateful fans and demanding media.

Daily Bruin co–sports editor Marc Dellins trailed Wooden into the hallway after the press conference and requested an additional interview for the special section the school paper would want to do to commemorate the end of an era. Call the room at 9:00 p.m., Wooden said, after the family gets back from dinner. Dellins followed instructions. Sure, Wooden answered, come on up.

At the end of an exhausting March 29, 1975, of beating protégé Crum in a Final Four and delivering one of the biggest college basketball headlines in years, about a half day before practice in preparation for a championship game and about forty-five hours before tip-off of his last game, Wooden on the couch in the hotel suite gave the school paper all the one-on-one time Dellins wanted. They talked about an hour, a relaxed Wooden clearly at peace with the monumental decision with his shoes off and legs extended to a foot cushion and a very unrelaxed Dellins struggling in his mind to get past "I can't believe I'm here with John Wooden." Wooden later even wrote him a thank-you letter when the edition came out.

Wooden went out with a 92–85 victory over Kentucky on March 31, a tenth title in twelve years, consecutive wins over opponents ranked No. 7, No. 4, and No. 2 to cap his final tournament, a 620-147 record in twenty-seven years at UCLA, 149-2 at Pauley Pavilion, and 885-203 in forty seasons counting Indiana State and high school. Being told by a Bruin backer in San Diego Arena in what should have been a time of pure celebration that the championship made up for letting fans down the year before became final confirmation to Wooden that he'd made the right decision to get out, a bitter memory he kept close the rest of his life as the symbol of wanting to quit. Then the Bartow hire was announced two days later as "a tremendous surprise" to Wooden. Crum would have been his choice, but Morgan never asked for input on a successor, a final arrogant act from boss to employee.

A Wooden appearance the next week in San Luis Obispo, 175 miles up the coast from L.A., drew a standing-room-only crowd of twelve hundred as an immediate sign of the popularity that would mark life in retirement. He did not want to be on campus when practice resumed in October, Wooden said as part of a two-hour conversation with the rapt audience, realizing that not working under the Wooden shadow would help Bartow, already facing the unenviable task of replacing a legend. He would continue the summer basketball camps, Wooden said, appear at clinics throughout the country, give lectures, and write. He would not pick an all-time Bruin team, but the first and last clubs, by coincidence, gave him the most satisfaction for playing with a focus and to their potential. Keith Wilkes made him the proudest,

Kareem Abdul-Jabbar was the most talented, UCLA-Louisville in the semifinals two weeks before was the best college game he ever saw.

San Luis Obispo would turn out to be the first step of Wooden spending the rest of his life as a revered figure whose immense popularity transcended basketball, reached well beyond Southern California, and turned him into a gentle elder dispensing wisdom. The demanding Wooden who drove his Bruins hard, who stressed himself into sleepless nights and chirped at referees and opposing players from behind a program, became more unrecognizable with each year. The older he got the more frail he became the more endearing he seemed. The former English teacher wrote books and contributed to the works of others, traveled widely for appearances as a sage, got fifteen hundred requests a year into his nineties for an autographed copy of the Pyramid of Success, and turned into America's kindly grandfather.

. . .

Former UCLA guard Andy Hill, a former source of conflict for Wooden, became a highly successful executive in movies and television while the difficult relationship with Wooden in school had turned into a complete break in the 1990s, until the day his playing partner told Hill during a round of golf to not hurry the 2-iron shot and get his balance. Being quick but not hurrying an activity and having balance in life being two Wooden philosophies, Hill felt his coach being channeled to the course, such a powerful presence it moved Hill to reconnect. Nervously calling the old phone number he had, unsure how he would be received, Hill got the answering machine, started to leave a message with "Hi, Coach, this is Andy Hill . . . ," when Wooden picked up as soon as hearing the name.

"Andy, where are you, where have you been?" Wooden said in a welcoming tone that put Hill in a time machine to the 1960s.

The conversation went so well they agreed to meet that day at Wooden's condominium in Encino. The talk lasted hours, the distance quickly falling away. Hill never let go again, visiting often and driving Wooden to breakfast and after everything ending up a devoted Wooden fan.

Bill Seibert took a job coaching and teaching in Australia. John Wooden put in a good word to help him get hired. When UCLA held a fortieth anniversary reunion for the 1970 champions and invited every team member to say a few words, Seibert reached the microphone and said, "I didn't think I'd ever get to speak at this place again." He got big laughs.

Wooden and Bill Sweek never had a bad moment after the near fight in the shower at the 1969 Final Four, putting the incident in the past once the team discussed it at breakfast the next day. Wooden even encouraged an Italian team to sign Sweek and another time wrote a letter of recommendation at Sweek's request for a teaching job in Paris.

Don Saffer always blamed himself, not Wooden, for quitting during 1968–69 in frustration over not getting his starting job back after an injury. Saffer came to see it as a rash act of youth, later regretted the decision, and wrote Wooden to apologize for walking out in the middle of the season. They exchanged letters several times, had pleasant conversations at reunions, and ended on good terms.

There is no indication Wooden and Edgar Lacey ever reconciled or even talked again after Lacey dropped out of school within days of the Game of the Century. Lacey played one season with the Los Angeles Stars of the ABA, coached by Wooden friend Bill Sharman, and quit basketball. He died in 2011.

Ralph Drollinger and Wooden remained friends, connected for decades by their shared strong faith. Drollinger, the first player to go to four Final Fours, later earned a master of divinity, started a ministry, and held Bible studies around the world and with top officials in the Trump administration. The friendship with Walton that reached back to high school also endured despite their being on opposite ends of the political spectrum.

Drollinger was in the three-on-three game on January 5, 1988, in Pasadena, California, when Pete Maravich said, "I feel great," during a break and collapsed. The timing of the fall immediately after upbeat words led everyone to believe he was going for comedy, until Maravich started foaming at the mouth. Drollinger and another player performed CPR while waiting for the ambulance and were at the hospital with others when Pistol Pete was pronounced dead at age forty from what was later discovered to be an undetected heart defect.

. . .

The playing surface in Pauley Pavilion was dedicated Nell & John Wooden Court on December 20, 2003. With all of Pauley set for renovations after the 2010–11 season, February 26, 2011, against Arizona marked the final home game after forty-six years in the original arena, a nostalgic afternoon that included the Bruins wearing retro uniforms from the 1963–64 squad, the first championship team. Nearly nine months after his passing, a wreath was on the railing next to the second-row aisle seat Wooden had in retirement.

Coach Ben Howland sent Tyler Trapani, late in his third season as a walk-on guard, in for the final minute of the eventual 71–49 victory. Trapani had yet to score a point in his career. He had only taken 2 shots, had played 3 games, and was a guard, not the position to ordinarily be in place for an offensive rebound. But when a teammate badly missed a 3-pointer with 25 seconds remaining, Trapani rushed in to grab the air ball and score.

His grandmother looked to the ceiling, but really the sky, and his father said, "What are the odds that it would end like this? Just think about that. For him to even have the ball in his hands at that moment, you have to think his great-grandfather had something to do with this."

John Wooden's great-grandson who for three years barely played and shot even less made the final basket in the original Pauley Pavilion.

. . .

H. R. Haldeman remained passionate about his favorite team the rest of his life and found special comfort in attending home games in the 1976–77 season while awaiting a ruling on his appeal of five guilty verdicts in the Watergate scandal. "He even has his own rooting section at the UCLA basketball games," his wife, Jo, wrote. "Whenever he raises his arms during halftime, a group of students across the court stands up and cheers." The family kept the same season tickets after Haldeman died in 1993 and purchased two of the actual seats when the school sold portions of the interior of Pauley Pavilion for souvenirs as part of the renovation. The Haldemans still had season tickets, in the new Pauley, as of the end of the 2022–23 season.

Haldeman served eighteen months at the minimum-security federal prison in Lompoc. His friend John Wooden made the 260-mile roundtrip drive to visit.

. . .

J. D. Morgan worked himself to death—"That's what killed him," his track coach Jim Bush said. The devotion to the school and his kingdom in particular turned obsessive in his refusing to delegate authority and declining to share department business even with high-ranking administrators sent by Young. Protecting his turf meant Morgan would answer to the chancellor and only the chancellor and handle every major decision, regularly making him the last to leave the office and then continuing at home until two or three in the morning. Wooden in the early years of retirement saw the same aggressive athletic director as before, only with Morgan, unable to find time to exercise, up to 240 or 250 pounds on his five-eleven frame by the mid-1970s.

He underwent open-heart surgery on December 20, 1978, and followed with long stretches of working from home, unable to muster the energy to come to the campus he loved and the office he once ruled as practically a physical force. Family, friends, and colleagues wanted to throw a testimonial dinner a few months later as part of his turning sixty on March 3, but the guest of honor was too ill. It was held for his sixty-first birthday instead, with NCAA executive director Walter Byers coming from Kansas to attend in a sign of Morgan's national stature. Top assistant Bob Fischer was made acting athletic director in October 1979, before taking over the permanent role as Morgan became a consultant but spent months on medical leave before officially retiring on June 30, 1980. His seventeen years as athletic director had included ten national championships in basketball, seven in volleyball, six in tennis, four in track and field, and three in water polo, in addition to the seven he won before that as tennis coach.

"They're going to miss my style," Morgan said as he headed into retirement, though it was unclear whether he was going for sarcastic or serious.

He died at home at sixty-one on December 16, 1980, from heart disease and hypertension. The building that housed most coaches and athletic administrators was rededicated as the J. D. Morgan Center in 1984 to honor an immeasurable contribution to the university.

· · ·

Abdul-Jabbar was awarded the Presidential Medal of Freedom by Barack Obama in 2016. Richard Lapchick attended as his guest as practically a lifelong friend and a reminder five decades later how history might have been different if St. John's had not forced Lapchick's father to retire as high school senior Lew Alcindor weighed college options.

Wooden was awarded the Presidential Medal of Freedom by George W. Bush in 2003. In the most John Wooden move ever, he hung the nation's highest civilian honor on a coatrack in the living room of his condominium, next to a medal on a ribbon one of his granddaughters made for his being the best grandfather.

· · ·

"I remember him coming over to the house," Rick Phelps said of Sam Gilbert. "I remember him coming out maybe a couple times. He really wanted my dad out at UCLA. I remember that. I remember my dad talking about it. Describing the life that would have been.

"I remember he was just a really nice, kind of jovial grandfatherly type guy, and he was super-nice to everybody in the family. I kind of knew who he was because my dad told me that he's from UCLA and that he was trying to probably get my dad to go out. My dad didn't specifically say that, but I put two and two together then. I just remember him being a really super-nice guy. I thought he was very endearing as well.

"I think my mom and dad talked about it. I remember them saying things. I think Sam painted a pretty picture of Hollywood, kids being celebrity kids doing Hollywood. Driving around in Porsches and all that stuff. Sam was making those types of promises. I remember specifically something like 'Rick would be driving a Porsche when he turns sixteen,' which my parents would never, ever let happen, by the way. My mom being the professor. I think there might have been a bit of a lure for my dad to some extent, but I don't think he ever really fully would have been in the position to say, 'You know what, this is a real tough decision for me,' because I think he just always kind of had it for Notre Dame. They were both concerned about kids being in the spotlight and all that stuff and thought L.A. would have been just too wild.

"I should have told Sam, 'I'll take the job.'"

. . .

Dick Vermeil left UCLA after one season as offensive coordinator to become quarterback coach for the Rams and returned to Westwood as head coach in 1974, the start of Wooden's last season. Vermeil invited Wooden to join the Bruins football team for breakfasts during training camp on campus because the personal connection built at the start of the decade remained as well as the professional admiration. Wooden did his five miles in Drake Stadium, then put in an extra quarter mile to the Student Union for the morning meal, usually sitting next to Vermeil.

Vermeil found him more relaxed emotionally and in the same good shape physically, still keeping a vigorous pace during morning loops around the track, not passing time with a leisurely stroll. Contrary to the potential of being bored with his morning routine, Wooden in his sixties appeared as focused on his regimen as when he returned to work in 1972 with doctor's orders that his career, and maybe more, depended on exercise. He was just as structured, naturally, when the regimen eventually shifted to the neighborhoods around his Encino condominium, saving the fifteen-mile drive to campus. White Oak Place up to Burbank Boulevard, right turn on Burbank to Balboa Park, through the park, down Balboa Boulevard to Ventura Boulevard, and Ventura back to White Oak, year after year, sometimes reciting biblical quotations as he goes, other times speaking a favorite poem or verse aloud. Except for the mornings Wooden added a detour to Winchell's for his sugar fix, a glazed doughnut and a coffee, not to be confused with the day former student manager George

Morgan visited and saw two dozen Krispy Kremes on the counter to be put in the freezer for future withdrawals, or when Wooden being taken home after a speech had the driver stop for doughnuts.

Vermeil over time morphed into another former Bruin basketball player receiving counsel. Wooden saw him soon after a disappointing recruiting period in 1974, Vermeil's first as UCLA head coach, noticed the sadness at losing several top targets to rival USC, and had Vermeil come to the basketball office. Don't focus on the prospects you didn't get, Wooden told him, but instead put the energy into making sure every player you did get maximizes his potential, and everything will take care of itself. Vermeil kept the advice close and preached the same message of focus to assistants when he took over the 4-10 Philadelphia Eagles in 1976 and the 6-10 St. Louis Rams in 1997 and led both to successful turnarounds. When the Rams lost eight in a row that first season, Wooden without prompting and without having seen Vermeil for years called his friend in Missouri on one of the glum Mondays with the direction to trust in himself and not let doubt creep in.

Fifty-two years after watching the Wicks-Rowe-Bibby championship team practice in Pauley Pavilion, forty-eight years after becoming a head coach himself on the same campus, and twenty-five years after the surprise phone call in St. Louis as a much-needed emotional life preserver, Dick Vermeil was inducted in the football Hall of Fame with an acceptance speech that included one minute five seconds on a basketball coach.

. . .

Wooden took his high school sweetheart to the hospital for the last time on Christmas morning 1984. Nell had previously survived a coma and had scares other times, staring down illnesses with the same indomitable spirit as she backed John, but lost the fight to cancer at age seventy-three on March 21, 1985, after fifty-two years of marriage.

Her husband pushed forward, but never fully recovered. He declined to redecorate the way she'd left the Encino condo the couple had shared since 1974 and certainly refused to move when friends and former players offered to buy him a newer place. John talked with his Nellie every night, visited her at the cemetery every Sunday when physically able, and wrote her love letters every month, folded them to about four inches by four inches, placed them in envelopes, put a ribbon around a group at the end of the year, and set them on her side of the bed, along with one of her nightgowns.

Wooden got to know Rick Reilly of ESPN as interviews through the years for articles and TV features grew into a warm working relationship. Reilly suggested during one of his Encino visits about fifteen years after Nell's passing that the notes would make a wonderful book, maybe "How to Make Love Last" by John and Nell Wooden, and donate proceeds to charity. Wooden loved the idea. They scheduled an appointment for about a month later, and Reilly rang the buzzer on the outside gate at the arranged time. No answer.

He tried again. No answer. There had been scares before, rumors in Los Angeles sports circles that Wooden had passed, sometimes credible enough that a UCLA official would take a deep breath and call the condo, desperately hoping for an answer. Dellins, in 1975 the *Daily Bruin* reporter granted an exclusive interview the night Wooden announced his retirement, in 2009 as the school's sports information director got the answering machine and started to leave a message explaining the purpose of the call when Wooden picked up. "Not yet," he told Dellins, "but well on my way." This time, with Reilly outside the condo, there was still no response after several attempts with the buzzer. Wooden was always punctual, he was in his late eighties or early nineties, so Reilly worried.

He hopped the fence and went to Wooden's condo.

Knock on the door.

Still no answer.

Ring the bell.

Same.

Step out to the courtyard to look around.

No Wooden.

"Coach!"

Pause.

"Coach!"

Nothing.

Reilly grew more scared. Finally, after an eternity, the door opened four inches, enough to see Wooden with tears streaming down his face.

"It's too soon." I can't do it, Wooden told Reilly. Fifteen years after Nell's passing was too soon.

• • •

Someone among what became a flow of visitors to the condo as a sports pilgrimage—former members of his program, friends, friends of friends, Bruins, other college or professional teams—secretly went into the bedroom and read the love letters. Wooden refused to identify who invaded his privacy, even to his son. But no one saw the notes again. Jim Wooden believes his father, shaken by the violation, destroyed the writings before another soulless guest could sink to the same depths.

• • •

The NCAA paid Jerry Tarkanian a $2.5 million settlement in 1998 to avoid a trial after Tarkanian sued the organization for conspiring to drive him out of college basketball, vindication for the coach who long claimed unfair treatment. "If the UCLA teams of the 1960s and early 1970s were subjected to the kind of scrutiny Jerry Tarkanian and his players have been, UCLA would probably have to forfeit about eight national championships and be on probation for the next 100 years," Walton wrote in his 1978 book. Years of support from Walton prompted Tarkanian to include him in the ceremonial role of presenter when Tarkanian was inducted in the Hall of Fame in 2013.

Tom Burleson spent several decades struggling with the memory of the parking structure at the 1972 Summer Olympics and the sounds of Israeli hostages being moved to the bus that would take them to their death, an agony that stayed with him from North Carolina State to seven NBA seasons and far into retirement. "I hear them . . . in my sleep!" he said at a 2012 reunion of the U.S. basketball squad, before rushing out of a ballroom where he and Munich teammates spoke on the fortieth anniversary of the Games.

Woody Hayes was fired as Ohio State football coach in 1978 after punching an opposing player in the throat during a game. When a student manager cleaned out Hayes's desk, dozens of checks worth thousands of dollars were discovered, payment Hayes received for charity speeches but never cashed. Hayes died in 1987. Former president Richard Nixon gave the eulogy at First Community Church near Columbus. Jeb Magruder, the deputy communications director in the Nixon White House, was a reverend there.

Swimmer and water polo player Kiki Vandeweghe fell in love with basketball in the years after freshman Bill Walton would walk through the unlocked front door and into the home on Bentley Circle and nonchalantly seize Kiki's dinners. Vandeweghe during junior high spent so much time at UCLA and dreaming of being a Bruin that he learned the best door to sneak in to watch John Wooden practices, before eventually being spotted among the top rows of Pauley Pavilion and being told to leave. Later, when Bartow asked one of the regulars for an appraisal of high school senior Vandeweghe, Marques Johnson gave such a strong endorsement that Vandeweghe received a scholarship and forever credited Johnson with changing his life. Vandeweghe became an all-conference forward for the Bruins and played thirteen seasons in the NBA before working as a general manager, coach, and league executive.

Danny Nee, Lew Alcindor's Power teammate, was transferred out of Vietnam and honorably discharged in 1968, became a high school coach in 1972, and eventually a college head coach at Ohio, Nebraska, Robert Morris, Duquesne, and the U.S. Merchant Marine Academy. His stops as an assistant coach included four seasons with Digger Phelps at Notre Dame from 1976 to 1980.

Peter Norman, the Australian who finished second in the 200-meter dash at the 1968 Olympics and supported the silent protest by Americans Tommie Smith and John Carlos, died in 2006 and had a funeral near Melbourne that ended with the theme music from *Chariots of Fire*. The coffin exited the town hall with Smith and Carlos the two front pallbearers.

Carl Peterson, Freddie Goss's friend and former roommate as Sproul Hall next-door neighbors to future tennis Hall of Famers Arthur Ashe and Charlie Pasarell, returned to UCLA from West Point to earn undergraduate and master's degrees in kinesiology and a doctorate of higher education in 1970. Peterson worked as receiver coach for the Bruin football team, had a lasting friendship with Wooden, and later became director of player personnel for the Philadelphia Eagles and general manager, president, and chief executive officer with the Kansas City Chiefs. He donated $1.25 million in 2017 to help build football offices near Pauley Pavilion and the Morgan Center.

Dale Brown went from assistant coach at Utah State and Washington State to LSU head coach for twenty-five years, making the NCAA tournament thirteen times and the Final Four twice.

Pennsylvania high school quarterback Joe Montana accepted a scholarship to Notre Dame, although it is unlikely attending the basketball game against UCLA on the recruiting visit in January 1974 played a major role in the decision. Montana had been a Fighting Irish fan his whole life and they were his father's favorite team. Had Montana instead taken the North Carolina State offer to go to Raleigh for football and basketball, he would have been a freshman eligible for the varsity in David Thompson's senior season with the Wolfpack as defending national champions.

. . .

Young, Morgan, and campus counsel Alan Charles met for lunch at the Hotel Bel-Air near campus in 1977 and slid into one of the red leather booths in the dining room. Something, Young said, had to be done about Sam Gilbert, whose influence in the post-Wooden years had grown to also include the first known involvement in recruiting. "Chu-uuuuck," Morgan interjected in his usual tone so ponderous that he dragged the chancellor's first name out to two syllables, "you'd better watch for your life if you do anything with Sam."

Young took the warning seriously from a man he trusted, that Young "might be attacked or killed or whatever if you cross Sam," but was not worried. He had received death threats before, even several at a time as a visible figure in an incendiary era. The words did stick in his mind, though, as a reminder of the potential implications of building a wall between Gilbert and his Bruins.

NCAA investigator Brent Clark the same year saw so much evidence of wrongdoing that he recommended his office look into the basketball program and Gilbert with the certainty that "if I had spent a month in Los Angeles, I could have put them on indefinite suspension." Clark's bosses in the enforcement division did not follow his advice and dropped the probe before it started. UCLA, he concluded, is "a school that is too big, too powerful, and too well respected by the public, that the timing was not right to proceed against them."

The NCAA moved forward in 1981, after the influential Morgan had died and Wooden was six years into retirement, far removed from daily details as part of the transition into adored university ambassador. Under the initial Clark proposal, Wooden would have been gone just two years, close enough to become part of the investigation with players he recruited and coached still in uniform. The NCAA could have forced active team members to consent to interviews, but not former athletes. Manipulating the calendar created the distance Clark believed his superiors wanted, and also made the NCAA an accomplice in the dynasty escaping official scrutiny.

Wooden admitted mistakes may have been made in dealing, or not dealing, with Gilbert, but insisted his conscience was clear regarding the years of cheating in his program. "Maybe I had tunnel vision," he said. "I still don't think he's had any great impact on the basketball program." The same Wooden so emphasized integrity in retirement that he paid for the stamps to reply to fan letters when the envelopes could easily and ethically have been included among outgoing mail in the athletic department. When he became friends with volleyball coach Al Scates, a great success himself, and Scates invited Wooden to the postseason banquet, Wooden's mailed RSVP included a check to cover his meal. Scates returned the money to Wooden and explained the volleyball team would be pleased to have him as its guest. Wooden sent the check again.

A 1977 infraction was the earliest violation cited in the December 1981 announcement of UCLA basketball being placed on probation for two years, being barred from the 1982 tournament, and having to vacate its second-place finish in 1980. The investigation could not have been more intensive, Charles Young said. The NCAA did not single out Gilbert by name, but he and Young both strongly implied Gilbert's involvement while spinning the transgressions into a fatherly benefactor being overzealous in wanting players to have a place for home-cooked meals. They took the stance that he cared too much.

Two *Los Angeles Times* sportswriters, Alan Greenberg and Mike Littwin, needed about seven weeks to turn the so-called intense inquiry into a mockery. Having conversations the NCAA purposely avoided for years, their interviews, even minus the ability to compel university cooperation, included players saying Gilbert arranged cars, stereos, clothes, and airline tickets at little or no cost and got scalpers' prices for basketball season tickets, sometimes four years' worth in advance for the freshmen to buy cars. He arranged and paid for abortions for girlfriends of Bruins.

"Should I press a button on my desk and have two guys come and throw you out the window?" Gilbert told one of the *Times* reporters who came to Gilbert's twelfth-floor office for an interview as part of the series. Gilbert later said he was kidding. When the two writers approached him in the building's garage another day, still trying to get a comment from the main figure in the controversy, Gilbert declined again except to say, "I'm warning you to stop harassing me. . . . If you know my history, you'll stay out of my hair. . . . There's something you don't understand. There are some things I'd be willing to go to jail for."

Bartow as coach and athletic director at the University of Alabama at Birmingham wrote David Berst, the NCAA assistant executive director for enforcement, on November 1, 1991, "to say 'Thank you' for possibly saving my life." "I believe Sam Gilbert was Mafia-related and was capable of hurting people," Bartow continued in the five-page message. "I think, had the NCAA come in hard while I was at UCLA, [Gilbert and others associated with the program] would have felt I had reported them, and I would have been in possible danger." Bartow said in 1993 he did not recall the reference, but also that he could have written something in jest about Gilbert, following other Bartow public comments through the years that he did not fear Gilbert.

The FBI knocked on Gilbert's door in Pacific Palisades on November 24, 1987, to arrest him on charges of racketeering and money laundering in a federal indictment related to a marijuana-smuggling ring in Florida. They did not know he died three days earlier at seventy-four following a two-year battle with cancer and heart disease. Former Cal coach and athletic director Pete Newell, retired as Lakers general manager, insisted for years Gilbert faked his death to avoid prosecution and was living under a fake identity, perhaps in South America.

. . .

Jerry West raced from his home in Bel Air to Rancho Santa Fe in northern San Diego County the morning of November 17, 2008, hoping to make it in time for a final visit with Newell, his coach on the 1960 Olympic team and later a father figure. One of the close friends caring for Newell called during the drive to tell West to hurry. "We're losing him." West pulled in the driveway to be told Newell died about ninety seconds before.

The profound loss left West disoriented and heartbroken as well as angry, at himself for not reaching Rancho Santa Fe in time. But it also became one of several events that put him on a path of wanting to do better at appreciating loved ones, friends, and special moments when he had the chance. He began to think more about his own mortality and wanting to end in a better place than the previous lifetime of swimming in loneliness, stress, and self-loathing. A 2011 autobiography became part of the attempted catharsis—*West by West* came with the honest subtitle *My Charmed, Tormented Life*—as a candid reveal of his painful youth and the emotional difficulties that clouded his adult life.

His adoration for John Wooden never waned. When it became obvious Wooden had entered his final days, West on the floor of Staples Center before tip-off of another Lakers-Celtics Finals showdown was nearly in tears discussing his college opponent, fellow everyday guy from Hollis Johnson's, and decades-long friend he deeply respected and enjoyed. It said something that West in later years held many former Bruins in high personal regard, from Gail Goodrich and Keith Erickson from the initial championship teams to Kareem Abdul-Jabbar in the middle of the dynasty to Jamaal Wilkes on the next-to-last Wooden squad.

"They always throw the word *icon* around. I don't know if we've seen an icon like him," West said. "He's one of the most remarkable men that I've ever been around in my life. The most uplifting person. I don't know if there's anyone wiser or smarter. I loved that guy. I absolutely loved him. He left a mark on this city that's never going to be forgotten. An incredible person."

West confronted the battlefield death of his older brother on a trip to South Korea in 2010. Jerry had already been to the Korean War Veterans Memorial in Washington and felt an eerie silence as he walked near the nineteen stainless-steel statues of men trudging through fields in ponchos and combat gear, but standing in the rough, hilly terrain where David gave his life was true face-to-face. That it reminded the younger brother of the part of West Virginia they once called home was both comforting and unsettling. But Jerry West left feeling closure.

. . .

The three pillars of the greatest dynasty in college basketball history became testaments to the power of transformation.

The same Wooden who gnawed on referees and opposing players from the bench and who had to be held back from going after Bill Sweek in the shower turned into a symbol of serenity, humility, and wisdom who welcomed at least hundreds of visitors to his condominium over the years, maybe thousands. In great demand for public appearances well into his nineties, Wooden told inquiring companies to make one offer and one offer only and he would decide, not wanting a negotiation and as unmotivated as ever by money. He visited with countless others for free, usually charities, schools, and others from basketball. Wooden became so bad at turning people down that his family, especially daughter Nan, became caring but vigilant gatekeepers once too many tried to take advantage of her father's good nature. The family eventually asked the school to announce that John would no longer visit with fans or sign autographs at games, and an usher was posted near his well-known spot in Pauley Pavilion to turn admirers away.

Wooden before his health turned bad welcomed the chance to share life lessons and basketball strategy, depending on the audience, a teacher to the end, and made more money the first two years of retirement than in twenty-seven years at UCLA. When Chuck Young became president of the University of Florida and invited Wooden to speak, some six hundred people filled a campus auditorium nearly thirty years after he retired and twenty-five hundred miles from where he became famous. Seeing the interest level in Gail Goodrich, Mike Warren, Lucius Allen, and others, in 2003 and on the other side of the country, became the ultimate perspective to John Sandbrook of how much of a dynasty his friend had built.

Taking care of John in the early 2000s led to the blessing of Jim Wooden and his father building the deep connection that did not exist during the schedule demands of running a goliath sports program. They always had a positive relationship, but became much closer in later years, just as Wooden did with many Bruins once he had more time and they had graduated, going from the necessary boundaries of a player-coach partnership to friends. The former college students had also matured.

Newell received hundreds of condolence cards in the weeks after the death of his wife in 1984, not only taking the time to read each but also to write back. The one from John and Nell Wooden left him stunned, three handwritten pages filled with sorrow, sincerity, and wishes for comfort in a difficult time, a beautiful letter, not a signed card with a quick note, that obviously took time. Pete and Florence did not care much for the Woodens, seeing them pompous when, in fact, John and Nell were the opposite, but the letter changed everything. Pete melted and made sure other family members read it, too. As with the others, Wooden and Newell became closer and made appearances together as co-legends who respected each other as coaches but in the end also had a friendship.

Kareem Abdul-Jabbar was in the middle of one of many visits to the Encino condo when Wooden brought up Jack Donohue, the Power Memorial coach who went on to the same role with the Canadian national team for sixteen years. Wooden detailed the time Donohue spent in 1965 to start the recruiting process that ended with Lew Alcindor at UCLA. The phone rang. Donohue, in Los Angeles, just happened to be calling. Abdul-Jabbar, having previously moved past the animosity of the racist comment in high school, gladly took the phone from Wooden, had a cheerful conversation, and made plans to meet in person later. Wooden wanted to make sure they had gotten to a good place before it was too late.

Wooden remained mentally sharp well into his nineties, but the years showed physically as using a wheelchair became a requirement, the back injury from the pickup game in the navy turned into a pronounced stoop, and he tired more easily. He was ninety-eight when the family halted public appearances. By ninety-nine, "Coach had become philosophical about death," Abdul-Jabbar wrote. "He spoke about it as if it were nothing more than an inconvenient appointment he had to rotate his tires. A nuisance more than something to be feared."

"I'm not afraid to die," he said one day in the den in Encino as they watched college basketball, Abdul-Jabbar hating where the conversation was obviously headed in the way a child might flinch at parents wanting to read their will out loud. Abdul-Jabbar stared at the TV screen, hoping the subject would change.

"They asked me the other day about my memorial at UCLA," Wooden continued. "What I wanted."

"Oh."

"The truth is, I don't think I've ever recovered from Nellie's death. Not really. So, I'm not afraid to die because I'll be with her again."

"I know you will, Coach."

"Mark Twain said, 'The fear of death follows from the fear of life. A man who lives fully is prepared to die at any time.'" Wooden paused. "Did I say that right?" he said out loud but obviously to himself, internally double-checking the statement, before nodding that he had. "I can't think of anyone who's had a fuller life than I."

Walton, seeing Wooden struggle more and more to hold conversations, said goodbye in February 2010, not knowing how much time Wooden had left and in what state if they did get to talk at the very end. Walton called Larry Bird the same day so one Indiana legend could chat a final time with another, with Bird doing most of the talking.

Abdul-Jabbar received word in Europe that Wooden had been taken to Ronald Reagan UCLA Medical Center suffering from dehydration and was not expected to live long. A do-not-resuscitate order had been taped to the refrigerator in the condo, in case a first responder entered for a rescue. Wooden's first superstar center rushed back to Los Angeles and straight to the hospital on June 4, 2010, the same drive Power senior Lew Alcindor made to meet Wooden for the first time forty-five years before except for the last mile. Walton hurried from the Bay Area after Andy Hill called with the news. Reaching the room, Walton walked silently to the bed, bent down to kiss Wooden, and whispered, "Thanks, Coach. I love you. And I'm really sorry for ruining your life." Gary Cunningham broke off a vacation in the mountains. Jamaal Wilkes answered his phone to hear Mike Warren urging him to get to the hospital. Dodgers manager Joe Torre, a longtime friend, paid a final visit. Keith Erickson came, gently held the fingers on one of Wooden's hands, spoke to Coach, and got a little smile in response as well as a few words Erickson could not understand.

Emotions swirled around Abdul-Jabbar as he walked through the maze of hospital hallways, the pain that "my last parent was dying," the pride of being in the building where one of his sons had excelled on a rotation in the trauma department in training to become a surgeon, and the good fortune of making it in time to see Wooden sedated but alive. He put a hand on one of Wooden's, leaned closer for a small amount of privacy, and told his surrogate father, "Thank you, thank you for everything you've given me." He added a Muslim prayer in a whisper: "Truly we belong to Allah. Truly we will return to him. Peace and blessings." Abdul-Jabbar then stepped back and sat in the shadows for an hour, waiting, going over their recent conversations to make sure Wooden knew how much Abdul-Jabbar cared about him, scolding himself for not being with him more often. "But then I looked over at him lying there and felt calmness. I had become the man he'd wanted me to be. I had followed my path, which is all he'd ever encouraged me to do. I had raised my children to be kind and compassionate. I had fought for justice whenever I saw injustice. I had lived one of his golden rules: 'Be more concerned with your character than your reputation, because your character is what you really are, while your reputation is merely what others think you are.'"

John Robert Wooden died at 6:45 p.m. on June 4, 2010, in the massive campus medical complex a half mile from Pauley Pavilion, sixty-two years after he came to UCLA, thirty-five years after he retired, and four months and ten days before he would have turned one hundred. Loved ones were at his bedside, others in a waiting room, and another group, most appearing to be college age, stood vigil outside the hospital. "It wasn't a sad ending," to Jim Wooden, comforted that his father did not appear to be in pain and, most of all, that John and Nell were together again. "It was a happy ending in a sense because he was going where he wanted to go. It was good. It was nice."

The ninety-minute public memorial on June 26, 2010, Wooden did not want but agreed to included his two children, seven grandchildren, and thirteen great-grandchildren, with the first great-great-grandchild on the way, former players and colleagues. "Galway Bay," popularized by Bing Crosby, was played on a guitar in homage to his Irish heritage, and his Pauley seat in retirement had been roped off and bathed in a spotlight. No one would ever watch from Section 103B, Row 2, Seat 1, again, Athletic Director Dan Guerrero announced to applause from the approximately four thousand people in the arena. Walton attended, but long before declined Wooden's request to speak, certain he had no chance to make sense through the inevitable tears at the podium. Just asking, though, became the bottom-line Wooden statement on their forty-year relationship, no matter how many times Walton said he ruined his coach's life. Exactly the opposite.

Walton had by then completed his improbable journey from early-twenties rebel who didn't talk much and was often rude when he did to adult with flowing words and kindness. As easy as it was during the UCLA years to imagine him reaching the Hall of Fame, no one would have predicted Walton with a career of decades as a basketball commentator and the new challenge of getting him to not talk. His analysis was often stream of consciousness about music, another event near the game, a historical figure—anything—just as he would often appear at fundraisers and become the most vocal person there on behalf of the charity. He even indirectly became part of the Establishment by signing with major TV networks.

He also went from college Walton rolling his eyes at Wooden's sayings to the father who would write the same Wooden maxims on lunch bags before his four sons left for school. They became the ones rolling their eyes at Bill as he turned into the most public Wooden flag bearer. He doted on his former coach, calling Encino so often and wanting to talk for so long that Wooden joked he would set the phone down, come back a minute later, interject a "Yes, Bill," and set the phone down again.

Abdul-Jabbar and Wooden likewise evolved in unimaginable ways, from partners in basketball—two mechanics—to former player and coach occasionally in touch to close friends who watched baseball and western movies together and comforted each other as parents and wives passed. "We had had our days of glory together," Abdul-Jabbar wrote in the 2017 recounting of their relationship. "Our triumphs. Our accolades. That was easy. But we had endured so much heartache together, weathered so many sorrows, waded through so much grief, always pulling each other to safety when one of us faltered. That had been the true test of friendship, and Heaven had rewarded us both."

His personal evolution the same years came to include Abdul-Jabbar writing numerous commentaries and appearing on TV to share views on race in America. The NBA created an award in 2020 to recognize players standing up for social justice and named it after him, the racist teenager now an adult being held up as an example of working to improve race relations. He followed his own path, as Abdul-Jabbar said to himself in the hospital room, and remembered one of many Wooden sayings:

Things work out best for the people who make the best of the way things work out.

ACKNOWLEDGMENTS

I approached Indiana Pacers executive and broadcaster Quinn Buckner as he stood on the baseline near the home bench inside Bankers Life Fieldhouse in Indianapolis, not by scheduling an interview in advance. He said he would be glad to talk but that he only had a few minutes before a VIP event elsewhere in the arena. The conversation lasted longer, about 10 minutes of impressive recall and candor before Buckner excused himself.

To meet the chairman of the Joint Chiefs of Staff.

Buckner gave extra time when he could have been with the highest-ranking military officer in the United States, Army Gen. Martin E. Dempsey, four stars better than me. Just maybe that conversation at a goodwill appearance before tipoff would have been more interesting. Yet Buckner stayed for a conversation on Far East travel itineraries, demanding fathers and 1970s hoops, gracious throughout before pushing himself away.

There were dozens of similar moments through years of research and writing. Some people interrupted vacations to step into the time machine, others set aside health issues to keep scheduled interviews, many granted multiple sessions through conversation or email, and most made clear I should not hesitate to call again if additional questions came up. When I first mentioned the idea for this project to Bill Walton, just in conversation at the time, he not only predicted his fellow Bruins of the era would participate, but that they would enjoy the chance to remember a unique era in American history.

He was right, and soon I lost count of the number of people who said with sincerity how much they enjoyed reminiscing.

I kept coming back to the words of Andy Hill, a guard for three titles and later a good friend to retired John Wooden: "My teammates at UCLA were just great fuckin' guys. They really were." They really still are. To be able to say with the same sincerity that I did not have one bad conversation makes me the envy of every author. Whatever success this book has will be because I spent time with a lot of smart, giving, fun people.

My only adjustment to Hill's statement is that it wasn't just his years, wasn't just the players, wasn't just the Bruins and wasn't just guys. Former student manager George Morgan showed patience as I pressed for specifics on the proper technique for cutting the oranges the detail-driven Wooden wanted in the locker room at games. In half? Quarters? (Morgan became quick with knives, but thankfully did not hurry.) Good luck finding anyone with a bad word to say about Gary Cunningham. I asked Stan Morrison for an hour of conversation, we went an hour 43, he told me to call again – and then mailed a card thanking me for my time. Digger Phelps and his family talked about the village of Notre Dame as a community spirit, not a location, and showed me around. Jo Haldeman got her kids involved to help with fact checking, even taking pictures to help me document long-ago moments.

While I was unable to speak with Wooden for this book before his death in 2010, I had the great fortune of many earlier conversations on the phone and in Pauley Pavilion as he supported the Bruins of the late-1990s. I still remember feeling smarter or happier at the end of each. The countless others who also crossed paths with him, whether briefly or for decades, will be pleased to know some of his best qualities have been passed down to son Jim and grandson Greg, just as kind and helpful as I'm sure Coach would have been if I'd started this project sooner. I appreciate the trust they showed in me to tell the story.

Agent Susan Canavan from Waxman Literary believed in the idea, lent expertise in shaping the direction and handling the deal and expressed confidence we would find the right fit for a publisher. Atria and parent company Simon & Schuster were the right fit. More specifically, Sean deLone was the right editor, a full partner in sharing the original vision we should not turn out a typical sports book, not when everything about the program and the times were atypical. His input and encouragement to stick to the plan of atmosphere and emotions over box scores, and finally the editing process itself, was invaluable.

I am grateful for the assistance of the UCLA sports information department, especially associate director Alex Timiraos as the lead on men's basketball. Dragging former SID stars Marc Dellins and Bill Bennett out of retirement was beneficial in a work sense and enjoyable as the chance to hang out again. I am indebted to them in many ways. Thanks also to Jane Collings at the UCLA Library for help with archive material.

Any attempt at listing colleagues and friends who played a direct part or otherwise supported this finished product many years in the making would double the size of the book. For now, I am grateful for the contributions and inspiration of Skip Nicholson, Nick Todd, Roland Lazenby, Mark Whicker, Fran Blinebury, Jeff Fellenzer, Keith Bereskin, Dwight Chapin, Bill Plaschke and Doug Kelly. The same goes for the impossible of naming the media members of the time whose coverage in the 1960s and '70s greatly aided my work in the 2020s. All books, newspapers, magazines, websites and podcasts are cited in the end notes, but nothing tops the daily coverage from the beat writers and columnists on the scene.

Taylor, Jordan and Nora get credit for everything else, especially after pushing past initial hesitation. I would have said something about being thankful for the next 88 years, and not just for the backing during this book, but it's better to say they make each day my masterpiece. I think John Wooden would like that.

NOTES

Introduction

1   *went through proper channels:* Katie Mettler, "The Day Anti-Vietnam Protestors Tried to Levitate the Pentagon," *Washington Post*, October 19, 2017, https://www .washingtonpost.com/news/retropolis/wp/2017/10/19/the-day-anti-vietnam -war-protesters-tried-to-levitate-the-pentagon/.

1   *The man in charge of permits: Time*, "The Banners of Dissent," October 27, 1967, https://content.time.com/time/subscriber/article/0,33009,841090-1,00.html.

1   *"We shall raise":* Mettler, "Day Anti-Vietnam Protestors."

2   *Another organizer flew home:* Larry "Ratso" Sloman, Michael Simmons, and Jay Babcock, "Out, Demons, Out! The 1967 Exorcism of the Pentagon and the Birth of Yippie!," *Arthur*, November 2004, https://arthurmag.com/2011/04/13/out -demons-out-the-1967-exorcism-of-the-pentagon-and-the-birth-of-yippie-arthur -no-13nov-2004/.

2   *When the day finally came:* Mettler, "Day Anti-Vietnam Protestors."

2   *He spent decades feeling bad:* Author interview with Jeff Fellenzer, April 7, 2023.

2   *He first shot hoops:* John Wooden with Steve Jamison, *My Personal Best: Life Lessons from an All-American Journey* (New York: McGraw-Hill Education, 2004), 1.

4   *"If it takes a bloodbath":* Wallace Turner, "Reagan Remark a Campaign Issue," *New York Times*, April 19, 1970, 43, https://www.nytimes.com/1970/04/19/archives /reagan-remark-a-campaign-issue-bloodbath-comment-fuels-oratory-in.html.

4   *"grandfatherly approach":* Neville L. Johnson, *The John Wooden Pyramid of Success: The Ultimate Guide to Life, Leadership, Friendship and Love Created by the Greatest Coach in the History of Sports* (Los Angeles: Cool Titles, 2000), 38.

4   *"victims of a permissive society":* Ibid.

4   *statistics later compiled:* vietnamveteranproject.org, https://vietnamveteranproject.org /statistics-2/.

5   *"I did not know how":* Author interview with Bill Walton, June 16, 2023.

1. On the Eve of Destruction

7   *staged a 7-Foot Party:* Author interview with Danny Nee, April 30, 2009.

8   *"I have an announcement to make":* Robert Lipsyte, "Alcindor Accepts U.C.L.A. Basketball Scholarship from 60 College Offers," *New York Times*, May 5, 1965, 56, https://www.nytimes.com/1965/05/05/archives/alcindor-accepts-ucla-basketball -scholarship-from-60-college-offers.html.

8   *Alarms sounded:* Author interview with Joe Jares, August 21, 2009.

8   *"refreshingly modest":* "Alcindor, 7-1 Cage Whiz, Picks UCLA," *Los Angeles Times*, May 5, 1965.

8   *"Can't talk anymore":* Lipsyte, "Alcindor Accepts," 56.

8   *"very confused":* Ibid.

8   *No, he replied to another:* "Alcindor, 7-1 Cage Whiz."

9   *"tremendously pleased":* Lipsyte, "Alcindor Accepts," 56.

9   *"His high school press clippings":* John Hall, "No More 'Camps,'" *Los Angeles Times*, May 5, 1965.

9   *When his parents sent:* Kareem Abdul-Jabbar and Peter Knobler, *Giant Steps: The Autobiography of Kareem Abdul-Jabbar* (New York: Bantam Books, 2003), 45–49.

10   *It felt like being:* Mark Whicker, "Kareem Appreciates Obama Journey," *Orange County Register*, November 5, 2008.

10   *He couldn't help:* Kareem Abdul-Jabbar and Raymond Obstfeld, *Becoming Kareem: Growing Up On and Off the Court* (New York: Little, Brown, 2017), 72.

10   *"You're acting just like":* Ibid., 101. Abdul-Jabbar in later years told the stories with slightly different wording at different times, but always with the same racist term and the same scene. The basics of what happened never changed.

10   *Absentmindedly doodling:* Lew Alcindor with Jack Olsen, "My Story," *Sports Illustrated*, October 27, 1969.

11   *"I sat there":* Ibid.

12   *Yet he was:* Kareem Abdul-Jabbar, *Coach Wooden and Me: Our 50-Year Friendship On and Off the Court* (New York: Grand Central Publishing, 2017), 190.

12   *a distant father:* Abdul-Jabbar and Obstfeld, *Becoming Kareem*, 13.

12   *would in retirement remember playing:* Ibid., 16.

12   *narrowed his college choice:* Ibid., 156.

12   *St. John's had the lure:* Author interview with Richard Lapchick, August 24, 2022.

13   *the school clearly unaware:* Ibid.

14   *Knicks management once sent:* David Wolf, *Foul! The Connie Hawkins Story* (New York: Holt, Rinehart and Winston, 1972), 46.

14   *"exceptionally fine record":* Franklin D. Murphy Archives at UCLA, via John Matthew Smith, "'It's Not Really My Country': Lew Alcindor and the Revolt of the Black Athlete," *Journal of Sports History*, Summer 2009.

15   *twelve-year-old San Diego resident:* Bill Walton with Gene Wojciechowski, *Nothing But Net: Just Give Me the Ball and Get Out of the Way* (New York: Hyperion, 1994), 13.

15   *If he had to leave town:* "Aids Handle UCLA Basket Recruiting," *St. Louis Post-Dispatch*, April 24, 1966.

16   *"That's the year":* John Hall, "Chess Master," *Los Angeles Times*, May 15, 1965, 27.

16   *Alcindor never forgot:* Author interview with Kareem Abdul-Jabbar, December 18, 2015.

16   *Seventeen-year-old Alcindor:* Abdul-Jabbar and Obstfeld, *Becoming Kareem*, 136–38.

16   *"Drink it or wear it":* Abdul-Jabbar and Knobler, *Giant Steps*, 84.

17   *Donohue heard a man:* George Walsh, "Wooing of a Seven-Foot Wonder," *Saturday Evening Post*, March 14, 1964.

17   *"We know what getting":* Ibid.

17   *"Jack Donohue has":* Ibid.

17   *"it's like":* Fox 71, "A Look Back: 'Alcindor Picks UCLA,'" bruinsnation.com, May 5, 2015, https://www.bruinsnation.com/ucla_basketball/2015/5/5/8545833/a-look-back -kareem-abdul-jabbar-lew-alcindor-picks-ucla.

18   *Alcindor was quickly taken:* Abdul-Jabbar, *Coach Wooden and Me*, 21.

18   *"We expect":* Ibid., 22.

18   *"so square":* Jim Murray, "John Wooden: With or Without Lew, He's Still the Best," *Los Angeles Times*, March 29, 1970, D1.

18   *"heavily muscled fellows":* Phil Pepe, "Alcindor Matures . . . but Forgets Coat," *New York Daily News*, December 27, 1968, 76.

18   *"Oh, you mean":* Red Auerbach and John Feinstein, *Let Me Tell You a Story: A Lifetime in the Game* (New York: Little, Brown, 2004), 224.

19   *"He wanted to see UCLA":* Sid Ziff, "Education's Tall Cost," *Los Angeles Times*, May 7, 1965, pt. 3, p. 3.

19   *At the end of the visit:* John Wooden, "Right Man at the Right Time: J. D. Morgan," interviewed by David A. Rose for UCLA Oral History Program, March 12, 1982, 349.

19   *"You owe it to me":* Abdul-Jabbar and Knobler, *Giant Steps*, 110.

19   *"If you come here":* Ibid.

20   *Morgan not only insisted:* Wooden, "Right Man at the Right Time," 349.

20   *"was afraid we wouldn't":* Author interview with Jerry Norman, August 23, 2022.

20   *"Worst thing to happen":* Ibid.

20   *his fourth or fifth:* "Aids Handle UCLA Basket Recruiting," 90.

20   *the only school to be invited:* Abdul-Jabbar, *Coach Wooden and Me*, 28.

20   *But the meeting felt:* Norman interview.

20   *"it's only a matter":* Lawrence Ferchaw, "King for a Day," *Daily Bruin*, February 24, 2000. For King's entire speech on April 27, 1965: https://newsroom.ucla.edu/stories /archivist-finds-long-lost-recording-of-martin-luther-king-jr-s-speech-at-ucla.

21   *set up through the Mets:* Author interview with Phil Pepe, May 7, 2009.

21   *Some Dodgers treated:* Ibid.

22   *"This is no place":* Peter Bart, "New Negro Riots Erupt on Coast; 3 Reported Shot," *New York Times*, August 13, 1965, 1, https://archive.nytimes.com/www.nytimes.com /learning/general/onthisday/big/0811.html.

22   *heard the loud pop:* Author interview with Jamaal Wilkes, June 7, 2023.

22   *"L-S-M-F-T!":* Rick Perlstein, *Nixonland: The Rise of a President and the Fracturing of America* (New York: Scribner, 2008), 14.

22   *"rather well in hand":* Matthew Dallek, *The Right Moment: Ronald Reagan's First Victory and the Decisive Turning Point in American Politics* (New York: Free Press, 2000), 130.

23 *"First one drops their hands"*: "Hell in the City of Angels," KTLA, August 15, 1965, via Perlstein, *Nixonland*, 16.

24 *"Have you ever been"*: Alexander Wolff, "Something Special about the First: How '64 Bruins Made John Wooden," *Sports Illustrated*, June 4, 2010, https://www.si.com /more-sports/2010/06/05/wooden-1964.

24 *"a six-five Bill Russell"*: Ibid.

24 *"If Lewis doesn't want"*: Seth Davis, *Wooden: A Coach's Life* (New York: Times Books, 2014), 247.

24 *"He practically begged"*: Ibid., 248.

24 To the Bruins' top assistant: Norman interview.

24 *"the stifling shadow"*: Abdul-Jabbar and Obstfeld, *Becoming Kareem*, 156.

24 He was sentimental: Abdul-Jabbar and Knobler, *Giant Steps*, 121.

2. Unveilings

25 so deep in contemplation: Abdul-Jabbar and Knobler, *Giant Steps*, 122.

25 *"a theme-park"*: Kareem Abdul-Jabbar with Raymond Obstfeld, *On the Shoulders of Giants: My Journey through the Harlem Renaissance* (New York: Simon & Schuster, 2007), 248.

25 *The first night*: Abdul-Jabbar and Obstfeld, *Becoming Kareem*, 174.

25 shot pool in Dykstra: Author interview with Gary Beban, September 1, 2022.

26 He mumbled in appreciation: Abdul-Jabbar and Obstfeld, *Becoming Kareem*, 175.

26 It took three days: Alcindor with Olsen: "My Story."

26 Alcindor wheeled around: Ibid.

27 *"And not only"*: Ibid.

27 *"I quickly discovered"*: Ibid.

28 *"From the minute"*: John Wooden and Steve Jamison, *Wooden on Leadership* (New York: McGraw-Hill, 2005), 138.

28 Wooden saw the grooming: Ibid., 141.

28 Alcindor considered pointing out: Abdul-Jabbar, *Coach Wooden and Me*, 93.

28 used the chalkboard: Wooden and Jamison, *Wooden on Leadership*, 151.

28 he liked balanced: Jares interview.

29 *"Phlegm, like shoestrings"*: Wooden and Jamison, *Wooden on Leadership*, 139.

29 Student managers through the years: Author interview with George Morgan, September 13, 2022.

29 *The staff often spent*: Fellowship of Christian Athletes, *The Greatest Coach Ever: Tony Dungy, David Robinson, Tom Osborne, and Others Pay Tribute to the Timeless Wisdom and Insights of John Wooden* (Grand Rapids, MI: Revell, 2010), 48.

30 freshman team on October 15, 1965: Abdul-Jabbar and Obstfeld, *Becoming Kareem*, 74–75.

31 Not stopping at: Wooden with Jamison, *My Personal Best*, 147.

31 *"kept myself a little aloof"*: Abdul-Jabbar, *Coach Wooden and Me*, 124.

31 still found Alcindor: Author interview with Gary Cunningham, September 1, 2022.

31 Wooden offered Cunningham: Cunningham interview.

31 *The best Wooden could offer*: Eddie Einhorn with Ron Rapoport, *How March Became*

Madness: How the NCAA Tournament Became the Greatest Sporting Event in America (Chicago: Triumph Books, 2006), 120.

32 *bullied the prized recruit:* Earl Gustkey, "Carty Talks About a Kid Named Lew," *Los Angeles Times*, June 5, 1972.

32 *"I jumped on him":* Ibid.

33 *He planned to get:* Wooden with Jamison, *My Personal Best*, 80.

33 *Wooden considered a lot:* "Interview: John Wooden Basketball Coaching Legend," Academy of Achievement, February 27, 1996.

34 *In an era of:* Seth Rosenfeld, "Secret FBI Files Reveal Covert Activities at UC / Bureau's Campus Operations Involved Reagan, CIA," *San Francisco Chronicle*, June 9, 2002, https://www.sfgate.com/news/article/Secret-FBI-files-reveal-covert-activities-at-UC-3307655.php.

34 *Bruin Hoopsters, who met weekly:* H. R. Haldeman, interviewed by Dale E. Treleven for UCLA Oral History Program, for the California State Archives State Government Oral History Program, June 18, 1991.

35 *"was the greatest thing":* Sam Farmer, "L.A. in Wooden's Words," *Los Angeles Times*, March 30, 2006, https://www.latimes.com/archives/la-xpm-2006-mar-30-sp-125 wooden-story.html.

36 *that surprised Alcindor:* Mike Lopresti, "Remembering the Start of UCLA's Dynasty, 50 Years Later," ncaa.com, March 3, 2017, https://www.ncaa.com/news/basketball -men/article/2017-03-03/ucla-basketball-and-beginning-its-golden-age-50-years-later.

36 *after a varsity reserve:* Joe Jares, "The Hot Brubabes," *Sports Illustrated*, December 6, 1965, 46.

36 *already better than:* Author interview with Bill Bertka, September 29, 2009.

36 *"He made us all":* Lopresti, "Remembering the Start."

36 *Unsure how to proceed:* Cunningham interview.

36 *The impromptu plan:* Ibid.

37 *"from that point on":* Lopresti, "Remembering the Start."

37 *"John," Harshman finally said:* Author interview with Marv Harshman, August 12, 2009.

37 *California players entered:* Author interview with Russ Critchfield, August 10, 2022.

38 *Washington's Mac Duckworth:* Earl Luebker, "Sports Log," *Tacoma News Tribune*, December 20, 1965, B-2.

38 *Wooden and Cunningham:* Gustkey, "Carty Talks About a Kid."

38 *Midway through the next:* Ibid.

38 *"At Christmastime":* Lew Alcindor with Jack Olsen, "UCLA Was a Mistake," *Sports Illustrated*, November 3, 1969, 34.

39 *"He seemed to be coping":* Pepe interview.

39 *"I wouldn't want":* Bob Pille, "The True Lew Needs a Challenge to Explode," *Binghamton Press and Sun-Bulletin*, January 29, 1967, 2-D.

39 *but privately:* Abdul-Jabbar, *Coach Wooden and Me*, 80.

39 *What Alcindor came:* Ibid.

39 *he became particularly concerned:* Bob Johnson, "My Nickel's Worth," *Spokane Daily Chronicle*, February 8, 1966, 13.

40 *"a little better":* Ibid.

40   *"I would discourage":* Dwight Chapin and Jeff Prugh, *The Wizard of Westwood: Coach John Wooden and His UCLA Bruins* (Boston: Houghton Mifflin, 1973), 303.

40   *Alcindor decided the racist South:* Mary Kaye Schilling, "Kareem Abdul-Jabbar in 1967 Was Dominant, Smart and Rightfully Annoyed: From the *Newsweek* Archives," *Newsweek*, February 14, 2019, https://www.newsweek.com/2019/02/22/kareem-abdul-jabbar-1967-ucla-dominant-smart-annoyed-newsweek-archives-1329138.html.

40   *"I had always been":* Alcindor with Olsen, "My Story."

40   *then reading:* Abdul-Jabbar and Obstfeld, *Becoming Kareem*, 213.

41   *"where a small minority":* New York Times, May 14, 1966, and *Los Angeles Times*, May 13, 1966, via Perlstein, *Nixonland*, 83.

42   *Reagan didn't have actual:* Clark Kerr, *The Gold and the Blue: A Personal Memoir of the University of California, 1949–1967* (Berkeley: University of California Press, 2003), 288.

42   *"sexual orgies so vile":* Ibid.

42   *"made it so difficult":* Pete Newell, "UC Berkeley Athletics and a Life in Basketball: Coaching Collegiate and Olympic Champions; Managing, Teaching, and Consulting in the NBA, 1935–1995," interviewed by Ann Lage, University of California University History Series, April 5, 1994, 229.

43   *"No, I'm not":* Ibid.

43   *"You don't want":* Ibid.

43   *Newell's wife:* Author interview with Greg Newell, July 11, 2022.

44   *What schools are you considering?:* Author interview with John Shumate, January 5, 2010.

44   *decided to sign with:* Author interview with Quinn Buckner, April 5, 2015.

44   *preferred trying to build:* Author interview with Paul Westphal, March 16, 2020.

45   *you know:* Michael Reagan, "Reagan: Public Shouldn't Eat Campaign Dirt," *East Valley Tribune*, eastvalleytribune.com, July 20, 2012, https://www.eastvalleytribune.com/opinion/columnists/reagan-public-shouldn-t-eat-campaign-dirt/article_6e2cc71a-d200-11e1-91e0-001a4bcf887a.html.

45   *"the last bastion":* Chapin and Prugh, *Wizard of Westwood*, 255.

45   *"was the regularity":* Author interview with Gene Bleymaier, March 19, 2005.

3. Boy King

47   *"There was no doubt":* John Wooden, as told to Jack Tobin, *They Call Me Coach* (Waco, TX: Word, 1972), 145.

48   *He had a list:* Si Burick, "Lew Was Wooden's Easiest Recruiting Coup," *Dayton Daily News*, March 26, 1967, D-1.

48   *"I am not":* Arnold Hano, "Winning," *New York Times*, December 2, 1973, 329.

48   *thought Norman had:* Newell interview.

48   *His idea of scouting:* Davis, *Wooden*, 121.

48   *"trained the mind":* Swen Nater, "John Wooden and Mental Toughness," *Swen Nater* (blog), August 10, 2018, http://swennater.blogspot.com.

49   *Wooden estimated he spent:* Wooden, as told to Tobin, *They Call Me Coach*, 146.

49   *Wooden considered him:* Wooden and Jamison, *Wooden on Leadership*, 263.

49   *"They don't come":* Kareem Abdul-Jabbar with Mignon McCarthy, *Kareem* (New York: Random House, 1990), 92.

49   *save up to buy:* Frank Deford, "'Lewie Is a Minority of One," *Sports Illustrated,* December 5, 1966.

50   *"I couldn't stand":* Alcindor with Olsen, "UCLA Was a Mistake," 38.

50   *and a university official:* Mal Florence, "Bruins Still Keep Alcindor 'Under Wraps,'" *Los Angeles Times,* December 1, 1965, 37.

50   *"I guess you have":* Sid Ziff, "Lights! Camera! Action—and Alcindor Speaks," *Los Angeles Times,* October 15, 1966, pt. 2, p. 3.

50   *"potentially the most":* Jeff Prugh, "Cage Teams Plot 'War on UCLA,'" *Los Angeles Times,* November 30, 1966, pt. 3, p. 1.

51   *"Why, I'd say":* Jeff Prugh, "Naulls Works to Smooth Out Lew's 'Rough Edges,'" *Los Angeles Times,* November 16, 1966, pt. 3, p. 4.

51   *"This team":* Steve Jacobsen, "UCLA: Wait Until Next Year . . . ," *Newsday,* March 27, 1967, 72.

51   *He could almost:* Abdul-Jabbar, *Coach Wooden and Me,* 192.

51   *"bigger—and more intimidating":* Abdul-Jabbar and Obstfeld, *Becoming Kareem,* 219.

51   *"That way it should":* "College Basketball: What to Do about Lew," *Time,* December 16, 1966, https://content.time.com/time/subscriber/article/0,33009,836670,00.html.

51   *"was like test-driving":* Lopresti, "Remembering the Start."

52   *"He even frightens me":* Jeff Prugh, "Alcindor Scores 56 as Bruins Conquer Trojans," *Los Angeles Times,* December 4, 1966, D-1.

52   *The announcement earlier:* "Bruin Cagers Get '68 Date in Astrodome," *Los Angeles Times,* December 4, 1966, D-8.

52   *Hey, Alcindor thought:* Scott Howard-Cooper, *The Bruin 100: The Greatest Games in the History of UCLA Basketball* (Lenexa, KS: Addax Publishing Group, 1999), 140.

52   *"He had a willing":* Ibid.

52   *"By last week":* "College Basketball: What to Do."

52   *"He can shoot":* Joe Falls, *Sporting News,* January 7, 1967.

52   *"Can Basketball Survive":* Rex Lardner, "Can Basketball Survive Lew Alcindor?," *Saturday Evening Post,* January 14, 1967.

52   *"The idea is":* Associated Press, "It's True—Alcindor (56) Great!," *Spokesman-Review,* December 5, 1966, 10.

52   *To ensure his Cougars:* Associated Press, "Harsh Uses 'Props' in Drills for Lew," *Spokesman-Review,* January 5, 1967.

53   *a player strapping:* Author interview with Dick Fry, July 7, 2009.

53   *The practical student:* WSU *Daily Evergreen* photo caption, January 6, 1967.

53   *The host athletic director:* Bob Johnson, "Give 'Em Room," *Spokane Chronicle,* December 13, 1966, 17.

53   *sounded like:* Dwight Chapin, "Bruins Escape from Pullman Still on Top," *Los Angeles Times,* March 1, 1971, pt. 3, p. 7.

53   *Wooden already considered:* Jeff Prugh, "Pullman Turns Out to Get First Look at Lew and Bruins," *Los Angeles Times,* January 7, 1967, pt. 2, p. 1.

53 *"And just to make sure":* Ibid.

53 *two traffic lights:* Ibid.

54 *"You keep thinking":* Author interview with Jim McKean, September 11, 2009.

54 *"Everyone wants to see":* "Basketball: Proof of the Promise," *Time*, February 10, 1967, https://content.time.com/time/subscriber/article/0,33009,840829,00.html.

55 *"Tell them they can":* Ibid.

55 *"Lew's bodyguard was":* "Alcindor Threatened, Had Police Bodyguard," *Los Angeles Times*, February 1, 1967. pt. 3, p. 1.

55 *"What's your problem":* Jack Rickard, "Rick's Ramblings . . . ," *Corvallis Gazette-Times*, February 23, 1967, 16.

55 *Alcindor signing:* Abdul-Jabbar, *Coach Wooden and Me*, 136.

55 *"He can't get on":* Jacobsen, "UCLA: Wait Until Next Year . . ."

55 *At California:* Abdul-Jabbar, *Coach Wooden and Me*, 133.

55 *"This bothers me sometimes":* Jeff Prugh, "Aloofness a Mask for Lew," *Los Angeles Times*, February 3, 1967, pt. 3, p. 1.

56 *He could be:* Author interview with Lyle Spencer, July 11, 2022.

56 *He brought records:* Author interview with Don Saffer, April 25, 2023.

56 *"At center":* Jeff Prugh, "Lew Alcindor Takes Chicago by Storm, Scores 45 Points," *Los Angeles Times*, January 30, 1967.

56 *suggested* UCLA *should now:* Abdul-Jabbar, *Coach Wooden and Me*, 133.

56 *He still found:* Mitch Chortkoff, "Here's Why Lew Dislikes UCLA," *Los Angeles Herald Examiner*, February 15, 1967, D-1.

56 *Wooden more than once:* Wooden, as told to Tobin, *They Call Me Coach*, 148.

57 *"mere presence created problems":* Ibid., 150.

57 *The implosion in the making:* Mitch Chortkoff, "Alcindor May Leave UCLA," *Los Angeles Herald Examiner*, February 12, 1967, D-1.

57 *"There are a lot":* Ibid.

58 *Wooden and the assistants:* Cunningham interview and Norman interview.

58 *never gained momentum:* Jeff Prugh, "'Trotters Owner Won't Raid UCLA to Sign Alcindor," *Los Angeles Times*, February 13, 1967, pt. 3, p. 1.

58 *"how beautiful the campus":* Brendan Quinn, "Lew Alcindor, Michigan and the Mystery of the Big What-If?," *Athletic*, December 8, 2017.

58 *"made a pretty compelling":* Ibid.

58 *"where some other":* Abdul-Jabbar and Knobler, *Giant Steps*, 154.

58 *Alcindor regretted:* Alcindor with Olsen, "My Story."

58 *Naulls spent 1966–67:* Prugh, "Naulls Works to Smooth Out."

59 *Within the locker room:* Davis, *Wooden*, 280.

59 *"a friend of":* Franklin D. Murphy, "Right Man at the Right Time: J. D. Morgan," interviewed by David A. Rose for UCLA Oral History Program, February 10, 1982, 82.

59 *he had never met:* Mal Florence, "UCLA's Good Sam," *Los Angeles Times*, March 20, 1974, pt. 3, p. 1.

59 *"A bundle of dynamite":* Alan Greenberg and Mike Littwin, "To Those Who Know Him, Gilbert Is the Godfather," *Los Angeles Times*, February 1, 1982, pt. 3, p. 1.

59 *"He's soft-spoken":* Ibid.

60 *Gilbert believing:* Florence, "UCLA's Good Sam."

60 *"they had gotten":* Ibid.

60 *"Once the money thing":* Abdul-Jabbar and Knobler, *Giant Steps*, 158.

60 *"that we would pretend":* Alcindor with Olsen, "UCLA Was a Mistake."

60 *"If not for":* Davis, *Wooden*, 282.

60 *"Lucius and I said":* Alcindor with Olsen, "UCLA Was a Mistake."

60 *Wooden instead chose:* Davis, *Wooden*, 282.

61 *"It's true":* Steve Jacobson, "Alcindor: A Towering Boy with Towering Problems," *Newsday*, March 27, 1967, 25A.

61 *"my most trying year":* Jeff Prugh, "Wooden Baffled, Remorseful, over Sudden Move by Lacey," *Los Angeles Times*, January 30, 1968, pt. 3, p. 1.

61 *which way to face:* Lopresti, "Remembering the Start."

63 *disliked physical play:* Prugh, "Aloofness a Mask."

63 *could not help but admire:* Abdul-Jabbar, *Coach Wooden and Me*, 158.

63 *"Ah, another big fan":* Abdul-Jabbar and Obstfeld, *Becoming Kareem*, 195.

63 *Alcindor found Ali:* Ibid., 195–96.

63 *at a Los Angeles party:* Ibid., 198–99.

64 *"I had plenty":* Ibid., 201.

64 *Alcindor did note several snide:* Ibid., 233.

64 *"Socially I often":* Wooden with Jamison, *My Personal Best*, 92.

65 *"I felt like":* Abdul-Jabbar and Obstfeld, *Becoming Kareem*, 233.

65 *without needing so much as:* Ibid.

66 *Maybe, Muhammad told:* Author interview with John B. Wooten, August 1, 2022.

66 *"Get the gang together":* Ibid.

66 *"Ali loved":* Ibid.

67 *proud and flattered:* Thomas Hauser, *Muhammad Ali: His Life and Times* (New York: Simon & Schuster, 1991), 177–79.

67 *"a jury in assessing":* Abdul-Jabbar, *Coach Wooden and Me*, 161.

67 *"pretty heated":* Ibid.

67 *Wooten's decision:* Wooten interview.

67 *its suddenness scared Alcindor:* Abdul-Jabbar and Obstfeld, *Becoming Kareem*, 235.

67 *"I personally":* Author interview with Walter Beach, August 19, 2022.

68 *"It was what":* Abdul-Jabbar and Obstfeld, *Becoming Kareem*, 235.

4. Churches and Stadiums

71 *"The capital of Alabama":* *Wall Street Journal*, December 7, 1967, via Hampton Sides, *Hellhound on His Trail* (New York: Anchor Books, 2010), 45.

71 *One of Wallace's true believers:* Sides, *Hellhound on his Trail*, 65.

71 *had been energized:* Abdul-Jabbar and Obstfeld, *Becoming Kareem*, 232.

72 *Working with kids:* Loel Schrader, "Lew: Harlem's Helping Hand," *Long Beach Independent*, February 11, 1969, C-1.

72 *but also as a student:* Kareem Abdul-Jabbar, "Kareem Abdul-Jabbar: A Candid Conversation with the Greatest Basketball Player of All Time," *Playboy*, June 1, 1986.

72   *It took only:* Abdul-Jabbar and Obstfeld, *Becoming Kareem*, 246.

73   *"I dedicated myself":* Ibid., 248.

73   *"If I'd been white":* Abdul-Jabbar and Knobler, *Giant Steps*, 160.

73   *"The game is about":* Abdul-Jabbar, *Coach Wooden and Me*, 108.

73   *"ugly shot," "nothing but brute force":* Ibid.

73   *Wooden didn't even agree:* Greg Johnson, "Chronicle of the Jam," ncaa.org, July 30, 2007, https://ncaanewsarchive.s3.amazonaws.com/2007/Association-wide /chronicle-of-the-jam---07-30-07-ncaa-news.html.

73   *was more concerned:* Abdul-Jabbar and Obstfeld, *Becoming Kareem*, 237.

73   *Houston coach Guy V. Lewis:* Johnson, "Chronicle of the Jam."

74   *The collaboration:* Abdul-Jabbar, *Coach Wooden and Me*, 106.

74   *"We worked on it":* Abdul-Jabbar and Obstfeld, *Becoming Kareem*, 225.

74   *a symbol to Alcindor:* Abdul-Jabbar, *Coach Wooden and Me*, 108.

75   *Approximately two hundred athletes:* Jonathan Rodgers, "A Step to an Olympic Boycott," *Sports Illustrated*, December 4, 1967. Other reports, including also in *Sports Illustrated* in later years, estimated attendance at fifty to sixty. Rodgers, however, was the only media member inside the meeting.

75   *"Well, what do you":* Ibid. Some reports said the vote was unanimous. Rodgers's story claimed no vote was even necessary.

75   *was among the proponents:* Ibid.

75   *Alcindor could not accept:* Abdul-Jabbar and Obstfeld, *Becoming Kareem*, 139.

75   *"If you live in":* Jeff Prugh, "Alcindor Says Olympic Boycott Doesn't Bind Him Personally," *Los Angeles Times*, November 25, 1967, pt. 2, p. 1.

76   *a* Sports Illustrated *writer:* Rodgers, "Step to an Olympic Boycott."

76   *"unpleasant commotion":* Lew Alcindor with Jack Olsen, "A Year of Turmoil and Decision," *Sports Illustrated*, November 10, 1969.

76   *He was, however:* Ibid.

76   *The reserve unit:* "And the Big Good Bruins," *Time*, January 5, 1968.

77   *"There isn't a kid":* Jimmy Claus, "Sporting Around," *Terre Haute Tribune*, January 7, 1968, 47.

77   *Beban became one:* Beban interview.

77   *The announcement from:* Ibid.

78   *"just sort of":* Ibid.

78   *Six hours later:* Chapin and Prugh, *Wizard of Westwood*, 162.

78   *Teammates had no idea:* Bill Libby, *The Walton Gang* (New York: Coward, McCann & Geoghegan, 1974), 163.

79   *Morgan's first love:* Robert A. Fischer, "Right Man at the Right Time: J. D. Morgan," interviewed by David A. Rose for UCLA Oral History Program, March 9, 1982, 66.

80   *Bruin assistants grew:* Cunningham interview and Norman interview.

80   *Everyone knew the target:* Author interview with Tom Hansen, April 8, 2009.

80   *"Boy," one coach said:* Fred Hessler, "Right Man at the Right Time: J. D. Morgan," interviewed by Rick C. Harmon for UCLA Oral History Program, October 26,

1982, 490. Hessler identified Bob Boyd as the coach. Other versions have been told with Marv Harshman as the coach. Asked by the author in 2009, Harshman said, "That could be true. I remember something happening."

80   *"a typical second-guesser":* Wooden, "Right Man at the Right Time," 343.

80   *"extremely forceful," "supremely confident":* Ibid., 358.

80   *also rated Morgan:* Ibid., 338.

80   *On occasions Wooden disagreed:* Ibid., 337.

81   *Wooden borrowed the same:* Ibid., 348.

81   *negotiated the TV contracts:* Fischer, "Right Man at the Right Time," 56.

81   *"I think he was":* Wooden, "Right Man at the Right Time," 359.

82   *"we were playing a game":* Einhorn with Rapoport, *How March Became Madness,* 22.

82   *Staffers in the:* Wells Twombly, "UCLA-Houston Game Excites Texas Fans," *Sporting News,* January 20, 1968, 7.

82   *Lewis and an assistant:* Ron Rapoport, "Inside and Outsized," *Los Angeles Times,* January 20, 2008, D1.

82   *Some forty thousand tickets:* Twombly, "UCLA-Houston Game Excites."

82   *The publicity director:* Rapoport, "Inside and Outsized."

83   *"It's hard to imagine":* Chapin and Prugh, *Wizard of Westwood,* 164.

83   *"We'll be worn-out":* Ibid.

83   *"Use the restroom now":* Wooden with Jamison, *My Personal Best,* 156.

83   *A vendor who usually:* J. R. Gonzales, "The Game of the Century: Looking Back 40 Years," *Houston Chronicle,* January 20, 2008, https://blog.chron.com /bayoucityhistory/2008/01/the-game-of-the-century-looking-back-40-years/.

83   *"Basketball, as seen from":* Ibid.

83   *"Slow down":* Rapoport, "Inside and Outsized."

84   *shout orders to wait:* Ibid.

84   *Alcindor went to:* Wooden with Jamison, *My Personal Best,* 157.

84   *Warren raised the possibility:* Rapoport, "Inside and Outsized."

84   *Houston guard Chaney:* Ibid.

84   *advertisers from around:* Einhorn with Rapoport, *How March Became Madness,* 51.

84   *"And some of":* Elvin Hayes and Bill Gilbert, *They Call Me "the Big E"* (Englewood Cliffs, NJ: Prentice-Hall, 1978), 60.

85   *"one of the phenomenal":* Jerry Wizig, "It's Been 20 Years Since They've Played the Game of the Century," *Houston Chronicle,* January 20, 1988, https://web. archive.org/web/20121004131333/http://www.chron.com/CDA/archives/archive. mpl?id=1988_517381.

85   *"I couldn't get away":* Hayes and Gilbert, *They Call Me the Big E,* 62.

85   *"God, how long":* Ibid., 63.

85   *Shackelford saw him enter:* Davis, *Wooden,* 292.

86   *earned the two athletic departments:* Wizig, "It's Been 20 Years."

86   *"Why didn't Coach use Lacey?":* Chapin and Prugh, *Wizard of Westwood,* 167.

86   *"He knew why":* Abdul-Jabbar and Knobler, *Giant Steps,* 162.

86   *"had this morality thing":* Alcindor with Olsen, "Year of Turmoil and Decision."

86 *Alcindor waited:* Jeff Prugh, "Lacey Quits UCLA Team, Fires Blast at Wooden," *Los Angeles Times*, January 29, 1968.

87 *Lacey threw the newspaper:* Author interview with Jeff Prugh, April 2, 2009.

87 *"My remark was correct":* Prugh, "Lacey Quits UCLA."

87 *"one of the few times":* Davis, *Wooden*, 197.

87 *Lacey took college freshman:* Kareem Abdul-Jabbar, "Kareem Abdul-Jabbar: Remembering Central Avenue, L.A.'s Jazz Oasis," *Los Angeles Times*, July 18, 2020, https://www.latimes.com/california/story/2020-07-18/central-avenue-los -angeles-jazz.

87 *"It caused us":* Davis, *Wooden*, 297.

88 *"What have you done":* Prugh interview.

88 *The reaction ten months after:* Steve Bisheff, *John Wooden: An American Treasure* (Nashville, TN: Cumberland House, 2004), 68.

88 *"Some say it was":* Wooden, as told to Tobin, *They Call Me Coach*, 155.

88 *he saw the new attack:* Ibid.

89 *"would get a heck":* Jim Van Valkenburg, "Alcindor Declines Bid to Trials for U.S. Olympic Basketball Team," *Glens Falls Times*, February 28, 1968, 14.

89 *turned down the invitations:* Associated Press, "Alcindor Approves 'Boycott,'" *Shreveport Times*, March 12, 1968, 31.

89 *Another wave:* Abdul-Jabbar and Obstfeld, *Becoming Kareem*, 256.

89 *"Lew Alcindor's first step":* Carl Porter, "No Thanks, Uncle Sam," *Tucson Citizen*, March 1, 1968, 29.

89 *"probably based on":* Paul Zimmerman, "Olympic Bids Rejected by 3 Bruins, Trojan," *Los Angeles Times*, February 28, 1968, B1.

89 *"victimized by those":* Arthur Daley, "Sports of the Times," *New York Times*, via Smith, "'It's Not Really My Country.'"

89 *"outside influences":* Ibid.

90 *"I feel we've got":* Ibid.

90 *As in the immediate:* Abdul-Jabbar, *Coach Wooden and Me*, 141.

90 *"bigger," Alcindor wrote:* Abdul-Jabbar and Knobler, *Giant Steps*, 163.

91 *"We're gonna beat you":* Ibid., 164.

91 *"pride, not quitting":* Joe Jares, "Two Routs to a Title," *Sports Illustrated*, April 1, 1968, 12.

91 *"That's the greatest":* Ibid.

91 *"If they'd thought":* Abdul-Jabbar and Knobler, *Giant Steps*, 164.

92 *felt anticlimactic:* Ibid.

92 *"the greatest basketball team":* Jares, "Two Routs to a Title."

92 *"in the history of":* Ibid.

92 *Alcindor called Norman:* Norman interview.

92 *he needed a career:* Norman, by all accounts, became a tremendous success in the financial world.

92 *Norman left with:* Norman interview.

93 *early in the offseason was wondering:* Davis, *Wooden*, 313.

5. Clenched Fists

95 *appear on the* Today: Associated Press, "UCLA Star Tells Boycott Reasons," *Spokane Chronicle*, July 20, 1968, 8.

96 *"I'm in full sympathy"*: Milton Richmond, "The Sports Parade," *Franklin (PA) News-Herald*, August 1, 1968, 18.

96 *"I think what"*: Ibid.

97 *"Man, just pick one"*: Abdul-Jabbar and Obstfeld, *Becoming Kareem*, 259–60.

97 *"as if at last"*: Ibid., 264.

97 *particularly hurtful*: Ibid., 263.

97 *He returned to Los Angeles*: Abdul-Jabbar and Knobler, *Giant Steps*, 183.

97 *"I withdrew"*: Ibid.

97 *"worked past the age"*: Alcindor with Olsen, "Year of Turmoil and Decision."

98 *"a third straight"*: Abdul-Jabbar and Knobler, *Giant Steps*, 183.

98 *"From the start"*: Curry Kirkpatrick, "The Week He Finally Got Rid of the Yoke," *Sports Illustrated*, March 31, 1969, 18.

98 *"We'd done the whole"*: Abdul-Jabbar and Knobler, *Giant Steps*, 182.

98 *He instead quit school*: Seth Davis, "The Wizard and the Giant," *Sports Illustrated*, January 13, 2014.

99 *"If I had to do it"*: Jack Scott, *Bill Walton: On the Road with the Portland Trail Blazers* (New York: Thomas Y. Crowell, 1978), 186.

99 *he wished he had*: Loel Schrader, "The Alcindor Story: Shy but Confident," *Long Beach Press-Telegram*, February 10, 1969, C-1.

99 *"I try not to"*: Ardie Ivie, "Fiendish in the Valley with Lew Alcindor," *Los Angeles Times West Magazine*, March 16, 1969, 30.

99 *Wooden still saw*: Wooden, as told to Tobin, *They Call Me Coach*, 160.

100 *"He was fighting"*: Abdul-Jabbar, *Coach Wooden and Me*, 97.

100 *"He wanted to protect"*: Ibid.

100 *"had a faith"*: Ibid., 98.

100 *"A lot of people"*: Jeff Prugh, "Basketball Is His Game, Winning Is His Trademark," *Los Angeles Times*, February 4, 1969, pt. 3, p. 1.

101 *The coach and athletic director*: Wooden, "Right Man at the Right Time," 340.

101 *"I sometimes wonder"*: Jeff Prugh, "Wooden's Greatest Reward Is Working with Young Men," *Los Angeles Times*, February 8, 1969, pt. 3, p. 1.

102 *"I can honestly say"*: Davis, "Wizard and the Giant."

102 *"I don't know whether"*: Johnson, *John Wooden Pyramid of Success*, 52.

102 *"I think he was happier"*: Cunningham interview.

102 *little, if any, conversation*: Author interview with Spencer Haywood, February 14, 2013, and Jo Jo White, April 4, 2015.

102 *"No," said the new*: Haywood interview.

103 *"I'll stand with you"*: Martin Flanagan, "Olympic Protest Heroes Praise Norman's Courage," *Sydney Morning Herald*, October 10, 2006, https://www.smh.com.au/sport/olympic-protest-heroes-praise-normans-courage-20061010-gdokc5.html.

103 *"I saw love"*: Ibid.

103 *"Tommie, if anyone"*: Kenny Moore, "A Courageous Stand," *Sports Illustrated*, August 5, 1991.

103 *Carlos did the same:* Kenny Moore, "The Eye of the Storm," *Sports Illustrated*, August 12, 1991.

104 *"nearly two hundred":* Sam Dillon, "A General Illuminates '68 Massacre in Mexico," *New York Times*, June 29, 1999, A6, https://www.nytimes.com/1999/06/29/world/a-general-illuminates-68-massacre-in-mexico.html.

104 *Alcindor found himself:* Abdul-Jabbar and Knobler, *Giant Steps*, 171.

104 *"I was a freshman":* Haywood interview.

105 *If anything, Alcindor assessed:* Alcindor with Olsen, "Year of Turmoil and Decision."

105 *The conversation grew:* Author interview with Bill Sweek, April 6, 2023.

105 *"Coach Wooden did not look":* Alcindor with Olsen, "Year of Turmoil and Decision."

105 *"we became a different group":* Ibid.

106 *"He thought that everybody":* Ibid.

106 *"It's nice to look out here":* Joe Doyle, "Scholar-Athletes Praised by Joyce at N.D. Banquet," *South Bend Tribune*, December 6, 1968, 45.

106 *had been so dramatic:* Sweek interview.

106 *"deeply special":* Davis, *Wooden*, 308.

106 *Saffer so didn't want:* Author interview with Don Saffer, April 25, 2023.

106 *"Well, Curtis":* Jeff Prugh, "Pressure on UCLA Cagers? Not on the Road," *Los Angeles Times*, February 20, 1969, pt. 3, p. 9.

107 *"I need to know":* Bisheff, *American Treasure*, 150.

107 *said he talked Wicks:* Chapin and Prugh, *Wizard of Westwood*, 299.

107 *Wicks contended:* Bisheff, *American Treasure*, 151.

108 *Wooden did not see:* Wooden and Jamison, *Wooden on Leadership*, 127.

6. In Case of Attack

109 *a chartered bus:* Pepe, "Alcindor Matures."

109 *"This is where":* Jeff Prugh, "Alcindor Home; Bruins Hit N.Y.," *Los Angeles Times*, December 27, 1968, pt. 3, p. 4.

109 *"was always looked upon":* Author interview with Brendan Malone, March 9, 2011.

109 *"To those who have":* Pepe, "Alcindor Matures."

109 *"I can see":* Ibid.

110 *Goss had been military:* Author interview with Freddie Goss, January 14, 2023.

110 *Peterson in the same:* Author interview with Carl Peterson, May 17, 2023.

111 *So being sent:* Goss interview.

111 *This was after some jets:* Perlstein, *Nixonland*, 154.

111 *Goss as the officer:* Goss interview.

111 *Alcindor's former Power teammate:* Nee interview.

112 *Bruin guard Don Saffer:* Saffer interview.

112 *The threat of the draft:* Associated Press, "Namath Plans to Run More," *Raleigh News and Observer*, June 19, 1966, pt. 2, p. 9.

112 *"I'd rather fight":* Mike Rathet, "Military Duty Pending for Jets' High-Priced Rookie Signal-Caller," *Selma Times-Journal*, August 12, 1965, 12.

112 *Saffer in the downtown:* Saffer interview.

113 *He brought the:* Paul Hornung, "Woody'll Head for Viet Nam," *Columbus Dispatch*,

July 3, 1966, reprinted October 2, 2015, https://www.dispatch.com/story/sports
/college/2015/10/02/the-woody-hayes-archive-coach/10884647007/.

113 *That grew into:* Homer Brickey Jr., "2 Coaches Visit Vietnam Troops," *Columbus Dispatch,* June 18, 1968, reprinted October 2, 2015, https://www.dispatch.com /story/sports/college/2015/10/02/the-woody-hayes-archive-coach/10884647007/.

113 *Hayes considered the high point:* Michael Rosenberg, *War as They Knew It: Woody Hayes, Bo Schembechler, and America in a Time of Unrest* (New York: Grand Central Publishing, 2008), 4–7.

114 *One of the Bruin student managers:* Author interview with George Morgan, September 13, 2022.

114 *was disappointed to flunk:* Peterson interview.

114 *Two of Pete Newell's sons:* Newell interview.

115 *Dentists around Los Angeles:* Christian G. Appy, *Working-Class War: American Combat Soldiers and Vietnam* (Chapel Hill: University of North Carolina Press, 1993), 33.

115 *When the dreaded:* Morgan interview.

115 *Football star Gary Beban:* Beban interview.

115 *Gilbert got Lucius Allen:* Abdul-Jabbar and Knobler, *Giant Steps,* 156.

115 *would in months decline:* Sweek interview.

116 *Don Saffer quitting:* Saffer interview.

116 *"This plane is going":* Prugh, "Pressure on UCLA Cagers?"

116 *"It's got to be":* H. Anthony Medley, *UCLA Basketball: The Real Story* (Galant Press, 1972), 148.

116 *Alcindor had also:* Loel Schrader, "$1.4 Million Gamble!," *Long Beach Independent,* April 2, 1969, C-1.

116 *The 1968–69 woes:* "Wooden Hints Lew Was Affected by Father's Accident," *Los Angeles Times,* March 4, 1969.

117 *with sixteen-year-old:* Walton with Wojciechowski, *Nothing But Net,* 13.

117 *He went through:* Dave Hicks, "'Tails' Eclipses Sun Hopes for Alcindor," *Arizona Republic,* March 20, 1969, 49.

117 *but he did know:* Jerry Crowe, "Suns Got the Tail End of Coin Flip," *Los Angeles Times,* March 15, 2009.

117 *"a swinging town":* Alcindor with Olsen, "Year of Turmoil and Decision."

117 *"where the winners live":* Ibid.

117 *Faced with two:* Crowe, "Suns Got the Tail End."

117 *"too hot, too small":* Scott Bordow, "Phoenix, Milwaukee Awarded NBA Expansion Franchises 50 Years Ago," *Arizona Republic,* January 22, 2018, https://www.azcentral .com/story/sports/nba/suns/2018/01/22/phoenix-milwaukee-awarded-nba-expansion -franchises-50-years-ago/1056335001/.

118 *"dreamed long and hard":* Author interview with Jerry Colangelo, April 22, 2009.

118 *Colangelo plotted out:* Ibid.

119 *with 54 percent of the vote:* United Press International, "Coin Flip Win Not First for Pavalon," *Fremont (CA) Argus,* March 20, 1969, 11. Jerry Colangelo put the number at 51.2 percent, but years later.

119 *"I'm going to put"*: Robert Lipsyte, "The Coin Kept Turning Up Tails for Kennedy," *New York Times News Service* via *Arizona Republic*, March 20, 1969, 53.

119 *"The coin has come up"*: Ibid.

119 *"We will get together"*: Associated Press, "Bucks Celebrate Biggest Victory," *Janesville Daily Gazette*, March 20, 1969, 14.

119 *Pavalon's lit cigarette*: Bill Dwyre, "Commentary: Kareem Abdul-Jabbar Will Always Be No. 1 for His Post-NBA Career Work," *Los Angeles Times*, February 8, 2023, https://www.latimes.com/sports/story/2023-02-08/kareem-abdul-jabbar-lebron-james-nba-scoring-record.

119 *"We would have called"*: United Press International, "Coin Flip Win Not First."

119 *Adding to the body blow*: Hicks, "'Tails' Eclipses Sun Hopes."

119 *choosing from among*: Ibid. The Suns ended up taking Neal Walk.

119 *He steered*: Colangelo interview.

119 *The commissioner in New York*: Hicks, "'Tails' Eclipses Sun Hopes."

120 *"Maybe I am"*: Kirkpatrick, "Week He Finally Got Rid."

120 *frustrated at not getting*: Ibid.

120 *Kentucky coach Adolph Rupp*: Scott Bosley, "Sneak Preview for Lew," *Akron Beacon Journal*, March 23, 1969, B1.

120 *prompted Alcindor to rank*: Lee Fensin, "Lew Cuts Leg, Celebrates Birthday and Plays Hookie," *Waukesha Daily Freeman*, 10.

120 *"There weren't that many"*: Ibid.

121 *Determined to make a point*: Davis, "Wizard and the Giant."

121 *Remembering it was almost*: Sweek interview.

122 *Wooden struggled to maintain*: Wooden, as told to Tobin, *They Call Me Coach*, 200.

122 *"Coach looked like"*: Abdul-Jabbar, *Coach Wooden and Me*, 202.

122 *The only thing*: Sweek interview.

122 *"You wanna fight me"*: Abdul-Jabbar, *Coach Wooden and Me*, 200.

122 *A lot of players laughed*: Ibid.

122 *You're right, Coach*: Sweek interview.

122 *Wooden standing close enough*: Ibid.

123 *"a little trouble"*: Wooden, as told to Tobin, *They Call Me Coach*, 162.

123 *Players who spent years*: Gary Schultz, "Lew Sidesteps Question on NBA or ABA," *Louisville Courier-Journal*, March 23, 1969, C1.

124 *Alcindor's UCLA career*: Lou Younkin, "Booed at 3:54, Alcindor Nets Prize at 6:04," *Louisville Courier-Journal*, C3.

124 *being replaced by*: Kirkpatrick, "Week He Finally Got Rid."

124 *Wooden walked over*: "The Lew Alcindor Era: Perplexity, Perfection," *Bradenton (FL) Herald*, April 2, 1969, 8-D.

125 *"I'll just say"*: Ibid.

125 *The din and darkness*: Ibid.

125 *"The experience of playing"*: Bosley, "Sneak Preview for Lew."

126 *the ABA had the Nets*: Terry Pluto, *Loose Balls: The Short, Wild Ride of the American Basketball Association* (New York: Simon & Schuster, 1990), 108–9.

126 *"wasn't the quality"*: Bosley, "Sneak Preview for Lew."

126 *The upstart league:* Alcindor with Olsen, "Year of Turmoil and Decision."

127 *three days at the Desert Inn:* Pluto, *Loose Balls,* 191.

127 *"wanted to know":* Ibid. .

128 *The package was worth:* Jeff Prugh, "Alcindor's Pact: Diary of a $1 Million Deal," *Los Angeles Times,* May 18, 1969, C1.

128 *It took little conversation:* Ibid.

128 *he phoned Kennedy:* Ibid.

128 *Alcindor still preferred:* Alcindor with Olsen, "Year of Turmoil and Decision."

128 *"He doesn't want":* Associated Press, "ABA, Nets Offer Lew $3.25 Million," *Louisville Courier-Journal,* March 30, 1969, C1.

128 *"me feel like":* Jeff Prugh, "Alcindor Receives New Super Offer from ABA," *Los Angeles Times,* March 30, 1969, 43.

129 *"He was as easy":* Hano, "Winning."

129 *"I always felt":* "Lew Alcindor Era: Perplexity, Perfection."

130 *"With Lewis gone":* Ibid.

130 *"Yes sir," he said:* Ibid.

7. BB

131 *with a request:* Author interview with Andy Hill, July 29, 2022.

131 *"Andy, you don't have":* Ibid.

131 *He confessed to cussing once:* Davis, *Wooden,* 10.

132 *"I wish just once":* Ron Rapoport, "B &%&!L &!$E &%($E !$% P," *Los Angeles Times,* June 22, 1973, EI.

132 *"He had a great":* Author interview with Hank Nichols, September 6, 2012.

132 *reasoning it as:* Author interview with Steve Bisheff, October 3, 2022.

132 *had a TV hooked up:* H. R. Haldeman, *The Haldeman Diaries: Inside the Nixon White House* (New York: G. Putnam's Sons, 1994), 110, via Rosenberg, *War as They Knew It.*

132 *When candidate Nixon:* United Press International, "Starr Hits the Campaign Trail on Nixon's Behalf," *Green Bay Press-Gazette,* March 9, 1968, 9.

132 *Arnold Palmer appeared:* Author interview with Dwight L. Chapin, September 9, 2022.

132 *Incumbent Nixon even paused:* Perlstein, *Nixonland,* 743.

133 *He had built:* Chapin interview.

133 *"It's easy to manipulate":* Tom Wells, *The War Within: America's Battle over Vietnam* (Berkeley: University of California Press, 1994), via Perlstein, *Nixonland,* 420.

133 *"organize one of the":* Jeff Shesol, *Mutual Contempt: Robert Kennedy, Lyndon Johnson and the Feud That Defined a Decade* (New York: W. W. Norton, 1998), 429.

133 *And, Wooden was:* Author interview with Jim Wooden, September 27, 2022.

134 *but BB was the clear:* Author interview with Jo Haldeman, September 22, 2022.

134 *"It was just who":* Ibid.

134 *The coach likewise:* Wooden interview.

134 *Yet there is no indication:* Haldeman interview and Wooden interview.

135 *"If you guys think":* Wells, *War Within,* 294.

135 *"ideological criminals," "new barbarians":* Rob Kirkpatrick, *1969: The Year Everything Changed* (New York: Skyhorse, 2019), 111.

135 *Vice President Spiro Agnew:* Marjorie Hunter, "Agnew Says 'Effete Snobs' Incited War Moratorium," *New York Times*, October 20, 1969, 1, https://www.nytimes.com/1969/10/20 /archives/agnew-says-effete-snobs-incited-war-moratorium-agnew-asserts-effete.html.

135 *"Those who want":* Lou Cannon, *Governor Reagan: His Rise to Power* (New York: Public Affairs, 2003), 291.

135 *before saying a day later:* United Press International, "'Bloodbath Needed' Reagan Says Remark Is Figure of Speech," *Desert Sun*, April 8, 1970, https://cdnc.ucr .edu/?a=d&d=DS19700408.2.17&e=-------en--20--1--txt-txIN-------.

135 *"when extremists halt classes":* "Harvard and Beyond: The University Under Siege," *Time*, April 18, 1969, https://content.time.com/time/subscriber /article/0,33009,844757,00.html.

135 *"If there was one word":* "The Campus Upheaval: An End to Patience," *Time*, May 9, 1969, https://content.time.com/time/subscriber/article/0,33009,844795,00.html.

136 *"I am looking forward":* Davis, *Wooden*, 321.

136 *Wooden rated it:* Wooden, as told to Tobin, *They Call Me Coach*, 164.

136 *He happily called:* Wooden with Jamison, *My Personal Best*, 161.

136 *counted the days:* Wooden, as told to Tobin, *They Call Me Coach*, 163.

136 *Sharing a table with Freddie Goss:* Goss interview.

137 *"When I went":* Davis, *Wooden*, 312.

137 *one of the few times:* Wooden interview.

138 *was so consistent:* Wooden, as told to Tobin, *They Call Me Coach*, 167.

138 *"I didn't get it":* Bisheff, *American Treasure*, 151.

138 *Wooden was impressed:* Wooden, as told to Tobin, *They Call Me Coach*, 164.

138 *"Not immediately":* Ibid., 168.

138 *"I'm going to tell":* Alcindor with Olsen, "My Story."

139 *Milwaukee's season-ticket sales:* Jeff Prugh, "Everyone Loves Bucks Now—Thanks to Lew," *Los Angeles Times*, October 24, 1969, pt. 3, p. 7.

139 *a view of downtown:* Bijan C. Bayne, "50 Years Ago, Alcindor and O.J. Were Both Leaving L.A., but Their Paths Quickly Diverged," *Andscape*, September 3, 2019, https://andscape.com/features/50-years-ago-alcindor-and-o-j-were-both-leaving-l-a -but-their-paths-quickly-diverged/.

139 *"UCLA WAS A MISTAKE":* Alcindor with Olsen, "UCLA Was a Mistake."

139 *"I could no longer":* Alcindor with Olsen, "Year of Turmoil and Decision."

139 *"Well," Wooden answered:* Charles Maher, "Mad Man," *Los Angeles Times*, November 5, 1969, pt. 3, p. 2.

140 *"If Lewis felt":* Chapin and Prugh, *Wizard of Westwood*, 182.

140 *"distressed to learn":* Libby, *Walton Gang*, 171.

140 *chose to occasionally:* Abdul-Jabbar, *Coach Wooden and Me*, 206.

140 *There were times:* Ibid., 94.

140 *"Any game films":* Dwight Chapin, "Playing UCLA Is New Game for Bruin Foes," *Los Angeles Times*, December 5, 1969, pt. 3, p. 9.

140 *he remained dedicated:* Wooden and Jamison, *Wooden on Leadership*, 161.

140 *"Oh":* Ivie, "Fiendish in the Valley."

141 *Practicing against Alcindor:* Chapin and Prugh, *Wizard of Westwood*, 183.

141 *He tended:* Dwight Chapin, "Henry Bibby Finds Whole New World as Bruin Star," *Los Angeles Times*, January 8, 1970, pt. 3, p. 1.

141 *still almost chose:* Ibid.

141 *"Even Lynn didn't get":* Ibid.

142 *"Pete Maravich," Wooden said:* Mark Kriegel, *Pistol: The Life of Pete Maravich* (New York: Free Press, 2007), 61.

142 *create a wretched odor:* Author interview with Michael Hunt, March 8, 2023.

143 *The rowdies turned:* Ibid.

143 *Wooden rated him:* Kriegel, *Pistol*, 61.

143 *"Mr. Maravich will now":* Wayne Federman and Marshall Terrill in collaboration with Jackie Maravich, *Pete Maravich: The Authorized Biography of Pistol Pete* (Carol Stream, IL: Tyndale House, 2006), 114.

143 *Wooden dreaded the thought:* Jares interview.

144 *"taken such a terrible":* Jeff Prugh, "Maravich: Hair Flops, Socks Sag—but What Moves!," *Los Angeles Times*, December 23, 1969, pt. 3, p. 1.

144 *Out came socks:* Federman and Terrill in collaboration with Maravich, *Pete Maravich*, 54.

144 *"Two broomsticks":* Ibid., 53.

144 *"It just kills him":* Prugh, "Hair Flops, Socks Sag."

144 *"You don't understand":* "Pete & Press," *Campbell University Magazine*, September 23, 2015, https://magazine.campbell.edu/articles/legendary-campbell-basketball -school/5/.

144 *"It was a game":* Federman and Terrill in collaboration with Maravich, *Pete Maravich*, 144.

145 *A high school senior:* Walton interview.

145 *Walton fell in love:* Larry Burnett, "Vice Sports Q&A: Bill Walton," *Vice*, February 9, 2016, https://www.vice.com/en/article/jp7qwk/vice-sports-qa-bill-walton.

145 *"in absolute awe":* Walton with Wojciechowski, *Nothing But Net*, 12.

145 *was the evidence:* Walton interview.

145 *wearing Alcindor's No. 33:* Bill Walton, *Back from the Dead: Searching for the Sound, Shining the Light, and Throwing It Down* (New York: Simon & Schuster, 2016), 158.

145 *"Basketball was my":* Burnett, "Vice Sports Q&A."

145 *he spun the story:* Davis, *Wooden*, 339.

145 *the first college to make:* Walton with Wojciechowski, *Nothing but Net*, 13.

145 *decided on enemy ground:* Walton interview.

146 *Crum drove his:* Davis, *Wooden*, 338.

146 *"Well," Wooden finally said:* Ibid.

146 *"He is as good":* Earl Gustkey, "San Diego Prep Rated Among Best in the Country," *Los Angeles Times*, March 10, 1970, pt. 3, p. 1.

146 *"he's like Alcindor":* Ibid.

146 *congenital defects:* Walton, *Back from the Dead*, 5.

146 *"I grew up thinking":* Ibid., 6.

147 *feeling sorry for Pistol Pete:* Walton interview.

147   *Walton's trips were:* Ibid.

147   *Wicks suddenly the best:* Dwight Chapin, "Sidney Wicks—Big, Tough, Agile—Fancies Grid Career," *Los Angeles Times*, February 27, 1970, pt. 3, p. 1.

147   *"In many ways":* Ibid.

148   *"This team is":* Dwight Chapin, "Bruins Turn Aggie Dream Into Nightmare—93–77," *Los Angeles Times*, March 20, 1970, pt. 3, p. 1.

148   *His growth had come:* Andrew Hill with John Wooden, *Be Quick—But Don't Hurry!: Finding Success in the Teachings of a Lifetime* (New York: Simon & Schuster, 2001), 29.

148   *"Not everyone gets":* Curry Kirkpatrick, "It's More Fun Without Lew," *Sports Illustrated*, February 2, 1970, 9.

148   *"We're so much more":* Ibid.

148   *"UCLA has five men":* Chapin, "Playing UCLA Is New Game."

149   *Aggies assistant coach:* Author interview with Dale Brown, April 26, 2009.

149   *"Now, Curtis":* Ibid.

149   *"Cut hard":* Ibid.

149   *These are drills:* Ibid.

149   *H. R. Haldeman marked:* Haldeman interview.

150   *"They do what":* Dwight Chapin, "Bruins Pit Speed, Discipline Against Dolphins' Height," *Los Angeles Times*, March 21, 1970, pt. 3, p. 1.

150   *Williams wore:* Joe Jares, "Victory by Mystique," *Sports Illustrated*, March 30, 1970.

150   *There could not have been:* Ibid.

150   *"That name":* Chapin, "Bruins Pit Speed, Discipline."

150   *Wooden the next day:* Jares, "Victory by Mystique."

150   *"the most intimidating man":* Ibid.

150   *"I think Gilmore was surprised":* Ibid.

151   *"Everybody was looking forward":* Ibid.

151   *Patterson, among others:* Dwight Chapin, "Bruins Get Heroes' Welcome Home," *Los Angeles Times*, March 23, 1970, pt. 3, p. 2.

152   *On the days:* Sam Allen, "Great Coach Was a Better Friend," *Daily Bruin*, June 6, 2010, https://dailybruin.com/2010/06/06/great-coach-was-better-friend.

152   *"The Kent State Four!":* James Michener, *Kent State: What Happened and Why* (New York: Random House, 1971), 429, 435–36.

152   *a Gallup poll soon:* Ibid.

153   *When he finished:* Curry Kirkpatrick, "UCLA: Simple, Awesomely Simple," *Sports Illustrated*, November 30, 1970. Also Hill interview.

153   *One guest threatened:* Libby, *Walton Gang*, 87.

153   *"just an unfortunate incident":* Ibid., 68.

154   *"We, the undersigned":* Letter acquired by author.

154   *The statement went on:* Ibid.

155   *He would rather:* Hill with Wooden, *Be Quick*, 38.

155   *Pick your new school:* Hill interview.

155   *Enough concern existed:* Hill with Wooden, *Be Quick*, 34.

155   *But the idea:* Hill interview.

155 *Even Wooden had to:* Hill with Wooden, *Be Quick*, 36.

155 *"had made us closer":* Ibid.

156 *"There's no limit":* Chapin, "Bruins Get Heroes' Welcome."

8. Orange Crates in the Alley

157 *"Are the Grateful Dead":* Dennis McNally, *A Long Strange Trip: The Inside History of the Grateful Dead* (New York: Broadway Books, 2002), 381.

157 *"reality suspended":* Ibid.

157 *"the only foreign tour":* Hunter S. Thompson, "The 'Hashbury' Is the Capital of the Hippies," *New York Times*, May 14, 1967, sec. SM, p. 14.

158 *"bums":* Bob Spitz, *The Beatles: The Biography* (New York: Back Bay Books, 2005), 707.

158 *with a migration:* Ronald Brownstein, *Rock Me on the Water: 1974—The Year Los Angeles Transformed Movies, Music, Television and Politics* (New York: Harper, 2021), 51.

158 *talked about forming:* Lisa Robinson, "An Oral History of Laurel Canyon, the 60s and 70s Music Mecca," *Vanity Fair*, February 8, 2015, https://www.vanityfair.com /culture/2015/02/laurel-canyon-music-scene.

158 *"like the gold rush":* Brownstein, *Rock Me*, 43.

158 *Other nights were spent:* Ibid., 116.

159 *But especially the Troubadour:* Ibid., 73.

159 *Led Zeppelin played:* Troubadour, https://troubadour.com/history/#:~:text=After%20 playing%20the%20LA%20Forum,"%20and%20"Mystery%20Train.

159 *Assigned the same:* Walton, *Back from the Dead*, 68.

159 *"I was more than ready":* Ibid., 66.

159 *Skimming the* Daily Bruin*:* Ibid., 68.

160 *"so much better":* Ibid., 69.

160 *"because I was":* John Papanek, "Climbing to the Top Again," *Sports Illustrated*, October 15, 1979.

160 *He entered the B.O. Barn:* Author interview, July 22, 2022.

160 *with a postmatch celebration:* Ibid.

160 *Had he waited:* Ibid. "Bill could have been great," Scates told the author in 2022 of Walton's volleyball potential. Regarding Chamberlain in volleyball, Scates said, "He would have dominated. Karch Kiraly was voted the best player in the world. He [Chamberlain] never would have been an all-around player like Karch, but he would have been the best hitter in the world and I would have taught him how to block. He would have been the best blocker in the world if he would have just asked somebody for a little information who knew what he was doing."

160 *Walton and Lee soon became:* Author interview with Kiki Vandeweghe, May 31, 2023.

161 *"I'm better than":* Spencer interview.

161 *growing up with:* Jerry West and Jonathan Coleman, *West by West: My Charmed, Tormented Life* (New York: Little, Brown, 2011), 12.

161 *"the ice house":* Ibid., 18.

162 *his marriage continued:* Ibid., 88.

162 *Reading* Helter Skelter*:* Ibid., 89.

163 *The actual experts:* Norman interview.

163 *Gary Cunningham became:* Cunningham interview.

163 *"two small-town, everyday guys":* West and Coleman, *West by West*, 215.

163 *"Jerry," Wooden said:* Ibid., 216.

163 *Jerry Norman occasionally took recruits:* Norman interview.

164 *West wanted to tell him:* Author interview with Jerry West, January 10, 2012.

164 *West had been:* Walton, *Back from the Dead*, 25.

165 *"I would be wolfing":* Roland Lazenby, *Jerry West: The Life and Legend of a Basketball Icon* (New York: Ballantine, 2009), 300.

165 *"almost reminded me":* West interview.

165 *"he was about to give":* Walton, *Back from the Dead*, 70.

165 *Wooden removing his own:* Ibid.

165 *"We thought at the time":* Ibid., 71.

166 *Just as importantly:* Author interview with Jim Nielsen, March 4, 2023.

166 *Walton showed the same:* Thomas Bonk, "Losing Never Came to Mind," *Los Angeles Times*, March 26, 1991, C1.

166 *"Sidney!":* Hill interview.

167 *Wilkes looked at:* Author interview with Jamaal Wilkes, June 7, 2023.

167 *A thirty-four-year-old:* Author interview with Dick Vermeil, November 28, 2022.

167 *The afternoon basketball sessions:* Ibid.

168 *I'd like to meet:* Ibid.

168 *The upperclassmen serving:* Ibid.

168 *football coaches for months:* Peterson interview.

169 *Wooden could understand:* Wooden, "Right Man at the Right Time," 347.

169 *"Well, I was out":* Ibid., 343.

169 *"So it was forgotten":* Ibid.

169 *"They execute so well":* Jeff Prugh, "Here's a Scout's-Eye View of Trojan and Bruin Cagers," *Los Angeles Times*, February 3, 1971, pt. 3, p. 1.

169 *"It will take":* Joe Jares, "The Week," *Sports Illustrated Vault*, December 14, 1970, https://vault.si.com/vault/1970/12/14/the-week.

170 *Wicks in particular:* Earl Gustkey, "Cowboy Scouts Keep Tabs on Cage Stars," *Los Angeles Times*, March 26, 1971, pt. 3, p. 5.

170 *"He's probably too tall":* Ibid.

170 *"a complete basketball player":* Dwight Chapin, "Wicks, Rowe Brilliant in Bruins' 94–75 Victory," *Los Angeles Times*, December 23, 1970, pt. 3, p. 1.

170 *Wooden thought Wicks had:* Wooden, as told to Tobin, *They Call Me Coach*, 189.

170 *"Damn!":* Dwight Chapin, "Washington Escape! UCLA, USC Rally to Win," *Los Angeles Times*, March 2, 1971, pt. 3, p. 1.

170 *"Isn't that disgraceful":* Author interview with Dwight Chapin, March 25, 2009.

171 *Wicks and Rowe suddenly walking:* Jerry Tarkanian and Terry Pluto, *Tark: College Basketball's Winningest Coach* (New York: McGraw-Hill, 1988), 93.

171 *"We look like":* Ibid.

171 *When Tarkanian recounted:* Ibid., 94.

172 *once Tark settled on:* Author interview with Danny Tarkanian, August 19, 2013.

172　*Tarkanian saw Morgan:* Author interview with Jerry Tarkanian, April 20, 2009, and Danny Tarkanian interview.
172　*"I don't always agree":* Bisheff, *American Treasure,* 111.
172　*Tarkanian considered being invited:* Tarkanian and Pluto, *Tark,* 49.
172　*"John Wooden and I":* Ibid., 90.
173　*He declined without hesitation:* Wooden interview and Cunningham interview.
173　*Tarkanian couldn't wait:* Bisheff, *American Treasure,* 110.
174　*Wooden in the moment:* Dwight Chapin, "Bruins Pull Another Houdini—Escape 57–55," *Los Angeles Times,* March 21, 1971, D1.
174　*"We had 'em":* Ibid.
174　*"You're nothing but a bunch":* Chapin and Prugh, *Wizard of Westwood,* 9.
174　*"Watch number forty-three!":* Tarkanian and Pluto, *Tark,* 95.
174　*"was a screw job":* Ibid.
175　*he couldn't walk away now:* Bisheff, *American Treasure,* 110.
175　*"You're out there alone":* Jeff Prugh, "The Dome: A Place Not Dear to UCLA, Except to Its Bankroll," *Los Angeles Times,* March 24, 1971, pt. 3, p. 1.
175　*Organizers, responding to:* Ibid.
175　*Tempers flared repeatedly:* Earl Gustkey, "Lack of 'Home Team' Hurts Astrodome Gate," *Los Angeles Times,* March 26, 1971, pt. 3, p. 12.
176　*"Look out, here I come":* Dwight Chapin, "UCLA Beats Kansas, 68–60; Villanova Final Foe," *Los Angeles Times,* March 26, 1971, pt. 3, p. 1.
176　*"Halt":* Ibid.
176　*"I'm the coach":* Jeff Prugh, "Louisville's Crum Confronts Ex-Boss Wooden in Semifinals," *Los Angeles Times,* March 20, 1972, pt. 3, p. 1.
176　*"Many building custodians":* Wooden, as told to Tobin, *They Call Me Coach,* 105.
177　*Wooden would recount:* Author interview with John Sandbrook, April 5, 2022.
177　*"I teach homely values":* Libby, *Walton Gang,* 169.
177　*"the sword that chopped":* Bonk, "Losing Never Came to Mind."
178　*"You're the national champions!":* Chapin and Prugh, *Wizard of Westwood,* 206.
178　*"Bruins are bush!":* Jeff Prugh, "It's Routine as UCLA Wins 5th Straight Title," *Los Angeles Times,* March 28, 1971, C1.
178　*"I might as well":* Bonk, "Losing Never Came to Mind."
178　*"It's been a nice":* Chapin and Prugh, *The Wizard of Westwood,* 206.
178　*"You're really something":* Ibid.
178　*among his five favorites ever:* Jerry Crowe, "Wooden's Five Favorite Teams," *Los Angeles Times,* October 14, 1990, C16. Wooden did not rank them in order, but in addition to the 1970–71 squad, he put the Bruins of 1948–49 (his first at UCLA), 1961–62, the 1963–64 champions, and 1974–75 in the top five.

9. A Most Unusual Young Man
179　*"It has been":* Wooden, as told to Tobin, *They Call Me Coach,* 178.
179　*He was optimistic:* Ibid., 179.
180　*no Wooden player:* Ibid., 180.
180　*"Every expert sees":* Ibid.

180 *"Only a lamebrain"*: Prugh, "It's Routine as UCLA Wins."

180 *"superclub"*: Wooden, as told to Tobin, *They Call Me Coach*, 181.

180 *"one of the most"*: Dwight Chapin, "Road Games Tough Challenge for Southland Basketball Teams," *Los Angeles Times*, December 14, 1971, pt. 3, p. 7.

181 *students camped outside:* Jeff Prugh, "A Real Freakout for Bruin Fans," *Los Angeles Times*, February 25, 1972, pt. 3, p. 1.

181 *"kindred to a"*: Chapin and Prugh, *Wizard of Westwood*, 29.

181 *Wooden family members:* Ibid.

181 *Season tickets had:* Ibid., 30.

181 *"It gives the students"*: Ibid.

181 *"I wouldn't have been happy"*: Libby, *Walton Gang*, 105.

182 *his high school coach sent:* Author interview with Larry Farmer, April 18, 2009.

182 *The recruiting visit included:* Ibid.

183 *The same battalion commander Farmer:* Ibid.

183 *"It really hurts me"*: Libby, *Walton Gang*, 106.

183 *The public relations staff:* Chapin and Prugh, *Wizard of Westwood*, 209.

184 *but the passion:* Libby, *Walton Gang*, 31.

184 *"He's better than Alcindor"*: Ibid.

184 *"He is a young man"*: Ibid., 171.

184 *"is a most unusual"*: Ibid.

184 *"It bothers Bill"*: United Press International, "Bruce Walton Only Gets Upset When Called 'Bill,'" *Chico Enterprise-Record*, September 23, 1972, 3B.

184 *When reporters tried:* Author interview with Doug Krikorian, September 26, 2022.

184 *"I'm just starting"*: Bill Libby, "Reluctant All-American," *Los Angeles Times Magazine*, October 1, 1972.

185 *"He's the best"*: Chapin and Prugh, *Wizard of Westwood*, 210.

185 *"That kid, Bill Walton"*: Jeff Prugh, "Indians Wiped Out by Walton & Gang," *Los Angeles Times*, January 15, 1972, pt. 3, p. 1.

185 *Dallmar's players came to see:* Author interview with Rich Kelley, August 1, 2022.

185 *"Well," Wooden said:* Jeff Prugh, "Walton Blitzes Hawes as Bruins Roll, 109–70," *Los Angeles Times*, February 13, 1972, D1.

185 *"Alcindor?"*: Ibid.

186 *so much unnecessary bloodshed:* Digger Phelps with Tom Bourret, *Digger Phelps's Tales from the Notre Dame Hardwood* (Champaign, IL: Sports Publishing, 2004), 21.

186 *Phelps saw the respected:* Ibid.

186 *"John," Phelps responded:* Ibid.

186 *"had very few fans"*: West interview.

187 *felt like the little brother:* Ibid.

187 *"When we were up"*: Nater, "John Wooden and Mental Toughness."

187 *"UCLA players were"*: Ibid.

188 *"We didn't have a meeting"*: Jeff Prugh, "Wooden's Winning Way," *Los Angeles Times*, January 14, 1972, pt. 3, p. 1.

188 *"but I hope"*: Ibid.

188 *A Bruin on a trip:* Saffer interview.

189 *seven players arrived:* Mike Littwin and Alan Greenberg, "NCAA Missed the Iceberg in Westwood," *Los Angeles Times*, January 31, 1982, pt. 3, p. 1.

189 *They likewise did not say:* Farmer interview.

189 *"That was the cheapest":* Jeff Prugh, "Walton: Riley Hit Me on Purpose," *Los Angeles Times*, March 11, 1972, pt. 3, p. 1.

189 *Walton said he got elbowed:* Ibid.

189 *"Every year we play":* Dwight Chapin, "Battered Ratleff Accuses Refs of Protecting UCLA," *Los Angeles Times*, March 19, 1972, D1.

190 *"Walton is strong":* Jeff Prugh, "Walton Difference; UCLA Wins 96–77," *Los Angeles Times*, March 24, 1972, pt. 3, p. 1.

190 *"I never saw anything closer":* Jim Klobuchar, "Normandy Beach at the Arena," *Minneapolis Star*, January 26, 1972, 9A.

190 *A rarely used:* William F. Reed, "An Ugly Affair in Minneapolis," *Sports Illustrated*, February 7, 1972.

190 *"I believe crowds":* Dwight Chapin, "Violence, Vulgarity—and Basketball," *Los Angeles Times*, March 19, 1972, D1.

190 THIS IS FOR: Ibid.

191 *"Students are quick":* Associated Press, "Fury Taints Basketball," *Wisconsin State Journal*, February 15, 1972, sec. 3, p. 2.

191 *"The principal turmoil":* Chapin and Prugh, *Wizard of Westwood*, 28.

191 *"relatively undisciplined":* Charles Maher, "Fight On!," *Los Angeles Times*, February 6, 1972, D1.

191 *"In past years":* Chapin, "Violence, Vulgarity."

191 *the welcome assignment:* Brown interview.

191 *WSU booster club:* Chapin and Prugh, *Wizard of Westwood*, 27.

192 *"I'd have to say":* Bud Furillo, *Los Angeles Herald Examiner*, date unknown, via Andy Furillo, *The Steamer: Bud Furillo and the Golden Age of L.A. Sports* (Solana Beach, CA: Santa Monica Press, 2016), 403.

192 *His friend Marv Harshman:* Prugh, "Walton Blitzes Hawes."

192 *"I'm not sure":* Bonk, "Losing Never Came to Mind."

192 *"it's inconceivable to me":* Furillo, *Steamer*, 403.

192 *had already started to cause:* Walton, *Back from the Dead*, 95.

193 *"have to be down":* John Hall, "Emmy Too Thin," *Los Angeles Times*, March 22, 1972, pt. 3, p. 3.

193 *Wooden turned icy:* Ibid.

193 *"The NCAA tournament?":* Libby, *Walton Gang*, 117.

193 *the reason Provo and Stanford:* Walton, *Back from the Dead*, 94.

193 *Tarkanian finally gave up:* Libby, *Walton Gang*, 118.

194 *watching Florida State practice:* Ibid., 126.

194 *Lee needed one varsity game:* Bonk, "Losing Never Came to Mind." "I'll admit it was not the most astute quote, although it was accurate," Lee said in the same article when the topic came up in 1991. "I still shouldn't have said it. Wooden was outraged—I was

belittling the opposition. Actually, if you want to know the truth, they were like a real solid high school team."

194 *"Now I've got a nice"*: Jeff Prugh, "Another Perfect Ending for UCLA," *Los Angeles Times*, March 26, 1972, C1.

194 *"beautiful," "freaked out"*: Libby, *Walton Gang*, 233.

194 *"It gets to be old"*: Prugh, "Another Perfect Ending."

194 *"There are a lot"*: Ibid.

194 *"I felt like"*: Ibid.

194 *"They didn't mean it personally"*: Dwight Chapin, "Wooden Defends UCLA's Dominance," *Los Angeles Times*, March 28, 1972, pt. 3, p. 1.

195 *he planned to be more*: Ibid.

195 *unveiled his custom home*: Jerry Crowe, "Recalling the Devilish Details in Wilt's Pyramid of Excess," *Los Angeles Times*, October 13, 2009, C3; and Robert Cherry, *Wilt: Larger than Life* (Chicago: Triumph Books, 2004), 273–80.

195 *"Wilt-style"*: Fran Blinebury, "Traces of Chamberlain Still Remain at His Old L.A. Palace," nba.com, undated.

195 *Jerry West saw*: West and Coleman, *West by West*, 187.

195 *an ostentatious setting*: Cherry, *Wilt*, 273–80.

196 *Wooden was misquoted*: Dwight Chapin, "Wooden Isn't Amused Over False Quotes," *Los Angeles Times*, September 10, 1971, pt. 3, p. 5.

196 *"I guess I should"*: Jeff Prugh, "Angry Wooden Rakes Critics of Bruin Schedule," *Los Angeles Times*, December 7, 1971, pt. 3, p. 1.

196 *He called Krikorian*: Krikorian interview.

196 *Even being aware*: Spencer interview.

196 *had so obviously disappeared*: Wooden with Jamison, *My Personal Best*, 172.

197 *"Fellows," Wooden told them*: Ibid.

197 *He left the room*: Ibid.

10. Nixon's Trap

199 *"He seemed to lead"*: Wooden with Jamison, *My Personal Best*, 169.

199 *declared no one older*: Curry Kirkpatrick, "Who Are These Guys?," *Sports Illustrated*, February 5, 1973.

199 *Wooden was eventually heard*: Author interview with Ralph Drollinger, September 26, 2022.

199 *High-profile Walton*: Author interview with Don Casey, September 5, 2022.

200 *Chancellor Charles Young agreed*: Author interview with Charles Young, April 6, 2022.

200 *The American and state flags*: John Kendall, "Violent Demonstrations Taper Off in California," *Los Angeles Times*, May 12, 1972, pt. 1, p. 3.

200 *Phones began ringing*: Cunningham interview.

200 *officials estimated*: Ted Thackrey Jr., "Students Protest War; Berkeley Rally Violent," *Los Angeles Times*, May 10, 1972, pt. 1, p. 3.

200 *"They told us"*: Farmer interview.

200 *Walton remained defiant enough*: Spencer interview.

201 *"There's no in-between"*: Cunningham interview.

201 *"Today is the day":* Walton, *Back from the Dead,* 104.

201 *Walton was among the group:* Ibid., 105.

201 *civil disobedience had for years:* John Darnton, "Hundreds Are Arrested in Antiwar Demonstrations," *New York Times,* May 11, 1972, https://www.nytimes .com/1972/05/11/archives/hundreds-are-arrested-in-antiwar-demonstrations .html.

202 *In California:* Associated Press, "War Protests Sweep California Campuses," *Long Beach Independent,* May 10, 1972, A1.

202 *A plan to snarl traffic:* David Shaw, "Car Traffic Slowdown at Airport Thwarted," *Los Angeles Times,* May 13, 1972, pt. 1, p. 3.

202 *The gas had been:* Kendall, "Violent Demonstrations Taper Off."

202 *Furniture began to rain:* Author interview with Jim Ober, August 8, 2022.

202 *described his role:* Walton, *Back from the Dead,* 105.

203 *others spotted nothing worse:* Chapin and Prugh, *Wizard of Westwood,* 278.

203 *"The whole world":* Libby, *Walton Gang,* 150.

203 *Walton, sitting handcuffed:* Walton, *Back from the Dead,* 106.

203 *"Fuck you, Chuck!":* Ibid., and Young interview.

203 *He held up:* Young interview.

203 *laughed off both:* Ibid.

203 *as Walton came to realize:* Walton interview and Young interview.

204 *"a few unpleasant":* Walton, *Back from the Dead,* 106.

204 *Walton remained intentionally vague:* Walton interview. "Everybody was involved," he said in 2023. "I somehow, some way, ended up by myself in a car with John Wooden driving back to UCLA." Also, "Bruce was involved, and I don't know who else was involved."

204 *"He got special treatment":* Young interview.

204 *Young always considered Walton:* Young interview.

204 *"emotional youngster":* "'Walton's Conduct Out of My Hands,' says Wooden," *Long Beach Press-Telegram,* May 13, 1972, S-1.

204 *"The chancellor, some feared":* Kirkpatrick, "Who Are These Guys?"

205 *"I plan to continue":* Shaw, "Car Traffic Slowdown."

205 *Photographer Jim Ober:* Ober interview.

205 *Sam Yorty failing badly:* Libby, *Walton Gang,* 150.

205 *At least one proud:* Wooden interview.

205 *"Don't," John told him:* Ibid.

205 *He was not surprised:* Morgan interview.

206 *"mindless rioters," "professional malcontents":* Richard Nixon, *RN: The Memoirs of Richard Nixon* (New York: Grosset & Dunlap, 1978), 353.

206 *"these bums, you know":* Juan de Onis, "Nixon Puts 'Bums' Label on Some College Radicals," *New York Times,* May 2, 1970, 1, https://www.nytimes .com/1970/05/02/archives/nixon-puts-bums-label-on-some-college-radicals -nixon-denounces-bums.html.

206 *"Good!":* Richard Reeves, *President Nixon: Alone in the White House* (New York: Simon & Schuster, 2001), 57.

206 *Nixon's trap:* Kendall, "Violent Demonstrations Taper Off."

206 *there was no hint:* Dwight L. Chapin interview and Haldeman interview.

206 *If anything:* Dwight L. Chapin interview.

207 *"I just don't want":* "Bruins' Walton Plans to Skip Games Trials," *Los Angeles Times,* May 4, 1972, pt. 3, p. 2.

207 *but it passed Walton:* Walton with Wojciechowski, *Nothing but Net,* 51.

207 *but the coach:* Davis, *Wooden,* 383.

207 *Wooden speaking out:* Chapin and Prugh, *Wizard of Westwood,* 312.

207 *the compromise choice:* Bill Dwyre, "Munich Olympics 30 Years Later," *Los Angeles Times,* August 27, 2002, D3.

207 *He may have recalled:* Ibid.

207 *"But under the circumstances":* Walton with Wojciechowski, *Nothing but Net,* 50.

208 *"This environment":* Author interview George Karl, December 16, 2012.

208 *"Of course, when you talk":* Red Auerbach with Joe Fitzgerald, *On and Off the Court* (New York: Bantam, 1985), 68–69.

208 *"a little standoffish":* Auerbach and Feinstein, *Let Me Tell You a Story,* 224.

209 *"We, the plebes of basketball":* Karl interview.

209 *"not playing for his country":* Bob Knight with Bob Hammel, *Knight: My Story* (New York: Thomas Dunne Books, 2002), 130.

209 *"Practices are games":* Kirkpatrick, "Who Are These Guys?"

209 *"He was kind of":* Bisheff, *American Treasure,* 168.

210 *that would lead Wooden:* Ibid.

210 *"was like a superstar":* Author interview with Jack Herron, June 29, 2002.

210 *"He cleaned up":* Ibid.

210 *"to be an exceptional teacher":* Swen Nater, "The Truth about Sam Gilbert and John Wooden," *Swen Nater* (blog), August 3, 2018, http://swennater.blogspot.com.

210 *leading vote getter:* Herron interview.

210 *"All the other players":* John Hall, "$600,000 Smile," *Los Angeles Times,* July 21, 1972, pt. 3, p. 3.

211 *when events in Vietnam:* Bruce Spinks, "Coach Says Nater 'Making Excuses,'" *Honolulu Advertiser,* July 22, 1972, D-3.

211 *Unable to get:* Ibid.

211 *"Now isn't that":* Ibid.

211 *"Nater wouldn't have liked":* Ibid.

211 *"a case of intensity":* Ibid.

211 *He wasn't even:* Rich Roberts, "U.S. Olympic Cager Now Warier, Wiser," *Long Beach Independent,* August 13, 1972, S-2.

213 *"Son," he told Burleson:* Steve Aschburner, "'72 Olympic Team Still Haunted by Tragedy in Munich Games," nba.com, August 29, 2012.

213 *Walton watched on TV:* Walton interview.

214 *"If he plays":* Marc Stein, "Unhappy Endings," ESPN, August 9, 2012, https://www.espn.com/olympics/summer/2012/basketball/story/_/id/8245769/remembering-1972-us-olympic-squad-40-years-later-three-endings.

11. Force du Jour

215 *pronounced himself ready:* "Wooden Starts 25th Year as Bruin Coach," *Los Angeles Times*, October 17, 1972, pt. 3, p. 9.

215 *"Some people enjoy":* Wooden and Jamison, *Wooden on Leadership*, 210.

215 *He wrongly projected:* Ibid.

215 *Matching Wooden's mood:* Dwight Chapin, "Ho-Hums Mix with Rah-Rahs on Bruin and Trojan Fronts," *Los Angeles Times*, November 16, 1972, pt. 3, p. 1.

216 *America's favorite TV bigot:* Perlstein, *Nixonland*, 698.

216 *"Most people look":* Chapin, "Ho-Hums Mix with Rah-Rahs."

216 *had been scrapped in 1970:* Ibid.

217 *returned sure it would happen:* Walton, *Back from the Dead*, 115.

217 *"Okay, that's starting":* Ibid.

218 *"Whatever playing time":* Ibid., 90.

218 *Wooden also remembered:* Wooden, as told to Tobin, *They Call Me Coach*, 181.

218 *"Wooden inhibits":* Libby, *Walton Gang*, 233.

219 *Drollinger eventually realized:* Drollinger interview.

219 *"there is no togetherness":* Libby, *Walton Gang*, 149.

220 *Walton and other returnees:* Walton, *Back from the Dead*, 116.

220 *"ridiculous":* Ibid., 122.

220 *The University of the Pacific:* Author interview with Stan Morrison, January 13, 2023.

220 *grew particularly concerned:* Ibid.

221 *"I love what you ran":* Ibid.

221 *"the finest amateur basketball team":* Ron Rapoport, "Bruins Win 48th Straight with 81–48 Romp over Pacific," *Los Angeles Times*, December 3, 1972, D1.

221 *did not notice anything:* Morrison interview.

221 *lunch at Hollis Johnson's:* Libby, *Walton Gang*, 182.

221 *He had quit completely:* Wooden, as told to Tobin, *They Call Me Coach*, 104.

221 *When he collapsed:* Libby, *Walton Gang*, 186.

222 *"like death warmed over":* United Press International, "Wooden Begins 26th Season," *Zanesville Times Recorder*, November 25, 1973, 4-B.

222 *cardiologists determined:* Ibid.

222 *the encouraging news:* "Heart Condition Cause of Wooden Confinement," *Los Angeles Times*, December 14, 1972, pt. 3, p. 1.

222 *Cunningham was more like:* Wooden interview.

223 *"In Hospital":* Wooden and Jamison, *Wooden on Leadership*, 276.

223 *"I have never seen":* Ron Rapoport, "Bruins Give Wooden Get-Well Card, Win 49th in Row, 98–67," *Los Angeles Times*, December 17, 1972, D1.

223 *with permission from:* "Wooden Returns Today, to Lead Team on Weekend," *Los Angeles Times*, December 21, 1972, pt. 3, p. 1.

223 *Wooden might step away:* Cunningham interview.

224 *"no more chili sizes":* Mal Florence, "Deliberate, Wan Wooden Returns to Coaching Duties," *Los Angeles Times*, December 22, 1972, pt. 3, p. 1.

224 *In December 1972:* Young interview.

224 *no serious conversations:* Young, Sandbrook, and Cunningham interviews.

224 *Nor did Wooden ever:* Cunningham interview and Wooden interview.

225 *Wooden entered:* Libby, *Walton Gang*, 196.

225 *"I've always told my players":* Florence, "Deliberate, Wan Wooden."

225 *and also found:* Farmer interview.

225 *"We didn't really pay":* Walton, *Back from the Dead*, 117.

225 *"When we had arrived":* Ibid.

225 *"Hey, hey":* Ted Green, "The Enigma of Westwood," *Los Angeles Times*, February 11, 1974, pt. 3, p. 1.

225 *resulted in a:* Libby, *Walton Gang*, 197.

226 *accepted a Grecian urn:* Ibid., 198.

226 *"a little heart problem":* Wooden with Jamison, *My Personal Best*, 196.

226 *he sent Christmas cards:* John Hall, "Talk of the Town," *Los Angeles Times*, December 22, 1972, pt. 3, p. 3.

226 *"We count on":* Libby, *Walton Gang*, 16.

227 *"It's so easy for us":* Ibid.

227 *TWA Flight 24:* Kirkpatrick, "Who Are These Guys?"

227 *"no sense trying":* Ron Rapoport, "Streak Can't Last Forever—Wooden," *Los Angeles Times*, January 25, 1973, pt. 3, p. 1.

227 *brought little outward reaction:* Libby, *Walton Gang*, 226.

227 *"We'll win":* Ibid.

227 *Finding an opening:* Farmer interview.

228 *"That was fun":* Libby, *Walton Gang*, 227.

228 *"boring, frustrating":* Walton, *Back from the Dead*, 92.

228 *"excessively violent":* Ibid., 121.

228 *"you know what he'll do":* Libby, *Walton Gang*, 23.

228 *"It's a two-way street":* Ibid.

228 *three football players:* Phelps with Bourret, *Tales from the Notre Dame Hardwood*, 22.

228 *older players feeling:* Libby, *Walton Gang*, 228.

228 *and replied:* Kirkpatrick, "Who Are These Guys?"

228 *"This isn't the greatest":* Libby, *Walton Gang*, 24.

229 *"Dear 'Digger'—":* The *Philadelphia Inquirer* reprinted the letter on February 15, 1973, C1.

229 *"bag it":* Kirkpatrick, "Who Are These Guys?"

229 *A former roommate:* Ibid.

230 *finally pushed Wooden:* Dwight Chapin, "Wonderful World of Walton—It's UCLA, 87–66," *Los Angeles Times*, March 27, 1973, pt. 3, p. 1.

230 *"the only time":* Associated Press, "Wooden Hails Members of Bruins' Walton Gang," *New York Times*, March 27, 1973, 57, https://www.nytimes.com/1973/03/27/archives /wooden-hails-members-of-bruins-walton-gang-wooden-praises-walton.html.

230 *"He was the best":* Author interview with Aki Hill, July 15, 2022.

230 *"bony chin was set hard":* Chapin, "Wonderful World of Walton."

230 *"We're almost ready to go":* Zack McMillan, "The Biggest Game," *Memphis Commercial Appeal*, April 5, 2003, D1.

230 *"Half his game":* Ibid.

231 *Sitting about ten rows up:* Morrison interview.
231 *J. D. Morgan tracked:* Wiles Hallock, "Right Man at the Right Time: J. D. Morgan," interviewed by Rick C. Harmon for UCLA Oral History Program, November 29, 1982, 574.
231 *Hallock believed reached:* Ibid.
232 *Wooden would rank:* Howard-Cooper, *Bruin 100*, 19.
232 *"as great a game":* Jack Kiser, "Walton Agrees to Offer But Will He Play?," *Philadelphia Daily News*, March 28, 1973, 83.
232 *"the best collegiate player":* Chapin, "Wonderful World of Walton."
232 *Bill, Drollinger told:* Drollinger interview.
232 *"The seventh straight":* Jimmy Smith, "John Wooden—the Man, the Moment, the Message," *Nola*, April 2, 1993, https://www.nola.com/sports/retrospective-john-wooden---the-man-the-moment-the-message/article_68c3480c-64fb-5df1-928c-2853593bb671.html.
233 *Yet he politely sat:* Kiser, "Walton Agrees to Offer."
233 *"Maybe if we fly":* Dick Weiss, "Walton Still Hunting . . . Ditto Sixers," *Camden Courier-Post*, March 30, 1973, 40.
233 *Nothing from the pros:* Walton, *Back from the Dead*, 120.
234 *working his way through:* Kelley interview.
234 *Nell's hopes:* Chapin, "Wonderful World of Walton."
234 *"Maybe we should":* "Letters," *Los Angeles Times*, February 24, 1973, pt. 3, p. 3.

12. The Cross in the Pocket

235 *Morgan was barely:* Walton, *Back from the Dead*, 130.
236 *"I was a twenty-year-old":* Ibid.
236 *In Canton, already steaming:* William Johnson, "Courting Time in Peking," *Sports Illustrated*, July 2, 1973.
236 *one player tossed:* Buckner interview.
237 *Sneakers became a thing:* Kelley interview.
237 *chosen with high character:* Author interview with Chuck Neinas, July 22, 2022.
237 *visits to numerous:* Johnson, "Courting Time," and Neinas interview.
237 *Wilkes and Lee were also:* Wilkes interview.
237 *"by far":* Walton, *Back from the Dead*, 134.
238 *"Sadly":* Ibid.
238 *"Sometimes with Bill":* Green, "Enigma of Westwood."
238 *"He's a complex person":* Ibid.
238 *When he won:* Ibid.
238 *"I would say":* Ibid.
238 *He was to the point:* Krikorian interview and Dwight Chapin interview.
239 *driving Green and Lee:* Green, "Enigma of Westwood."
239 *allowed Walton to use:* Walton, *Back from the Dead*, 135.
239 *"We had to bring":* Bud Withers, "UCLA's Basketball Dynasty Began Its Demise 30 Years Ago in Oregon," *Seattle Times*, February 10, 2004, https://archive.seattletimes.com/archive/?date=20040210&slug=bruins10.
239 *opened the door to find:* Herron interview.

239 *to daydream about:* Green, "Enigma of Westwood."

239 *"Bob Marcucci, who did":* SI staff, "The Top Twenty," *Sports Illustrated,* November 26, 1973.

240 *"When you're under":* Ibid.

240 *"UCLA may be":* Jamaal Wilkes with Edward Reynolds Davis Jr., *Jamaal Wilkes: Memoirs of the Original Smooth as Silk* (Los Angeles: 88 STR8 Enterprises, 2015), 148.

240 *Wooden striding with determination:* Walton, *Back from the Dead,* 135–36.

241 *"begging, pleading":* Ibid., 137.

241 *A* New York Times Magazine*:* Hano, "Winning."

242 *Indeed, when freshman Drollinger:* Drollinger interview.

242 *"He's more like a minister":* "The Wooden Style," *Time,* February 12, 1973, https://content.time.com/time/subscriber/article/0,33009,903847,00.html.

242 *"We thought we had":* Ibid.

242 *Wooden's occasionally watching:* Abdul-Jabbar, *Coach Wooden and Me,* 7.

242 *Wooden chose to stay behind:* Casey interview.

243 *had put so much focus:* Author interview with Tom McMillen, March 9, 2023.

243 *aggressive in sharing:* Drollinger interview.

243 *he went there rather:* Ibid.

243 *never more obvious:* Ibid.

244 *Walton told his alleged opponent:* Ibid.

244 *particularly trying:* Ibid.

244 *Wooden received word:* Ibid.

245 *Tickets that went for:* Jeff Prugh, "The 79th Win: Behind the Scenes in St. Louis," *Los Angeles Times,* December 19, 1973, pt. 3, p. 1.

245 *"Win or lose":* Ibid.

245 *"Imagine":* Ibid.

246 *the North Carolina State band:* Ibid.

246 *yelled at referees:* Ibid.

246 *"Watch 'em pushing away":* Frank Dolson, "Writer Reveals the 'Other' John Wooden," *Shreveport Times* via Knight Newspapers, December 19, 1973, 41.

246 *"That's an offensive foul":* Ibid.

246 *"Oh, for crying out":* Ibid.

246 *"Feeling good?":* Ibid.

246 *"John Wooden—despite what":* Ibid.

247 *Encouraging his teammate:* Drollinger interview.

247 *He took Walton's advice:* Ibid.

247 *and fell back:* Dwight Chapin, "Drollinger to the Rescue," *Los Angeles Times,* December 16, 1973, pt. 3, p. 1.

247 *then returned:* Jeff Prugh, "Wooden: Bruins Still Could Lose," *Los Angeles Times,* December 17, 1973, pt. 3, p. 1.

247 *"I'd like to be":* Howard-Cooper, *Bruin 100,* 83.

247 *Towe spent the flight:* Norm Sloan and Larry Guest, *Confessions of a Coach* (Nashville, TN: Rutledge Hill Press, 1976), 90.

248 *"We'll have one":* Chapin, "Drollinger to the Rescue."

248 *as part of what:* Jim McCormack, "NCAA Kayoes 49ers—3-Year Ban," *Long Beach Press-Telegram*, January 7, 1974, C-1.

248 *"Wanna take a shot?":* Dwight Chapin and Ted Green, "Long Beach vs. the NCAA," *Los Angeles Times*, January 18, 1974, pt. 3, p. 1.

248 *"Hey, Tark":* Ray Kennedy, "The Payoff," *Sports Illustrated*, June 17, 1974.

249 *Washington State coach George Raveling:* Jeff Prugh, "UCLA Wins 85th Straight; Bill Walton Hurt," *Los Angeles Times*, January 8, 1974, pt. 3, p. 1.

249 *keep a large file:* Ibid.

249 *"Who am I":* Ibid.

249 *"despicable act":* Nick Canepa, "Back Pain Nearly Drove Bill Walton to End It All," *San Diego Union-Tribune*, April 17, 2010, https://www .sandiegouniontribune.com/sdut-back-pain-nearly-drove-bill-walton-to-end-it-all -2010apr17-story.html.

249 *The crowd that booed:* Bob Johnson, "The Wizard Holds Court," *Spokane Daily Chronicle*, January 8, 1974, 11.

250 *later found to be:* Canepa, "Back Pain Nearly Drove."

250 *his confidence growing:* Drollinger interview.

13. The Lost Season

251 *"the devil himself":* Walton, *Back from the Dead*, 121.

251 *Troubling news was often:* Richard "Digger" Phelps with Jack Colwell, *Undertaker's Son: Life Lessons from a Coach* (Guilford, CT: Lyons Press, 2007), 22–23.

252 *had a shamrock:* Phelps with Bourret, *Tales from the Notre Dame Hardwood*, 4.

252 *arrived with visions:* Author interview with Frank McLaughlin, July 26, 2022.

252 *"the surprisingly poor":* Richard "Digger" Phelps and Larry Keith, *A Coach's World* (New York: Thomas Y. Crowell, 1974), 68.

252 *Phelps was pleased:* Ibid., 67.

252 *"Digger lived and died":* Michael Coffey, *Echoes of the Hardwood: 100 Seasons of Notre Dame Men's Basketball* (Lanham, MD: Taylor Trade, 2004), 135.

253 *he considered:* Phelps and Keith, *Coach's World*, 68.

253 *"Someday you will tell":* Phelps with Bourret, *Tales from the Notre Dame Hardwood*, 24.

253 *telling friends for weeks:* Frank Dolson, "Pent-Up Irish Sophs Stun UCLA . . . Only in Digger's Dream World," *Philadelphia Inquirer*, January 28, 1973, D1.

253 *So many out-of-towners:* Ibid.

254 *"Dear John":* Phelps with Bourret, *Tales from the Notre Dame Hardwood*, 26.

254 *Shumate the same Friday night:* Shumate interview.

254 *It was the same:* Coffey, *Echoes of the Hardwood*, 108.

254 *When you're announced:* Shumate interview.

254 *Shumate gathered himself:* Ibid.

255 *The team gathering:* Ibid.

255 *"The chances are good":* Coffey, *Echoes of the Hardwood*, 27.

255 *"I had a dream":* Shumate interview.

256 *Phelps stared at:* Ibid.

256 *the rest of the crowd:* Author interview with Rick Phelps, April 27, 2023.

256 *"I know in my":* Author interview with Adrian Dantley, March 7, 2009.

256 *Dantley's message:* Ibid.

257 *"Hey, I remember":* Ibid.

257 *"with some of the worst":* Ibid.

257 *players saw the passion:* "30 Years Later," *Observer,* January 30, 2004.

257 *"If you don't believe":* Ibid.

257 *"Never did I want":* Davis, *Wooden,* 122.

258 *Phelps gained the insight:* Author interview with Digger Phelps, April 26, 2023.

258 *In the Alcindor days:* Hansen interview.

258 *Twice Tommy Curtis looked:* Jeff Prugh, "Curtis Apologetic, but He Still Wants to Beat the Irish," *Los Angeles Times,* January 24, 1974, pt. 3, p. 1.

258 *"I personally lost":* Dwight Chapin, "Blame Me—Wooden," *Los Angeles Times,* March 27, 1974, pt. 3, p. 2.

258 *"I know I was guilty":* Jeff Prugh, "UCLA Will Work This Week on How to Meet the Press," *Los Angeles Times,* January 22, 1974, pt. 3, p. 1.

258 *"came out of the stands":* "You Are There," *Referee,* March 8, 2021, https://www.referee.com/ucla-streak-snapped/.

258 *Revelers charged the court:* Author interview with David Israel, August 17, 2022.

259 *He landed nose first:* Shumate interview.

259 *"I love you":* Ibid.

259 *When Phelps recognized:* Phelps interview.

259 *"Intensity!":* Jeff Prugh, "No. 1! Who Are Those Guys?," *Los Angeles Times,* January 25, 1974, sec. 3, p. 1.

259 *"UCLA came to play":* Ibid.

259 *J. D. Morgan quickly hunted:* McLaughlin interview.

259 *Hey, don't worry:* Dantley interview.

260 *a group of Notre Dame:* McLaughlin interview.

260 *just inside the entrance:* Author interview with Rod Hundley, January 6, 2009.

260 *plans went into action:* "Hometown Hails Phelps," *New York Times,* January 21, 1974, 21, https://www.nytimes.com/1974/01/21/archives/hometown-hails-phelps.html.

260 *a high school senior:* Joe Montana with Dick Schapp, *Montana* (Atlanta: Turner Publishing, 1995), 27.

261 *in the neighborhood:* Rick Phelps interview.

261 *also close enough:* Author interview with Karen Phelps Moyer, April 27, 2023.

261 *Unattached Phelps assistant:* McLaughlin interview.

261 *Oh, proud smart-ass:* Ibid.

261 *"Why don't you respect":* Ibid.

261 *Wooden soon began speaking:* "John Wooden's Simple Strategy," *Time,* February 25, 1974, https://content.time.com/time/subscriber/article/0,33009,879295,00.html.

262 *"every time we didn't":* Mark Whicker, "Recollecting the Day When a Dynasty Fell," *Orange County Register,* December 27, 1993.

262 *"These should have been":* Johnson, *John Wooden Pyramid of Success,* 53.

262 *John was hardly sleeping:* Ibid.

262 *but also noticed:* Dantley interview.

262 *The most emotional:* Shumate interview.

262 *"What did he want?":* Ibid.

263 *Players were heard:* Author interview with Ron Rapoport, September 6, 2022.

263 *"Walking Antique":* Thomas Stinson, "War Raged and UCLA Reigned," *Atlanta Journal-Constitution*, March 31, 2007, F6.

263 *"they listen but":* "John Wooden's Simple Strategy."

263 *"We thought everything":* Einhorn with Rapoport, *How March Became Madness*, 30.

263 *"It kind of made":* Withers, "UCLA's Basketball Dynasty Began."

263 *"and they're ten points ahead":* Ibid.

263 *hit in the chest:* Walton, *Back from the Dead*, 144.

263 *the Ducks could not hear:* Withers, "UCLA's Basketball Dynasty Began."

264 *Few coaches:* Ibid.

264 *He said the rest:* Wooden with Jamison, *My Personal Best*, 98.

264 *none maximized potential more:* Ibid., 120.

264 *turned Wooden livid:* Walton, *Back from the Dead*, 144.

264 *Players had already taken:* Withers, "UCLA's Basketball Dynasty Began."

265 *"He's got to be":* Frank Dolson, "Dick Harter: USC Has Best Team in College Basketball," *Los Angeles Times* via Knight News Service, February 19, 1974, pt. 3, p. 1.

265 *"just too sure":* Wooden with Jamison, *My Personal Best*, 174.

265 *"A coach needs":* Ibid.

265 *"The 1974 Bruins may have":* Ibid., 178.

265 *Also, Bob "Die-lyn":* Walton, *Back from the Dead*, 144.

266 *"I think the fact":* Dwight Chapin, "UCLA Barely Survives Triple Overtime, 111–100," *Los Angeles Times*, March 15, 1974, pt. 3, p. 1.

266 *A drinking problem:* David Thompson with Sean Stormes and Marshall Terrill, *David Thompson: Skywalker* (Chicago: Sports Publishing, 2003), 121.

267 *"Really, all you've got":* A. J. Carr, "State's High Wire Act," *Raleigh News and Observer*, March 16, 1974, 9.

267 *At the heights:* A. J. Carr, "Pitt Defense Poses Problem for Soaring Pack," *Raleigh News and Observer*, March 16, 1974, 9.

267 *with a thud:* Thompson with Stormes and Terrill, *Skywalker*, 91.

267 *"My teammates feared":* Ibid., 92.

267 *Spence said he cried:* A. J. Carr, "Wolfpack Cried, Prayed and Won," *Raleigh News and Observer*, March 17, 1974, sec. 2, p. 1.

268 *people calling with offers:* Thompson with Stormes and Terrill, *Skywalker*, 95.

268 *felt the Wolfpack:* Sloan and Guest, *Confessions of a Coach*, 97.

268 *Wooden even delivered:* Walton, *Back from the Dead*, 79.

268 *The cliché request:* Author interview with Tim Peeler, July 20, 2022.

269 *"stunned us":* Wilkes with Davis Jr., *Memoirs of the Original Smooth*, 159.

269 *a call that irritated:* Sandbrook interview.

269 *Walton carrying a chair:* Ross Newhan, "Walton, Other Bruins May Sit Out Last Game," *Los Angeles Times*, March 24, 1974, pt. 3, p. 1.

269 *"We got careless":* Ibid.

269 *A solemn bus ride:* Cunningham interview.

270 *Even Wooden in the privacy:* Drollinger interview.

270 *top NCAA executives:* Author interview with Tom Jernstedt, June 2, 2009.

270 *"For the first time":* Chapin, "Blame Me—Wooden."

270 *"If I'm back":* Ibid.

270 *"I enjoyed working":* Ibid.

271 *"got out of there":* Walton interview.

271 *"I'm sorry, Coach":* Walton, *Back from the Dead*, 148.

271 *"if you took":* Wooden with Jamison, *My Personal Best*, 169.

272 *"I mean, we hardly":* Green, "Enigma of Westwood."

272 *a franchise coached by Wilt Chamberlain:* Chamberlain was mostly regarded as the figurehead coach of the San Diego Conquistadors in 1973–74, on the job for publicity purposes while respected assistant Stan Albeck did the work. Chamberlain lived in his Bel Air mansion and commuted to home games with a flight from Los Angeles that arrived at 6:30 or 6:45 p.m. before he was driven to the arena for 7:30 starts. He once missed games on back-to-back nights without an explanation beyond the general manager noting Wilt was sick, Albeck claiming Chamberlain was scouting, the team owner saying the coach was attending to company business, and Chamberlain appearing shocked that the press would wonder why the coach wasn't showing up. (Bob Wolf, "Wilt the Coach? It Was Different," *Los Angeles Times*, July 4, 1990, https://www.latimes.com/archives/la-xpm-1990-07-04-sp-230-story.html.

272 *"I'm no longer":* Sam Goldaper, "Blazers Win Draft Rights to Walton on a Coin Toss," *New York Times*, March 28, 1974, 49, https://www.nytimes.com/1974/03/28/archives /blazers-win-draft-rights-to-walton-on-a-coin-toss-previous-history.html.

272 *Jerry West praising Portland:* Walton interview.

272 *The participating teams:* "Trail Blazers Win Rights to Walton," *Los Angeles Times*, March 28, 1974, pt. 3, p. 1; and Goldaper, "Blazers Win Draft Rights."

272 *talking openly for six months:* "It's Walton or Bust," *Long Beach Independent*, January 8, 1974, 20.

273 *"Cut my throat":* "Blazers Win Flip—Walton Their Choice," *Long Beach Independent*, March 28, 1974, C-1.

273 *There was just one thing:* Walton interview.

14. Epilogue

275 *"Are the ladies":* Dwight Chapin, "Walton Still Lets Actions Do Talking," *Los Angeles Times*, September 28, 1974, pt. 3, p. 1.

275 *Walton arrived:* Ibid.

275 *"I've done a lot":* Ibid.

276 *Planning for 1974–75 included:* Wooden and Jamison, *Wooden on Leadership*, 281.

276 *Placing two of the most:* Ibid.

277 *got involved too late:* Author interview with Larry Bird, March 3, 2009. Bird chose Indiana, but dropped out before playing. He later attended Indiana State.

277 *"What about Tarkanian?":* Byron Atkinson, "Right Man at the Right Time: J. D. Morgan," interviewed by David A. Rose for UCLA Oral History Program, March 23, 1982, 227.

277 *Morgan topped:* Davis, *Wooden*, 431.

277 *The news broke:* Associated Press, "Wooden to Quit, Says Coach," *Oakland Tribune*, March 9, 1975, 5C.

277 *"Several sources":* Ibid.

278 *While Meyers and Trgovich:* Ted Green, "Bruins Hear 'Sad' News," *Los Angeles Times*, March 30, 1975, pt. 3, p. 1.

278 *Wooden was reading:* Loel Schrader, "Unknown Element in Wooden Decision," *Long Beach Independent*, March 31, 1975, C-1.

278 *Nell Wooden said:* Dwight Chapin, "Wooden's Successor Still a Mystery Man," *Los Angeles Times*, March 31, 1975, pt. 3, p. 1.

278 *John had been telling reporters:* Loel Schrader, "By Any Other Name, Wooden Still a Wizard," *Long Beach Independent Press-Telegram*, March 30, 1975, S-1.

278 *He was even:* Spencer interview.

278 *"Perhaps it was":* Wooden with Jamison, *My Personal Best*, 195.

278 Daily Bruin *co–sports editor:* Author interview with Marc Dellins, August 10, 2022.

279 *"I can't believe I'm here":* Ibid.

279 *"a tremendous surprise":* Wooden, "Right Man at the Right Time," 366.

279 *Crum would have been:* Curry Kirkpatrick, "Wise in the Ways of the Wizard," *Sports Illustrated*, November 30, 1981.

279 *Morgan never asked:* Wooden, "Right Man at the Right Time," 366.

279 *He would not pick:* Pete Dunan, "'Wizard' Spellbinds Huge SLO Audience," *San Luis Obispo Telegram-Tribune*, April 11, 1975, 1.

280 *got fifteen hundred requests:* Robyn Norwood, "The Pyramid Stands the Test of Time," *Los Angeles Times*, June 13, 2010, V5. Wooden in the same story said friends urged him to copyright the Pyramid of Success, but he never did. When one told Wooden he did not have a marketing bone in his body, Wooden replied, "I hope not."

280 *Hill felt his coach:* Hill with Wooden, *Be Quick*, 49–55.

281 *"I didn't think I'd ever":* Davis, *Wooden*, 512.

281 *never had a bad moment:* Sweek interview.

281 *always blamed himself:* Saffer interview.

281 *Ralph Drollinger and Wooden remained:* Drollinger interview.

281 *"I feel great":* Rich Roberts, "He Was Doing What He Loved, Playing a Game," *Los Angeles Times*, January 6, 1988, pt. 3, p. 1.

282 *"What are the odds":* Bill Plaschke, "The Finale at Pauley Is Heaven-Sent," *Los Angeles Times*, February 27, 2011, C1.

282 *"He even has his":* Jo Haldeman, *In the Shadow of the White House: A Memoir of the Washington and Watergate Years, 1968–1978* (Los Angeles: Rare Bird Books, 2017), 405.

283 *"That's what killed him":* Jim Bush, "Right Man at the Right Time: J. D. Morgan," interviewed by David A. Rose and Rick C. Harmon for UCLA Oral History Program, March 16, 1982, 384.

283 *"They're going to miss":* "A League of His Own," UCLA Alumni, undated, https://alumni.ucla.edu/ucla-history-13/.

284 *"I remember him coming over":* Rick Phelps interview.

285 *Wooden in his sixties appeared:* Thomas Bonk, "He Walks Alone with His Memories," *Los Angeles Times*, December 25, 1988, sec. 3, p. 1.

285 *Wooden added a detour:* Wooden interview.

286 *Don't focus on:* Vermeil interview.

286 *When the Rams lost:* Ibid.

286 *Wooden took his:* Bonk, "He Walks Alone."

287 *wrote her love letters:* Author interview with Rick Reilly, April 28, 2022.

287 *They scheduled:* Ibid.

287 *"Not yet":* T. J. Simers, "Wooden Has Too Much Life in Him to Call It Quits," *Los Angeles Times*, May 1, 2009, C2.

287 *This time:* Reilly interview.

288 *secretly went into:* Wooden interview.

288 *"If the UCLA teams":* Jack Scott, *Bill Walton: On the Road with the Portland Trail Blazers* (New York: Thomas Y. Crowell, 1978), via Michael James, "Because of Jerry Tarkanian and UNLV What Happened in Vegas Didn't Stay in Vegas," *Tribe Sports* (blog), February 11, 2015, https://www.thetribesports.com/thanks-to-tark-what-happened-in-vegas-didnt-stay-in-vegas/.

288 *I hear them":* Aschburner, "'72 Olympic Team Still Haunted."

288 *When a student manager:* Rosenberg, *War as They Knew It*, 301.

289 *so much time at UCLA:* Vandeweghe interview.

289 *When Bartow asked:* Author interview with Marques Johnson, January 10, 2020.

289 *forever credited:* Vandeweghe interview.

289 *The coffin exited:* Martin Flanagan, "Olympic Protest Heroes Praise Norman's Courage," *Sydney Morning Herald*, October 10, 2006, https://www.smh.com.au/sport/olympic-protest-heroes-praise-normans-courage-20061010-gdokc5.html.

290 *although it is unlikely:* Montana with Schapp, *Montana*, 27.

290 *Young, Morgan, and campus counsel:* Young interview.

290 *"Chu-uuuuck":* Ibid.

290 *"might be attacked":* Ibid.

290 *"if I had spent":* Mike Littwin and Alan Greenberg, "Former NCAA Investigator Tells of a Coverup," *Los Angeles Times*, January 31, 1982, pt. 3, p. 1.

291 *"a school that is":* Ibid.

291 *"Maybe I had":* Ibid.

291 *Wooden so emphasized:* Scates interview, July 22, 2022.

291 *Wooden's mailed RSVP:* Ibid.

291 *The investigation could not:* Littwin and Greenberg, "NCAA Missed the Iceberg."

292 *included players saying:* Ibid.

292 *"Should I press":* Greenberg and Littwin, "Gilbert Is the Godfather."

292 *"I'm warning you":* Ibid.

292 *"to say 'Thank you'":* Danny Robbins, "Bartow Was in Fear of UCLA Booster," *Los Angeles Times*, August 4, 1993, C1.

292 *The FBI knocked:* William Overend and William Nottingham, "Man Indicted in Drug Case 4 Days After Death," *Los Angeles Times*, November 26, 1987, pt. 2, p. 11.

293 *insisted for years:* Morrison interview.

293 *Jerry West raced:* West and Coleman, *West by West*, 251–54.

293 *The profound loss:* Ibid., 265.

293 *"They always throw":* Scott Howard-Cooper, "Wooden Leaves a Legacy Unmatched in Hoops History," nba.com, June 5, 2010.

294 *felt an eerie silence:* West and Coleman, *West By West*, 292.

294 *The family eventually asked:* Dellins interview.

294 *made more money:* Wooden interview.

295 *Seeing the interest level:* Sandbrook interview.

295 *left him stunned:* Greg Newell interview.

295 *Wooden detailed the time:* Abdul-Jabbar, *Coach Wooden and Me*, 125.

296 *"Coach had become":* Ibid., 266.

296 *"I'm not afraid":* Ibid., 266–67.

296 *said goodbye:* Walton, *Back from the Dead*, 312–13.

296 *Abdul-Jabbar received word:* Abdul-Jabbar, *Coach Wooden and Me*, 268–69.

297 *Walton hurried:* Walton, *Back from the Dead*, 313.

297 *"Thanks, Coach":* Ibid.

297 *Jamaal Wilkes answered:* Associated Press, "Filled with Love," *Port Charlotte Sun*, June 6, 2010, 7.

297 *"my last parent":* Abdul-Jabbar, *Coach Wooden and Me*, 271.

297 *"Thank you, thank you":* Ibid., 271–72.

298 *"It wasn't a sad":* Wooden interview.

298 *The ninety-minute public memorial:* Associated Press, "Saying Goodbye to 'Coach,'" *Waterville (ME) Morning Sentinel*, June 27, 2010, C8.

298 *long before declined:* Author interview with Bobby Field, March 17, 2023.

299 *He also went:* Walton, *Back from the Dead*, 266.

299 *"We had had our days":* Abdul-Jabbar, *Coach Wooden and Me*, 250.

299 *Things work out best:* Ibid., 187.

Acknowledgments

302 *"My teammates at UCLA":* Hill interview.

BIBLIOGRAPHY

Abdul-Jabbar, Kareem. *Coach Wooden and Me.* New York: Grand Central
  Publishing, 2017.

Abdul-Jabbar, Kareem, and Peter Knobler. *Giant Steps: The Autobiography
  of Kareem Abdul-Jabbar.* New York: Bantam Books, 1983.

Abdul-Jabbar, Kareem, with Mignon McCarthy. *Kareem.* New York:
  Random House, 1990.

Abdul-Jabbar, Kareem, and Raymond Obstfeld. *Becoming Kareem: Growing
  Up On and Off the Court.* New York: Little, Brown, 2017.

Abdul-Jabbar, Kareem, with Raymond Obstfeld. *On the Shoulders of Giants: My
  Journey Through the Harlem Renaissance.* New York: Simon & Schuster, 2007.

Appy, Christian G. *Working-Class War: American Combat Soldiers and Vietnam.*
  Chapel Hill: University of North Carolina Press, 1993.

Auerbach, Red, and John Feinstein. *Let Me Tell You a Story: A Lifetime in the
  Game.* New York: Little, Brown, 2004.

Auerbach, Red, with Joe Fitzgerald. *On and Off the Court.* New York: Bantam, 1985.

Axthelm, Pete. *The City Game: Basketball from the Garden to the Playgrounds.*
  New York: Penguin, 1970.

Berges, Marshall. *The Life and Times of Los Angeles: A Newspaper, a Family
  and a City.* New York: Atheneum, 1984.

Bisheff, Steve. *John Wooden: An American Treasure.* Nashville, TN:
  Cumberland House, 2004.

Branch, Taylor. *At Canaan's Edge: America in the King Years, 1965–68.*
New York: Simon & Schuster, 2007.

Brokaw, Tom. *Boom! Talking About the Sixties.* New York: Random House, 2008.

Brownstein, Ronald. *Rock Me on the Water: 1974—The Year Los Angeles Transformed Movies, Music, Television and Politics.* New York: Harper, 2021.

Cannon, Lou. *Governor Reagan: His Rise to Power.* New York: Public Affairs, 2003.

Chapin, Dwight. *The President's Man: The Memoirs of Nixon's Trusted Aide.*
New York: William Morrow, 2022.

Chapin, Dwight, and Jeff Prugh. *The Wizard of Westwood: Coach John Wooden
and His UCLA Bruins.* Boston: Houghton Mifflin, 1973.

Cherry, Robert. *Wilt: Larger than Life.* Chicago: Triumph Books, 2004.

Coffey, Michael. *Echoes of the Hardwood: 100 Seasons of Notre Dame Men's
Basketball.* Lanham, MD: Taylor Trade, 2004.

Dallek, Matthew. *The Right Moment: Ronald Reagan's First Victory and the
Decisive Turning Point in American Politics.* New York: Free Press, 2000.

Davis, Seth. *Wooden: A Coach's Life.* New York: Times Books, 2014.

Einhorn, Eddie, with Ron Rapoport. *How March Became Madness: How the
NCAA Tournament Became the Greatest Sporting Event in America.* Chicago:
Triumph Books, 2006.

Enberg, Dick, with Jim Perry. *Dick Enberg: Oh, My!* Champaign, IL: Sports
Publishing, 2004.

Federman, Wayne, and Marshall Terrill in collaboration with Jackie Maravich.
Pete Maravich: The Authorized Biography of Pistol Pete. Carol Stream, IL:
Tyndale House, 2006.

Fellowship of Christian Athletes. *The Greatest Coach Ever: Tony Dungy, David
Robinson, Tom Osborne, and Others Pay Tribute to the Timeless Wisdom
and Insights of John Wooden.* Grand Rapids, MI: Revell, 2010.

Frum, David. *How We Got Here: The 70's; The Decade That Brought You
Modern Life—(For Better or Worse).* New York: Basic Books, 2000.

Furillo, Andy. *The Steamer: Bud Furillo and the Golden Age of L.A. Sports.*
Solana Beach, CA: Santa Monica Press, 2016.

Godwin Phelps, Teresa. *The Coach's Wife: A Memoir.* New York:
W. W. Norton, 1994.

Goss, Freddie. *The Adventures of Uncle Son (New York Willie) Momma and Me (One of John Wooden's UCLA Boys)*. 2 vols. Self-published, 2021.

Halberstam, David. *The Breaks of the Game*. New York: Alfred A. Knopf, 1981.

Haldeman, H. R. *The Haldeman Diaries: Inside the Nixon White House*. New York: G. Putnam's Sons, 1994.

Haldeman, Jo. *In the Shadow of the White House: A Memoir of the Washington and Watergate Years, 1968–1978*. Los Angeles: Rare Bird Books, 2017.

Haskins, James. *From Lew Alcindor to Kareem Abdul-Jabbar*. New York: Lothrop, Lee & Shepard, 1972.

Hauser, Thomas. *Muhammad Ali: His Life and Times*. New York: Simon & Schuster Paperbacks, 1991.

Hayes, Elvin, and Bill Gilbert. *They Call Me "the Big E."* Englewood Cliffs, NJ: Prentice-Hall, 1978.

Hill, Andrew, with John Wooden. *Be Quick—But Don't Hurry!: Finding Success in the Teachings of a Lifetime*. New York: Simon & Schuster, 2001.

Howard-Cooper, Scott. *The Bruins 100: The Greatest Games in the History of UCLA Basketball*. Lenexa, KS: Addax Publishing, 1999.

Jenkins, Bruce. *A Good Man: The Pete Newell Story*. Berkeley, CA: Frog, 1999.

Johnson, Neville L. *The John Wooden Pyramid of Success: The Ultimate Guide to Life, Leadership, Friendship and Love Created by the Greatest Coach in the History of Sports*. Los Angeles: Cool Titles, 2000.

Kaiser, Charles. *1968 in America: Music, Politics, Chaos, Counterculture, and the Shaping of a Generation*. New York: Grove Press, 1988.

Kerr, Clark. *The Gold and the Blue: A Personal Memoir of the University of California, 1949–1967*. Berkeley: University of California Press, 2003.

Kirkpatrick, Rob. *1969: The Year That Changed Everything*. New York: Skyhorse Publishing, 2011.

Knight, Bob, with Bob Hammel. *Knight: My Story*. New York: Thomas Dunne Books, 2002.

Kriegel, Mark. *Pistol: The Life of Pete Maravich*. New York: Free Press, 2007.

Krikorian, Doug. *Los Angeles Sports Memories*. Charleston, SC: History Press, 2013.

Kurlansky, Mark. *1968: The Year That Rocked the World*. New York: Random House Trade Paperback, 2005.

Lazenby, Roland. *Jerry West: The Life and Legend of a Basketball Icon.* New York: Ballantine, 2009.

———. *The Lakers: A Basketball Journey.* New York: St. Martin's Press, 1993.

———. *The Show: The Inside Story of the Spectacular Los Angeles Lakers in the Words of Those Who Lived It.* New York: McGraw-Hill, 2006.

Libby, Bill. *The Walton Gang.* New York: Coward, McCann & Geoghegan, 1974.

———. *We Love You Lakers.* New York: Sport Magazine Press, 1972.

Lombardo, John. *A Fire to Win: The Life and Times of Woody Hayes.* New York: Thomas Dunne Books, 2005.

MacMillan, Margaret. *Nixon and Mao: The Week That Changed the World.* New York: Random House, 2007.

McNally, Dennis. *A Long Strange Trip: The Inside History of the Grateful Dead.* New York: Broadway Books, 2002.

Michaels, Al, with L. Jon Wertheim. *You Can't Make This Up: Miracles, Memories, and the Perfect Marriage of Sports and Television.* New York: William Morrow, 2014.

Michener, James. *Kent State: What Happened and Why.* New York: Random House, 1971.

Montana, Joe, with Dick Schapp. *Montana.* Atlanta: Turner Publishing, 1995.

Nixon, Richard. *RN: The Memoirs of Richard Nixon.* New York: Grosset & Dunlap, 1978.

Perlstein, Rick. *Nixonland: The Rise of a President and the Fracturing of America.* New York: Scribner, 2008.

Phelps, Digger, and Tim Bourret. *Digger Phelps's Tales from the Notre Dame Hardwood.* Champaign, IL: Sports Publishing, 2004.

Phelps, Digger, with Jack Colwell. *Undertaker's Son: Life Lessons from a Coach.* Guilford, CT: Lyons Press, 2007.

Phelps, Digger, with Larry Keith. *A Coach's World.* New York: Thomas Y. Crowell, 1974.

Pluto, Terry. *Loose Balls: The Short, Wild Life of the American Basketball Association.* New York: Simon & Schuster, 1990.

Reeves, Richard. *President Nixon: Alone in the White House.* New York: Simon & Schuster, 2001.

Rice, Russell. *Adolph Rupp: Kentucky's Basketball Baron.* Champaign, IL: Sagamore Publishing, 1994.

Rosenberg, Michael. *War as They Knew It: Woody Hayes, Bo Schembechler, and America in a Time of Unrest.* New York: Grand Central Publishing, 2008.

Scott, Jack. *Bill Walton: On the Road with the Portland Trail Blazers.* New York: Thomas Y. Crowell, 1978.

Shesol, Jeff. *Mutual Contempt: Robert Kennedy, Lyndon Johnson and the Feud That Defined a Decade.* New York: W. W. Norton, 1998.

Sides, Hampton. *Hellhound on His Trail.* New York: Anchor Books, 2010.

Sloan, Norman, with Larry Guest. *Confessions of a Coach.* Nashville, TN: Rutledge Hill Press, 1991.

Smith, Red, edited by Dave Anderson. *The Red Smith Reader.* New York: Random House, 1982.

Spitz, Bob. *The Beatles: The Biography.* New York: Back Bay Books, 2005.

Springer, Steve, and Michael Arkush. *60 Years of USC-UCLA Football.* Stamford, CT: Longmeadow Press, 1991.

Tarkanian, Jerry, and Terry Pluto. *Tark: College Basketball's Winningest Coach.* New York: McGraw-Hill, 1988.

Tarkanian, Jerry, with Dan Wetzel. *Runnin' Rebel: Shark Tales of "Extra Benefits," Frank Sinatra and Winning It All.* Champaign, IL: Sports Publishing, 2005.

Thompson, David, with Sean Stormes and Marshall Terrill. *David Thompson: Skywalker.* Chicago: Sports Publishing, 2003.

Towle, Mike. *I Remember Pete Maravich: Personal Recollections of Basketball's Pistol by the People and Players Who Knew Him Best.* Nashville, TN: Cumberland House, 2000.

Walton, Bill. *Back from the Dead: Searching for the Sound, Shining the Light, and Throwing It Down.* New York: Simon & Schuster, 2016.

Walton, Bill, with Gene Wojciechowski. *Nothing But Net: Just Give Me the Ball and Get Out of the Way.* New York: Hyperion, 1994.

Wells, Tom. *The War Within: America's Battle Over Vietnam.* Berkeley: University of California Press, 1994.

West, Jerry, and Jonathan Coleman. *West by West: My Charmed, Tormented Life.* New York: Little, Brown, 2011.

Wilkes, Jamaal, with Edward Reynolds Davis Jr. *Jamaal Wilkes: Memoirs of the Original Smooth as Silk.* Los Angeles: 88 STR8 Enterprises, 2015.

Wolf, David. *Foul! The Connie Hawkins Story.* New York: Holt, Rinehart and Winston, 1972.

Wooden, John, and Steve Jamison. *Wooden on Leadership.* New York: McGraw-Hill, 2005.

Wooden, John, as told to Jack Tobin. *They Call Me Coach.* Waco, TX: Word, 1972.

Wooden, John, with Steve Jamison. *My Personal Best: Life Lessons from an All-American Journey.* New York: McGraw-Hill Education, 2004.

———. *Wooden: A Lifetime of Observations and Reflections On and Off the Court.* Chicago: Contemporary Books, 1997.

INDEX

MAR 1 9 2024

WITHDRAWN

DATE DUE

BEST
SELLER

7 DAY

MAR 2 8 2024

APR 2 3 2024

AUG 2 6 2024

PRINTED IN U.S.A.